# Handbook of
# BUYING
# and
# PURCHASING
# MANAGEMENT

## Harry E. Hough
### James M. Ashley

**PRENTICE HALL**
Englewood Cliffs, New Jersey 07632

Library of Congress Cataloging-in-Publication Data

Hough, Harry E.
    Handbook of buying and purchasing management /
by Harry E. Hough and James M. Ashley.
        p.   cm.
    Includes index.
    ISBN 0-13-374190-7
    1. Industrial procurement—Handbooks, manuals, etc.   I. Ashley,
James M.   II. Title.
HD39.5.H68   1992                                     92-11987
658.7'2—dc20                                          CIP

*Printed in the United States of America*

*10   9   8   7   6   5*

**PRENTICE HALL**
Career & Personal Development
Englewood Cliffs, NJ 07632
A Simon & Schuster Company

On the World Wide Web at http://www.phdirect.com

Prentice-Hall International (UK) Limited, *London*
Prentice-Hall of Australia Pty. Limited, *Sydney*
Prentice-Hall Canada Inc., *Toronto*
Prentice-Hall Hispanoamericana, S.A., *Mexico*
Prentice-Hall of India Private Limited, *New Delhi*
Prentice-Hall of Japan, Inc., *Tokyo*
Simon & Schuster Asia Pte. Ltd., *Singapore*
Editora Prentice-Hall do Brasil, Ltda., *Rio de Janeiro*

# About the Authors

HARRY E. HOUGH started his business career at Ford Motor Company where he held supervisory positions in manufacturing management before becoming Senior Purchasing Analyst at Ford Division. After leaving Ford he held top purchasing positions in various industries. Among the positions he held were director of Purchasing and Materials for American International Aluminum, Vice President of North American Car Corporation, and Director of Purchasing for domestic and international purchases at the Ekco Housewares Company. He has been a consultant to companies in both the manufacturing and service industries.

Dr. Hough studied Mechanical Engineering at Drexel University, received a Bachelor of Arts degree with a major in Economics from the University of Pennsylvania, an MBA from the University of Chicago Executive Program, and a Ph.D. from Columbia Pacific University.

Dr. Hough has taught courses at several colleges in the Detroit and Chicago areas. He founded the American Purchasing Society and helped establish the first certification program which requires high ethical standards as well as special business knowledge for purchasing professionals. His time is now spent as a consultant to companies in both manufacturing and the service industries, as chief executive of the American Purchasing Society, and in giving seminars for the Society, the American Management Association and other professional organizations.

JAMES M. ASHLEY has a 30-year background in negotiations for the purchasing and sales functions. During over ten years at IBM he served in many capacities from buyer to manager. He was Far East negotiator responsible for contracts administration and managing suppliers for the IBM personal computer. Mr. Ashley is now a consultant and is certified by the American Purchasing Society as a purchasing professional.

# Acknowledgments

When I first entered the field of purchasing there were very few sources of information on the subject. There was only one book that I know of on the subject of negotiating and that was aimed at labor negotiators. There were very few books on the general subject of purchasing. A notable exception is *Purchasing, Principles and Applications* by Stuart Heinritz and Paul Farrell which is an excellent introduction to purchasing and is now in its 8th edition. I owe much to what I learned from it during my early years in purchasing.

Neither were there many courses offered by colleges or universities. The American Management Association held seminars on the fundamentals of purchasing and on purchasing research. I learned a great deal from those sessions and appreciate the AMA's continuing efforts to provide training for those who have all levels of purchasing experience.

However, I learned most on the job at Ford Motor Company, which had a highly developed purchasing function long before the value of purchasing activities were appreciated. Bud Chicoine and the late Ben Mills, who were vice presidents of Ford's Purchasing Operations built strong departments.

I owe a lot to Bud who gave me the opportunity to join the purchase analysis team and exposed me to the many bright individuals who contributed to excellence in purchasing. I learned much about analyzing suppliers from my friend and fellow worker Gus Bloomquist. More recently, I want to thank Mr. G. C. Hague who supplied current information about Ford's purchasing operation.

Thanks to the many other business associates, too numerous to mention, who contributed their knowledge of business transactions. They include my former bosses, colleagues, and suppliers.

A special thanks to James Ashley who wrote chapters 6, 9, 10, 11, and 16 and provided insights based on his personal experience. Jim is an experienced, knowledgeable businessman who gave me ideas and made comments that helped make the book better.

My thanks to Ellen Kadin, Gerry Galbo, and Ruth Mills, my editors at Prentice Hall. I particularly appreciate the advice and comments received from Ruth Mills and her long patience in seeing me through to the completion of this project.

While all of the above supplied me with valuable information the responsibility for any errors of omission or commission is entirely mine.

Last, but not least, thanks also to my wife, Lynne; my daughter, Caroline; and my son, Richard, for their support and encouragement.

*Harry E. Hough*

# What This Book
# Will Do for You

*The Handbook of Buying and Purchasing Management* is a comprehensive guide that covers the A's to Z's of purchasing, from the recognition of a need for a product or service to the delivery and satisfaction after delivery. It is suited for the new buyer who wants a thorough understanding of the principles of purchasing as well as the seasoned purchasing manager who wants to learn the latest concepts and to learn how to solve the problems that every purchasing operation encounters.

Whether you work for a small company or a giant organization, using the guidelines in this book will help you do a better job and be prepared to solve the problems you have or will encounter. The first chapter explains the importance of purchasing and the common mistakes to avoid. Chapter 2 explains how to set-up and organize the department to fit your company needs. Chapter 3 explains the essentials of law that you need to know to buy and what you need to know to avoid getting into trouble. The fourth chapter gives you the details of the normal business buying process, from the issuance of a requisition to the receipt of the product. In Chapter 5 you will learn how you can use proper product description to improve quality and reduce the rate of rejections. Chapter 6 explains the various kinds of cost that you must be aware of to buy products intelligently.

If you buy many products and services, once in a while you will need to find a new source. Chapter 7 tells you how to find and qualify the best sources and then Chapter 8 tells you how to negotiate with the sources you locate or already have.

Chapter 9 gives you what you need to know to prepare a policy and procedure manual, a necessity for a well-run purchasing operation. Chapter 10 introduces you to the use of the computer for purchasing operations to make your job easier and give you the modern tools necessary to do the best possible purchasing job.

In Chapter 11 you will find out how to buy properly to obtain the best quality and in Chapter 12 you will learn how to eliminate shortages and obtain delivery when you want it. Chapter 13 gives you the essentials of how to buy different types of products. Chapter 14 gives you the information you need to manage a purchasing department efficiently, and chapter 15 discusses the common problems that purchasing departments encounter and gives you the ways you can solve those problems.

—————————— **THIS BOOK WILL TELL YOU:** ——————————

- The tremendous profit opportunities available from good purchasing and how you can obtain those profits.
- How to set up your purchasing organization to gain negotiating strength and minimize duplication of effort.
- How to protect your company from costly legal mistakes when you buy.
- How to use administrative procedures that make buying less risky and provide the information necessary to minimize future cost.
- How to describe the products and services you want to purchase so that you will receive the quality you want and keep cost under control.
- How to analyze cost so that you are able to negotiate from strength.
- Where to find the suppliers you need and how to determine if they are qualified.
- When, where, and how to negotiate even if you have never done so before.
- How to follow-up and expedite shipments to get the best results.
- How to avoid the common purchasing mistakes.

# Contents

## CHAPTER 4:   SIMPLIFYING THE BUYING PROCESS WITHOUT SACRIFICING CONTROL   55

## CHAPTER 5:   HOW TO OBTAIN THE PROPER SPECIFICATIONS TO HELP YOU AVOID COMMON PURCHASING PROBLEMS   101

## CHAPTER 6:  WHAT YOU NEED TO KNOW ABOUT PRICING AND COSTS  115

## CHAPTER 7:  HOW TO FIND AND QUALIFY SOURCES  143

## CHAPTER 8:  HOW TO NEGOTIATE THE BEST DEAL  167

## CHAPTER 9:   HOW TO ESTABLISH POLICIES AND PROCEDURES THAT WILL MAINTAIN CONTROL   187

## CHAPTER 10:   HOW TO USE COMPUTERS TO INCREASE PURCHASING PRODUCTIVITY   217

## CHAPTER 11: WHAT THE BUYER NEEDS TO KNOW ABOUT QUALITY 245

## CHAPTER 12: OBTAIN DELIVERY WHEN YOU WANT IT   000

## CHAPTER 13: HOW TO USE DIFFERENT BUYING TECHNIQUES FOR DIFFERENT PRODUCTS   297

# SELECTED BIBLIOGRAPHY   383

# APPENDIXES   389

# INDEX   444

# CHAPTER ONE

# Proper Purchasing Principles to Make More Money for Your Company

If you are a purchasing manager or full-time buyer, you are fortunate in being able to significantly affect the performance of your company. Purchasing is probably the most neglected function in business. Companies spend huge amounts on advertising and sales promotion. They devote most of their time to increasing the amount of sales. Often the profits on these sales are minimal. If the company is a manufacturing organization, tremendous effort goes into reducing manufacturing cost. Particular attention is spent on reductions in staffing since management believes that most of the operating costs are in labor and they believe that labor cost is the easiest to control. Yet the savings potential in reducing the cost of material may far exceed any labor savings.

A typical company will make a profit of 5% to 20% on every dollar sold. On the other hand savings by purchasing go directly into profit. In other words, 5 cents will be earned for an extra dollar sold, but $1 will be earned for every dollar saved by purchasing.

## HOW THIS BOOK WILL HELP YOU IMPROVE YOUR BUYING AND MAKE MORE ——————— MONEY FOR YOUR COMPANY ———————

Every business has someone who is responsible for buying goods and services. In the smallest of businesses perhaps the president or a secretary may place the orders. If the dollar volume of the purchase is low the order may be placed with little comparison shopping. No attempt is made to negotiate the price. There is often an unnecessary added cost for many items purchased. As the company grows the methods used do not always change to adapt to the growth. The same personnel may handle the buying and use the same or similar methods that were more appropriate for a smaller operation.

This book will help you understand the necessity of changing and give you the knowledge to buy in a professional manner. This book will show you how to set up the required policies and procedures for an efficient purchasing department. It will show you how to eliminate unnecessary extra cost. This book will improve your purchasing by telling you how to avoid the eight common purchasing mistakes. It will show you how to use proactive and imaginative buying techniques and how to manage purchasing effectively.

## 8 COMMON PURCHASING MISTAKES ——————— AND HOW TO SOLVE THEM[1] ———————

### Mistake #1: Not Shopping

The question is not if you should shop but how much. The more time that you spend looking for a better product or a better price the more chance that you will make a better choice. It is not unusual to see price differences in the 20% to 30% range and experienced buyers find occasions when the differences are much higher. The limit on shopping efforts is determined by comparing the cost of your buyers' time, the urgency of the need for the product, and the suitability of the product to satisfy the need. The buyer and management alike often are saddled with a lesser or more expensive product because they rushed to purchase an item without thoroughly shop-

---

[1] Adapted from "Common Purchasing Mistakes You Want to Avoid," 1989, American Purchasing Society, Inc., Port Richey, FL

ping to learn what was available. See Chapter 7 on how to find and qualify sources.

## Mistake #2: Not Understanding the Market

It is important to know the distribution method used for the product you are buying. For example, if you are buying steel you may buy directly from the mill or you may buy from a steel warehouse distributor. You may also buy from a broker or an importer. There are reasons for choosing each of these different types of sources and using the wrong type can be costly. For information on how to buy steel, see Chapter 13.

It is also important to know if the product you are looking for is in scarce supply. Are customers on allocation? Is there a strike or a threat of one? These factors affect the price, the quantity that you can buy, and how quickly you will receive delivery. You can waste a great deal of time trying to negotiate when suppliers are not that interested in obtaining new business. Once in a while the suppliers will tell you openly that they are not interested in your orders, but more often the message will be disguised in the form of higher prices and slow delivery or service. You may call or write several times to get a salesperson to call. If the volume of your order is small or the dollar amount insignificant it is possible that no salesperson will take the time to call on you. If you send out a dozen requests for bids and the only ones you receive say, "Decline to quote at this time," something may be going on that you do not know about.

The market always changes. It may change slowly or quickly but it is only a matter of time before conditions will be different. Perhaps the market will shrink and suppliers will go out of business. That is exactly what happened in the casting industry. Back in the 1960s, there were many foundries of all sizes. There were many "Mom and Pop" operations and prices were low. The industry was fiercely competitive. Then the Environmental Protection Agency (EPA) made some rules to clean up the environment. Many of the smaller firms did not like all the rules and could not afford the investment in equipment necessary to clean the atmosphere. Hundreds closed their businesses. The survivors raised their prices and it became difficult for buyers to find sources that could deliver quality castings without paying large price increases. In addition, delivery time was stretched. This required better inventory planning by the purchaser. Many companies decided to accept the cost of higher inventories to avoid out-of-stock situations.

In the 1970s and 1980s, foreign competition started to undercut the domestic foundries. Smart buyers went overseas looking for better prices and they found them. But that is not the end of the story. The buyers found the quality was not as good as they had been previously receiving from the domestic sources. In addition the exchange rate made it less economical to buy overseas. So many of the things that were bought overseas to save money were resourced again to suppliers in the United States.

The market changes for various reasons:

- Raw material becomes scarce.
- Labor rates go up.
- Foreign imports become a factor.
- The price of the dollar changes.
- New products are developed which make the old product obsolete and less attractive—in which case, a surplus in productive capacity will provide pressure for price reductions.

When buyers are aware of the market they can take prompt action to protect supply, to obtain reductions in price or postpone increases, to search for alternative products. In general, they can take measures which will improve or protect the company's profit picture.

## Mistake #3: Not Knowing the True Cost

Many executives and salespeople have a very low opinion of buyers because they feel sourcing decisions are based on price alone. Prices do have a major influence on buyers, but always buying the lowest price results in sometimes receiving inferior quality and poor service. The ultimate cost of the product is therefore much higher.

As consumers, unconsciously we usually consider other factors when we buy. We consider the reputation of the brand or the manufacturer and the perceived quality and the service that we expect to receive. When buying for business it should be no different except we may not actually see the product we are buying. Thus it is important to get in the habit of thinking in terms of buying the lowest cost item rather than the lowest priced item.

To buy a product or service without giving sufficient attention to price is just as much of a mistake as it is to consider price alone as the basis for the buying decision. Price is expressed in dollars. The difficulty lies in putting dollar figures on the other components of cost. Nevertheless, it can be done, although not always as precisely. For example, if a product is needed to keep a factory running, calculate the cost of shutting down operations or losing sales because of an out-of-stock situation. Comparing such cost to the differences in price between one supplier and another may more than justify buying from the supplier with the higher price. See Chapter 6 for a further discussion of prices and costing.

## Mistake #4: Letting Your Emotions Influence Your Buying Decision

Being friendly with the people you do business with would seem to make it easier. It is certainly more enjoyable. It also can be very costly and in the end you may lose the friendship. It is not possible to be overly friendly with your supplier without letting your emotions influence your buying decision. Keep suppliers' sales representatives and supplier management at a certain arm's length. Companies who have several buyers can get around this problem by rotating buyer assignments. In this way strong attachments to particular suppliers are not established.

Those who go into sales work do so because they say they like people. It is generally accepted that a pleasant outgoing personality suits one for sales. The implication is clear: buyers are influenced by the personality of the salesperson. Good buyers must resist the tendency to be influenced by salespeople they like or dislike.

For centuries salespeople have used flattery and other devices to appeal to buyers' emotions. In recent times many of us assume that enlightened companies sell their products by emphasizing the features and benefits. We may be lulled into the false feeling that the facts speak for themselves, and we can pick the best product and the best supplier simply by comparing one product or supplier to another. But if it is possible that salespeople can influence our unconscious, purchasing management and buyers must make an extra effort to remove personal prejudice and emotional factors from the buying decision.

Without considering the ethical issue, the buyer's ability to remain unemotional when making a purchase is affected when lavish entertainment or gratuities are accepted from the seller.

## Mistake #5: Only Looking at the Short Run

There are times when you can obtain your desired objective very quickly but the long-term effect will be disadvantageous. For example, you might be able to force a significant cost reduction because of market conditions or because the supplier thinks he needs your business to survive. However, the added business, rather than preventing the supplier's downfall, reduces profits and only speeds up his business failure. Now you are faced with finding a new supplier who may charge you more than you were previously paying.

Resourcing to obtain a short-term gain may have an equally unfortunate result. The new source may have bid low to get your business. After he has it, he finds it necessary to raise prices. Going back to your old source may not help. Your original source may have been reluctant to ask for higher prices because he did not want to risk losing your business, but now he realizes that even though his prices were low you still changed sources. He therefore feels justified in now asking for more. In addition he may have made up for your lost volume by selling it elsewhere and now he does not have the capacity to handle your account without adding resources.

If you feel you are getting a low price, good quality, and prompt delivery it is easy to become complacent and forget about planning for future needs. That could cause trouble ahead if your company is growing rapidly. Your present sources may not be able to furnish all the material that you require. They simply may not have the resources to do so. Even if they have the equipment and capacity to handle your business, they may choose not to take it because they do not want most of their business with one customer. Rather than divulge their thinking directly, they increase the price or extend delivery time far into the future.

## Mistake #6: Not Timing Your Purchases

The cost of keeping material in stock prevents many companies from buying at the right time and in the right quantities. You pay more for fresh fruit when it is not in season. You pay more for products and services in any of the following situations:

- When supply is scarce or when the raw materials going into the products cost more.
- When orders have to be rushed because the supplier has to pay overtime rates or cause inefficiencies in his operation by rescheduling.
- When you buy small quantities rather frequently than if you ordered larger quantities less often.
- When you constantly surprise the supplier with unexpected rush orders so that he cannot plan or time his purchases. He may have to order his raw material from a supplier that has higher prices and he may have to use a method of transportation that costs more.

## Mistake #7: Not Looking at the Details

Every buyer needs to read the fine print and analyze the details before signing agreements or accepting changes in terms. Average price increases stated in a cover letter are frequently distortions in favor of the supplier. Blanket price increases usually are not weighted for the volumes purchased by each customer. Prices may have remained the same or may have even been reduced on items that you buy in low quantities, whereas the items that you buy in large quantities may have large price changes.

## Mistake #8: Not Looking at the Big Picture

Any supplier is able to offer the lowest price or perform well on certain items, but dividing your purchase volume among hundreds of suppliers weakens your negotiating ability. Although a supplier may have a higher price for one or two items used in low volume, lower costs on the major items added to reduced administrative cost far exceed the advantages of having many unnecessary sources.

# USE PROACTIVE AND IMAGINATIVE ———————— BUYING TECHNIQUES ————————

Successful purchasing requires action. The buyer who sits back and waits for requisitions before shopping never has time to shop. The most effective buyers are in a state of constant activity. There never is enough time to learn all there is to know about every product you buy or about the suppliers and industries you buy from. Successful buyers also devote time to learning about their own company. That includes learning about the products your company sells and the people who work for your company. You especially need to know about the people and their idiosyncrasies. This helps to promote good communication and avoid the conflicts that hinder the best purchasing performance.

Every buyer needs to take steps to reduce prices, improve quality, improve delivery schedules, reduce paperwork, and improve communications. The following sections provide recommendations for how to achieve each of these goals.

## How to Ask for Price Reductions and Get Them

Suppliers do not often voluntarily reduce prices. It is up to the buyer to ask for reductions in price, but just because you ask does not mean you are going to succeed. In order to succeed you must know the market so that you make your request at the appropriate time. You need to be armed with all the facts that are available. Your request has a much greater chance to be granted if you can support it with valid reasons. For example, if you are buying a manufactured component that uses raw material such as plastic resin and you learn that resin prices have declined, then your supplier's cost is less and he can reduce prices to you without any loss of profit.

You can obtain raw material prices from various sources. Business magazines such as *Purchasing* print such information. *The Wall Street Journal* reports on prices and price changes as do many other major city newspapers.

Periodically you will obtain prices from new sources. Sometimes these may even be unsolicited. If they are at all lower than what you are paying you have ammunition to ask for a reduction from your present source. Hesitate before disclosing who has given you a lower price quotation or the amount, but simply mentioning that you have received a lower price and asking if your supplier cannot make some adjustment will often produce a beneficial result. The reduction from your present source often exceeds what the new source has quoted. See Chapter 8 for a discussion of methods of negotiating and Chapter 3 for information on price discrimination.

## How to Get Your Supplier to Improve Quality

Business managers often assume that the way to get better quality is to pay more, but higher prices and a higher degree of quality are not necessarily related. To be assured of a certain level of quality it is first necessary to provide clear specifications on what you want. If the product meets those specifications, then by definition, you have the quality level you want. The cause of an unsatisfactory quality level is either no specifications have been provided or the specifications are inadequate. Sometimes the specifications are totally incorrect for the purpose intended. For example, if the specification calls for carbon steel and you are unhappy because you are receiving rusty steel, perhaps you need one of the grades of stainless. If so, your specification should be changed and it should be changed in such a way that it will reflect the least expensive grade of stainless that will do the job. See Chapter 5 for more on establishing proper specifications. Also see Chapter 7 on qualifying sources and Chapter 11 on Quality.

## How to Get Your Supplier to Deliver When You Want

One of the most difficult jobs a buyer has is to get suppliers to deliver on time. Companies protect themselves from late deliveries by carrying "safety stocks" or, in other words, larger inventories than are necessary. In recent years managements have gone to stockless purchasing systems where they rely on the supplier to stock material. However, that only passes the delivery problem on to the supplier who compensates for the added cost of keeping inventory by eventually raising prices.

Nor is it better to get deliveries before the items are needed. A few suppliers ship early because they believe that the earlier they ship the better. Unless you really need the goods the early shipment disrupts your operation by requiring staff to unload and warehouse the product. If scheduling was proper those people were planned for other assignments. When suppliers ship early they usually invoice at the same time. This unnecessarily adds to your cost if you pay the invoice earlier than agreed because of the time value of money. If you do not pay when the invoices are due, your credit record will be affected. It is easier to remedy the early shipment problem than the late shipment problem. Usually a telephone call to the supplier is all that is necessary, although it is better to put it in writing so that there is a record of your request.

The cause of early or late deliveries is just as often the fault of the buyer as it is the seller. The buyer needs to clearly specify when goods are to be delivered and those delivery schedules must consider the minimum lead time quoted by the supplier. A supplier should only be considered behind schedule when he has agreed to make delivery on a certain date. You should instruct the supplier on the importance of meeting delivery schedules before you place the order and then the delivery date should be clearly and conspicuously spelled out when the purchase order is written. The proper kind of follow-up system is necessary to ensure on-time performance by tardy suppliers. For a detailed discussion of the delivery problem see Chapter 12.

## How to Reduce Paperwork and Improve Communications

To do a good job in purchasing it is necessary to write purchase orders, purchase order revisions, letters of agreement, letters of instruction, letters of complaint, and many other types of business communications. (For a complete guide to sample letters, see the *PURCHASING MANAGER'S GUIDE TO MODEL LETTERS, MEMOS, AND FORMS*, by Kenneth H. Killen and Robert L. Janson, published by Prentice Hall, © 1991.) It is necessary to maintain records of price histories to be used for future negotiations and records of all transactions for legal purposes. Some purchasing functions are responsible for keeping track of purchased goods by checking receiving documents. All these activities involve the handling of paper or forms and the volume can at times be staggering.

One measure of a purchasing department's performance is how well it handles this volume of paperwork. With limited staff resources, it is important to have an efficient paper handling system that provides all the information you need to buy in the best way but requires the smallest possible demand for time. There are purchasing departments with a dozen or more people spending 90% of their time just handling paperwork.

Although the burden is being sharply reduced by the introduction of the computer into the purchasing function, mechanization does not necessarily alleviate the problem. In fact, it can accentuate the volume because of the speed of the computer and because of additional data that pours out.

Most of a buyer's time should be spent in shopping, interviewing salesreps, and negotiating. See Figures 1-1, 1-2, and 1-3. A large portion of time should be spent studying the products, the markets, and the suppliers. To make time available for these duties, you must streamline your depart-

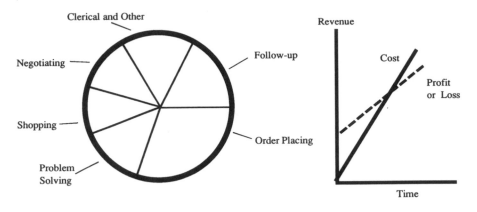

**Figure 1-1. The Use of Time—Profit Erosion**

ment's administrative procedures. Using blanket orders and releases against those orders eliminates the need to negotiate repeatedly for the same product. Limiting the number of suppliers used for the same product reduces paperwork and has the added advantage of giving the buyer more negotiating muscle.

The proper design of a requisition form saves a significant amount of time and improves communication. (For a full discussion see Chapter 4.) Buying larger quantities often means fewer purchase orders to write, fewer receiving transactions, and fewer invoices for the accounting department (the cost of added inventory must be compared with the reduced administrative cost before taking such action). Limiting the number of copies of forms will reduce paperwork. For example, similar companies use a vastly different number of copies of purchase orders. The number of copies of

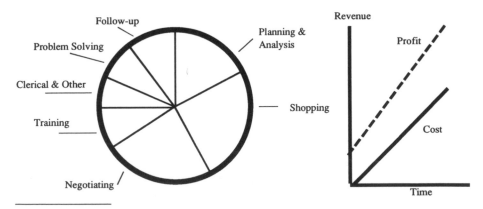

Copyright © 1990 by American Purchasing Society, Inc.

**Figure 1-2. The Use of Time—Profit Improvement**

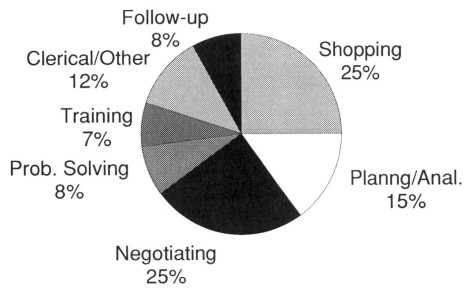

Approximate Percentages

**Figure 1-3. Purchasing Dynamics—Profitable Use of Time**

purchase orders varies between two to twelve. If certain departments find the need to see the purchase order, one copy can simply be forwarded from department to department and perhaps filed in the last department. This has the added advantage of reducing the printing cost of the form.

## Using Effective Purchasing Management Techniques

The management of the purchasing function is similar to the management of any other function. That is, it is involved in the seven functions of management: decision making, organizing, staffing, planning, controlling, communicating, and directing.[2] These functions differ for purchasing only in as much that they deal with the particular purchasing specialty:

*Decision Making.* Purchasing management decisions would involve establishing policies on the number of sources to use, how often a product will be reshopped, how often to visit suppliers, and so on.

*Organizing.* The organizing function in purchasing may run counter to what general management feels is the best policy. From a purchasing point of view a centralized organization is clearly superior to a decentral-

---

[2] *Essentials of Management*, 3rd ed. (Prentice Hall 1979), pp. 6–8

ized one, whereas general management may prefer local control. See Chapter 2 for the pros and cons of various organizational structures.

*Staffing.* Adding to your buying staff involves the selection of people who are adequately trained to do buying. Too often companies select someone who has a superior knowledge of one product but lacks the minimum necessary knowledge of business law or economics to keep the company out of difficulty.

*Planning.* Planning for negotiating sessions is perhaps a little different from planning a marketing campaign. However, planning for budgets and setting of objectives is somewhat similar to what a marketing manager might do.

*Controlling.* This is one of the most important but frequently overlooked duties of purchasing management. As purchasing manager, you are responsible to see that all purchases for the company are made for the benefit of the company. A violation of this principle by any buyer reflects poorly on the purchasing manager in charge.

*Communicating.* All management must communicate and usually the better the communication the better the performance. This is especially true for purchasing management. Purchasing Managers need to communicate with more people and at more levels than any other function. You need to communicate not only with your own staff and with general management, you need to communicate either directly or indirectly with every requisitioner, with suppliers, and with each department head. No other function deals directly with so many facets of the business.

*Directing.* Obviously, you direct each buyer and clerk in the purchasing operation, but you also direct the requisitioners by informing them what is available and what cost premiums they will incur if they insist on certain products. You also direct the suppliers on what to ship, when to ship it, and how to ship it.

## How to Minimize Operational Costs

One of the primary goals in the purchasing function is to minimize cost. Purchasing costs fall into two categories: product cost and administrative cost. You must establish objectives to reduce cost to the lowest possible level and take measures to keep them there. All of the above mentioned management functions are used to achieve these ends and we will discuss each one of them.

## Controlling Unauthorized Purchases

You need to establish policies and procedures to protect your company from unnecessary expenditures. Some of these expenditures may come from employees who are not aware of the company's priorities or who do not know what products or services are really needed. With the approval and support of general management, you need to establish levels of authority to authorize purchasing expenditures. Company budgets are often assumed to be sufficient authorization for purchases. However, the budget is usually prepared far in advance of the need to purchase and subsequent conditions change making the purchase unwise. Furthermore, budgets usually do not provide sufficient detail to make an intelligent purchase. Just because an item has been budgeted for a certain dollar amount does not mean the company has to spend that amount to get the goods. Salespeople sometimes try to find out how much was budgeted so they can quote a price that is near to that budget limitation. The smart buyer never tells the seller how much he has to spend. If the buyer does so, surely all of it will be needed.

## Forecasting, Measuring, and Controlling Authorized Purchases

The purchasing manager is usually called upon by the financial people or general management to forecast price changes or the total dollars that will be spent for a future period. These forecasts help management make financial plans and cash flow analysis. The same information is useful to the purchasing department to help establish objectives and highlight areas that need concentrated effort.

The best purchasing management ensures that adequate records are maintained so that performance can be measured. You should measure buyer performance and departmental performance against budgets, objectives, and previous results.

The accounting function can help your department control purchases. Obtaining the proper prior authorization for a potential purchase is only a fraction of adequate control. It does not ensure the lowest cost. To get that type of control calls for a requirement that there must be documented evidence of sufficient shopping effort.

Therefore, study the unit cost for an item as well as total expenditures for the same item or class of items. Such studies reveal possible problem areas that call for further investigation and possible corrective action. For example, one manufacturing company discovered that it was buying five times as many safety glasses every year as they had employees. Another company reduced an enormous annual expenditure for disposable pallets by 85% by using high quality returnable pallets. Years ago the automotive companies learned the importance of keeping track of their expenditures for raw material. When metal prices became too high or the steel companies would not negotiate, the designs were changed to use plastic. Automobiles then contained more items made of plastic. High quality plastic gears were substituted for metal gears. Plastic replaced sheet metal in fenders and hoods.

Good purchasing practices help make a company more profitable in the best of times and help prevent it from losing money when times are difficult. Purchasing operations vary in importance depending on the amount of expenditures made by a company. Generally companies that deal with tangible products spend more than service companies and would therefore tend to have bigger and more influential purchasing departments. However, there are exceptions.

For example, telephone companies and electric companies have high capital expenditures. It is not uncommon for even small manufacturing companies to spend 50% or more of their sales dollar in purchased goods. The purchasing manager responsible for so much of the company's capital is considered a very important part of the management team. To neglect the purchasing function or to allow incompetence is to risk significant loss and possible business failure. This book will show you how to set up the required policies and procedures of a professional purchasing department. It will show you how to eliminate those unnecessary extra costs.

# CHAPTER TWO

# How to Structure and Staff the Purchasing Operation to Fit the Company Organization and Maximize Profit Potential

It is easy for an organization to become too highly structured with too many layers of management. Responsibilities and authority can become so well defined that no one will step outside of those clearly established lines. When this happens, undefined problems often go unsolved because they do not fall under anyone's responsibility and no one is willing to step out of bounds. On the other hand, companies with little or no structure suffer from duplication of effort and lack of control. Somewhere between these extremes is the proper plan.

Perhaps purchasing more than any other department needs a minimum of company structure to properly control purchases. The purchasing department itself must be structured to operate efficiently within the organization.

Individuals within the department need to be carefully selected to make sure they are capable and then they must have proper authority to carry out their responsibilities. Once selected those individuals must be motivated to achieve the established company and departmental goals.

## HOW TO RELATE COMPANY STRUCTURE
## ———————— TO MANAGEMENT STYLE ————————

Companies (like governments) can have strong central control or delegate authority to branches, plants, or departments at lower levels. The former system is referred to as centralized management and the latter as decentralized. Purchasing may also be either centralized or decentralized. With centralized purchasing all buying is done from one location, usually at the corporate or home office. Figure 2-1 is an organization chart illustrating centralized purchasing. With decentralized purchasing buying is done at the local level by plant personnel, branch personnel, and sometimes delegated down to department heads or end users of the product or service being bought. Figure 2-2 provides an organization chart to illustrate decentralized purchasing.

Over the past 30 years, company organizations have shifted from highly centralized to decentralized back to centralized structures ad infinitum. The advocates for one type of an organization or another are convinced that their plan is the best for the most effective management of the company. A change in the structure may have more to do with the personality of the chief executive than with any proof of what is the best system. A dictatorial style of management logically favors the centralized system whereas those who prefer to delegate authority are inclined to prefer a decentralized system.

The advocates of centralized management believe that the system provides easier control. Those who favor decentralized management say that it is better to give local management control over most facets of the operation because decisions can be made quicker and better by those who are most familiar with the operation and its problems. The idea under the decentralized system is to give local management full authority in all but a few areas and then either good or bad performance is the result of local management decisions. Responsibility for profits or losses is therefore clearer and good performance can be properly compensated or action taken to improve poor performance. The theory is that managers are highly motivated by knowing that they will be compensated for their efforts and knowing that they have the authority to make decisions and determine their own destiny.

In practice, most businesses are not totally centralized or decentralized. A highly centralized company still delegates certain authority to department heads or branch managers. It would be impractical, if not impossible, to do otherwise in all but the smallest of operations. The most decentralized organization has authority limits or restricted areas that are reserved for central management. For example, corporate policy usually determines broad product areas of what will be sold even though a division has the authority to decide a particular item or design.

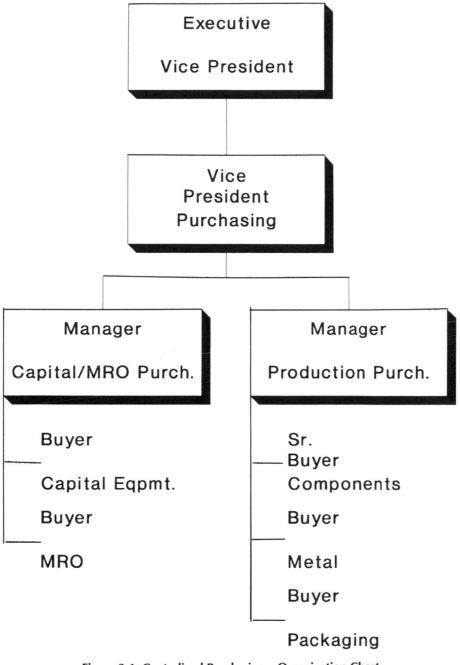

Figure 2-1. Centralized Purchasing—Organization Chart

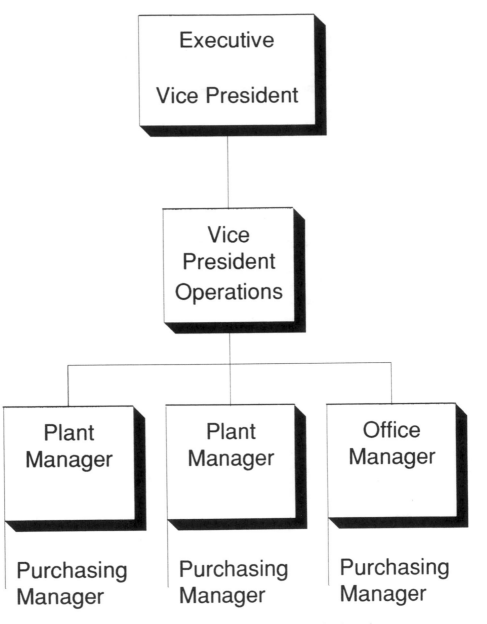

**Figure 2-2. Decentralized Purchasing—Organization Chart**

# HOW TO STRUCTURE
## _____ THE PURCHASING FUNCTION _____

Additional considerations are necessary when deciding the organizational structure of the purchasing department. There are advantages and disadvantages of either a centralized or a decentralized system that are unique to the purchasing function. Modification of the corporate structure may be required in order to maximize company profits.

If your company has decentralized management, the local managers believe that they are entitled to maintain control of local purchasing activities. They see various advantages of decentralized purchasing (see Figure 2-2) and often fail to see the disadvantages. Their viewpoint is understandable since performance by Purchasing affects the overall performance of the local operation and has an affect on local profits. Consequently, bonuses may be determined as much if not more by Purchasing performance than the performance of any other function.

Regardless of company structure there is always pressure for some degree of local control in buying decisions, for any or all of the following reasons:

- People like to buy.
- Sales efforts are being directed toward users of products and not necessarily toward professional buyers.
- There is a need for special user knowledge of products or services.
- The purchasing function is misunderstood.

None of the above beliefs should be the sole criterion for deciding how the Purchasing function should be organized. You should make your decision primarily on the advantages and disadvantages of the organizational structure from a Purchasing function viewpoint. Your decision should also consider the local viewpoint and how each type of structure will affect total company profits.

### Advantages of Decentralized Purchasing

_**Local Control.**_ This is cited as an advantage to decentralized purchasing by those who assume that local control assures better control.

_**Quick Response Time.**_ Local requisitioners can see a local buyer faster and can pressure the buyers to hurry an order. The fear is that a buyer far removed from the scene does not react as fast and may have other branches that take priority.

_**Good Communication.**_ Requisitioners working close to buyers can deliver messages quicker. They can answer questions and provide data easier. Because they are well acquainted with the buyer they understand each other and know each other's needs.

*Community Relations.* Local buyers get to know local suppliers well and place business locally. As a result the community gives the company more support. Employees may have friends or relatives working at other companies in the community and giving business to those companies helps assure continuing employment and economic security for the community.

## Disadvantages of Decentralized Purchasing

*Undue Pressure from Employees and Local Sources.* Employees and suppliers influence buying decisions without proper regard to cost.

*Different Priorities of Local Management.* The primary concern of management of a sales office is to obtain sales. The primary concern of a manufacturing plant is to make product. The highest priority of local management is therefore making sure that the goods or services needed are delivered on time and are of the best quality. Price and total procurement cost considerations are frequently neglected.

*Local Salaries Preclude Hiring Qualified Buyers.* The wage scale of knowledgeable buyers is sometimes higher than what managerial personnel get at the local level. Well-qualified people are thoroughly trained and therefore demand higher salaries. These higher salaries can be justified if they have sufficient responsibility in terms of dollars spent or volume of purchases. Buyers for branch operations seldom have high enough dollar responsibility to justify the higher salaries and the people they report to often earn modest remuneration. It would be illogical to pay a local buyer nearly as much or more than his or her supervisor makes.

*Buyer Specialization is Impractical.* Because many products are purchased in low volumes it is uneconomical to hire many buyers who know the products and can therefore obtain the lowest cost. Fewer buyers do not have the time to learn enough about the many products purchased.

*Insufficient Knowledge by Local General Management.* Inexperience and lack of purchasing knowledge sometimes allow incompetent buyers to be hired and continue on the job for many years without being discovered.

Local costs are given higher importance than total company cost. When the central or corporate office tries to obtain a national agreement beneficial to the total company, cost for some locations on certain items may be higher than could have been obtained locally even though the total company cost is lower. With local control or strong local influence, agreements of this type often fail.

## Advantages of Centralized Purchasing

*Item Prices are Reduced and Terms can be Improved.* Tremendous negotiating power is attained from the economies of scale. Combining the requirements from many requisitioners provides volumes to obtain better discounts from published lists. More important, volumes sometimes become large enough to obtain price reductions and improvements in terms and conditions beyond published figures.

*Category Prices are Reduced and Terms can be Improved.* Combining requirements from multiplant or branch offices provides high volumes of various classes of items. For example; although the volumes of purchases of individual corrugated cartons may be low and the designs may even be unique to one location, combining all corrugated items may provide a very large volume of corrugated carton usage.

*Buyer Specialization is More Economical.* If a company is large enough to have more than one or two purchasing agents, then it can gain many advantages by buyer specialization or simply assigning certain products or category of products to one individual and other products or categories to another individual. For example, if a company has three purchasing agents, one might be assigned all packaging goods, another all metal purchases, and the third maintenance supplies and capital equipment. There are many ways to divide the responsibilities but the most qualified buyer is usually given the most difficult category or the category with the highest dollar impact.

Limiting the number of products that one person handles allows the individual to become thoroughly familiar with the product, the suppliers, and the industry. It gives the buyer the chance to be on an equal footing with the sales representative who spends all his or her time becoming familiar with one product.

*Local Bias is Minimized.* The central buyer is not as apt to be influenced by local suppliers or by the agenda of other departments.

*Duplication of Effort can be Avoided.* Fewer suppliers are used resulting in less paperwork, from writing the purchase order to paying the invoices. The time spent for negotiations of similar products is reduced by the number of plants that could have duplicated the effort.

*There Tends to be One Set of Specifications.* This saves engineering effort and makes it much easier to measure and control quality.

*Lower Inventories are Required and Smaller Safety Stocks are Needed.* In an emergency, one location can help satisfy the needs of another.

*Total Company Costs are Lower.* Some local locations may pay more, however.

## Combining Centralized and Decentralized Purchasing— Using a Modified Structure

While the advantages of the centralized system over the decentralized system may seem obvious, in practice it is often difficult to establish without extreme organizational conflict. To obtain most of the benefits of the centralized organization it may be better to use a modified system. Many companies do just that and obtain most of the advantages of both systems.

A modified system may take several forms. For example, you might delegate the purchase of selected items or categories of items which represent the largest annual dollar expenditures to a central buyer or buyers. Or, some companies assign the purchase of all production goods (goods that are components or raw material going into products for resale) to central purchasing. Maintenance, repair, and operating supplies are often purchased at the local level. The responsibility for the purchase of capital equipment is frequently shared. The requisitioner or using location may shop for the item to obtain information to help them define the kind of equipment they need but the negotiations are conducted by a central buyer.

While in most cases, the amount of annual expenditures for a product determines who will buy the goods, it is easier to define by specifying the class of the goods. For example, production items and capital equipment will be bought by central purchasing; maintenance, repair, and operating supplies will be purchased at the plant level.

However, in large companies many MRO items represent significant dollar expenditures. National contracts are written which provide a much lower cost than what would be achieved by the local plant. Such agreements require a specification that will be used by all operations and proper control to make certain that local users do not ignore the national agreement and buy what they choose.

Managers and buyers at the local level may have different criteria in selecting a source than the national buyer has. In one case price may be the determining factor. In another case it may be brand name preference or specifications. The national buyer must consider what product or service best suits multiple locations even though one particular location could be better off with another choice.

Some central purchasing departments handle the buying from receipt of the requisition or bill of material to the verification of delivery. They may even help forecast needs and decide inventory levels or purchase quantities. At the other extreme are the central departments that simply locate the sources and negotiate the contract. The quantity to be ordered (released) against the master contract is done at the local level.

**Central Staff Functions.**

A classical definition of staff would be individuals who plan and advise rather than take an active part in day-to-day operations. Modern usage corrupts this definition by sometimes referring to those in the central office as staff. Thus the above mentioned central purchasing that negotiates contracts and allows local plants to release against those contracts is sometimes referred to as central staff purchasing. However, with the more traditional meaning, such buying would categorize those buyers as operating personnel or the department as an operating department rather than staff. Fig. 2-3 illustrates the organization of a central staff with a decentralized purchasing system.

Nevertheless a central staff purchasing function is extremely important to all but the smallest of businesses. Staff duties include planning, measuring, analyzing, forecasting, and advising general management of past performance, potential problems, and suggesting measures that need to be taken. A staff purchasing executive usually has the responsibility to write policies and procedures for the function. Another important responsibility is to conduct routine audits of purchasing activity. In smaller companies these duties are often combined with the responsibility of buying or managing the day-to-day operation of purchasing. Unfortunately, if the functions are combined the importance of staff duties is often overlooked and problems of daily business take priority over long range needs. While the operating function solves the daily problems repeatedly as they arise, successful staff performance solves them once by preventing their repetition.

## A Modified Centralized System

A typical purchasing organization for a medium-sized company is illustrated in Figure 2-4. The Director of Purchasing has responsibility to contract for purchase of production parts, capital equipment, and national contracts for selected items. All other maintenance, repair, and operating supplies are delegated to the plant level. The Director has staff responsibilities as well as operational duties and the staff function is indicated by a dotted line in Figure 2-3 and Figure 2-4. That is why staff functions are sometimes referred to as the dotted line responsibility.

A possible variation of a modified system allows buyers with multibranch buying responsibility to be physically located at a branch operation. If several branches employ purchasing agents, the agent at one branch can have the authority to buy a particular product or products for all branches while an agent at another plant has the authority to do the same for all branches including the first branch. This system has many of the advantages of a fully centralized system and still keeps a buyer available at

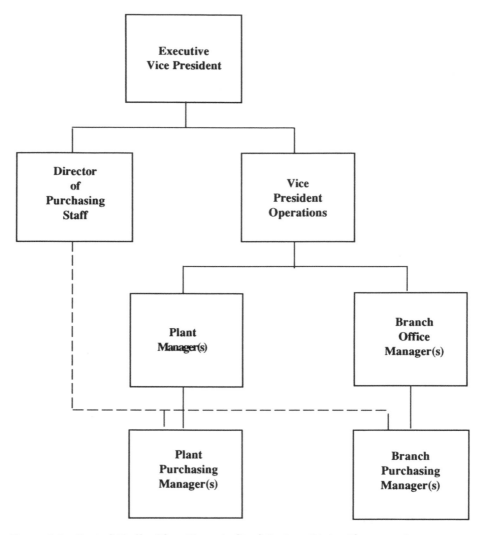

**Figure 2-3. Central Staff with a Decentralized System (Note: The reporting structure remains the same for multiple plants or multiple branches.)**

a local operation. The purchasing agent who buys the most of a particular product and who therefore may have most knowledge of that product has the responsibility to buy for the entire organization.

## HOW TO UNDERSTAND
## AND CLARIFY RESPONSIBILITY

Organizational charts such as those illustrated are sometimes scoffed at as unnecessary or restrictive. Critics believe that they are detrimental to team effort which has been such a successful management style in Japan.

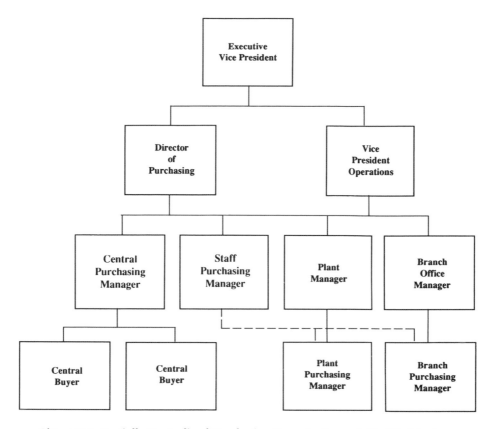

**Figure 2-4. Partially Centralized Purchasing Organization—A Modified System**

While there may be some truth in these arguments, it is especially important that everyone in a business organization has a clear understanding of reporting structure and purchasing lines of authority. Millions of dollars are wasted by unauthorized buying personnel. Usually this results from a vague understanding of who has responsibility and who has the authority to make purchases and to what extent. It can be clarified by up-to-date organization charts and well-defined policy and procedure manuals. Amazingly, many chief purchasing executives do not know what the limits of their authority are.

Buying is a skill that takes training and experience. Many people think they know how to buy wisely, perhaps because they enjoy it. Placing an order especially for a large dollar amount gives one a sense of power. However, placing an order, by our definition, is not buying any more than taking an order is selling. Non-purchasing department heads or even officers of companies make commitments which later turn out to be disastrous. They are experts in their field but learn too late that their training and experience in purchasing are insufficient.

Your company should have a procedure which defines who has the authority to requisition and to what level as well as who has the authority to buy. Some companies mistakenly use the budgeting process to authorize purchases. Because budgets are prepared well in advance of the purchase, cost figures become outdated. In addition, the requisitioner believes that because the budget has been approved the supplier who provided the cost information can be used without the need for further shopping. Costs obtained for budgeting are usually done quickly without proper shopping and almost always without sufficient negotiating effort. Furthermore, although the item was budgeted, it may no longer be required. An authorized requisition should still be prepared. Figure 2-5 illustrates authority levels for requisitions as well as purchases.

Armed with documents that show who is authorized to requisition and knowing how much authority is delegated, you will have the guide you need to help control unauthorized purchases. Help, yes. Control alone, no. General management must believe in the system and back up the procedures by forceful statements both in writing and orally. If violators go unpunished (even if it is only an oral reprimand), then the whole system breaks down. If the chief financial officer or controller does not help enforce the system, it has little chance for success. If invoices are sometimes paid without issuance of a purchase order, word quickly spreads that you do not have to go through the purchasing department. Without going through the purchasing department, effective budget control disappears, acquisition cost becomes higher than necessary, and most important of all insufficient records of transactions are maintained to measure loss of control or to resolve problems that routinely develop.

## HOW TO USE THE SCOPE AND LIMITATIONS ———— OF AUTHORITY TO ADVANTAGE ————

With clearly defined purchasing responsibility, buyers can concentrate their efforts on only the products and services assigned to them. Salespeople can be referred to the appropriate area responsible to purchase a particular product or service.

You can delegate the lowest cost transactions to the least skilled buyer and use the time of more experienced individuals where it will produce the best return.

Without written guidelines unauthorized purchases are difficult to correct. With a written and completely circulated statement employees are less likely to plead ignorance successfully although occasional written reminders of who is authorized to requisition or purchase are necessary. It

## Requisitioning Authority

| | |
|---|---|
| Clerks and other hourly workers | All requisitions must be approved by supervisor |
| First line supervision | Up to $500 in value |
| Department managers | Up to $1000 for expense items; capitalized items require prior budget approval. |
| Material control and inventory manager | Same as above except $10,000 for existing items used for the purchase of items for resale. New items for resale must have prior approval of the V.P. of marketing. |
| Officers | Up to $2500 for expense items without prior budget approval; up to $5000 for capital items without prior budget approval. No limitation on budgeted items. |

## Purchasing Authority (with a properly approved requisition)

| | |
|---|---|
| Buyers | Expense items up to $1000 per item or per order whichever less. Items for resale up to $5,000. |
| Senior buyers | Expense items up to $2500 per item or per order whichever less. Items for resale up to $10,000. Capital items up to $5000. |
| Purchasing managers | Expense items up to $10,000. Items for resale up to $50,000. Capital items up to $10,000. |
| Director of purchasing | Expense items up to $100,000. Items for resale, no limitation. Capital items up to $100,000. |
| Vice president | No limitation on approved requisitions except for capital items in excess of one million dollars which needs approval by the president and the board of directors. |

*Figure 2-5. Typical Authority Levels for Requisitioning and Buying*

is important that your company informs each new employee of certain purchasing policies and procedures—and those regarding authorization are key. If this information has been communicated then both the employee and the seller are responsible for any unauthorized purchase and usually the goods can be returned without cost if done so promptly.

When sellers circumvent or try to circumvent lines of authority by taking orders from unauthorized individuals, the responsible buyer or purchasing agent should inform the seller in the strongest language that such tactics are not appreciated and that no future orders will be awarded to the seller if the representative does not work through the proper channels. The controller should not pay any invoices without a properly authorized purchase order and no after-the-fact purchase order should be issued without making procedures clear to both the offending employee and supplier. Some buyers delay issuing after-the-fact purchase orders or delay payment and in some extreme cases even force the employee to pay for the goods or pay the difference in the lower price that would have been obtained if an authorized supplier had been used. This is particularly true when it is impossible to return the goods because they have been consumed.

## HOW TO FIND AND SELECT THE _____ BEST PURCHASING PERSONNEL _____

Highly qualified purchasing personnel are difficult to find. Some of the reasons are that formal training courses are few and those that are available are often inadequate. The best trained buyers and purchasing managers usually work for the largest companies because those companies recognize the importance of purchasing and reward those in the profession accordingly. Ideally a buyer should have a thorough knowledge of business law and accounting, be a psychologist, have excellent communication skills, be assertive, have good mathematics skills, and have a clear understanding of economics. A knowledge of negotiating techniques should have been learned through reading the available material on the subject and applying it. In many cases a background in engineering is helpful if not necessary.

A purchasing manager needs all this and more. The best management of purchasing requires a knowledge of statistics and management know-how. Today, knowing how to use the computer is almost essential. For companies heavily involved in international trade, one or more foreign languages is helpful but not absolutely necessary.

Where do you find such an individual? Hiring someone with an MBA gives you much of the above background. On-the-job experience helps. When hiring for purchasing, keep in mind the very significant impact that person will have on the overall performance of the company. A plant manager may control less in company expenditures than a buyer or purchasing manager. The potential for profit improvement may be much more from reducing the cost of purchased product than higher sales volume.

The best source for experienced buyers is through professional associations such as the American Purchasing Society. Not only does it have a list of buyers from every part of the United States and even some from other countries, it has the know-how to evaluate their skills and investigate their reputation in business. Another way to find purchasing personnel is by advertising in the periodicals read by professionals in purchasing. Examples of such periodicals are *Purchasing* and *Electronic Buyers News*. Another publication widely read by buyers and purchasing management who are looking for the best positions is *The Wall Street Journal*. Newspapers in major cities will also provide you with some candidates, but generally those replying to city newspaper advertisements are often less qualified. Although replies to advertisements may provide you with a stack of resumes, selecting qualified candidates from that stack requires a thorough knowledge of purchasing techniques described in this book. Product knowledge is not as important as the knowledge of buying techniques. Product knowledge usually can be learned rather quickly whereas purchasing know-how takes years of training and experience. Many purchasing people are hired without having to answer one question about their specialty simply because personnel interviewers do not know what to ask.

Again the American Purchasing Society can come to your aid either by interviewing the candidates in your behalf or through the certification program they offer.

## HOW TO TRAIN AND MOTIVATE PURCHASING PERSONNEL ———— TO OBTAIN OUTSTANDING PERFORMANCE ————

Buyers and purchasing managers are hired without much direct purchasing experience because those that have it are difficult to locate or want salaries that are beyond the budget of the employer. Those hired sometimes do a fairly decent job intuitively and others are hopelessly inadequate. The former can be developed into top-notch professionals through proper training; the latter may be salvaged by proper training.

A few will read all the available literature and the periodicals, and given the opportunity, will attend seminars that give them the knowledge they need. Most will need to be nudged into action. It is doubtful they will read any of the text in the field unless they are forced to upgrade their skills by attending seminars and taking the courses to fill in the deficiencies in their knowledge. Everyone in purchasing should have at least one course in general business law which includes an emphasis on contract law or preferably two courses with one devoted to contract law. Everyone in purchasing should have at least some formal training in economics. One or more courses should cover macroeconomics and one course should cover microeconomics. Everyone in purchasing should attend at least one seminar on purchasing. Anyone planning to stay in the field or who is interested in a purchasing management position should take courses covering the general principles of purchasing, purchasing management, and international purchasing.

If you require your buyers to improve their purchasing skills, they will be motivated to learn those skills. Set aside a portion of the purchasing budget for education. If buyers are to obtain the best products at the lowest cost, then they must know about those products. Learning about products is part of their education and they can learn most about products and alternative products by attending trade shows and conventions. Allocate funds for buyers to travel to trade shows.

You can motivate buyers by taking a great interest in what they are doing, by seeing that goals are established, and by measuring their performance. Goals must be realistic—that is, attainable. They must be measurable and a completion date should be specified. When certain goals are met, new ones should be given. One of the goals could be to complete the study of a purchasing textbook, attend a seminar on purchasing, or take a particular course at a local university which will help them do a better job. Certainly some of the goals will have a more direct effect on the performance of the department and its contribution to the company profits. For example, there will be a $10,000 reduction in the cost of widgets for the coming year.

Purchasing people are motivated the same as all employees—by having them set attainable goals, stroking them with praise when they succeed or do a good job, and offering constructive suggestions and guidance when they need it. Proper monetary compensation is important too but high salary alone does not achieve maximum effort.

These authors and others who see the unnecessarily high prices paid by most companies suggest motivating buyers by tying their compensation to the results they achieve. Giving them a sort of reverse commission. Whereas you pay salespeople a percentage of the sales revenue they generate, buyers would be paid a percentage of the reduction in costs they obtain. For example, you might pay them 10% of all verifiable cost reductions achieved during any one year.

The critics of this proposal claim that buyers would sacrifice quality to obtain price reductions. However, that problem can be easily overcome if the specifications are clearly defined. If the product meets the specifications, there is no quality problem. If the product does not meet the specifications, the goods or services are unacceptable and the buyer receives no compensation for the reduced price. Obviously this program would need to be spelled out in detail, but we are convinced such a system would yield high returns for both the buyer and the company. In practice, compensation would probably include some base salary plus the percentage of costs saved.

## SUMMARY

Companies may have either a centralized or decentralized organization but additional factors need consideration when establishing the organization of the Purchasing department. A modified centralized system may provide most of the benefits of both systems. Regardless of the system chosen, a central staff purchasing function is necessary.

Organization charts help clarify lines of authority and pinpoint responsibility. However, a policy should also be written to define the limitations of requisitioning and buying authority. With well-defined authority limitations it is easier to make buyer assignments and control unauthorized purchases. Suppliers are then told who has the authority to purchase and that their sales efforts must be directed through proper channels.

Purchasing requires many skills which are difficult to find in any one individual. Assistance in searching for qualified buyers and purchasing management is available through the professional associations such as the American Purchasing Society. Advertising in magazines read by those in purchasing is a good method of obtaining potential candidates. Selection of the best qualified individual must include some checking of professional purchasing competence.

Purchasing professionals are trained through college level business programs, purchasing textbooks, seminars, and attendance at trade shows and conventions.

Buyers and purchasing management are motivated by methods similar to other workers. Proper goal setting, appropriate praise, attentive management, and monetary rewards are all strong motivators of purchasing personnel.

# CHAPTER THREE

# What the Successful Buyer Must Know About the Law to Stay Out of Trouble

One thing that separates truly professional buyers from amateurs is their knowledge of the law. Obviously you can get along for a while without any legal knowledge but if you buy enough over a period of time you are bound to get into trouble. That is, at the least, you will cost yourself embarrassment; quite possibly, lack of knowledge of the law will also cost you financially. You may end up paying more for goods or services, you could be fined because you broke the law, and you could even be imprisoned.

Today the business world is filled with rules and regulations that our predecessors did not have to worry about. If you are going to buy, you are well advised to learn about the legal requirements and how to keep out of trouble. Businesses that ignore this advice find themselves spending thousands of dollars defending themselves and often in vain.

Of course, you can buy without knowing all these rules and regulations and if you are lucky you may go for years without encountering a problem. On the other hand, if you are unlucky, you may run into a problem with your next purchase. For example, one of your major suppliers might go bankrupt, or you might have a legal problem due to an oversight of a term added to a proposal. Or a supplier might violate the anti-trust laws.

This chapter is intended to give you some knowledge of most, if not all, of the law necessary to buy. If you know the law discussed here, it should keep you out of trouble most of the time. There are libraries of material written on the subjects we will be discussing here. Not only that, but the law is constantly changing. Judicial interpretations differ from place to place and from one time to another.

There are various laws that may be applicable to your type organization and your geographic location. You should consult your legal counsel to make certain that you are aware of all laws that affect your particular business.

## HOW TO PROTECT YOUR ——————— COMPANY AND YOURSELF ———————

When purchasing people buy, they make contracts. This chapter describes what a contract is and how you should create one. Only certain people have the authority to make contracts. You need to know:

- How that authority is established and the responsibilities of those who have such authority
- That it is illegal to make certain kinds of agreements and how such agreements may be used against you
- How you are protected by warranties and how to be sure that you are protected
- The importance of patents and the care you as a buyer must take not to infringe on patents

This chapter provides this information.

When you complete this chapter, you may wish to further your study of purchasing law. (*The PURCHASING MANAGER'S DESK BOOK OF PURCHASING LAW*, by James J. Ritterskamp, Jr. is one source of information on this topic. It is published by Prentice Hall and is supplemented annually to keep you up to date on critical legal issues.) You will find it very difficult to find any so named course in law schools, although certain individuals do give seminars to the purchasing community. Undergraduate courses in colleges and universities are much more general and usually are entitled, Business Law or Introduction to Law. Such courses will include some of the things we address in this chapter. One reason for not having a course in purchasing law is that there are many aspects of the law that affect purchasing. Another reason is that traditionally the law that most affects purchasing has been approached from the other side, the sales side.

## Essential Background

The law in the United States is based on English common law, which has a history going back hundreds of years. (The state of Louisiana is an exception; its' law is derived from the French system.) *Common law* is law that is a result of a decision given by a judge. Subsequent similar cases tend to be settled in the same manner. Thus, lawyers search through previous cases to see how they were handled in the past. They then cite the various cases of a similar nature to support a decision in their favor. However, judges in different jurisdictions may interpret things differently. If the lawyer can show many cases in many jurisdictions that were settled in a way that would favor the client, the stronger the likelihood that the case will be settled in the same way. Of course, the lawyers for the opposing side look for past cases that support their position. More recent decisions carry more weight than older decisions.

If a legislative body decides to pass a law, it is written into the books and becomes *statute law*. Often the statutes do not clearly cover all situations or, because of the wording in the statute, there is some doubt what the legislators meant. When a case then comes to court, the judge must interpret the law. Such interpretation is then added to the mass of common law and may be cited in future similar cases.

## Understanding the Uniform Commercial Code (UCC)

Because the interpretation of law and the statutes varied from jurisdiction to jurisdiction (city, county, state, federal), conducting business across boundaries became more and more difficult. In an attempt to simplify the situation, a group of lawyers decided to work on a document that would be acceptable to the legislatures of each state. The document sponsored by the bar association became known as the Uniform Commercial Code (UCC). The document is over 100 pages in length. It was started in 1942 and improved in 1952 with revisions in 1957, 1958, 1962, 1966, and 1977. Although it has been approved in all states except in Louisiana, there are minor differences from state to state. Nevertheless, the general principles of the code are the same and every professional in purchasing should be familiar with the document.

If your purchase is for goods (as opposed to services, which fall under the common law), and the order is between two merchants (business people, purchasing agents, and salespeople are considered merchants), your purchase is under the guidelines established by the Universal Commercial Code which is printed in the appendixes. Read the Code and become familiar with its requirements for a contract. This is much easier than before when every transaction was open to interpretation. True, there are some vague areas in the Code that are open to interpretation, but at least you have a document that eliminates much of the guess work.

The UCC is especially important because it has changed many of the principles of common law that heretofore would determine the outcome of a case.

- Article 1 explains the purpose of the law and provides definitions.
- Article 2 deals with sales.
- Article 3 discusses commercial paper.
- Article 4 talks about bank deposits and collections.
- Article 5 describes letters of credit.
- Article 6 is about bulk transfers.
- Article 7 discusses warehouse receipts, bills of lading and other documents of title.
- Article 8 is on investment securities.
- Article 9 is on secured transactions, sales of accounts and chattel paper.
- Article 10 is the effective date and repealer.

Although you may have some interest in the entire document, the major area is in article 2. This article is only 23 pages long and for most part is easily understandable. As a purchasing professional, you should learn its major provisions.

## UNDERSTANDING THE LAW OF AGENCY
## —————— AND YOUR LEGAL RESPONSIBILITIES ——————

The law of agency helps define your legal responsibilities and provides you with valuable information on the responsibilities of the salespeople calling on you. However, before we get involved in the more technical aspects of agency law, make sure you understand your responsibility in relation to other members of your own purchasing department.

Regardless if you are a junior buyer, buyer, purchasing manager or vice president of purchasing, you may be responsible for purchases that are made by your company if you have been so delegated when you were hired or transferred into the department. Such delegation may have been done very informally. Furthermore, the law treats you as a professional and you are assumed to know what the regulations and customary business practices are. To use what has become an old cliche, *ignorance of the law is no excuse.*

Those of you who delegate some of your purchasing authority to subordinates are in part responsible for the action of those subordinates. Your company is responsible to honor agreements that have been made by those subordinates. That is one reason managers of purchasing earn more than buyers, and directors of purchasing earn more than managers. We constantly see buyers making commitments and then defaulting on those contracts. This damages the reputation of the buyer, the company itself, and the purchasing profession. Purchasing management should make certain that contracts are honored. That is not to say that cancellations should not be made. It only means that cancellations must be made in a legal fashion. A buyer learns nothing if you allow him or her to renege on an agreement for even a small purchase. In fact, it is establishing dangerous habits which may end up costing the company heavily when the amount of the expenditures is high.

## Authorizing Agents to Make Binding Buy or Sell Contracts

When a company grows beyond a one-person operation so that someone must be delegated to conduct a portion of the business, the law of agency comes into play. An agent is appointed by the owner or by another agent who has the authority to hire or appoint someone to carry out the business as needed. Agents are created to buy or to sell. (Salespeople are agents too.)

There are various kinds of agents. There are special agents with limited authority that are only authorized to perform certain functions. There are general agents that are authorized to perform all the duties connected with a portion of the business. They may be hired for certain divisions or for certain projects.

The *principle* is the person or corporation that is doing the hiring. A universal agent is an unlimited general agent and may conduct all of the principal's business.

Anyone who has not been delegated as an agent may not transact business for the organization. Any agreement made by an unauthorized agent can be disavowed. However, an organization may acknowledge such an agreement formally or sometimes by doing nothing as we shall see.

Salespersons may be special or general agents just as purchasing managers may be special or general agents. If you as a buyer are negotiating with a salesperson for a price reduction and that salesperson does not have the authority to make such a reduction, you could be wasting your time. If such a salesperson agrees to a reduction and you accept it and your company bases other major business decisions on that reduction you may be in big trouble.

**TIP:** Make certain you understand the limits of authority of the person you deal with.

## Recognizing the Limits of Purchasing Authority

An agent is created by the principal when there is a so-called meeting of the minds. That is, both the principal and the designated person who will be the agent consent to the agreement. No written document is necessary to create the agency agreement. When you were hired as a buyer, purchasing agent, or purchasing manager, both your employer and you understood or should have understood what you were being hired for. You knew that you were going to be buying certain products but perhaps not other products. Or perhaps you were promoted into the position or transferred from another department. It makes no difference; if you consented to the offer, it is assumed you knew what authority you were being given and the limitations on that authority.

If this is not the case then you should immediately get it clarified. One way of doing this to make certain that you are not exceeding the bounds of your authority is to prepare a memo detailing what you believe to be your authority and send it to the person to whom you report. Although it is best to get a written reply or an approval signature on your memo you can write the memo so that you are protected if there is reluctance in giving you a written reply. Simply say that this is your understanding of the authority that you have and you will exercise such authority unless you receive a correction to your memo within the next three days or some other reasonable period of time.

Often very little thought is given to what authority and duties are being delegated to purchasing personnel, but this is very important and you should have it clarified. Executives will sometimes carelessly say, purchasing does all the buying, or they have the authority to buy everything, but when certain products or services are specified, they begin to realize that those are exceptions. For example, accounting services, large capital expenditures such as mainframe computers, real estate, advertising, and legal services are just a few of the items that are frequently excluded from the purchasing department jurisdiction. They do not have to be. If you want jurisdiction over those areas, include them in your memo and give management the opportunity to think about it. On the other hand, if you do not feel qualified to handle certain areas or do not have the hours to cover all areas properly, alert the proper people that you are not responsible for those areas.

***Express Authority.*** There is express authority and implied authority given to an agent. Express authority may be given orally or in writing and it provides the guidelines of what you are responsible for or what products you may buy and to what extent. It may limit the dollar amount you can spend or contract for, or it may limit the quantity that you are permitted to buy.

*Implied Authority.* Implied authority is the unstated authority that is necessary to carry out your duties for the benefit of your employer within the guidelines established by policies and procedures of the organization.

The agency agreement is often implied by the buyer's conduct. If you indicate to suppliers that you are authorized to make purchase contracts and management indicates by its actions that it supports your statement, you are an agent.

*Apparent Authority.* There is what is called agency by estoppel and necessity. If a supplier believes that someone has the authority to make a purchase and the principal does not deny or object to that belief, an agency relationship has been established. If you allow your shipping clerk or a secretary to place orders and the company receives the merchandise and pays the invoices without objection, an agency relationship has been created and those persons can then make future contracts with that supplier in behalf of your organization.

## Delegating Purchasing Authority

Agents may delegate some of their authority to subagents. Thus the Personnel Manager may hire a Purchasing Manager and indicate the areas of responsibility. The purchasing manager may hire buyers and give them authority to perform all of the functions of a buyer. Keep in mind that anyone who has been given the authority to buy becomes a purchasing agent. In past years only the person in charge of the department had the title purchasing agent, but the actual title does not matter. Junior buyers, buyers, senior buyers, purchasing managers or any other title you choose can all be purchasing agents in the eyes of the law.

## UNDERSTANDING THE OBLIGATIONS OF PURCHASING AGENTS AND THE RIGHTS OF THE EMPLOYER

### Purchasing Agents Must Protect the Employer's Interest

A buyer or purchasing agent may act only as authorized. It is the duty of such an agent to disclose all important facts to the supervisor or the person who gave the authority. The agent may not act against his or her employer, nor may the agent have any private interest that conflicts with the interest of the employer. Using your time for your own benefit that your employer has paid for in the form of wages to you is against the interest of your employer. An agent may not engage in competition or make a personal profit from the position as agent.

An agent cannot disclose any confidential information about his or her employer. Be careful what you say. Sometimes seemingly innocent remarks may come back to haunt you if the information was useful to competitors of your employer or proved embarrassing to your employer.

If you receive money or property in the course of your dealings which is intended for your employer, you are responsible to keep it safe and to deliver it to your employer at once.

## Employers Have a Legal Right to Benefit from Your Efforts

An employer is entitled to all of the benefits resulting from a purchasing agent's actions taken in behalf of the employer. If you use the name of your employer in making a contract with a supplier, the supplier is bound to perform for your employer just as if the employer were dealing directly with the supplier.

## Employers Must Back Up Your Agreements

Your employer has certain obligations to you, as buyer or purchasing agent. Whoever gives you authority, in your organization, must have the authority to delegate to you. If, per chance, that person did not have such authority, you are still entitled to be compensated for work you performed.

Your employer has the duty to compensate you for the work you perform as agent. Unless otherwise agreed, your employer has the duty to reimburse you for reasonable expenses incurred as a result of your purchasing business. Use your judgment, depending on your position and the type of organization, in deciding how much you should spend without getting prior approval. A written guideline or budget limitation is helpful and avoids the necessity of running for approval every time you need to spend a few dollars.

Your employer has the duty to compensate you for any loss you sustain if a supplier tries to hold you personally responsible for some act that you did in behalf of your employer.

Your employer must not interfere unreasonably with your work as a purchasing agent. As long as you follow specific instructions and adhere to the limitations of authority that have been given to you, you have a certain degree of freedom to carry out purchasing duties.

## Obligation of Your Employer

Your employer is liable if he fails to carry out the duties explained above. He is also liable for mistakes that the purchasing agent makes although such liability does not necessarily excuse the purchasing agent from the same liability.

You and your employer may be held liable if you break laws involving your duties as a purchasing agent.

Your employer is obligated to honor the contracts that a purchasing agent makes as long as the contract falls within the area of delegated responsibility.

Thus, it is easy to understand why an employer is concerned about the activities of the purchasing department and sometimes is reluctant to delegate full authority for all purchasing transactions.

## HOW TO MAKE
## ———————————— FAVORABLE CONTRACTS ————————————

First let us clear up a common misunderstanding. Some buyers think that they do not make contracts. In fact some company presidents and other corporate executives have been heard saying that they will allow purchasing to do only the buying; they will not delegate work involving the making of contracts to purchasing. Some non-lawyers are confused because they only think of a contract as a very formal document prepared by lawyers and which contains a great deal of legal jargon. Not so. A contract can be made between any two capable and qualified people. It does not always have to be in writing. Buyers are routinely making contracts all day long.

Perhaps your major concern in purchasing is how to make a good contract, a contract beneficial to your company. Making a contract is easy. Knowing when a contract has been made and how to make one that protects your company from all kinds of business problems is not so easy.

In order to create a good contract you have to understand the meaning of a contract. A contract is an agreement, but there are certain requirements to make it valid:

- A contract must be made by people that are adults and sane.
- A contract must not violate the law. For example, an agreement to smuggle goods into the country would not be enforceable.
- There must be an offer.
- There must be an acceptance of the offer.
- There must be consideration. "Consideration" is the word used to describe the benefit that both parties get. One party to the contract obtains the goods or service, the other party is paid in cash or in some other form of compensation.

### Recognizing and Accepting the Offer

What constitutes an offer? Sales brochures and catalogs are not offers. If you, as a buyer, call a supplier and ask for information and the supplier sends you a description of the product or a catalog, they would not normally be considered offers. If you prepare a request for a quotation and the supplier sends you a reply in the form of general sales literature, it probably is not an offer.

On the other hand, your requests can take the form of an offer. To make certain it does, indicate on the form that you are offering to buy. Indicate the amount that you wish to buy and the price you are willing to pay.

For any offer to be an acceptable offer, the offeror must intend to make an agreement, the offer must be specific, and the offeree must receive notice of that intent.

Under the common law, an offer is accepted in its entirety without any changes whatsoever. If any changes are made, it is no longer an acceptance. It becomes a counteroffer. Under the Uniform Commercial Code additional or different terms may be made and still be treated as an acceptance providing they are made in a reasonable time unless the offer contains a condition that the entire offer must be accepted without any additions, deletions or changes.

The typical purchase order form can be used as an acceptance or as a document to make an offer. If the seller changes the price, the terms, or the conditions, your offer may not have been accepted and those changes may constitute a new offer.

This old system created what has been named, *the battle of the forms*. The buyer and the seller keep making changes and firing back their own form with a new offer. Eventually one party gives in and accepts what may be unfavorable terms or less frequently the sale is never made. Often the goods are shipped before complete agreement is made. In such cases, the determination of what was the offer, the acceptance, and if there was a valid contract may become unclear. If there is a dispute it then is up to the court to decide these matters. Of course, the purchaser can refuse delivery of the goods if no contract has been made, but in practice the goods are usually needed and they may even be used before the buyer is aware of the delivery. If such is the case, the interpretation would more than likely favor the last document delivered.

Arguments about pending purchasing contracts may be about price or delivery schedules or various other items. While these items are important, the most serious difference usually revolves around a clause by either party trying to escape liability for consequential damages. The dollar impact of this responsibility normally amounts to many times the value of the goods. Clauses regarding consequential damages are inserted by lawyers in the *boiler plate* on the back of sales order forms and purchase order forms. Signing and returning acknowledgment copies of these forms may indicate acceptance of all the terms on the forms including the consequential damage clause.

For this reason alone, it is very important to read any sales order form before you sign. Check your own acknowledgment forms that have been returned to see if any changes have been made (this can be done by a trusted clerk having them bring any changes to your attention). Frequently suppliers will return their acknowledgment forms instead of yours. In such cases, the forms should be read carefully for objectionable clauses and the supplier should be notified immediately in writing that such terms are not acceptable.

Because most purchasing departments are understaffed and simply do not have enough time to thoroughly check all documents, their companies are exposed to significant risk. To solve this problem, some buyers are including a clause on their purchase order which may protect them. The clause is similar to the following.

> *When this purchase order is interpreted as an offer, acceptance is limited to the exact terms of this offer and XYZ (name of company) hereby notifies the seller of our objection to any additional, missing, or different terms in the buyer's acceptance. When this purchase order is interpreted as an acceptance of seller's offer, this acceptance is expressly conditioned on seller's assent to any additional, deleted, or different terms (from seller's offer) on this form.*

This is strong language and will more than likely protect you until sales forms start containing a similar message. Nevertheless, you are urged to set up a procedure to review the forms associated with a purchase and to object in writing to any that do not satisfy you. Smart managers delegate routine checking to clerical help and spend their time on transactions that involve high expenditures and carry high risks. The cost of the material alone should not be the sole criterion. A small bolt with little value may be crucial to keep an airplane flying or in preventing a machine from breaking and seriously injuring someone. Such accidents could result in law suits costing millions of dollars.

As stated previously, contracts may be oral as well as written, although the Uniform Commercial Code, which deals with goods rather than services, requires *a writing* for any amount of $500 or over. In practice, buyers place many orders by telephone and thereby make contracts. Confirming the order by purchase order will not change the terms of the contract. Therefore, to make sure that there is agreement to the oral order, indicate on your purchase order that it confirms the contract made by telephone. Indicate the name of the person you made the contract with and the date of the conversation. Be certain that you use the words *confirming the contract.*

## Terms and Conditions to Include in Your Contract

Your purchase contract should consider a number of items to protect you and get as many benefits as possible. These terms may be preprinted on the front or back of your purchase order form or typed in with each order. You can use a personal computer and a word processing program to store standard terms and conditions or those you most frequently use. You can then pick and choose the ones that are most appropriate to the particular purchase.

Most purchase orders have a minimum number of common terms and conditions printed on the form. Those that call for particular emphasis are placed on the front, sometimes in large type. Those on the back are also important and should not be ignored. Make sure that the type on the back of the form and for that matter all of the type is not so small or so light in color that it is difficult to read. If this happens, the court may rule them invalid.

Some of the most commonly used terms for problem areas are given below. (Also for actually used terms and conditions refer to the sample purchase orders in Chapter 4.) Consider each of these carefully before deciding not to include them in your contract:

- **Patent or copyright infringement**—The seller should provide assurances in writing that any goods supplied do not infringe on any patents or copyrights.

- **Overshipments**—Some industries have a practice of shipping larger quantities than ordered and billing you for the larger quantities. Although there are legitimate reasons for this practice, sometimes it is abused. If you do not want overshipments include a clause stating such in your contract.

- **Packaging charges**—Suppliers will sometimes add charges for packaging material or labor. Others will have a minimum charge which might be more than that stated on your purchase order. If you only want charges allowed that are shown on your purchase order, that should be clearly spelled out.

- **Property protection**—When you order items that require special tooling, dies, fixtures, artwork, or photos, you may supply them or the supplier may supply them and bill you for them. Make certain that the contract indicates that in either case, such material is your property and must be returned to you upon request.

- **Product design protection**—In addition to tooling, you may either supply your own drawings or designs to a supplier or pay a supplier to produce them for you. It is normal practice to restrict the supplier from using your drawings, designs, or tooling to produce goods for another customer.

- **Property insurance**—Make sure the contract includes a clause requiring the supplier to have insurance for any of your property in his possession.

- **Payment discounts**—Indicate what point in time will be used in qualifying payment discounts. Some suppliers start counting when they send the invoice and some when they ship the goods. It is better for the purchaser to measure the time from whichever is later, the scheduled delivery date, the invoice date, or the actual delivery date. If you omit this clause the UCC states that ". . . the credit period runs from the time of shipment but postdating the invoice or delaying its dispatch will correspondingly delay the starting of the credit period" (UCC Paragraph 2-310).

- **Delivery changes**—The Buyer should have the right to hold up shipments because of strikes, accidents, or other causes of work stoppage at the Buyer's plant.

- **Shipment delays**—You may wish to include a clause giving you the right to cancel if the goods are not shipped on time. It is suggested that you use the phrase *TIME IS OF THE ESSENCE ON THIS ORDER* and place it in bold, large letters on the face of your order. This should be done in addition to the cancellation clause.

- **Defective goods**—The seller should warrant that goods are free of defects.

- **Quality inspection**—The Buyer should have the right to inspect the goods even though prior payments were made.

- **Product testing**—Additional time may be needed to inspect or test machinery in use at the Buyer's facilities.

- **Returns due to poor quality**—You may want to include a clause that gives you the right to return poor quality material and charge the supplier for both inbound and outbound transportation.

- **Buyer's rights**—Payment for the goods should not end the Buyer's rights under this contract.

- **Price changes**—Do not ship if the price is higher than agreed. The price is a firm price.

- **Order cancellations**—The Buyer should have the right to cancel the order if the supplier fails to comply with the terms of the agreement.

- **Worker safety insurance**—If the order is for services on your premises you should have a *hold harmless* clause in case a supplier's worker is hurt. You should also require that the supplier have a specified amount of Workers' Compensation, Occupational Disease, and public liability insurance and that proof of such insurance be furnished to the Buyer.

- **Contract revisions**—You may wish to include a statement that no revisions to the terms of this contract are permitted by anyone other than an authorized buyer.

- **Legal warranty**—A clause is often included that requires the seller to warrant that he has complied with all the federal, state, and local laws.

• **Rights to use creative work**—A *work-for-hire clause* is sometimes necessary. When receiving and paying for photographs or what may be interpreted as artistic or creative works, it is important to make it understood that you are buying all rights to use the material as often as you wish without further compensation to the individuals involved.

**CAUTION:** Be careful what you sign. Under what is known as the *Parol Evidence Rule,* the UCC says that once an agreement is made in writing, it ". . . may not be contradicted by evidence of any prior agreement or of a contemporaneous oral agreement . . ." Make sure you understand all of the terms and conditions and they correspond to what was discussed.

## HOW TO AMEND A CONTRACT

Prior to the Universal Commercial Code you could not make a contract without being definite. Under the UCC certain missing terms do not prevent the formation of a contract. Agreement under the UCC is not enforceable for the purchase of goods of $500 or more unless the agreement is in writing. Furthermore, the UCC pertains to transactions between merchants only. It does not apply to the purchase of services nor does it apply to transactions involving consumers.

If however, you form a contract and it falls under the UCC, you may omit the price, the place of delivery, or even the time for delivery and the payment terms. If you do omit any of these items, the law will decide what the provisions should be. The interpretation for missing payment terms was explained previously under common clauses. An open price term usually means a reasonable price. Place of delivery, if not specified, means ". . . the seller's place of business or if he has none his residence; but" if the goods are identified ". . . which to the knowledge of the parties at the time of contracting are in some other place, that place is the place for their delivery . . ." (Paragraph 2-307). Time for delivery will be a reasonable time.

**TIP:** Be as detailed as you can be and specify what you want. If you don't, you may find that you are agreeing to a contract that is either unacceptable to your organization or that your company cannot enforce.

## CANCELLING A CONTRACT

You can cancel a contract if the seller defaults. For example, you may be able to cancel because of the inability of the supplier to deliver on time especially if you had included the phrase *TIME IS OF THE ESSENCE ON THIS ORDER* in the contract. You may have to prove default; therefore make sure you spell out all the terms and conditions and document the transaction carefully. Record all conversations in writing with the time and date and who you spoke to. Place everything in a file folder with the contract and all letters, memorandums, and even sales literature that may contain statements and drawings that will be useful if legal action is necessary.

You can also cancel a contract for the convenience of the buyer, but the seller must not incur any loss. And, a contract may be canceled by mutual consent. Never assume that you cannot cancel a contract without a penalty. Sometimes a supplier is able to use the material that was intended for you. It is also possible that no work has been performed and no special material has been ordered in your behalf in which case the supplier may not incur any loss.

To avoid cancellations sometimes a supplier will claim that the material is in process or ready to ship. In one instance, I asked to immediately see such material and offered to send our truck to get the partially completed goods. It was discovered that the material was nowhere to be found.

Contracts that fail to specify quantities or the length of time of the agreement can usually be canceled by the buyer or the seller as long as the other party is notified.

## HOW TO OBTAIN WARRANTIES THAT ———————— REALLY PROTECT THE BUYER ————————

There are express warranties and implied warranties. The Uniform Commercial Code says that, "It is not necessary to the creation of an express warranty that the seller use formal words such as 'warrant' or 'guarantee' or that he have a specific intention to make a warranty, . . ." An express warranty may take the form of a sample or a model. The law expects that the products you order should look and perform something like the sample. Or the seller may state what the product will do in specific terms. For example, the salesperson may say that the machine will produce 2,000 widgets per hour. Statements with specific quantities or measures normally would be considered an express warranty (See the UCC, Paragraph 2-313). However, many sales presentations include statements that are called *puffery*. These include statements such as, "This is the best little widget in the world" or "This is the finest widget you will ever find." Sales puffery statements are not express warranties.

Express warranties may be either given orally or in writing. They may be included in sales literature, in memos, in letters, or in any other written document you receive from the supplier. As with so many other things in purchasing, oral statements are difficult to prove. However, you may protect yourself to a large degree by making a written record of what has been said and including it in the file with the sales literature, letters, and the like. Record who made the statement, the date, where it was said, and who was present to witness the statement. It is even better to get verification of the statement from a higher authority in the company. Send a letter to the company indicating your understanding of the conversation and requesting any necessary correction to your understanding.

There is an implied warranty of merchantability when goods are sold by a company dealing in such goods. There is an implied warranty that the goods are fit for a particular purpose (See UCC, Paragraph 2-314). It is a good idea to tell the seller what you are going to use the product for if it is for other than the obvious intended purpose. Obtain assurances from the supplier that the product will meet your needs and perform as you expect. As always, spell it out in writing how you are going to use the product and ask the supplier to notify you if the product will not do the job you want (See UCC, Paragraph 2-315).

Watch out for exclusions. Express warranties and limitations on those warranties need to be consistent. Limits on the implied warranty of merchantability must be in writing and conspicuous (See UCC, Paragraph 2-316).

The laws concerning warranty have significantly changed in recent years. The old doctrine called *privity of contract*, which held that a buyer could only sue the seller, has been rejected. The Magnuson-Moss Warranty Act of July 4, 1975 to protect consumers and the Federal Trade Commission Improvement Act made everyone connected with a product failure potentially liable. Liability today is based on the no-fault concept. If a consumer uses a product and gets injured, he may sue the person who sold him the product, the company that manufactured the product, the company that made a component that was used in the assembly, and the producer of the raw material going into the component.

This way of looking at product liability puts a heavy burden on purchasing personnel to be cautious about what they buy, particularly when the product may end up as a component of a finished product that will be sold to consumers. Not long ago a consumer sued the maker of a plastic cooking utensil that exploded while in use. The manufacturer of the cooking utensil discovered that the raw material going into its product was defective and in turn sued the raw material producer. However, the raw material producer claimed the material was not made by its company. The cooking utensil manufacturer could not prove that it was that particular raw material producer since it used several sources and its records were not adequate to show which material went into the product.

Knowing the law and making your agreements specific and in writing helps prevent this and other legal problems. Solving legal disputes revolves around keeping very good records. Spell out details on purchase orders, provide detailed specifications, and update records constantly.

# WHAT YOUR BUYERS NEED TO KNOW
## ——————— ABOUT ANTITRUST LAWS ———————

The Sherman Act of 1890 made it illegal to make contracts or enter into conspiracies that unreasonably restrain trade. It prohibits monopolization or attempts to monopolize. In 1914 the Clayton Act was passed. It makes it illegal to sell or lease a product or service with the requirement that the buyer cannot buy from another supplier and it may result in injury to competition. The Clayton Act also prohibits mergers and acquisition that may lessen competition.

In 1936 the Robinson-Patman Amendment closed some of the loopholes. It makes it illegal for a supplier to discriminate in prices of the same product if competition will be hurt. For buyers, possibly the most important part of the Robinson-Patman Act is where it makes it illegal to knowingly try to obtain or receive an improper discrimination in price. The Act also makes it illegal to sell goods at an unreasonably low price to eliminate the competition.

Not much proof is needed to hold either a buyer or seller guilty of violating these acts if they are accused of doing so. There is a *per se doctrine* that will assume buyers are guilty if they meet with other buyers from different companies to discuss pricing or service about a particular supplier or potential supplier. Competitive salespeople who hold a meeting together are subject to similar risks.

While a company cannot offer a buyer a price different from what is being offered to other customers, it can match a lower price to meet competition. However, there is usually a problem learning what that price is since ethical buyers are not willing to give out such information (except when required for government purchasing). Many buyers will not even divulge the identity of the competition. Of course, if the company trying to obtain the pricing information knows who the competition is, it may try to telephone the low price supplier, but even if the information were willingly supplied, both companies are at risk because they are competitors and are discussing price.

## How to Deal With the Robinson-Patman Act and Avoid Criminal Charges

If you, as a buyer, give false information about what you are paying or what another supplier has bid, you can be found guilty of violating Robinson-Patman and using an unfair trade practice and may be subject to severe penalties. It is perfectly acceptable to tell a supplier that the price is too high, or that he is not the lowest bidder (if that is really so). You may even say that it is necessary to reduce his prices by 10% in order to get the business (such a statement is not to imply that any other supplier bid 10% less).

A supplier can establish different prices for a product if the product is in some way different or there is a difference in actual cost. Differences in volume do not always justify different prices. There must be real cost differences. Minor differences in packaging or slight differences in transportation probably would not be sufficient to allow price differences. Cost differences must be known and documented before prices are established, not after a company has been accused of discrimination.

Keep in mind that violations only occur when they may lessen competition. As a buyer, unless you are working for a large company or a company that makes a substantial impact in the marketplace of a particular product, it is unlikely you will be accused of violating these laws. However, you should be aware of the possibilities of other buyers or sellers who may violate these laws to your detriment. If you believe this is the case it may be to your advantage to discuss solutions with your attorney. Also be aware of the severe penalties for those who are found guilty of violations: prison, fines, and treble damages, and harm to the reputation of you and your company.

### International Antitrust Laws

When dealing in international trade there are different sets of laws to consider. The Wilson Tariff Act of 1913 applies to any illegal combination between two or more parties either of whom is engaged in importing into the United States. The Revenue Act of 1916 prohibits the importation of items at a price substantially less than the value of such articles in the foreign country at the time of exportation. The Tariff Act of 1930 makes it illegal to use unfair methods of competition in the importation of articles into the United States.

Up until recently, there was little antitrust legislation outside of the U.S., but Germany passed such a law in 1957, the Dutch passed an anticartel law in 1956, England passed an antimonopoly law in 1948, and in the Treaty of Rome in 1957 an antitrust law was agreed to for the European Common Market. Spain, Ireland, and Austria now have anticartel laws.

## WHAT BUYERS NEED TO KNOW ABOUT PATENTS

A patent is issued by the United States Government to inventors or designers of new products. It gives the owner of the patent the sole right to make, produce, and sell the item for a period from 14 to 17 years, depending on the type of patent. If someone wishes a patent, he or she must pay to have the records searched at the patent office to see if anyone has already patented a similar device. Patents may be issued to do the same function in a different way. For example, there are a number of patents for articles used to open bottles or cans. There are various types of patents with different rights. There are mechanical, process, composition, manufacturing, and design patents.

When a patent has been applied for, the applicant has the right to have *patent pending* or *patent applied for* on the product. If a company wishes to buy or make such a product without waiting to see if the patent is issued, it is at risk that it will be accused of infringement or at least would have to stop the sale or production of the item until permission is received from the patent holder. On the other hand, there is no way of knowing how long it will be before the patent will be issued or rejected. The wait may take months if not years. Buyers should keep this in mind when purchasing an item that is patent pending.

## How to Avoid Charges of Patent Infringement

A charge of patent infringement may result if, without authorization, you use, make, purchase, or sell a product that has been patented. In other words, as the buyer you could innocently purchase a finished product or component and have it confiscated without reimbursement. If such a product happens to be included as a component of another product you make and sell, the cost of recovery could be enormous. Particular attention should be paid to products being imported because having a patent in one country does not mean that it is patented in another. Recently, a shipment arriving from Hong Kong was stopped by U.S. customs, and destroyed because it violated a U.S. patent although it broke no Hong Kong law.

Buyers should always question a supplier about where it obtained the design for a product and if a patent search was either attempted or if any components have patents, and who owns the patents. It may be necessary to check with the patent owner to determine if the supplier has been licensed to use the item. Include a clause in your contract that requires the supplier's assurance of no patent infringement and that protects you from liability.

Penalties for violations of patents are not always severe. You may simply be told to stop using the product or to pay the patent holder for his loss of revenue which might be minimal. Nevertheless, the risk is present so you should protect yourself.

## Beware of False Patents

Sometimes sellers will claim to have a patent when they do not. Their purpose might be to give you a reason for a higher price or more likely to discourage you from trying to make the item or buy somewhere else. Ask for the patent numbers. Have your attorney check to see if there is a valid patent and what it covers. You will find that the patent is often for a minor feature that is easily eliminated or changed. Or you may find that the patent is about to expire.

## OTHER LAWS BUYERS
## MUST BE AWARE OF

A buyer should be concerned about obeying all federal, state, and local laws regardless of the type of business involved. If you currently have or might have any military or government business you should pay particular attention to the regulations for doing business with the government. The government requires your sources to conduct their business in a certain manner. If you do not make certain that your suppliers conform to methods required, your company runs the risk of losing government business. A clause in your purchase contract or purchase order is helpful but you should also question the supplier to make certain that the required policies and procedures are being used.

Some of the laws you should reference in the terms and conditions section of a purchase order are:

- the Fair Labor Standards Act
- the Civil Rights Act of 1964, Title VII, Executive Order 11246, as amended; and 11375, the Vietnam-Era Veterans Readjustment Act of 1972, as amended
- the Rehabilitation Act of 1973 as amended
- the Federal Toxic Substances Control Act
- the Federal Insecticide, Fungicide, and Rodenticide Act
- the Federal Occupational Safety and Health Act
- the Explosive and Combustible Act of 1960
- the Transportation Safety Act of 1974
- other applicable Federal, State, or local laws, ordinances or regulations.

Consult your in-house counsel for further information on these laws.

## CONCLUSION

The law often uses the terms *due consideration, what is reasonable, customary and usual, good faith, what is fair, what is unfair, unconscionable,* and others which illustrate sincere efforts to be fair and just. If you are honest, try to be fair, and pay attention to what you are doing, you will stay out of legal trouble most of the time.

Remember, your supplier does not want to lose your business even if he has a good case against you or has the letter of the law on his side in a particular situation. If you make an honest mistake and it is not costly, the supplier will usually work with you to help solve the problem. This is why it is a good policy to spend the time finding honest and capable suppliers that are interested in doing business for the long term. Admittedly, you may be able to save some cost by changing your sourcing, but make sure the savings are more than temporary. Make sure the new sources have some staying power and will work with you.

# CHAPTER FOUR

# Simplifying the Buying Process Without Sacrificing Control

This chapter covers the purchasing process used by most businesses. It takes you from the recognition and documentation of the need for a product or service to delivery and payment of the invoice.

An efficient purchasing system makes buying easier and keeps operating cost at a minimum while maintaining the necessary purchasing controls. An efficient system makes buying easier by requiring the least amount of paperwork and the least amount of effort to use the required forms and obtain the material and services needed. Proper control prevents unauthorized purchases, provides legal protection for the buying organization, and provides assurance of economic purchases.

In an effort to keep paperwork at a minimum, some companies have oversimplified forms by omitting essential data. Other forms have been eliminated or overlooked. Consultants and practitioners have even advocated paperless purchasing (The Uniform Commercial Code requires purchase contracts of goods for $500 or more to be in writing in order to be enforceable). While the objectives of these measures are praiseworthy, the results can prove to be very costly. An efficient purchasing system is not created easily. It requires thought and careful planning whether it is a manual or computerized system.

Most purchasing systems generate an enormous amount of paperwork. In spite of the mass of paperwork, many of these organizations still lack the documentation necessary for good management and control. Without adequate records:

- You cannot objectively measure supplier performance.
- You cannot control prices.
- Negotiating attempts are hampered.
- Cost control is inadequate.
- The risks of losing possible legal arguments become high.
- You cannot properly evaluate the performance of buyers and purchasing management.
- It becomes difficult to measure workload.

One important reason to measure workload is to obtain the very profitable benefits of adequate staffing and avoid the problems that result from inadequate staffing. When purchasing has sufficient time, costs are reduced and are kept to a minimum. When purchasing is inadequately staffed, buyers take shortcuts to maintain supply, but at a cost to the organization. Maintaining a staff sufficient to handle the routine daily purchasing during low volume periods provides time to perform other important purchasing functions that are often neglected.

Accumulating and recording data need not always mean more paperwork. The data may be entered and stored in the computer and calculations may all be done by the computer. It is usually advisable to have hard copies of certain forms, such as, request for quotations, requisitions, purchase orders, and purchase order revisions. Entering the information on these forms may be done manually or by computer. Some purchases require manual handling or at least interaction with the computer system.

You can reduce documentation time by systemization:

- Use standard clauses in your contracts to eliminate the need to compose new terms and conditions for every transaction.
- Use default statements to eliminate the need to enter data for every term.
- Design forms that are completed manually so that the forms reduce eyestrain and the amount of writing or typing necessary. For example, preprint as much information as possible. Your company name, address, telephone number are normally preprinted. Where there is more than one billing address or shipping address, have them all preprinted and provide boxes to be checked. This saves time and effort if the form is handwritten or typed.
- Plan the system considering the whole process. Each item on the requisition should be in the same sequence as they will be on the

request for quotation or the purchase order. Such arrangement eliminates the need to search one form for the next item to be filled in on another form.

- Have forms printed so their spacing allows typewriters to tab to the next item and line advance to the next printed line without adjustment. Considerable time is saved by doing this.

## HOW TO SIMPLIFY THE PURCHASING PROCESS ——————— BY STANDARDIZING REQUISITIONS ———————

In many companies, the requisition process is haphazard—which complicates the purchasing function. For example, someone in need of a product or service may approach one of your buyers in the office hallway and tell him what he needs. Other times the message may be yelled in at the door of the buyer's office. Many times the requests are received by telephone. These requests may be received from the lowest echelon all the way up to and including the chairman of the board.

When you receive more than one or two such oral requests within a short period of time, it is easy to forget the details of the requests. It is not unusual for purchasing departments to receive hundreds of requests for material every day. Add to this volume the many pressures of daily business and it is easy to understand that you may forget about oral requests. If you take special pains to remember the request for the chief executive, which may be for a relatively unimportant stationery item, you may neglect the more important item needed to satisfy the outside customer needs.

Just as it is important for all contracts to be documented in writing, it is also important to have the internal requests documented in writing. Written documents offer a predefined and uniform format that makes the purchasing job easier by improving communication of the essential data.

As purchasing manager, you need to make certain that there is a procedure and the proper forms to document requests for material and services. Some purchasing departments are responsible to prepare requisitions and source documents for other departments. *This is not the normal function of purchasing.* It diverts purchasing personnel from their intended purpose of finding sources, negotiating the transaction, and assuring delivery of the goods or service. When purchasing agents prepare source documents, it gives them the responsibility of determining the needs of the requisitioner and preparing specifications that may or may not satisfy the requirements of the using department. (See Chapter 5 for a full discussion of specifications.) It also makes it difficult to measure normal purchasing workload and compare activities to other purchasing departments.

If your company is organized with a materials management function that also manages purchasing rather than an independent purchasing department, you might handle requisitioning. Nevertheless, even if the same person does both the determination of need and the buying, the time required should be allocated to the correct function. Wherever possible, requisitions should be prepared by the users, by inventory control or the production control function.

Requirements for maintenance, repair, and operating supplies should always be documented by the person or persons responsible for those functions.

## Types of Requisitions

Source documents may be in several different forms. The classic requisition form is normally used for maintenance, repair, and operating supplies, but in some cases is used for all material and services that a company requires.

Manufacturing organizations usually, but not always, have separate forms for material that is needed for production. These forms are referred to as *bills of material* (see Figure 4-1). In some cases, bills of material are used to generate separate requisitions although this method may be needlessly complicated. This is believed to be justified when several buyers are employed and the bill of material does not segregate the items by the buyer's responsibility. Other companies expect buyers to select their own items from the bill of material, assuming that they should know their areas of responsibility. There is some risk in this assumption because the boundaries of responsibility are not always clearly defined and unless the bills are clearly formatted, an item may be temporarily missed. With the computer, items can be buyer coded, and a separate sort made so that each buyer receives only the items that he or she needs to order.

Production items require a significant amount of time for the initial order. In most cases, such items represent relatively high-dollar expenditures. Consequently, more time is spent in finding the most capable and competitive source. Once the source has been found, the negotiations concluded, and the initial order has been prepared, additional orders for the same item become routine. Bills of Material normally carry very few details about the requested item. Since Bills of Material are usually for production material that is purchased again and again and more than likely from the same source or sources, the detailed description is on file with the supplier. Purchasing then orders by part number or refers to a specification or drawing number.

While many MRO items fall into a similar pattern, others are purchased for one-time use or so infrequently that reshopping efforts are

Indented Bill of Materials
#9 Pin-up Lamp

Date
March 5, 1992

Mfg. Code
1020314

Approved
AES

| 1st level component number | 2nd level component number | Description | Quantity Required | Source | Remarks |
|---|---|---|---|---|---|
| X18 | | Switch | 1 | Purchase | |
| Y2L | | Socket | 1 | Manufacture | |
| | 10314 | Switch | 1 | Purchase | |
| | Y2L-S | Shell | 1 | Manufacture | |
| | Y2L-B | Base | 1 | Manufacture | |
| | Y2L-SI | Shell Insulator | 1 | Purchase | |
| | Y2l-BI | Base Insulator | 1 | Purchase | |
| | Y2L-XI | Screw stem | 1 | Manufacture | |
| 9P | | Shade | 1 | Manufacture | |
| 414 | | Hanger | 2 | Manufacture | |
| 4107 | | Cord Set | 1 | Purchase | |

**Figure 4-1. Sample Bill of Material**

Adapted from *Production and Inventory Control* by G. W. Plossl & O. W. Wight, Prentice-Hall, 1967, p. 140

necessary. For a manufacturing company, these supply items take a disproportionate amount of time compared with their cost. There are various methods to reduce the time required such as blanket orders and systems contracts. Another method is the use of an efficient requisitioning system.

### How a Good Requisition Can Save You Time and Reduce Cost

Many of the problems associated with purchasing are caused by a poorly designed requisitioning system. The major problems caused by a poor requisitioning procedure are:

- Needed material is delayed or late.
- Orders are duplicated and excess inventory is accumulated.
- Multiple requests for the same item within a short period of time result in multiple purchases at unnecessarily high low-volume prices.
- Receiving docks, aisles, and store areas become crowded because material is being received that is not immediately needed.
- Requisitioners and purchasing department employees bicker, each blaming the other for incompetence.
- Dozens of sources are used for similar low volume items which creates an excessive workload for purchasing, receiving, and accounts payable.
- Buyers pay higher prices than necessary for low volume items which are multiple sourced.

### Eight Common Requisitioning Problems and How to Prevent Them

*How to Prevent Delayed or Late Material.* Requisition volume flowing into the purchasing department fluctuates and needs to be monitored. There may be very high volume at certain times of the year. At other times, the volume may be low. Certain days of the week and hours of the day produce more requisitions. But the exact times differ from company to company and industry to industry.

It is helpful to keep records of how many requisitions arrive and when they arrive. To do so, each requisition should be prenumbered and dated. Numbering requisitions provides an easy reference when the requisitioner needs to know the status of an order. Prenumbering is a way of knowing that the document is for a new order. Follow-up messages should not use a prenumbered form. Dating the requisition establishes one element in prioritizing handling and scheduling.

Good purchasing management will make it a policy to handle requisitions within a certain period of time after receipt. Dating the requisition provides a base point. Some purchasing departments also date stamp the document when it is received. Purchasing is frequently criticized for delays in processing requisitions. Investigation into the cause for these delays has revealed significant discrepancies between the dates on the documents and the times actually received by purchasing.

**How to Keep Track of Requests for Price Information.** Some companies such as job shops constantly require price information from outside sources. Most companies have capital budgets and various department heads need prices of items that they are going to buy to help prepare their budget requests. These requests for pricing should be given to purchasing so that purchasing is involved at the earliest stages of supplier contacts. Frequently, because no firm order is intended prior to approval of the budget, no requisitions or other documentation of the price information request is prepared. This is a mistake. Without keeping track of these requests, any accurate analysis of purchasing workload is impossible. An easy way to keep track of such requests is to use the normal requisition form and include a space which should be checked if the request is for price information only.

**How to Ensure On-Time Delivery.** Purchasing procedure should require a specific date that material is needed. It is common for requisitioners to indicate ASAP (meaning, as soon as possible) or RUSH on a requisition. This is a poor practice: these terms are vague and almost meaningless. "As soon as possible" is only a day for off-the-shelf items from a local supplier, whereas it can be over a year for large capital equipment items. It is difficult to establish priorities for handling shipments and making schedules when vague terms are used.

The practice of using ASAP and RUSH rather than specific dates was so common with one manufacturing firm in the Detroit area that 85% of the requisitions were so marked. As a result many items that were needed at once were handled after those that could have waited a few days. Requisitioners should be required to indicate a specific date when the material is needed, even if it is the day the paperwork is issued.

**How to Prevent Duplicate Orders and Resulting Excess Inventory.** Using prenumbered forms and dating will also help prevent duplicate requisitions for the same item. Requisitioners should be made to understand that every time they write a requisition, it will be handled as a separate order. Follow-up messages by written note, requisition copy, or telephone should reference the original requisition number and date. There are many varieties of purchase requisitions. Some are simple stock forms which can be obtained from most office supply stores (see Figures 4-2 to 4-4) but take particular note of Figures 4-5 and 4-6 which illustrate a multipart requisition form which includes a copy to be retained by the requisitioner for reference information. Without a copy, requisitioners sometimes forget whether or not they have ordered the product and then proceed to write a duplicate.

# PURCHASE REQUISITION

No. _____

Date _____

**Purchasing Department**
Please purchase the following named items:

INDICATE SOURCE OF SUPPLY IF KNOWN

| Quantity | Number | Description |
|---|---|---|
| | | |
| | | |
| | | |
| | | |
| | | |
| | | |
| | | |
| | | |
| | | |

Purpose or Use _____

When wanted _____

For _____ Dept.

To be filled in by Purchasing Dept.

Date ordered _____ Order No. _____

From _____

Approved _____

TOPS FORM 3243 – LITHO IN U.S.A.

**Figure 4-2. Purchase Requisition**

PURCHASE REQUISITION

PLANT NO. ______ DELIVER AT ______ PURCHASE REQUISITION 234013 PURCHASE ORDER NO. ______

ORDER FROM ______ F.O.B. POINT ______

ADDRESS ______ SHIP VIA ______ TERMS ______

| REFERENCE | DATE WANTED | CHARGE ACCOUNT | CHARGE DEPT. | FOLLOW-UP | INQUIRY NO. |
|---|---|---|---|---|---|
| | | | | | |

| QUANTITY | DESCRIPTION | PRICE |
|---|---|---|
| | | |
| | | |
| | | |
| | | |
| | | |
| | | |
| | | |
| | | |
| | | |

TO BE USED FOR ______

ORIGINATOR ______ DEPT. ______ APPROVALS ______ ACCOUNTING ______ BUYER ______

DATE ______ SUBJECT TO SALES TAX YES ☐ NO ☐

PURCHASE REQUISITION

Figure 4-3. Purchase Requisition

# REQUEST FOR PURCHASE

| | DATE PREPARED | DATE REQUIRED |
|---|---|---|

SUGGESTED
VENDOR NAME _____

| DEPT. NO. | DEPARTMENT NAME |
|---|---|

VENDOR NUMBER _____

REQUESTED BY _____

VENDOR ADDRESS _____

APPROVED BY _____

| P.O. NUMBER | P.O. DATE |
|---|---|

| SHADED AREAS TO BE COMPLETED BY PURCHASING | DELIVERY REQUIRED ON OR BEFORE |
|---|---|

| TERMS | F.O.B. SHIPPING POINT ☐ DEST. ☐ | SHIP VIA | FREIGHT ALLOWED ☐ | NOT ALLOWED ☐ | PREPAID ☐ | COLLECT ☐ |
|---|---|---|---|---|---|---|

| ITEM NO. | ACCT. NO. | QUANTITY | U/M | DESCRIPTION | UNIT LIST PRICE | % DISC. | UNIT NET PRICE | TOTAL PRICE |
|---|---|---|---|---|---|---|---|---|
| | | | | | | | | |
| | | | | | | | | |
| | | | | | | | | |
| | | | | | | | | |
| | | | | | | | | |
| | | | | | | | | |
| | | | | | | | | |
| | | | | | | | | |
| | | | | | | | | |

**NOTE: THE BELOW CONTROL REQUEST IS TO BE COMPLETED IF THE REQUESTOR FEELS THAT THE ITEM REQUESTED SHOULD BE PLACED IN INVENTORY.**

| ANTICIPATED MONTHLY USAGE | MAXIMUM STOCK | MINIMUM LEVEL | THIS ITEM REPLACES NO. | USE STOCK ON HAND | | CATALOG NO. OF NEW ITEM | CONTROL REQUEST PROCESSED BY |
|---|---|---|---|---|---|---|---|
| | | | | YES ☐ NO ☐ | | | DATE |

| EXPENSE SUB CLASS | DATE | GENERAL USE | SPECIAL INSTRUCTIONS | QUANTITY ON HAND | |
|---|---|---|---|---|---|
| | | YES ☐ NO ☐ | | | |

PURCHASING DEPT.

**Figure 4-4. Request for Purchase**

PRINTED BY THE STANDARD REGISTER COMPANY U.S.A. ZIPSET ®

| | | |
|---|---|---|
| **AIM** Companies, Inc. | **Purchase Requisition** LIST ONE CLASS OF MATERIAL ONLY | REQ. NO. **1364** |

Figure 4-5. Purchase Requisition

**How to Prevent Multiple Orders by Using a Standard Form.** A standard formalized requisition system provides a record of who is ordering, how much, and how frequently. Reviewing requisition records will disclose the need to keep stock in inventory and avoid the cost of repetitive small orders. One or two requisitioners may not order a sufficient quantity or frequently enough to stock the item, but if many people in the organization are also ordering small quantities frequently, a larger purchase will save the time of repeat orders and possibly can qualify for a lower price.

**How to Eliminate Crowded Storage Areas and Excess Transportation Cost with Realistic Delivery Dates.** Specific dates will help eliminate excess inventory. When unrealistic dates are placed on the requisition, the buyer will try to obtain those delivery dates, but will be unable to get delivery unless a premium is paid for overtime or premium transportation methods are used. The buyer should then check with the requisitioner or authorized

**SUPPLY / PURCHASE REQUISITION**

No._____

TO:  ☐ SUPPLY

PLEASE TYPE OR PRINT CLEARLY. COMPLETE ALL
UNSHADED AREAS AS THOROUGHLY AS POSSIBLE.

☐ PURCHASE REQUISITION

VENDOR

☐ DEPARTMENT TRANSFER

☐ SYSTEMS RELEASE

BILL AND SHIP TO THE ABOVE ADDRESS
UNLESS ALTERNATE IS SHOWN BELOW.

TO: (8)

P.O. NUMBER

P.O. DATE

(6)DATE WANTED
BE SPECIFIC

| JOB | TERMS | F.O.B. (DELIVERED UNLESS INDICATED) SHIP VIA | (LOWEST COST UNLESS INDICATED) | CERT. TAX EXEMPT ☐ | |
|---|---|---|---|---|---|
| REQN. NO. | REQT. FOR QUOTES | (3) CC. ACCT., AFE | VENDOR CODE | BUYER CODE | FOR CONSUMPTION BILL SALES TAX ☐ |

PLEASE ENTER OUR ORDER FOR THE FOLLOWING
SUBJECT TO THE TERMS AND CONDITIONS HEREON

| (11) ITEM NO. | (12) QUANTITY | PART NO. | (13) DESCRIPTION | CODE | UNIT MEAS. | PRICE | EXTENDED AMOUNT | AGREED SHIP SCHEDULE |
|---|---|---|---|---|---|---|---|---|
| | | | | | | | | |
| | | | | | | | | |
| | | | | | | | | |
| | | | | | | | | |
| | | | | | | | | |
| | | | | | | | | |
| | | | | | | | | |
| | | | | | | | | |

| (1) DATE REQN. PREPARED | (2) REQUISITIONER | (7) TOTAL ESTIMATED PRICE | (4) SHIP TO DEPT. |
|---|---|---|---|
| (5) SUGGESTED VENDOR(S) | | | |

| (9) AUTHORIZED SIGNATURE | DATE | (10) APPROVED SIGNATURE | DATE |
|---|---|---|---|

FORM P101 HEH 2-75 REV. 2-79

**PURCHASING/STORES DEPT.**

**SYSTEMS RELEASE OR SUPPLIER RECORD**

**REQUISITIONERS COPY**

**ADVISE COPY**

**Figure 4-6. Supply/Purchase Requisition**

individual to get approval for the added cost. More times than not, the
normal lead time is acceptable to avoid the excess charge. After several
instances of this type, the requisitioners become more realistic in specifying the dates material is required.

Purchasing can help the requisitioner by publishing a list of normal lead times for categories of items (see Figure 4-7). Such leadtimes should not be overly optimistic or based on wishful thinking. For the maximum creditability, they should be developed using averages from experience. Before that long-term project is completed, the next best substitute is the normal delivery time quoted by suppliers.

When the requisitioner follows the leadtime guidelines material will arrive close to the time actually needed rather than too early or too late. Requisitioners may not follow published guidelines for a variety of reasons:

- They believe the listed times are inflated.
- They are unable or unwilling to plan their needs.
- A true emergency requirement develops which requires material sooner than the normal lead time requires.

Providing you are diligent in obtaining accurate information when preparing your leadtime list, the requisitioner will soon learn that he should rely on the times shown. It helps to explain how the list was developed and to indicate that you are continually working on the list to keep it current. Leadtimes are always changing because of economic conditions. It is therefore important to revise the list periodically and send the new information to each requisitioner.

Individuals still submitting requirements with insufficient leadtime for normal delivery need to be told about the hardships that their ordering methods cause. They may claim that if purchasing had good relationships with suppliers the buyer could get quicker delivery. They may claim that they have had experience in dealing with the supplier and know they can get the material delivered when they want it without extra cost. These arguments are refuted by showing the NORMAL leadtime quoted by the supplier. Explain the elementary law of economics, that nothing is free. Routinely providing better delivery service than normal to one customer is eventually reflected in the price.

True emergencies require special handling. They may require expediting effort and added cost. Those added costs should be absorbed by the department that has the emergency. When the requisitioner realizes that he will be charged for the added cost of obtaining emergency requirements, he will limit such requests to actual emergency needs.

**How to Prevent Conflict Among Requisitioners and Purchasing.** You can minimize arguments among requisitioners and purchasing if the purchasing department reacts promptly to all requests and considers each and every requisitioner's request for material as important. With an efficient system, prompt attention can be given to every request. If all

## LEADTIME REPORT
## Average Leadtime In Days
## as of March 1992

| ITEM OR CATEGORY | SHOP FOR NEW ITEM | PLACE ORDER | P.O. DELIVERD | SUPPLIER SCHED. | SHIPPING TIME | TOTAL FOR SHELF OR REPEAT ITEMS | MAKE TOOLING | MANU-FACT-URING | TOTAL FOR NEW ITEM |
|---|---|---|---|---|---|---|---|---|---|
| Abrasives | 15 | 2 | 2 | 2 | 3 | 9 | 10 | 10 | 44 |
| Bearings | 15 | 2 | 2 | 2 | 10 | 16 | 9 | 12 | 52 |
| Castings | 25 | 2 | 3 | 3 | 5 | 13 | 25 | 14 | 77 |
| Chemicals | 12 | 2 | 2 | 2 | 5 | 11 | - | 23 | 46 |
| Corrugated | 6 | 2 | 2 | 2 | 2 | 8 | 11 | 2 | 27 |
| Forgings | 28 | 2 | 3 | 3 | 5 | 13 | 31 | 3 | 75 |
| Mill Supplies | 3 | 1 | 1 | 1 | 1 | 4 | - | 5 | 12 |
| Nickel | 15 | 2 | 2 | 3 | 5 | 12 | - | 3 | 30 |
| Paper Towels | 1 | 1 | 1 | 1 | 1 | 4 | - | 3 | 8 |
| Plastic Resin | 15 | 2 | 2 | 5 | 3 | 12 | - | 3 | 30 |
| Rubber Mats | 10 | 2 | 2 | 2 | 3 | 9 | 15 | 15 | 49 |
| Screws, Custom | 7 | 2 | 2 | 2 | 2 | 8 | 10 | 10 | 35 |
| Screws, Stanard | 3 | 2 | 2 | 1 | 1 | 6 | - | - | 9 |
| Stationery Supplies | 3 | 2 | 1 | 1 | 1 | 5 | - | - | 8 |

Figure 4-7. Sample Leadtime Report (Note: Length of leadtimes are not actual. Do not use for planning purposes.)

purchasing personnel are always busy on routine matters, rather than putting out fires, and requisitions still cannot be handled in a prompt manner, chances are the department is under staffed. Management should look carefully at the system before blaming purchasing personnel for poor performance.

***How to Save Time and Limit the Number of Suppliers Used for Similar Low Volume Items.*** Supplier selection is the responsibility of purchasing. Requisitioners and users have the responsibility of determining what they want and the specifications they need but do not and should not have the power to dictate which supplier to use. (See Chapter 5 for a full discussion of specifications.) Requisition forms usually have a space for inserting the name of the supplier. The sample requisition shown in Figure 4-6 has two such spaces, one for a suggested supplier (box marked (5) suggested vendor(s)) which may be filled in by the requisitioner, the other to be filled in by the buyer.

The name of a suggested supplier is helpful to the buyer when the item has never been purchased before and is not likely to be purchased frequently, if ever again. Items for repair fall into this category. The suggested supplier information also helps the buyer by saving time in looking up the information providing the buyer is familiar with the capabilities and competitiveness of the supplier.

The sample requisition form has a shaded box (marked (8)) for the name of the selected supplier. This form serves as either a supply requisition for release of material against a system contract or a purchase requisition. When used as a systems contract release, the supplier's name may be inserted by a stores clerk or some other authorized person outside of purchasing. When used as a requisition, the same space is reserved for the use of purchasing only.

When only one space is provided for insertion of the name of the supplier, the requisitioner almost invariably inserts a name. The name inserted may be the only source known by the user or it may be a preferred source. The buyer, under pressure to place the order promptly, uses the suggested source. In all but the smallest of companies, requisitions are received from dozens of departments and a hundred or more individuals. Many of these requisitions are for the same item, but show different suppliers. Using the requisitioner's source, the buyer places the order without realizing that the same item was previously ordered from a different source. Thus, the purchase volume from any one source is low. With low purchase volume, service is less and prices are higher. Additional records must be kept by purchasing and accounting. Purchasing may be solicited for more business from each of the sources used. This takes up more of your precious time.

## How to Design a Requisition Form That Saves Time and Money

Requisition forms come in all sizes and shapes. Some are only one page. Others are multipart forms. Some provide space for a minimum of information. While any standardized form is better than accepting oral requests or unformatted notes, a good design saves time and helps make purchasing more efficient.

The following lists 11 tips for designing an efficient, effective requisition form:

1. Provide spaces for a checklist of all needed purchasing information to assure consideration of each item.

2. Use a uniform format to save time usually spent searching for each piece of information.

3. Allow proper spacing to permit faster typing by use of tabs and line advance without adjustment.

4. Allow spaces for the buyer to insert information. This eliminates the need of having the buyer rewrite some or all the information on another source document to give to a typist or data entry clerk.

5. Use prenumbered and multipart forms. This permits the requisitioner to keep a copy for reference and follow-up purposes.

6. Provide an extra copy. This allows purchasing to notify the requisitioner when the material is scheduled for shipment and eliminates many time-consuming, fruitless telephone inquiries requesting the status of the order.

7. Include spaces for the signatures of both the requisitioner and the person authorizing the requisition. This assures the buyer that the purchase has been approved and provides the name of the user, so the buyer can save time contacting the proper individual if questions need to be answered.

8. Provide spaces for the purchase order number. This gives the buyer a cross reference when checking the requisition number. The user also receives this information when the advise copy is returned.

9. Provide a space for the request for quotation number. This saves time in looking for a bid file.

10. Provide spaces for both the date the goods are wanted and the supplier scheduled shipment date. This allows the buyer to notify the user routinely what is expected and permits the user to decide if emergency action is warranted. The user is often satisfied with promises that are only a day or two later than requested.

11. Print instructions on the back of the form. This makes it easier for people using the form for the first time (see Figure 4-8).

## HOW TO ASK FOR A QUOTATION
## ——————— AND GET THE BEST REPLIES ———————

As is the case for requisitions, requests for quotations may be either oral or written. Oral requests sometimes get quicker results, but there is a great possibility for misunderstanding. When specifications are lengthy or complicated it is far better to prepare a formal written request.

Many of the suggestions that apply to requisitions also apply to requests for quotation forms. One major difference is that RFQs should be prepared by the buyer rather than the user. That does not mean that the buyer is the person to establish specification (see Chapter 5). On the contrary, the user or an engineering department should do that. Specifications for material to be used in manufacturing are usually prepared by engineers. Other material requirements are usually furnished by the user.

**INSTRUCTIONS FOR PREPARATION
AND
HANDLING OF THIS FORM**

USER Fill in the unshaded area only. Please type or print clearly.

(1) DATE REQ'N. PREPARED - Please use the date you are preparing the requisition.
(2) REQUISITIONER - Name of the person preparing the form.
(3) DEPT. NO. OR COST CENTER - The department number of the person preparing the requisition and charged for the goods or services.
(4) SHIP TO DEPT. - The department to which the goods are to be shipped for use or storage.
(5) SUGGESTED VENDORS - The Sources that you know of that are reliable and have the product or service that you wish. These may not necessarily be the best or most competitive sources.
(6) DATE NEEDED - BE SPECIFIC - When the goods or services are actually needed. Avoid the use of terms such as ASAP, RUSH, or URGENT and use specific times which must be met.
(7) TOTAL ESTIMATED PRICE - Total estimated value of this order; for budget control.
(8) IF FORM IS FOR AN EMERGENCY ITEM TO BE PURCHASED AS A SYSTEMS RELEASE OR AGAINST A BLANKET ORDER, Fill in the name and correct address of the supplier in the shaded area (8)
(9) AUTHORIZED SIGNATURE - Authorized signature for the amount of this requisition.
(10) APPROVED SIGNATURE - Authorized signature when higher authority is required for the amount of this requisition.
(11) ITEM NO. - The first item of this requisition, the twentieth item on page of this requisition, etc.
(12) QUANTITY - Quantity needed and units; such as feet, quarts, pieces, gallons, etc. Your order may be filled with quantities slightly different because of packaging methods.
(13) DESCRIPTION - Provide as much information as possible; giving either detailed specifications or the function needed of the product.

**FORM COPY DISTRIBUTION (FLOW)**

USED AS A REQUISITION
Requisitioner forwards copies 1, 2 and 4 to supply for stock items and to purchasing for non-stocked items. If unsure if items are stocked, send to supply. Requisitioner keeps copy 3 for reference and follow-up.

Purchasing returns part 4 (advise copy) to the requisitioner with the shipment promised date filled in. If shipped from stock, the goods will be accompanied by number 4 copy.

USED AS A SYSTEM RELEASE

MAKE CERTAIN SYSTEM RELEASE BOX IS CHECKED

USER gets approval signatures. Copy 4 is sent to purchasing with receival from supplier which has been checked for proper quantities and quality. Receival should be signed by person authorized to take delivery of goods.

Copy 1 and 2 will be left with the supplier. Supplier will forward copy 1 to        Accounts Payable along with the covering invoice. Copy 2 may be kept by the supplier for their record. Copy 3, may be kept as a user record.

**Figure 4-8. Instructions for Handling Supply/Purchase Requisition Shown in Figure 4-6**

If the specifications are short, they may be typed on to a standard requisition form. Lengthy specifications which may include many pages of description as well as engineering drawings may be attached to the requisition form. In such cases, the description on the requisition is brief and indicates that the specifications are attached. The requisition should reference:

- the attached specifications by date
- specification number
- drawing number(s), if any
- drawing number date(s)
- drawing revision number(s), if any, and dates of those revisions.

Thorough documentation of this type eliminates later problems between buyer and seller if products are produced to the wrong specifications. When engineering drawings do not show a date or an approval signature, disputes arise between the buyer and seller whenever products are slightly revised and do not meet the required quality level.

Sometimes neither the user nor the engineer is sure what product is needed. They may not know what is available or how to write the specifications. In those cases, a brief functional specification may be written on the requisition. You will then look for the various alternative products that can be used to achieve the desired result. See Chapter 5 for a detailed discussion of specifications.

## Why Smart Purchasing Professionals Request Quotations

There are at least two reasons to send out requests for quotations.

- To obtain prices and specifications for different products performing the same function.
- To obtain prices of the same product from different suppliers to meet established specifications.

It may be easier to use the telephone to make your request when the decision on specifications has not yet been made. In this case you are more interested in what is available than in the best cost. You should tell the supplier that you are trying to decide what you need. The supplier should send you brochures, catalogs, standard specifications, and list prices. High value capital equipment needs are usually refined in this way. You will be able to review the catalogs and see the differences in specifications.

The buyer may assist the user in developing specifications for a formal request for quotation. You might notice very small differences in the specifications of certain models of a product from different suppliers. The difference may not really matter to the user. For example, two brands of fork lift trucks may have forks that are only one or two inches difference in length. By indicating a range in the specification for fork length, you do not exclude either supplier from bidding. Keep such information in mind later when negotiating the final agreement.

Requests for quotations to obtain prices on products with established specifications are sent at two different times.

- To find the most competitive and qualified sources for new products.
- To check the marketplace to see if your existing supplier is still the most competitive source.

In either case, a meaningful RFQ should be formally written and should include all the information necessary to make an intelligent quotation. Preferably you should use a standard printed form.

## How to Design a Request for Quotation Form to Save Time and Improve Response

There are standard off the shelf request for quotation forms (RFQs) that are available in padded form from any stationery supply store (see Figure 4-9). Use of these forms is certainly better than no form at all, unless you use them so infrequently that a custom letter does the job. Most of the standard forms only have space for one supplier address and contain little if any information regarding terms and conditions. It is acceptable to use these forms or use a letter if you give the supplier enough information to bid intelligently and if you send exactly the same information to each supplier that you ask to bid. If you do not do so, you are being at least unfair to one or more of the suppliers, and more than likely, you are not awarding the order to the best source. If suppliers are making their bids with different information, some of them may not be giving you their best offer. See Figure 4-10 for a custom RFQ used by Ford Motor Company.

One way to overcome this problem is to design the form so that more than one supplier can be included. Some forms have space for up to six suppliers. The top or original shows all suppliers but each copy only shows one, and each copy shows a different supplier with its address. This is accomplished by having different portions of the carbon cut out for each page so that only the name of one supplier and one address appears on the page going to the supplier. The top copy shows all suppliers and their addresses. This system saves time in typing or printing and ensures that all the information given to each supplier is exactly the same. See Figure 4-11, Sample Request for Quotation form, used by American International Aluminum. If the cost of this complex form seems very high, it may be less

## QUOTATION REQUEST

From ................................................................

Street Address ................................................................

City and State ................................................................

To

THIS IS AN INQUIRY—NOT AN ORDER

Inquiry No. ................................................................

Date ................................................................

Classification ................................................................

**PLEASE NOTE CAREFULLY**

This inquiry implies no obligation on the part of the buyer.

Unless otherwise specified, there is no restriction on the number of items that may be ordered.

In quoting, use duplicate copy of this form provided. Fill in complete information before returning.

Do not quote on articles you cannot supply. If substitutes are offered, make full explanation.

Delivery Point ................................................................
By ☐ Parcel Post  ☐ Freight ........................................... R.R.  If not indicated, suggest most practical way.
☐ Express  ☐ ................................................................

Prices Quoted F. O. B. ................................................  Freight Allowance ................................................................

Shipping Point ................................................................

Terms: ................ % Discount ................ Days  Net Cash ................ Days   No charge to be made for packing, boxing crating or delivery to Transportation Co.

| ITEM NO. | QUANTITY | ITEM AND SPECIFICATIONS | * | UNIT | LIST PRICE OF UNIT | DISCOUNT OFFERED | NET UNIT PRICE | ESTIMATED GROSS WT. |
|---|---|---|---|---|---|---|---|---|
| | | | | | | | | |

* Check-mark in this column indicates shipment can be made from stock.

Delivery of other items as follows: ................................................................

Subject to withdrawal ................................................  Date returned ................................................................

........................................................For Buyer

........................................................For Seller

**Figure 4-9. Quotation Request**

**Request for Quotation**          ADDRESS REPLY TO

| DATE OF INQUIRY | REPLY REQUESTED BY | MODEL YEAR | RELEASE NUMBER | BLUEPRINT DATE | CONTROL NUMBER |

| PART NUMBER | PART NAME | REPLACED PART |

PART USED ON PRODUCT LINE(S)

| OPPOSITE-HAND PART | REQUIRED TOOLING CAPACITY PER WEEK | PLANNING VOLUME PER WEEK | AVG PLANT WKLY USAGE (PACKAGE SIZING) |

**BIDDER MUST FURNISH THE FOLLOWING INFORMATION**

| MATERIAL COST PER CWT. | PACKAGING COST (INCLUDED IN PRICE) | ECONOMIC LEVEL DATES | | UNIT PRICE | | PIECE PRICE | TOOLING | U.S. $/FOREIGN FUNDS CONV. |
|---|---|---|---|---|---|---|---|---|
| | | MATERIAL | LABOR | | | | | |
| $ | $ | / / | / / | $ | U.S. $ | ☐ | ☐ | RATE _____ |
| | | | | | CANADIAN $ | ☐ | ☐ | EFF. DATE _____ |
| | | | | | OTHER | ☐ | ☐ | OTHER _____ |

TOOLING (SHOW BREAKDOWN OF TOOLS AND GAUGES BELOW OR ON SEPARATE SCHEDULE)

TOOL & GAUGE COST BY ITEM

$

TOTAL $

RETURN THIS COPY

| SAMPLE PROMISE FROM PRODUCTION TOOLS (DATE OR NUMBER OF WEEKS AFTER TOOLING AUTHORIZATION) | SAMPLE PROMISE FROM PRODUCTION TOOLS (NUMBER OF DAYS AFTER RECEIPT OF TOOLING AIDS) | PRODUCTION SHIPMENT PROMISE (NUMBER OF DAYS AFTER SAMPLE APPROVAL) |

| SHIPPING POINT (CITY & STATE OR PROVINCE) | SUPPLIER CODE | GROSS PART WEIGHT | NET PART WEIGHT | BLANK SIZE |
|---|---|---|---|---|
| | | LBS. | LBS. | |

| TOOLING CAPACITY (PIECES PER WEEK) | NORMAL SHIFT  MAXIMUM OVERTIME | TOOL SOURCE | PACKAGING TYPE | LIMITING OPERATION |
|---|---|---|---|---|
| | /WK      /WK | | | |

OTHER INFORMATION (EXPLAIN FULLY ANY DEVIATION FROM, OR EXCEPTION TO, THE ABOVE TERMS AND CONDITIONS)
NOTE: Manufacturing Feasibility Sign-Off is required as shown on the back of this form, <u>unless otherwise instructed.</u>

| FULL NAME OF FIRM SUBMITTING QUOTATION | SIGNATURE OF AUTHORIZED REPRESENTATIVE | DATE |

**TERMS**

Your quotation must be on the basis of the terms and conditions of Ford's usual purchase order, a copy of which is available upon request. Base your prices on delivery F.O.B. Seller's plant, transportation collect, and payment net 15th and 30th próximo, unless otherwise specified.

If you cannot meet any feature of the drawings or specifications, or if any feature thereof is likely to cause manufacturing or quality problems, advise Ford's buyer as soon as possible.

Ford Motor Company welcomes any suggestions you have for improving the design, processing, packaging or use of the supplies of this request for quotation. Such suggestions must be furnished on a nonproprietary basis although Ford does not acquire thereby any rights in your patents. Please furnish a separate quotation for supplies that embody such suggestions.

PURCH 290          7-88 Printed in U.S.A.

**Figure 4-10. Request for Quotation**

E-2-OUT ®

UARCO BUSINESS FORMS
CHICAGO

## american-international aluminum corporation

SEND QUOTES ●
TO ●

DATE OF
REQUEST ●

**REQUEST FOR QUOTATION**

No. 11519

THE ABOVE NUMBER MUST APPEAR ON ALL
QUOTATIONS AND RELATED CORRESPONDENCE
**THIS IS NOT AN ORDER**

| V E N D O R | TOTAL COST | PRICE | TERMS | F.O.B. | DELIVERY | TRANS. COST TOOL COST |
|---|---|---|---|---|---|---|
| | | | | | | |
| | | | | | | |
| | | | | | | |
| | | | | | | |
| | | | | | | |

SOURCING DECISION

ORDER PLACED WITH _____ IF NOT THE LOWEST QUOTE, STATE

REASON_____

IF F.O.B. IS NOT DESTINATION POINT, SHOW TRANSPORTATION COSTS SEPARATELY.
ALL PRICES QUOTED SHOULD BE IN UNITED STATES CURRENCY.

* ALL IMPORT, DUTIES, TARIFF & BROKER
COSTS MUST BE LISTED SEPARATELY.

BIDS MUST BE RECEIVED BY | DESTINATION OF MATERIAL | BUYER

| QUANTITY | D E S C R I P T I O N | PRICE PER – | TOTAL |
|---|---|---|---|
| | | | |
| | | | |

**TELEPHONE:**

IMPORTANT:  PLEASE FURNISH FOLLOWING INFORMATION; IF UNABLE TO QUOTE, PLEASE STATE REASON

TOTAL COST OF TRANSPORTATION IF NOT F.O.B. DESTINATION | TOTAL COST OF TARIFFS, DUTIES, IMPORT TAX & BROKER FEES.

FOR CASTINGS, FORGINGS, STAMPINGS, SCREW MACHINE PARTS, AND ETC.

| BLANK WGT. OR ROUGH WGT. IF CASTING OR FORGING | MATERIAL COST PER CWT. | |
|---|---|---|
| DELIVERY DATE REQUIRED IN OUR PLANT | WHAT IS YOUR BEST DELIVERY DATE | F.O.B. POINT | TERMS |
| DATE OF BID | VENDOR | BY | |

PUR. FORM NO. 1 (1967)

**Figure 4-11. Summary of Quotation**

expensive to have the computer print different pages for each address. Each case must be analyzed to determine which system is better.

The following sections provide additional tips on designing the RFQ.

*Include space for the quantity of the item you want.* Indicate the quantity you expect to buy or use over a stated period of time. This is especially important when comparing new suppliers with an existing supplier that knows your usage figures and your ordering pattern.

It is perfectly acceptable to ask for prices at different quantity levels. Some purchasing professionals believe that this is an unfair negotiating tactic. Not so; your decision on the order quantity cannot always be made until you can compare the lower cost of purchasing a larger quantity with your cost of possession.

*Include space for a description of the items you want.* The description may indicate that a certain drawing or specification number is attached. Make sure you reference the date of the drawing and the revision number and make sure that each supplier receives copies of the same drawing and specification.

Sometimes requests for quotation forms can be used without knowing exactly what product you want or what is available. In such cases, you can describe what you want the product to do. This is called a *functional description.*

*Make absolutely certain that all requests forms with their attachments are exactly the same.* They should all be mailed at the same time. Always indicate a date when you want the bids returned but allow sufficient time for the receipt of your request, for calculation of bids and for return of the bid to you. You can help speed the process by alerting each supplier to expect your RFQ and that you need a prompt reply. If you grant an extension of time to any supplier, you should notify all other suppliers that they have the same extension. Any deviation from this practice can effect the bids you receive.

If the bids received have different specifications, you cannot compare them with the other bids unless you quantify those differences. This is normally difficult to do and some buyers will automatically disqualify such bids. An alternative is to have every supplier requote with the new specifications. However, the supplier submitting the revised specifications may know that he is the only one who can make the product in that way or the only one who can produce it at a low cost.

*Specify Whether the Quotation is Considered Negotiable.* The quotation form can include one of two statements, "Your first price is your final price" or "All bids are subject to negotiation." The former statement tends to have suppliers quote their lowest price on the first bid, although some will not believe the statement. Using this method somewhat obligates you to accept the lowest cost bid. Note, we said lowest cost, not lowest price. If you do not feel that any of the bids are satisfactory, you have a slight problem if you try to negotiate. Where you have indicated that all quotes are subject to negotiation, suppliers tend to add a little "fat" so they have room to reduce their charges to you if necessary.

One way to overcome the situation is to omit either statement on your RFQ. This will not solve all your problems as there are some suppliers who will interpret your intentions one way or the other if they happen to be at a disadvantage. When they are told they will not be getting the business because you awarded it to another supplier with a lower cost, they will tell you that they understood all quotes are subject to negotiation and they deserve a chance to rebid. When you say that you are not satisfied with the quotes received and want to discuss how the quotes can be improved, they will tell you they believed that all bids were final bids. Whether they believe their interpretation or it is feigned is open to speculation. In either case, it does not matter. You should not be intimidated. Simply take the course of action that is best for the situation making sure that you give each qualified supplier the same opportunity.

## Sending RFQs to Multiple Suppliers

How many suppliers should you solicit for quotes? How many bids are enough? Experience shows that on the average the more RFQs you send out, the lower the cost you will get. However, there is a diminishing rate of return. It costs you time to speak to every bidder and you may not always get any better results by contacting 15 suppliers than you would by contacting five. The answer is as always, it all depends. It depends on the time you have available, the importance of the product, the size of the expenditure involved, and how frequently the product will be purchased.

On high dollar capital equipment items, try to get at least three valid bids. That means you may have to contact six to ten suppliers to obtain the three bids. If time permits, double the number. You will usually get better results.

On repeat items or those used in manufacturing production year after year there is a cost saving method of covering the market little by little. Initially get five or six good quotes. This is particularly important if high cost tooling is involved because you don't want to have to change sources quickly and you are hoping for a long-term relationship. Then request new quotes periodically every year or two dropping off the two or three suppliers with the highest bids and adding two or three new ones. Be aware, however, that conditions change, management changes, companies change their policies, their procedures, and their equipment. The high-priced supplier one year may be the low-priced one the following year. That is why you are shopping in the first place. The reverse may be true and your low-cost selection may have changed so that it is no longer competitive.

As stated, a good RFQ form allows you to type in the names and addresses of three to five suppliers on the original but each copy shows a different one of the suppliers' names and addresses. The spaces where the other suppliers would appear are blank because of cutouts in the carbon. The reason for this is so that the supplier does not know who the other bidders are.

Suppliers will often ask who you are obtaining quotes from. They may even ask secretaries and clerks in your office. They sometimes get the information from engineers or other employees in your operation who innocently give out the information not understanding its value to the seller. Well-informed salespeople know their major competition. They know who they lose business to because the other supplier has a lower price or a lower cost. They know which of their competitors have higher prices and who are difficult to deal with. Therefore, knowing who they are bidding against helps them decide how low or high they can price their product and still have a good opportunity to get the business. Make it a rule never to tell suppliers who they are bidding against. Inform the people in your organization that this information is not to be disclosed.

Once in a while you will not be able to find a second or third source for a product. The supplier may know that he is the only source and therefore feels he can quote any price he wishes. You sometimes can place doubts in his mind with the blanked out RFQ form. Instead of having his company name and address typed in the first available space on the form, have it typed somewhere in the middle, perhaps the third or fourth space. This gives the impression you have sent the RFQ to other suppliers. Eventually all products and services will have competition. It is simply a matter of time. Your supplier with a monopoly never knows for sure when that competition will start. Be prepared, however, to answer questions when you use this tactic. The supplier will tell you there is no competition. No other firm has the same product.

## What to Do If You Get No Response From Your RFQ

You may not receive a response if you send requests for quotations to companies you are not familiar with. Some of the reasons for a lack of responses are:

1. The sellers do not believe you intend to place an order. They think you are only looking for information to use in negotiating with other suppliers. They feel they will be wasting their time.

2. The company does not make or sell the product you asked for.

3. The company is fully booked with orders and cannot handle your order in a reasonable time or is afraid to quote because cost will be higher when the work will be done.

4. The company feels that it does not have the technical know-how to handle what you need.

5. Although it may not be true, you or your firm has a reputation of being a "tough buyer" and sellers would rather not do business with difficult customers.

6. Your deadline for submission of the quotation does not allow sufficient time to prepare the bid. Rather than ask for more time, they simply do not reply or reply with the statement, "decline to quote."

A preliminary telephone call before mailing the request or a follow-up call afterward will often reassure the supplier that you are serious about giving them business if they are competitive and meet your qualifications. You can also avoid sending the RFQs to companies that do not sell the product you want by calling them first.

The buying directories list companies by types of products they produce and this may be sufficient if you are willing to take a chance and send out enough RFQs. However, sometimes the listed product categories are very general and include many types of suppliers. For example, if you look under valves, you may find companies that produce hydraulic valves, electrical valves, and pneumatic valves and even within those categories there are vast differences. There are many types and sizes of hydraulic valves and companies may specialize in one or more types and a particular range of sizes.

If you send out a great many RFQs for a particular product and you get few or no replies, call and find out what the problem is. Your interest and reassurance may change the supplier's mind and a bid will be submitted.

Probably the most frequent mistake made by buyers when asking for bids is not allowing sufficient time to prepare the quotation. Pay attention to what you are asking for. If the product is simple or is usually a stock item, it is relatively easy to prepare a bid. If you are asking for prices on dozens of items, it will take time to calculate a volume order price.

If the item is complex or if drawings and engineering calculations need to be made, the bid will take much longer to prepare. A supplier may need to buy materials to make a custom designed item for you. In this case, he will want to check with his suppliers to find out what he must pay for such material. That will add to the time required to make his bid.

## WHAT TO DO AFTER YOU RECEIVE THE BIDS: ———————— WRITING A PURCHASE ORDER ————————

In spite of all your efforts, suppliers will send bids that differ from what you asked in one way or another. Many will use their own form rather than yours so they control or think they control the legal interpretation of any agreement based on what is written on their bid. Some suppliers will not be able to give you exactly what you want so they will change the specifications. In some cases this will be obvious. In others, you will need to look carefully to see how their bid differs from what you specified.

### How to Analyze and Compare Suppliers' Bids

You must analyze bids to determine which supplier is offering the lowest cost. Note: LOWEST COST, not lowest price. Lowest cost considers the best value rather than price alone. Thus, you need to look at many things.

Here are some of the items you should compare:

- Is a warranty offered? What does it cover? For how long?
- What is the delivered cost including any setup charges, piece price, freight, payment terms, and any extra cost?
- How long will the product or service last compared with what you really need?
- What is the reputation of the supplier? Are you sure the agreement will be fulfilled? Will delivery be made on time?
- Does the supplier have the capacity to deliver the quantities you need now or might need in the future?
- Does the supplier have the facilities to produce the specifications or quality level that you want?
- If the supplier is offering a revision to your requests, is a better product being offered that could save your company labor expense or improve your company's product?

You should try to place dollar values on as many items as possible and enter the values on a columnar pad, a bid analysis form, or in a computer spread sheet program such as Lotus 1-2-3 or Excel. See Figure 4-12, for a sample bid analysis form.

After your analysis is complete, depending on the policy described above, you may want to negotiate with one or more of the suppliers to obtain a better offer. When you are sure you have completed your negotiations, you are ready to document your agreement. That can be done by a

**PURCHASING DEPARTMENT — BID ANALYSIS SHEET**

R.F.G.# _____

COMMODITY _____  CONSIGNEE _____

R.F.G. DATE _____

| QUANTITY REQUESTED | U/I | DESCRIPTION | REQ'N. NO. OR NACCO PART NO. | QUOTE TO CLOSE _____ |

A F E OR PROGRAM

DELIVERY REQUESTED

WEIGHT — PER UNIT | PER SHIPMENT

| ANNUAL PURCHASE AMOUNT | |
|---|---|
| UNITS | DOLLARS |

| | | | | | |
|---|---|---|---|---|---|
| VENDOR | | | | | |
| QUOTE RECEIVED | | | | | |
| VENDOR PART NUMBER OR REFERENCE | | | | | |
| CASH TERMS | | | | | |
| F.O.B. POINT | | | | | |
| ROUTING | | | | | |
| DELIVERY | | | | | |
| UNIT PRICE | | | | | |
| TOTAL AMOUNT | | | | | |
| AMOUNT LESS CASH DISCOUNT | | | | | |
| + PLUS FREIGHT | | | | | |
| + OR − OTHER | | | | | |
| TOTAL DELIVERED AMOUNT | | | | | |
| DELIVERED UNIT PRICE | | | | | |

PURCHASE APPROVAL

BID CLOSED

COMMENTS

ORDER NO.

PURCH. 100  3/75

**Figure 4-12. Bid Analysis Sheet**

formal written contract, the kind often prepared by attorneys, by a written note or letter, or by issuing a purchase order. Most businesses use a purchase order form of some sort. The purchase order form is the most important document handled by purchasing.

## How A Good Purchase Order Form Saves You Time and Minimizes Risk

Although most businesses use purchase order forms, very few have forms that make purchasing easier while protecting the company from undue risk. Some companies, even very large ones, use forms that are generated by the computer without any clauses that protect the company's interest. Others use forms that are out of date. Still others use forms that are awkward to use and generate needless paperwork. Years ago, the average purchase order form consisted of eight copies and some had as many as 15 copies. Today, partially because of the use of the computer, the average is much lower, between three and four.

One of the reasons for this change is that instead of the information being placed in a file drawer by various departments needing it, it is placed in the computer which is accessible by those authorized to use it. Here is a break down of how the copies used to be distributed (and may still be in some companies) and what is most common today.

| Distribution of Copies | New Distribution |
| --- | --- |
| Original to supplier | Same |
| Acknowledgement to supplier | Same |
| Copy to purchasing, filed alphabetically by supplier name | Same |
| Copy to purchasing, numerical file | Eliminated |
| Copy to Accounts Payable File in Accounting | Same |
| Copy to Receiving Dept. File | Eliminated |
| Copy to Data Processing File | Eliminated |
| Copy to Quality Control File | Eliminated |
| Copy to Production Control File | Eliminated |

The original and the acknowledgement copy are sent to the supplier. Many companies do not use any acknowledgement copy because so few are returned. There are arguments pro and con about the merits of this policy. It is true that few of the buyer's forms are returned; the supplier often sends in his own. In either case, any returned forms need to be checked for agreement. It is preferable to include the acknowledgement: although its use has limited practical value on small orders, it can be of great help in confirming understanding of the contract where large sums are at stake.

Before widespread use of the computer most companies found it advantageous to keep two purchasing copies. Sometimes, one copy was kept as an open order file. That is, those were orders for material not yet received in full. The buyer or a clerk or expediter kept track of the progress on the order and contacted the supplier periodically to make sure the order was shipped.

If you are running a purchasing department that is not yet computerized, it is a great advantage to have two copies for reference purposes. One copy is kept in alphabetical order by supplier. The other copy is kept in numerical order by the purchase order number (a copy of the requisition can also be filed in numerical order or chronological order and be marked with the appropriate purchase order number for cross reference). It saves a great deal of time and eliminates many problems to maintain a good filing system and proper documentation of all transactions.

With the computer it is no longer necessary to keep two copies of the purchase order in purchasing. The computer can easily cross reference purchase order numbers to the appropriate supplier or vice versa. A simple sort or database program can handle this.

Remember, the purchase order may be your only documented proof of a contract. A very few companies do not maintain a copy of the purchase order in purchasing. This could turn out to be a very serious mistake. Purchasing seems the best place to keep all records regarding the agreement including the bids, purchase orders, and all other correspondence.

Unless, purchasing checks invoices and receiving documents to make certain they match the purchase order before the invoice is paid, accounting needs a copy to perform this function (it might also be done through the computer although this is not yet common). Incidentally, the accounts payable matching function should not be done by purchasing personnel in all but the tiniest of companies. It is considered poor financial control.

Receiving traditionally used a copy to check the shipment against what was ordered. Well-controlled companies made sure that the receiving copy had the prices blanked out since there is no valid reason why receiving clerks needed that information. After the receiving clerk noted any discrepancies (shortages, wrong stock, and so on), the copy was usually sent to accounting for payment or correction of the invoice. In some companies, the receiving operation used two copies, one for a permanent file or to handle split shipments and the other to forward to accounting. It was not unusual to see bootleg copies of the purchase order being made on copying machines for use by various departments including the requisitioner.

Today, where companies have computer systems that are on-line, the receiving clerk may look at a monitor screen with the appropriate purchase order information shown and simply enter what has been received or discrepancies directly into the computer. Communications are fast and efficient.

Prior to on-line systems, a data processing copy was used to give information to clerks so that it could be entered into the computer. With on-line systems, the information is more often input by buyers or typists in purchasing, receiving, and any other appropriate department (production control, quality control, and so on).

## Essential Information You Must Include in a Purchase Order

As is the case of the RFQ, stock purchase forms can be obtained from any stationery supply company and many mail order forms companies. See Figures 4-13 and 4-14. These may do the job for a very small company or one that is just getting started, but they are poor substitutes for a well-designed form. If you don't have one, make sure you get your own as soon as time permits and in general make sure it includes identified space for the essentials listed below. Exceptions may be possible for large companies that have unique terms and systems.

Since the purchase order form is so important, you should take sufficient time to design it carefully and get help if you need it. You should think about what terms and conditions are important to you and write them down. Review them with your company attorneys or outside counsel to obtain their opinion and their additions or deletions. Make sure that these terms are reviewed once in a while to include provisions for new laws. Once in a while we discover forms that have been used for 20 years without modification. Attorneys seldom ask to review purchasing forms. It is up to you to initiate a review. If your operation is very large or complex it is sometimes more efficient to have different design purchase order forms for different purposes. For example, see Figures 4-15 and 4-16. These are purchase order forms used by Ford Motor Company. One is designed for the purchase of supplies and services (Figure 4-15) and the other is designed for the purchase of tools, jigs, dies, and so on (Figure 4-16). However, to keep your operation efficient your objective should be to make the procedures as simple as possible while avoiding problems. If you can do the job with one style of purchase order form, which most companies can, then you should do so. Only use more forms if it improves communication or makes the job easier.

The following checklist itemizes the essential information for an adequate purchase order form:

- Your company name
- Your company's address

09442

# PURCHASE ORDER

| TO | | | | SHIP TO | | |
|---|---|---|---|---|---|---|
| ADDRESS | | | | ADDRESS | | |
| CITY, STATE, ZIP | | | | CITY, STATE, ZIP | | |

| DATE | DATE REQUIRED | TERMS | HOW SHIPPED | REQ. NO. OR DEPT. | FOR |
|---|---|---|---|---|---|
| / / | / / | | | | |

| QUANTITY | DESCRIPTION | PRICE | UNIT |
|---|---|---|---|
| | | | |
| | | | |
| | | | |
| | | | |
| | | | |
| | | | |
| | | | |
| | | | |
| | | | |
| | | | |
| | | | |
| | | | |
| | | | |
| | | | |

**IMPORTANT**

PURCHASE ORDER NUMBER MUST APPEAR ON ALL INVOICES - PACKAGING, ETC.

PLEASE NOTIFY US IMMEDIATELY IF YOU ARE UNABLE TO COMPLETE ORDER BY DATE SPECIFIED

PLEASE SEND _____ COPIES OF YOUR INVOICE WITH ORIGINAL BILL OF LADING.

PURCHASING AGENT

DC 8131                    ORIGINAL

**Figure 4-13. Sample Stock Purchase Order Form**

**PURCHASE ORDER**

No. 0347        Req. No._____        Date_____19_____

To_____        For _____

Address_____        Date Required_____

Ship To_____        How Ship _____

Address_____        Terms_____

| QUANTITY | PLEASE SUPPLY ITEMS LISTED BELOW | PRICE | UNIT |
|---|---|---|---|
| 1 | | | |
| 2 | | | |
| 3 | | | |
| 4 | | | |
| 5 | | | |
| 6 | | | |
| 7 | | | |
| 8 | | | |
| 9 | | | |
| 10 | | | |
| 11 | | | |
| 12 | | | |
| 13 | | | |
| 14 | | | |
| 15 | | | |
| 16 | | | |
| 17 | | | |
| 18 | | | |
| 19 | | | |
| 20 | | | |
| 21 | | | |
| 22 | | | |

**IMPORTANT**

OUR ORDER NUMBER MUST APPEAR ON ALL IN-VOICES, PACKAGES, ETC.
PLEASE NOTIFY US IMMEDIATELY IF YOU ARE UN-ABLE TO SHIP COMPLETE ORDER BY DATE SPECIFIED.

Please Send        Copies Of Your Invoice With Original Bill Of Lading

Purchasing Agent

1H 146  Rediform        ORIGINAL

**Figure 4-14. Another Example of a Stock Purchase Order Form**

**Instructions to Requisitioner:**

1. For in space (with information as available) indicated by asterisks or enclosed in bold outline

3. Forward balance of set to Controller's Office for

☐ F.B. ☐ F.D.

**For releases:** Comply with local procedures

**For requisitions:** Future items 1, 2 and 3

2. Separate last three copies including carbons; remove carbons, retain last copy, distribute remaining two copies

account classification and tax status

4. Use envelope number 896.

**Ford** **Purchase Notification**

☐ Release ☐ Purchase Order ☐ Requisition

**Ford Motor Company, buyer,** agrees to purchase and receive, and

**Seller,** agrees to sell and deliver supplies or services specified herein subject to the terms and conditions on the face and reverse side hereof.

**Show these numbers on shipping and billing documents**

| Blanket order number (if any) | Purchase Order number, or Release Authorization when blanket order is entered at left. |
|---|---|
| | No. 055368 |

F.O.B. (Title transfer point): ☐ Carrier seller's plant ☐ Destination | (other) | Date of order

Transportation terms: ☐ Collect ☐ Prepaid | (other) | Delivery date

Supplier's code | Payment terms: ☐ Net _____ prox. | (other) | Shipping point

Routing: ☐ Seller's delivery ☐ By destination traffic | (other)

*Ship to:
**FORD MOTOR COMPANY**

**SALES — USE TAX STATUS**

☐ Subject to sales or use tax. (Bill tax if you are (1) legally required and (2) licensed; otherwise, Ford will pay tax direct.)

☐ Do not bill sales or use tax. Reason: See reverse side, paragraph 16, clause _____

☐ Other:

*Invoice to:
**FORD MOTOR COMPANY**

| *Quantity | *Code | Show on all shipping papers | *Description of supplies or services | Unit | Unit Price |
|---|---|---|---|---|---|
| | | | | | |

SUPPLIER COPY

| Confirming reference: to-date | *For additional information contact: Name - phone No. | By_____ Ford Motor Company, Purchasing |
|---|---|---|

| Requested by (name, phone, room no.) | | Project & item no | | Account classification & work order no | | | |
|---|---|---|---|---|---|---|---|

| For use in (dept name & no.) | Date issued | Delivery req'd | Dict code | Value characteristics | | | | | |
|---|---|---|---|---|---|---|---|---|---|
| | | | | 1 | 2 | 3 | 4 | 5 | 6 |

| Purpose | Estimated cost | Accounting approval |
|---|---|---|

| Approved by | Approved by | Buyer | Date | Senior buyer | Date |
|---|---|---|---|---|---|

| Supplier | Del date | 1 | 2 | 3 | 4 | 5 | F.O.B. | Tran. cost | Pay't terms | Total |
|---|---|---|---|---|---|---|---|---|---|---|
| | | | | | | | | | | |
| | | | | | | | | | | |
| | | | | | | | | | | |

| Previous supplier | Previous order no | Quantity | Date | Price |
|---|---|---|---|---|

Supply Stf(P) **492b** (Previous editions may be used) Dec 79

**PURCHASING FILE**

**Figure 4-15. Purchase Order Form Used by Ford Motor Company to Order Supplies and Services**

☐ Ford Motor Company, S.A., A Mexican Corporation, Buyer

☐ Ford Motor Company, A Delaware Corporation, Buyer.

☐ Ford Motor Company of Canada, Limited, A Canadian Corporation, Buyer.

☐ Ensite Limited, A Canadian Corporation, Buyer.

*Ford* **Purchase Order**

Hereby agrees to purchase and receive, and

| | Date of order | Purchase order no. |
|---|---|---|
| | | **T  029781** |

| Supplier's name and address | Code | Buyer | Code | Tooling completion date |
|---|---|---|---|---|

Tools used at (city, state or province)

Seller shall not use tooling, either separately or in conjunction with seller-owned tooling for the manufacture of parts for sale to parties other than buyer.

Shipments to Canadian locations are exempt from Canadian federal sales tax. We certify that the goods ordered/imported hereby are to be used as outlined in Sections 1, 3 and 4 of Part XIII of Schedule III of the Excise Tax Act.

Seller, agrees to design and construct, or to rework, as provided herein, the tools, jigs, dies, fixtures, molds or patterns (hereinafter referred to as "tooling") specified herein, in accordance with the terms and conditions on the face and reverse side hereof and on any continuation sheets.

Do not charge Ontario retail sales tax: Ontario Vendor's Permit Numbers, Ford of Canada 13240609G, Ensite Ltd. 12031402G.

Invoice to:

☐ Central Account Services General Services Division P.O. Box 1718 Dearborn, Mich. 48121

☐ Ford of Canada P.O. Box 2900 Oakville, Ontario

☐ Ford of Canada P.O. Box 8900 Windsor, Ontario

**PAYMENT TERMS:**
☐ Net 15th and 30th prox. after approval of production samples ☐

☐ Engine Div. Gen. Ofc. P.O. Box 1647 Dearborn, Mich. 48121

☐ Cleveland Engine Plants P.O. Box 9898 Cleveland, Ohio 44142

☐ Dearborn Engine Plt P.O. Box 1616 Dearborn, Mich. 48121

☐ Essex Engine Plant P.O. Box 1627 Windsor, Ont. Canada

☐ Lima Engine Plant P.O. Box 177 Lima, Ohio 45802

☐ Ford Motor Company, S.A. c/o P.O. Box 1647 (Mexico) Dearborn, Mich. 48121

☐ T & C Division P.O. Box 2100 (T-1-D) Livonia, Mich. 48151

☐ Other

Tooling price

☐ U.S. funds  ☐ Canadian funds  ☐ Mexican funds  ☐ Other

| Related part number | Part name and description of tooling | |
|---|---|---|

| Ford Motor Company | Ford Motor Company of Canada, Limited | Ensite Limited | Ford Motor Co., S.A. |
|---|---|---|---|
| By: | By: | By: | By: |

| Weekly tool capacity | Model year | Vehicle | A.I. or E.R. or latest PCR/Dev. | Control item Yes ☐ No ☐ | PPR-PPCN |
|---|---|---|---|---|---|

☐ Competitively Quoted          ☐ Not Competitively Quoted

| Part number | | | PCR or deviation | | | Item no. | | Memo expense | Price |
|---|---|---|---|---|---|---|---|---|---|
| Prefix | Base | Suffix | Cau pre | Base | Supp. no. | Base | SFX | | |
| | | | | | | | | | |
| | | | | | | | | | |
| | | | | | | | | | |
| | | | | | | | Prior Authentication | | |

Approval

| Buying activity | Charge to: | Bill to: | Project no. | Controller approval | Total |
|---|---|---|---|---|---|
| Date: | | | | Date: | |

PT & C
FEB. 82 **Purch 2800**

**2-PURCHASING FILES**

**Figure 4-16. Purchase Order Form Used by Ford Motor Company to Order Tools, Jigs, Dies, etc.**

- Date of the order
- Name of supplier
- Address of supplier
- Payment terms
- Point where title passes (FOB point)
- Scheduled delivery date
- Routing
- Quantity
- Units of measure (may be custom inserted on each order)
- Description of goods or service
- Unit price
- Percent of price discount (may be custom inserted on each order)
- Amount (extension of price times quantity for each item)
- Buyer's name
- Authorized agent's name if different from buyer
- Necessary common terms and conditions (to protect your company or minimize your risk and applicable to all your orders)

The following items are often included. Although they are optional, some are highly desirable:

- Company telephone (recommended)
- Buyer's company telephone number or extension number
- Supplier identification or code number
- Item number
- Part number
- Account numbers
- Requisitioner's name (not recommended)
- Deliver-to address (if different from address on heading)
- Bill-to address (if different from address on heading)
- Requested delivery date
- Sales tax status and exemption numbers
- Total of amount column which should be the value of the order (highly recommended)
- Buyer identification or code
- Material classification or code
- Confirming line

- Title of buyer or agent
- Approving signature
- Name and title of purchasing executive (such as Director of Purchasing or Vice President of Purchasing)

Some of both the essential and optional items require more explanation.

**Date of Order.** This can be misinterpreted. Does it refer to the date the form is typed or the date the agreement was made? When orders are prepared and sent promptly there is little problem, but if a backlog develops, it is a good idea to use a confirming line saying that "this purchase order confirms the contract made on . . ." (use the date of the contract).

**Supplier Name.** You should be careful what supplier name you use on purchase orders. If the product is manufactured by one company but supplied by another, make certain that you are making an agreement with the appropriate and authorized party. For example, is the supplier an authorized dealer, representative, or agent? If not, the manufacturer may disavow any terms or conditions you discussed with the salesperson. You may mail an order to the representative, but you might be better advised to use the name of the manufacturer or actual supplier and show the representative's as only care of. For example, XYZ Mfg. Co., c/o John Jones Associates.

**Scheduled Delivery Date.** This may also be called the agreed delivery date. To clarify the need for the item, include an extra space for requested delivery date. Sometimes, the supplier is unable to ship when you want the product. Later when you call to complain about the product being one or two days late from the agreed upon date, the supplier says you expect too much and you are unreasonable. By showing the date when you need the goods it alerts the supplier that it is important to be on time. Furthermore, you should not blame the supplier if he meets the agreed schedule even though you needed the material sooner.

As is the case with requisitions, never use ASAP or RUSH as a scheduled delivery date. While you may have some ability to interpret such vague terms from your requisitioners, the supplier may not have an inkling when you really need the goods or what you mean by these terms.

**Units of Measure.** This is a very important piece of information. First it is important to match the units of measure of the quantity ordered to the units of measure used for pricing; otherwise the extended cost will be incorrect. Purchase histories should use the same units of measure for every purchase to avoid being misled about price movements.

***Other Essential Terms and Conditions.*** These may be printed on the face of the purchase order form or on the reverse side. You may use so many terms and conditions that it is impossible to include them all on the form. Rarely do all such terms and conditions apply to any one transaction. It is probably best to print only the ones that apply in most cases. Other terms can be typed in as you need them. Some purchasing operations customize each purchase order by use of the computer. Although all the terms reside in the computer memory, only those terms that apply are assigned by the buyer.

If preprinted, the terms and conditions (so-called boilerplate) should be large enough and dark enough to be legible; otherwise any dispute involving such terms may be adjudicated against your interest. If a particular clause is very important and you want it to apply to all or most of your orders, have it printed on the face of the form rather than on the back. The larger or more conspicuous it is the more likely it will be valid as long as there are no contradictory clauses or inconsistencies elsewhere on the form. You must be careful to be consistent. Refer to the list of 20 commonly used terms and conditions in Chapter 3 for terms you should consider including in your boilerplate.

***Supplier Identification or Code Number.*** This is often used by accounting and data processing and only needs to be included on the form if your particular system requires it.

***Ship-To and Bill-To Addresses.*** These can be preprinted on the form (to save typing time) for one or multiple locations. Provide spaces on the form for checkmarks beside the appropriate location where goods should be shipped or where billing should be sent. I have managed several different purchasing operations where we used a similar procedure. One had seven locations and another five. This is particularly useful for centralized systems and where shipments may be ordered for any combination of locations. See Figure 4-17, which is an example for AIM Companies, Inc.

***Sales Tax Status and Exemption Numbers.*** You can help eliminate an annoying and time consuming chore by preprinting your sales tax numbers on the purchase order and having a check box indicating that an item is exempt or nonexempt. This will not eliminate all requests for tax numbers because suppliers sometimes overlook to read this information on your purchase order. Nevertheless, if it reduces the requests you have gained time with little cost or effort.

***Total Amount of Order.*** Providing space for the total amount of the order and using that space to type in the order value has at least four advantages:

- It gives the information needed to determine authority signature levels necessary for approval of the order.

## PURCHASE ORDER

# AIM Companies, Inc.

| PURCHASE ORDER NUMBER |
|---|
| No. |
| THIS NUMBER MUST APPEAR ON ALL PACKAGES, PACKING SLIPS, INVOICES AND BILLS OF LADING. |

TO

SHIP TO

1 — PERMANENT MOLD DIE CO., 2275 EAST NINE MILE ROAD, WARREN, MICHIGAN 48091

2 — H. R. KRUEGER CO., 32471 INDUSTRIAL AVE., MADISON HEIGHTS, MICHIGAN 48220

3 — DRILLMATION CO., 1601 WANDA AVE., FERNDALE, MICHIGAN 48220

4 — PERMANENT MOLD DIE CO., INDUSTRIAL PARK, FLORENCE, ALABAMA 35630

5 — PERMANENT MOLD DIE CO., 820 WEST 84TH STREET, HIALEAH, FLORIDA 33014

← SHIP TO ADDRESS NUMBER SHOWN, IF NOT INDICATED ABOVE →

| 1 | 2 | 3 | 4 | 5 |
|---|---|---|---|---|

| VENDOR CODE | ACCOUNT NUMBER | JOB NUMBER | REQUISITION DATE | REQUISITIONER | DEPT. | DELIVERY DATE | REQ. NO. |
|---|---|---|---|---|---|---|---|

| SHIP VIA | DATE OF ORDER | TERMS | F.O.B. | | BUYER CODE | REQ. FOR QUOTE NO. |
|---|---|---|---|---|---|---|
| | | | DEST. | S.P. | | |

| PLANT CODE | P.O. DATE | SALES TAX | | BILL TO (SAME AS SHIP TO UNLESS OTHERWISE SHOWN) |
|---|---|---|---|---|
| | | EXEMPT | TAXABLE | |

| ITEM NO. | QUANTITY | DESCRIPTION | CODE | UNIT PRICE | % DISCOUNT | AMOUNT |
|---|---|---|---|---|---|---|
| | | | | | | |

SPECIAL INSTRUCTIONS OR REMARKS:

DUE TO OUR ACCOUNTING SYSTEM A PACKING SLIP IS A MUST, OR FREIGHT MAY BE RETURNED AT YOUR EXPENSE.

MAIL ACKNOWLEDGEMENT AT ONCE; AND ON DATE OF SHIPMENT SEND INVOICE IN **DUPLICATE TO**

ACCEPTANCE OF THIS PURCHASE ORDER IS EXPRESSLY LIMITED TO THE TERMS AND CONDITIONS SET FORTH HEREIN.

See reverse side for additional terms and conditions.

**AIM** Companies, Inc.

Buyer

Approved

**Figure 4-17. Purchase Order Form Used by AIM Companies, Inc.**

- It makes the buyer aware of the full extent that he or she is committing to a particular supplier. Only looking at the unit cost of a few cents or even at the extended amounts of each item is often misleading.
- It provides some help in comparing invoices and statements with the purchase order.
- It makes the supplier aware of the value of your business. This is perhaps the most important reason. When a salesperson sees he is receiving an order for a sixty cent item, he may not give you much service. When that price is extended by the quantity ordered and he sees the amount of one or two hundred dollars, he may pay more attention. However, if the order is totaled and is between $3,000 or $4,000, you should have his attention.

***Name and Title of Purchasing Executive.*** Printing the name and title of the top purchasing official on the form gives the supplier the name of someone to contact if there is a serious problem with supplier relations. If there is a delicate situation where a buyer uses tactics or methods that are excessively rude or even less than honest, the seller may want to discuss this with a higher level of management. It is better if you first give them the opportunity of contacting the director of purchasing rather than contacting the chief executive officer. It gives you the chance of solving a possible problem before it gets blown out of proportion.

## How to Change or Amend a Purchase Order

Every purchasing department sometimes needs to change an order after it has been sent to the supplier. Hopefully, it does not happen frequently, but the need does exist. Many companies do this by using an unnumbered purchase order form and simply typing in the same purchase order number as the original order with a revision number and date. Sometimes it is referred to as an amendment, or a purchase order change notice. Regardless of the name, the purpose is to notify the supplier and document any change to the original agreement.

It is extremely important to put changes in writing and to have any changes documented by purchasing. There are many cases where unauthorized personnel instruct suppliers to make changes and the supplier complies and then bills the company for extra product or extra work. Or oral instructions changing an order are ignored by the supplier and goods or services are delivered to match the original order. The supplier then may claim that he was never given official notification of the change or never agreed to the change. These situations often result in serious disputes and cause unnecessary grief. It makes it much easier to document changes in writing by using a standard form designed to do the job. A standard form saves time and looks more business like.

When you use the purchase order form, you run the risks of changing certain parts of the agreement that you do not intend to change unless you repeat all terms and conditions on the original. The revision form limits any changes to those changes only. Each form should contain a statement that, "all requirements, terms, and conditions of the original agreement remain in effect except as shown herein." A standard form can list the most usual changes and provide a box for each that may be checked where changes are to be made.

The following lists the most common changes that you will normally make.

- Change quantity
- Cancel entire order
- Change scheduled delivery date
- Add these items to the order
- Remove these items from the order
- Change specifications

As is the case with requisitions forms, purchase order forms, and requests for quotation forms, you can obtain stock forms for purchase order changes from most stationery supply stores (see Figure 4-18). These standard forms will not have your company's address, however; therefore, it is better to have your forms printed with your company name and address. Revision forms should have the same number of copies as purchase orders but distribution depends on the type of change. For example, if the change is in quantity, the receiving department needs to know, but if the change is for payment terms, the receiving department is not involved. See the sample purchase order change notice, Figure 4-18 and the Purchase Order Revision form, Figure 4-19. Also note Fig. 4-20, the Purchase Notice Revision form used by Ford Motor Company and Figure 4-21, the Tooling Purchase Order Amendment form. Using more than one form is helpful when you have sufficient volume to justify it, but most companies will find one form sufficient for all purchase revisions. The Purchase Order Revision form shown in Figure 4-19 is typical of that used by many companies.

## CONCLUSION-PAPERLESS PURCHASING VERSUS USING EFFECTIVE FORMS

Today good purchasing forms are essential for efficient purchasing administration. Modern management is stressing the advantages of paperless purchasing because of the abuses in the use of forms, but paperless purchasing creates a whole new set of problems. The computer and electronic

BROOKS & McMULLEN 537-1220

## Purchase Order Change Notice

PLEASE ACKNOWLEDGE THIS CHANGE IMMEDIATELY

☐ BY PHONE

☐ THRU YOUR REPRESENTATIVE

☐ ON YOUR FORM

TO

DATE

| OUR P.O. NO. & ENTRY DATE | SHOP COPY NO. | VENDOR ORDER NO. | CONFIRMING PHONE TO |
|---|---|---|---|

PLEASE CHANGE OUR ORIGINAL PURCHASE ORDER AS FOLLOWS:

☐ CHANGE QUANTITY ON FOLLOWING ITEMS TO:          ☐ SHIP TO:

☐ CHANGE DESCRIPTION TO READ:

☐ SHIP VIA:
☐ OTHER CHANGES (SEE REMARKS)
☐ HOLD SHIPMENT UNTIL FURTHER NOTICE.          ☐ CHANGE PURCHASE ORDER NUMBER TO:
☐ CANCEL ENTIRE ORDER
☐ CANCEL THE FOLLOWING ITEMS:
                                                  ☐ ADD THE FOLLOWING ITEM(S) TO OUR ORDER:

ALL TERMS AND CONDITIONS SHOWN ON ORIGINAL ORDER SHALL REMAIN UNCHANGED.

## Remarks

DATE                                             SIGNED

VENDOR

**Figure 4-18. An Example of a Stock Purchase Order Change Notice Form**

**PURCHASE ORDER REVISION**

TO: ⌐

| THIS NUMBER MUST APPEAR ON ALL PACKING LISTS PACKAGES, BILLS OF LADING, INVOICES AND CORRESPONDENCE. | |
| --- | --- |
| PURCHASE ORDER NUMBER | PURCHASE ORDER DATE |
| | |
| REVISION NUMBER | REVISION DATE |
| | |

TYPE OF CHANGE

☐ PRICE   ☐ QUANTITY   ☐ DELIVERY
☐ SPECIFICATION   ☐ OTHER

GENTLEMEN:
Please refer to our purchase order number and date above and make changes as noted below:

| ITEM # | PART # AND/OR DESCRIPTION | OLD PRICE | NEW PRICE | OLD QUANTITY | NEW QUANTITY | OLD SHIP DATE | NEW SHIP DATE |
| --- | --- | --- | --- | --- | --- | --- | --- |
| | | | | | | | |

All terms and conditions shown on original order shall remain the same unless specifically revised herein. No additions in price or charges for the change(s) shown herein will be accepted without prior written agreement.

Return signed acknowledgement at once to Purchasing Department.

Inquiries regarding these changes should be made to the issuing party.

SPECIFICATIONS, OTHER OR REMARKS

ISSUED BY_____    APPROVED BY_____

FORM P-100A HEH 11-78 REV. 5-79

**ORIGINAL**

**Figure 4-19. Typical Purchase Order Revision Form**

Instructions to the Requisitioner.

In order to change your requirements on a previously issued purchase requisition or an established purchase order please fill in the appropriate information in the space marked with an asterisk(*). Purchasing will complete the form and process it as an amendment when appropriate or use it as authority for issuing a regular amendment to the purchase order.

## Ford **Purchase Notice Revision**

Original PN No._____

| ★Requested by | | Room no. | ★Phone no. | ★Date issued | ★Accounting approval | | ★Project number | ★Item number |
|---|---|---|---|---|---|---|---|---|
| ★For use in *(Dept. name)* | | ★Dept. number | ★Delivery requested | | ★Account classification | | ★Ford Work Order number | |
| ★Purpose | | | | | ★Est. cost | ★Approved by | | ★Approved by |
| Date | Buyer | | Senior Buyer | | Date | | ☐ Used as Amendment | ☐ Amendment to be typed |
| ★Reason for change | | | | | | | | |

## Ford **Ford Motor Company**

★Purchase Order No._____

| ★Supplier's name and address | Amendment date |
|---|---|
| | Effective date |
| | Amendment number |

| ★Part or code number | ★Description of material |
|---|---|

★ The above Purchase Order is hereby amended by changing the

☐ Price   ☐ F. O. B.   ☐ Quantity   ☐ "Ship To"   ☐ Delivery

☐ Terms   ☐ Routing   ☐ Specifications   ☐ "Bill To"

| From | Price | To | Price |
|---|---|---|---|
| ★ | | ★ | |

Reason:

**For Distribution Purposes Only**

| Reference: Wire-letter-phone-verbal to | Buyer | Code number | ★ "Bill To" location | ★ "Ship To" location |
|---|---|---|---|---|

Delivery to remain unchanged unless indicated above.

This Purchase Order Amendment does not require acknowledgement. It is assumed that the provisions of this amendment are acceptable to you. If you do not accept it as written, please return it with your counterproposal immediately.

**Purchase Order**

**Amendment**   By _____

Purchasing

SUPPLY STF(P)
MAY 78 **495b**

ORIGINAL

**Figure 4-20. Purchase Order Revision Form Used by Ford Motor Company**

Ford

**TOOLING PURCHASE ORDER AMENDMENT**

| EFFECTIVE DATE | AMENDMENT NO. | PURCHASE ORDER NO. T |
|---|---|---|

☐ FORD MOTOR COMPANY, A DELAWARE CORPORATION, BUYER. ☐ FORD MOTOR COMPANY OF CANADA, LIMITED, A CANADIAN CORPORATION, BUYER.

BUYER'S NAME | CODE

SUPPLIER'S NAME AND ADDRESS | CODE

EXPLANATION OF CHANGE

RELATED PART NO.

TOOLS USED AT (CITY, STATE, OR PROVINCE) | EST. WEIGHT OF TOOLS | PART DESCRIPTION

INVOICE TO: ☐ CENTRAL ACCOUNTING SERVICES GENERAL SERVICES DIVISION P.O. BOX 1718 DEARBORN, MICH. 48121 ☐ FORD OF CANADA P.O. BOX 2900 OAKVILLE, ONTARIO ☐ FORD OF CANADA P.O. BOX 8900 WINDSOR, ONTARIO ☐ OTHER (SPECIFY)

THIS PURCHASE ORDER IS AMENDED ONLY WITH RESPECT TO THE MATTERS AND TO THE EXTENT INDICATED BELOW

| PAYMENT TERMS | TOOL COMPLETION DATE | ☐ U.S. FUNDS ☐ CANADIAN FUNDS | TOOLING PRICE FROM $ | TO $ |
|---|---|---|---|---|

OTHER ADDITIONS, DELETIONS OR CHANGES, IF ANY:

This purchase order amendment does not require acknowledgment. It is assumed that the provisions of this amendment are acceptable to you. If you do not accept it as written, please return it with your counterproposal immediately.

| FORD MOTOR COMPANY<br>BY: | FORD MOTOR COMPANY OF CANADA, LIMITED<br>BY: |
|---|---|

| WEEKLY TOOL CAPACITY | A.I. OR E.R. OR LATEST PCR/DEV. | | PROJECT NO. | PROJECT NO. |
|---|---|---|---|---|

| PART NUMBER | | | PCR OR DEVIATION | | | ITEM NO. | | MEMO EXPENSE | PRICE |
|---|---|---|---|---|---|---|---|---|---|
| PREFIX | BASE | SUFFIX | CAU PRE | BASE | SUPP NO. | BASE | SFX | | |
| | | | | | | | | | |
| | | | | | | | | | |
| | | | | | | | | | |
| | | | | | | | | | |
| | | | | | | | | | |

| MODEL YEAR | VEHICLE | PPR-PPCN | TOTAL MEMO EXPENSE | PRIOR AUTHENTICATION |
|---|---|---|---|---|

| APPROVAL | | | | | | | |
|---|---|---|---|---|---|---|---|
| BUYING ACTIVITY | DATE | PURCH. EST. ACTIVITY | DATE | CONTROLLER APPROVAL | DATE | THIS REQUEST | |
| | | | | | | TOTAL | |

PURCH2707A MAY 81 PRINTED IN U.S.A. 2-PURCHASING FILES

**Figure 4-21. Purchase Order Revision Form Used by Ford Motor Company for Changes to Tooling Orders**

processing will no doubt, in time, eliminate the need for hard copies. At present our legal system and most business enterprises are not set up to handle paperless purchasing efficiently. Although we have seen many software packages, they still do not provide the reliability and the thoroughness that a well-run purchasing department needs. Many save expenses in one area only to have the savings offset by inefficiency and excess cost in another area.

The largest companies develop their own systems and have the clout to get their suppliers to work with them, but the time is not here for complete paperless systems in the smaller company.

In the past, forms were poorly designed. It was not that there were enormous amounts of paper as much as the paper was used carelessly and improperly. There were too many copies generated without a purpose. However, a good forms management system can solve that problem and improve purchasing operations as well.

The entire purchasing system can be learned by knowing the forms and how to use them. It is difficult to learn and understand purchasing when all you have to deal with is a monitor. Not only do you have to learn about purchasing, you also must understand the computer and its software.

So, until the time that we do away with all forms you should make sure that you have the best designed forms available. The essential ones for purchasing are the requisition, the request for quotation, the purchase order, and the purchase order revision form. You may add others that are unique to your operation, but be sure that they have a useful purpose. Periodically review the need for each form and make changes accordingly.

Up to this point you have covered the essentials of the order processing. If everything always went smoothly you might be tempted to stop reading here, but in practice it seldom does. After the order is placed, many questions develop from the supplier. Suppliers do not ship the product or perform the service on schedule. Products that are shipped are not what you wanted. The invoices are incorrect. A multitude of problems plague the buyer every day. In poorly run purchasing departments there are more problems and in the best run departments there are far less. However, all of them routinely must remedy problems as they arise.

# CHAPTER FIVE

# How to Obtain the Proper Specifications to Help You Avoid Common Purchasing Problems

Proper specifications are the most valuable help that a requisitioner can give you. Without good specifications, purchasing cannot achieve the best results. Yet there is much confusion about specifications and why they are needed. Specifications are detailed descriptions of the product or service desired. The descriptions can be presented in various formats and with as little or as much detail as needed. Proper specifications are those that present sufficient detail to achieve the best purchase without excessive data that restricts the buyer or seller needlessly.

Some companies eliminate their engineering departments or limit their size and then depend on their suppliers to establish any needed specifications. These managers believe the internal savings are more important than creating their own specifications. They fail to measure the high cost of the purchase products, the restriction on purchasing power to negotiate or shop, and the inability to measure or check quality objectively and impartially.

## SIX WAYS PROPER SPECIFICATIONS HELP YOU BUY ——— *EXACTLY* WHAT IS NEEDED *AND* REDUCE COSTS ———

*1. Order the correct material the first time and avoid unnecessary extra cost.* For example, if a buyer receives a requisition for a pen, she may place an order with a stationery supplier. The salesperson will ask for the color desired and whether she wants a fine, medium, or heavy point. The same salesperson may inquire if the buyer wants a ballpoint, a felt tip, or a roller ball style. Actually, there are dozens of questions that the salesperson can ask, but it is more likely that a selection will be based on the price and availability rather than the ultimate cost or usefulness of the product. Obviously, this is an exaggeration of what often happens. Usually there are a few more details supplied by the requisitioner.

To carry the example to the extreme, let us assume that the requisitioner was exceptionally obtuse and did not really want a writing instrument, but wanted a pen for cattle. Judging from past experience, the company's business and environment, the buyer would probably guess or at least suspect the type of product wanted. Nevertheless, the buyer does not perform well if she must guess what is needed. Even in the best managed organizations, buyers order material that is received and must be returned because it is not what is needed. Many times this is the fault of the seller, but often it is because the product was not properly described to the seller.

What is worse, it is not always evident that products are inappropriate for the purpose intended. If a buyer orders low carbon steel when a specific grade of tool steel is needed, the result can be disastrous. Or if a chemical is purchased without the correct concentration or correct compounds, the product may be ineffective or do great harm.

Even without causing physical injury or resulting in lost customers, the cost of receiving the incorrect material, storing it, returning it, getting billing adjusted, and reordering the correct material, mounts up to a large expense over a year period. You can reduce this added expense substantially, if not eliminating it entirely, by establishing policies and procedures aimed at producing proper specifications.

*2. Send out requests for bids in writing to many suppliers with the assurance that all suppliers are using the same data.* Proper specifications are very important when a buyer wants to ask for quotations and compare the costs for the same goods or services from various suppliers. Without clear unambiguous descriptions of the product, it is likely that quotations will be for different products, even if the differences are slight. The differences may not be stated or even realized by either the buyer or the seller.

*3. Compare costs for the same product or service from different suppliers.* Sending out the same specifications also helps compare different suppliers' costs. Any cost differences between the products may be, in part, as a consequence of the difference in specifications and cannot be attributed to the competitiveness or efficiency of any of the bidders. To restate an old cliché, you must compare apples to apples to learn which is the better apple.

***4. Shop for and place orders for material and services without bias.*** Eliminate the prejudices of the requisitioner or buyer by giving copies of the same written specifications to each supplier asked to make a bid. Oral requests for bids may leave out one or more specifications or add other requirements to the description. No doubt this happens when one party deliberately wishes to favor a particular supplier or feels that one supplier has a better product and is not willing to trust the system to determine who has the better product. More often, it is done unconsciously by the requisitioner or buyer who neglects to communicate all the details to each potential source in exactly the same way.

***5. Measure the quality of the product or service.*** Detailed specifications include a complete description of the features necessary and objective measurements of the product ordered. These descriptions and measurements are vital for inspection by the receiving department or a quality control function so they can evaluate if the product has met the requirements of the purchase agreement as well as the requirements to do the job for which the goods were purchased.

***6. Measure the performance of your suppliers and reshop for the same product or service to obtain lower cost or a better product.*** Complete specifications allow you to continually shop for better products and better suppliers. Over a period of years, performance from a particular supplier may slip for a number of reasons. When such is the case, it may be weeks, months, or years for you to find capable alternative sources. The time required to do so is much shorter when complete and up-to-date specifications are available.

## ASSIGN RESPONSIBILITY FOR PROPER SPECIFICATIONS TO ———— OTHER DEPARTMENTS TO REDUCE COSTS ————

If the requirement is for raw material or items involved in a manufacturing process, the design or engineering function provides the specifications. Sometimes, the buyer helps establish or even totally decides on the specifications for the product although that is not the normal responsibility of purchasing. In a small- to medium-sized organization the requisitioner usually specifies capital equipment, maintenance supplies, and office equipment and supplies. A standard set of specifications is highly advantageous if more than one or two requisitioners use the product. Costs are thereby reduced through quantity discounts, reduction in administrative cost, smaller inventories of the product itself and smaller inventories of any stocked repair items.

Even though a company may have a large engineering department which is responsible for the establishment of product specifications, purchasing is frequently asked to obtain information from potential suppliers to help engineering learn what is available and to see what type of specifications are normally used in an industry. Larger companies provide many more details than sales literature usually shows.

## Minimize Sales Contacts Between Suppliers and Requisitioners

Requisitioners ask purchasing agents to obtain catalogs and sales literature on products of interest to them. The requisitioner then uses the sales information to write a requisition. If the salespeople have free access to the requisitioner, they can persuade the requisitioner to write the requisition in such a way that only their product meets the requirements. It is not unheard of for the salesperson to write the requisition for the requisitioner. It is therefore, important that purchasing has veto power over any proposed purchase where comparative information has not been obtained or where the reason for the source selection cannot be completely cost justified by need and where the selection of any source does not conflict with other agreements made by purchasing.

A well-qualified buyer needs to know many things. Unless he has the limited responsibility for only one product he cannot possibly know all the technical aspects of what he buys. Even in large companies where buyers are product specialized they depend on engineers and other technicians to develop product specifications which is a full-time job. In some cases buyers have engineering degrees but they still do not have the time to prepare complete specifications. That is not to say that they do not have much product knowledge. In some instances they may know more about the product than the engineer responsible for developing the specifications. It is simply not their function. The buyer is or should be another kind of specialist. The buyer must have a knowledge of the law. A buyer must be an experienced and effective communicator. A buyer must be familiar with business practices. A buyer must know how to find sources of supply. A buyer must know and be able to use the various techniques for successful negotiation. In short, purchasing personnel should not be burdened with the responsibility for specification development; they simply have too many other things to do.

Nevertheless, the buyer is in the best position to obtain information about products. He can furnish such information to the person responsible for specification development, be that engineer or any requisitioner from any department. The buyer's input should be solicited and his recommendations should be taken if there are no important reasons for not doing so.

A typical assignment for specification responsibility is as follows.

- Production Raw Material—Engineering Manager
- Software—MIS Manager
- Office Equipment and Supplies—Manager of Administration or Office Manager
- Plant Equipment—Manufacturing Engineering Manager or Plant Manager or Operations Manager
- Maintenance, Repair, and Operating Supplies—Maintenance Supervisor
- Leased Automobiles—Vice President of Sales or Marketing Manager
- Packaging—Packaging Engineer

## TYPES OF SPECIFICATIONS AND THEIR ADVANTAGES AND DISADVANTAGES

### Functional Specifications

Any verbal description of a product or service may be considered a specification, but ordinarily we think a specification needs detail that includes measurable items such as weights, tolerances, dimensions, quantities, and percentages. Good specifications ensure that this type of information is included and that it is necessary for the performance of the product being ordered.

Requisitioners know what they want the product to do. They then indicate what the product is going to be used for or what they want it to do, without further detail when placing the request. In other words they indicate the function that the product should perform. Such a specification is sometimes called a functional specification or a performance specification. Performance specifications put the responsibility for the design on the supplier. If the supplier agrees to accept the performance specification without a disclaimer, then he is responsible to make sure that the product does exactly what it is supposed to do.

Another way of avoiding product details in the specification is to use a brand name. The user believes the brand name carries some assurance that the product will do the job required given the quality level and reputation of the manufacturer. The reputation may be justified because of a high quality standard or it may be derived, at least in part, from the image generated through advertising. Producers of specifications should make every effort to avoid the use of brand names. They restrict the buyer's ability to shop or negotiate. Salespeople make every effort to have their brands specified on drawings or in specification descriptions. They usually work with engineers and architects to obtain this end. When successful, they obtain the business and in many cases they continue to receive repeat orders for their product for many years to come without the threat of serious competition. It is frequently very difficult for a buyer to have brand names removed from specifications once included.

When engineers or requisitioners have been made aware of the drawbacks of specifying by brand, they sometimes widen the opportunity for competition by adding the words "or equivalent" after the named brand. This has the advantage of avoiding the cost of determining the specification details of the product while to some degree giving the buyer the ability to shop and negotiate. However, it usually becomes difficult to prove that alternate sources have equivalent products. There are missing details and measurements that make comparisons hard. Most users tend to be biased in favor of the mentioned brand and very few products are 100% equal in every respect.

## Industry Standards

There are many trade associations, professional societies, and governmental organizations that develop standard specifications for products. For example, the American Association of Railroads (AAR) provides details on components of rail cars. The AAR even gives the names of which suppliers they approve of and consider capable of manufacturing the various components. Other organizations that provide specifications include:

- the Copper Development Association, Inc.
- the American Iron and Steel Institute
- the American Standards Association
- the American Society for Testing and Materials
- the National Electric Manufacturer's Association
- the American Society of Mechanical Engineers

This list names only a few. The American Society for Testing and Materials publishes a wide variety of specifications which are available for purchase. You can obtain their catalog by writing to the ASTM, 1916 Race Street, Philadelphia, PA 19103-1187 or calling (215) 299-5585.

## Proprietary Engineered or Technical Specifications

Some specifications describe the raw material or components to be used in the product and then describe how the product should be manufactured. These type specifications place the responsibility for the performance of the product with the buyer. They are best used when the buying company needs highly technical items and has the engineering know-how to make the product that is not available from outside suppliers.

Certain products sold in bulk or liquid form require a description of the product's physical and chemical constituents. For example, coatings (paint) will indicate the percentage of pigment solids contained per gallon.

Specifications for component parts, assemblies, and construction projects include drawings, layout, or sketches. The drawings are sometimes referred to as engineering drawings or blueprints. Drawings are frequently checked by the buyer. They should include the following information:

- All necessary dimensions.
- The allowable tolerances (plus or minus a specified amount).
- The date and a drawing number.
- Revision dates and numbers.
- The name of the draftsman as well as the name and approving signature of the authorized engineer or individual.

It is very important to ask buyers to give the latest drawing to suppliers at the start of the bidding process. Therefore, it is essential that drawings be properly maintained and controlled.

Various people in your organization may ask a supplier to slightly revise a product. If the product is one that has been or will be purchased for many years, many such slight revisions can take place. Every one of those revisions requires a revision to the drawing; otherwise when you send out for quotations you will not be able to obtain a valid bid or compare the bid with the product you are now receiving. Each revision should be numbered and dated so you can refer to the proper revision level. Even slight revisions may require revisions to other components. That is why one person should be responsible for approving all revisions.

When selling assemblies to your customer, the components of those assemblies must be traceable to a particular engineering level; otherwise you may not be able to supply the replacing repair parts that fit.

The draftsperson or specifier must take care to keep copies of each engineering level before revisions are made to the master copy. Without the copies it will be difficult, if not impossible, to know what the design originally looked like.

A description of the product contained in the agreement or purchase order may refer to a submitted sample and provide no other details on the specification or only minimal details. The use of samples alone has some serious drawbacks:

- Most samples will change because of age or wear.

- Because of cost and time considerations, it is impossible to send out for more than one bid at a time when only one sample is available.
- Samples get lost or damaged in transit.
- Revisions to the sample are difficult to make and when made destroy the original design.
- Substitution of a different incorrect sample is possible.

## HOW TO PRODUCE COMPLETE SPECS: ——— EIGHT ITEMS TO INCLUDE AND ONE TO AVOID ———

If you are very flexible with your requirements you need not provide a great deal of detail. The more detail you provide the closer the delivered product will always be to what you want. Here is a list of items that you should consider including in the description of the product or service you want.

***1. Specify LINEAR DIMENSIONS (with or without a drawing).*** If the product has a simple shape a drawing is not necessary. However if many dimensions are needed to describe the product, a drawing is always helpful, if not essential. Always indicate the measurement system being used (Standard or Metric).

***2. Describe the SHAPE (usually requires a drawing).*** Standard shapes are available when ordering steel and may be ordered by name, dimensions, and the type of steel.

***3. Indicate UNITS OF MEASURE.*** Always indicate the units of measure being used. For example, length may be given in inches, feet, millimeters, centimeters, and meters. Weight may be given in ounces, pounds, grams, kilograms, short tons, and long tons.

***4. Specify COLOR.*** There are many shades of the same color. Establishing a good specification for color is difficult but important when a product's color is important to you. Without a good color specification your supplier will have trouble producing the color you want. It will be difficult to get the same color on every rerun and a new supplier will not find it easy to match the color you were receiving. Color can be specified by various methods including standardized prenumbered plastic color chips, standardized color swatches, and by specifying the percentage of compounds necessary to make the pigment going into paint or ink.

***5. Specify FORMULAS.*** Raw material, chemical compounds, lubricants, drugs, coatings, and detergents can be specified by the formula needed to produce the product.

***6. Specify PACKAGING.*** Packaging products may be purchased on their own in which case you will definitely be interested in specifying what you want. If packaging is only being obtained as the portion of the purchase necessary for shipping the goods, you may or may not wish to provide details. Details include the type of material to be used, such as steel strapping, corrugated boxes, polyethylene film, and a crate made of a particular grade of lumber. You may only wish to specify the outside shipping container. When you are buying consumer goods or other goods for resale you may also wish to specify the inner box, and the shelf container including any graphics on all the containers. You no doubt would indicate the quantities in each container.

Remember, however that you are paying for the packaging even if the cost is not separately stated. By providing details you may increase or decrease the cost depending on the design you wish.

**7. *Describe the Required QUALITY AND TESTING.*** All specifications determine the level of quality you require, but a separate quality description can include how specifications are going to be verified, what will be considered acceptable or unacceptable within certain ranges, and the methods that will be used to measure, test, or analyze the product.

**8. *Include the CARRIER NAME AND ROUTING SPECIFICATIONS.*** If the buyer or buyer's traffic department wants a particular type of carrier or a particular common carrier, that may be so stated in the agreement or purchase order, but in addition the preferred routing may also be specified. Traffic departments in large companies determine the lowest cost transportation method, the fastest method, and the most reliable carrier and then either instruct the supplier directly or indirectly through the buyer.

**9. *Avoid BRAND NAMES.*** Avoid the use of brand names wherever possible. If the use of a brand name is absolutely necessary always include "or equivalent" with the name of the brand.

## HOW TO BENEFIT FROM USING YOUR PROPRIETARY DESIGN AND ───── YOUR OWN SPECIFICATIONS ─────

There are many benefits from designing your own product or providing your own specifications. You determine exactly what you want without compromise. Products made for many customers base specifications reflecting what the average customer wants or what the seller thinks the customer wants. If your needs are slightly different from the average and you are buying a stocked or shelf item you must settle for less.

Although it sounds contradictory, a custom-produced item can still be purchased with the seller's design and specifications. This happens when you tell the seller approximately what you want or what you want the product to do. The supplier then engineers the item to meet your requirements but all the details of the product are furnished by the supplier. The supplier may use the same specifications or with slight modifications to sell to other customers.

With your own design you are in a better position to control cost by specifying the lowest cost materials that you know will do the job you want. With your own design you can make tolerances on components as tight or loose as necessary. Looser tolerances cost less and are perfectly all right if they do the job without jeopardizing safety and give you the desired service life. Similarly, if you want closer tolerances for a higher level of quality or better material to increase the life of the product you can do so.

Producing specifications in-house makes you familiar with each component and gives you full knowledge of the product. It helps you to know what may or may not go wrong with the product and gives you the information necessary to buy material for service at the lowest cost.

You can establish your own specifications without regard to the available facilities or tooling of one supplier. Your own specifications allow you to shop and negotiate with any capable supplier regardless of their location. If necessary, you are then able to revise the specifications to meet the capabilities of any supplier and take advantage of lower cost conditions and other favorable offers. With your own specifications you are in a better position to determine the need for subcontracting and to control those sub-contractors.

Drawings and other specifications produced by you should be marked CONFIDENTIAL. Include a clause prohibiting the supplier from disclosing any information contained in those drawings or specifications to any third party or from using the information to produce the same item for any other customer. Designers and engineers frequently print or stamp such a clause directly on the documents. When left off by the specifiers, buyers can do the same thing before they give the packet to suppliers.

## REDUCING THE COST OF USING
## YOUR OWN DESIGN
## ———————— AND SPECIFICATIONS ————————

The major disadvantages of designing your own products and preparing your own specifications are the cost involved and the knowledge required. We all prepare our own specifications for some simple products we buy, but when the documentation job is long or difficult it is common to turn that job over to those who do it all the time whether they are in-house or work for the supplier.

The cost of providing specifications for highly technical products can be very high and many companies may not realize how much the costs are. Nevertheless, do not assume that those costs are prohibitive. They should be carefully estimated and compared with an estimated long run cost of not having your own.

In practice, compromise by using in-house specifications for some items and depending on the supplier for others. In-house specifications also vary on the amount of detail supplied. For an excellent guideline on specification policy see the Federal Acquisition Regulation, Selecting Specifications or Descriptions for Use, 10.004 (see Exhibit 5-1.) While this regulation was produced by and for the government, much of it can be applied to use in the public sector. Simply substitute your company name wherever the word "Government" appears.

Using your own specifications rather than an industry standard may increase the cost of supply in other ways. A larger inventory is required since items matching your specifications are probably not available elsewhere. Leadtimes are often longer because the quantities you want are for your use only and the supplier must schedule them between larger runs of standard items that will be distributed to many customers.

## WATCH OUT FOR SUPPLIER DESIGNS AND SPECIFICATIONS THAT RESTRICT YOUR PURCHASING FLEXIBILITY

A supplier designs a product and establishes specifications around the capabilities and facilities that are available. Avoid paying for expensive tooling only used on machinery that is available at your present source. Later when the supplier raises prices excessively, you will have a weak negotiating position because you will not be able to resource without a large capital outlay.

Suppliers sometimes design products that are uncommon in the industry. When you want to add other products used together with the first product you must go to the first supplier or purchase additional new equipment that does not match your original equipment. Not only do you have the added expense of additional equipment, there are extra charges for service contracts, and it may be necessary to spend more on training.

For example, one major computer manufacturer produced a microcomputer which had a unique operating system. It also had unique connecting devices that would not match with any other computer in the market. When buying printers for the microcomputer, the buyer found out that the only printer that would work well was from the manufacturer of the computer. In addition to being restricted in selection of the printer, the disposal value of the printer was far below that of other printers. The same applied to software which could only be used with the unusual operating system.

**Exhibit 5-1. Federal Acquisition Regulation, Selecting Specifications or Descriptions for Use, 10.004**

Paragraph 29,899, FAR 10.003[1]

10.004 Selecting specifications or descriptions for use.

(a) (1) Plans, drawings, specifications, standards, or purchase descriptions for acquisitions shall state only the Government's actual minimum needs and describe the supplies and/or services in a manner designed to promote full and open competition.

    (2) Items to be acquired shall be described

        (i) by citing the applicable specifications and standards or

        (ii) by a description containing the necessary requirements.

    (3) Specifications and standards shall be selectively applied and tailored in their application.

        (i) "Selective application" is the process of reviewing and selecting from available specifications, standards, and related documents those which have application to a particular acquisition.

        (ii) "Tailoring" is the process by which individual sections, paragraphs or sentences of the selected specifications, standards, and related documents are reviewed and modified so that each one selected states only the Government's minimum requirements. Such tailoring need not be made a part of the basic specification or standard but will vary with each application, dependent upon the nature of the acquisition.

(b) (1) When authorized by 10.006(a), or when no applicable specification exists, agencies may use a purchase description, subject to pertinent restrictions on repetitive use. An adequate purchase description should set forth the essential physical and functional characteristics of the materials or services required. As many of the following characteristics as are necessary to express the Government's minimum requirements should be used in preparing purchase descriptions.

        (i)    Common nomenclature.

        (ii)   Kind of material; i.e., type, grade, alternatives, etc.

        (iii)  Electrical data, if any.

        (iv)  Dimensions, size, or capacity.

        (v)   Principles of operation.

---

[1] From FAR, Federal Acquisition Regulation as of June 1, 1987, Department of Defense, General Services Administration, National Aeronautics and Space Administration

    (vi)   Restrictive environmental conditions.

    (vii)  Intended use, including—

        (A)  Location within an assembly, and

        (B)  Essential operating conditions.

    (viii) Equipment with which the item is to be used.

    (ix)   Other pertinent information that further describes the item, material, or service required.

(2) Purchase descriptions shall not be written so as to specify a product, or a particular feature of a product, peculiar to one manufacturer, thereby precluding consideration of a product manufactured by another company, unless it is determined, in accordance with agency procedures, that the particular feature is essential to the Government's requirements, and that other companies' similar products lacking the particular feature would not meet the minimum requirements for the item.

(3) Generally, the minimum acceptable purchase description is the identification of a requirement by use of brand name followed by the words "or equal." This technique should be used only when an adequate specification or more detailed description cannot feasibly be made available by means other than inspection and analysis in time for the acquisition under consideration. Agencies should provide detailed guidance and necessary clauses for use by contracting activities when using this technique.

(4) Purchase descriptions of services should outline to the greatest degree practicable the specific services the contractor is expected to perform.

(c) Except as provided in (b) above, when considering the acquisition of products sold or traded to the general public in the course of normal business operations at prices based on established catalog or market prices, agencies should consult Part 11 and implementing agency regulations for guidance on acquiring commercial products.

(d) *Foreign purchase descriptions.* Unless precluded by law, products that are acquired overseas may be acquired by using purchase descriptions prepared by foreign governments or foreign industry associations, if the description will satisfy the agency's actual minimum requirements.

(e) *Packing, packaging, and marking requirements.* In accordance with agency regulations, contracting offices shall require adequate packaging and marking of supplies to prevent deterioration and damage during shipping, handling, and storage. In acquiring commercial products, contracting offices should consult Part 11 and implementing agency regulations [FAC 84-5, 50FR 1736, 1/11/85, effective 4/1/85]

## KNOW WHEN TO BUY OFF-THE-SHELF
## —————————— ITEMS—AND WHEN NOT TO ——————————

If you are able to specify items that are in stock and available you have the advantage of keeping inventories lower. The cost of engineering and tooling are not necessary and you can expect performance within certain established standards by well recognized manufacturers. However, be careful of items that are stocked but off standard or in low demand. The manufacturer may decide to discontinue selling those items and they may be difficult to obtain later if you are looking for replacement parts.

## HOW TO MAKE SURE YOUR
## SUPPLIER KNOWS WHAT YOU
## —————————— NEED—AND DELIVERS IT ——————————

Good communication from buyer to seller is one of the elements of success in purchasing. Simply delivering the drawings and accompanying documents to the supplier does not insure understanding. I have experienced situations where the supplier produced the product from a poor sample without ever referring to the correctly written specifications and without paying attention to critical dimensions. You should review the drawings with the supplier to make sure that he has complete understanding of what is needed and that he has the capability to deliver. If you, as the buyer, do not feel technically qualified to do so alone, have an engineer make the review. However, you should be there to make certain that they cover all points and that you are sure the supplier understands. Being present also educates you about the product so that you are better able to handle future questions. You can then also handle similar presentations yourself in the future, and negotiate with suppliers having a good knowledge of the product.

If the supplier produces the drawings or specifications, ask for one or more copies for your company records. Copies of moderately short or simple specifications are normally provided free of charge. There may be a fee for sets of very large specifications. It is important to have these if you ever need to shop for an alternate source or if your own engineers wish to consider revision of the item. Some suppliers balk about giving you this information since they feel it can only be used against them. Although they may state their objections, it is more likely they will simply delay giving you the documents with the hopes that you will forget about it. Therefore, make sure you discuss this requirement while negotiating. After agreement insist on compliance. It is easy to enforce if it is included in your agreement by withholding payment until the job is complete. The work is not complete until the drawings are delivered as agreed.

# CHAPTER SIX

# What You Need to Know about Pricing and Costs

Many times the price of an item is merely pulled out of thin air in hopes of satisfying a seller's need or desire. That price is dependent on what the seller believes his cost is plus an anticipated profit. The actual cost may be different. To achieve the best possible purchasing results, answer the following questions about cost:

- Does the supplier really know his true cost?
- Are cost figures arbitrary or accounting based?
- Are profit goals clear? What are they based on? Are they realistic?
- Do cost figures for other customers apply to you?
- Does the supplier use a standard cost system?
- Are costs estimated, average or actual?

Knowing how prices are established, how costs are calculated, and the details of those costs makes the difference between buying at a savings for your company or paying an excessive amount. Adding the individual amounts for every transaction over a one-year period helps determine the profitability of your company. It can even be the difference between a profit and a loss.

There always seems to be a lower price for those willing to spend the time and effort to research the costing behind the pricing. This chapter provides different methods for establishing your company's needs and balancing those needs with the supplier's needs. You will investigate avenues available to you for imaginative cost analysis and price reduction. You will also expand your understanding of value analysis from the purchasing point of view.

## BUYING TO MEET YOUR NEEDS

A requisitioner fills out a purchase requisition form; she has a need. A judgment is made by someone or a group outside of purchasing on how the need will be filled (buy/lease, repair/replace, and so on). The purchasing function, however, may possess additional information that may modify the planned direction. Good buyers do not accept requisitions without questioning the appropriateness of the request. The questions need not always be addressed to anyone other than yourself. If you are satisfied that the product is needed as stated, your job is to fill the request, but first you need to make some choices and see if your decisions match the requisitioner's.

Six Cost-Related Choices You Must Consider:

- Repair versus replace
- Make versus buy
- Lease versus purchase
- New versus used
- Direct versus distributor
- Low volume versus high volume

You must make six cost-related choices to see your potential cost savings. The following sections describe each decision and the factors you need to consider before making your choices. Use this information to assist you in making the best decision for your company. The chart shown in Figure 6-1 will also help you be sure you have considered the various alternatives.

When making these choices, you will probably also find reasons for negotiating with the requisitioner. This may surprise you as most people perceive negotiating as something to be done only with outsiders, a sales rep, for instance. Nevertheless, you are privy to a greater variety of cost related information than the average requisitioner or many other parties involved in a purchasing decision. It is your input that will be valuable in assisting requisitioners to make cost effective decisions. Effective communication skills are as important when attempting to challenge a preconceived idea from within your own company as they are on the outside.

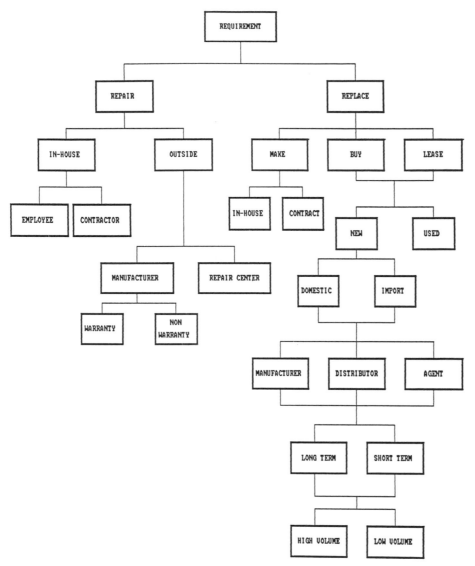

Figure 6-1. Flowchart of Buying Decisions

## Determining Whether to Repair or Replace Material

*Cost Considerations.* Is it better to repair the item or replace it with a new item? If the cost of repair is greater than X% of the cost of new—replace. "X" will vary from company to company and from time to time. It is dependent on the cost of money, the availability of funds, and the life of the repaired item compared with the life of a new item.

***Technological Advantages.*** Are there cost savings from technological advantages of a new product to replace the older item, or will the repaired older item function almost as well as a new item? For example, if the new item operates with less energy or at a faster speed, the higher initial price of replacement over repair may quickly be made up and yield a very good return on the investment.

***Duration of Product Need.*** You need to know if there is a short- or long-term need for the item. Why invest a relatively large amount if the product will not be needed? If the anticipated need will not pay for depreciation of the product, then it may be less expensive to repair the old item.

***Depreciation Cost.*** What is the remaining depreciated value of the present item? This is important for accounting purposes. If it is already fully depreciated, there will be no loss by selling or trading in the item. If the item still contributes a large depreciation expense which helps offset profits that are taxable, it may be costly to replace the item with a new product which does not provide the same amount of depreciation expense.

***Scrap Value.*** What is the scrap or trade-in value of the present item? Never be misled by the book value. It is rarely the market value although in theory it is supposed to be. Don't tell a prospective buyer of used equipment what your book value is. To some extent his bid will be based on that figure. Nor should you tell the book value to the supplier of new equipment. Any negotiated price may be raised or lowered and the trade-in value adjusted to fully write off your book value and satisfy the accountants.

## Deciding Whether to Make or Buy a Product

***Production Cost.*** Your decision is primarily based on your cost producing the item in-house compared with the cost of purchasing the product or service from outside suppliers. On the surface, this seems easy to determine; however in practice it is easy to overlook some of the details and miss some of the cost involved with going in either direction. All cost must be included for your decision to be correct and the most economical.

***Required Tooling.*** Many products require special tooling. Is the tooling available in-house? How much will it cost to obtain? Do you have the machinery to make the item or produce the goods?

***Scheduling Requirements.*** Do you have the time to produce the item? Can you wait for tooling and machinery to be delivered? Can you meet the same schedules as an outside supplier? Many companies base their make/buy decision on the ability to satisfy their own customers. Sometimes costs are a secondary consideration. When you produce your own goods you are often able to provide better service to your customers. You can control your own schedules. With this belief many companies switch from outside sourcing to in-house production but then find they cannot deliver the goods when needed.

***Needed Knowledge and Experience.*** Most products require a special knowledge to produce them properly. That knowledge is learned partly from books, but much of it is learned through experience. Does the supplier have the know-how and experience? Do your own people have more or less experience than a supplier has?

***Subcontracting.*** Consider the cost of subcontracting a portion of the work. What is the cost of giving some work outside compared with doing it in-house?

***Security.*** Is secrecy important for the product? Security is usually easier to control in-house, although not always.

***Check Patents.*** Are there patents on the product or a portion of the product? If you are considering making the item can you obtain licenses on patents. A major producer of printing machinery was faced with an exorbitant price increase from a supplier of a unique pallet designed for its machines. When the machinery producer announced that his company was going to produce the pallet for itself, the supplier disclosed that he had a patent on the product and would not license it or give permission to make the pallet without a large royalty on each pallet produced.

***Length of Time Needed.*** As in the repair versus replace decision, a make/buy decision depends on the duration of the product need. If it is only needed on a one-time basis or for a short period, it is not worth the investment to buy tooling and machinery. Perhaps extra people must be hired and trained to produce the product. When products are needed for short periods, it is better to use the existing in-house source or the existing outside source rather than try to change. Suppliers do not want to invest funds for short run business anymore than you do.

***Status of the Market.*** Is there only one outside supplier or are there many sources? Will there be more or less competition in the future? A major automobile manufacturer resourced plastic components from outside to its own manufacturing facilities even though there were hundreds of suppliers and the market was very competitive. The company had idle equipment and facilities that it wanted to utilize. There are some other possible reasons. You should consider each of them. There was a need for better quality that it felt it could control better. It wanted to gain knowledge and experience in the manufacture of plastic components. It believed there was so much competition that prices were too low to justify investment in research and facilities and that the industry was therefore not living up to its potential.

***Importance of Product Research.*** Is there a needed commitment to research and product improvement in-house or at outside suppliers? The same automobile company was going to resource windshield wiper blades from a long-time outside supplier and manufacture its own. The decision was reversed when it was discovered that the supplier had ten times as many engineers working on research and development as the manufacturer planned to use. The cost of such commitment to research and development may remain hidden unless you analyze all aspects of your relationship with a supplier or potential supplier. The above situation could just as easily have been reversed. The auto manufacturer could have been the one with the many engineers and the supplier with few. Looking at that situation, you can see how the supplier's cost would seem to be much lower. Each situation must be evaluated on its own without prejudice.

## Deciding Whether to Lease or Purchase Goods

***What Is the Cost of the Lease?*** Leasing is basically a financing decision. Keep in mind, however, that there is a cost of leasing and that cost must be measured against the purchase cost. The finance charges in a lease should be compared to the time value of money for your firm. Also keep in mind that financing for a lease may be provided by many sources, including banks, leasing companies, and the supplier of the goods. You may get a better lease cost from the supplier of the material but that should never be assumed.

The true cost of the lease compared with an outright purchase must include the tax effects. Either you or your tax specialist must interpret how tax law applies to your company and then calculate the effect. The supplier usually cannot do this for you even if he wants to because he does not have all the necessary information about your company. Furthermore, even if you provide the essential information, he is not a disinterested party and may consciously or unconsciously allow his own bias to influence his figures.

***Short-Term Requirement.*** As in our repair/replace and make/buy decisions, time is a factor that you should consider when deciding whether to lease or buy. If you will only need the product for a relatively short period of time, it may be better to lease. For example, suppose you need a computer for a special project that will take about a year, or suppose you need some rail cars to haul grain. Although the lease cost may be high, it still is much less than purchasing the equipment and then letting it sit idle. If you purchase it and then later have no use for it, it may be difficult to resell.

***Availability of Funds and Ease of Financing.*** Leasing is often a choice when capital is limited or not available. Leasing is usually easier to arrange for small or new companies than conventional bank loans. The cost of the lease or financing should be kept separate from the cost of the product itself. Do not allow financing to affect the product cost.

***Potential for Product Obsolescence.*** A major reason for leasing is to avoid purchasing products that become obsolete rapidly. The decision to lease computers is a typical example. It is often based on known or forecasted rapid technological changes in the product.

## Deciding Whether to Buy New or Used Equipment or Goods

***Cost of Used versus New.*** It is often easier to determine the price of new equipment than used. It takes more shopping effort to look for the type of used equipment you need. Used equipment may need some work and the cost involved in such work must be included to compare the total cost of the used item with the cost of the new item. There is some risk in buying used products as problems are not always apparent, but if you are knowledgeable and careful, you can get real bargains.

***Availability of Capital.*** Many companies buy used equipment because the price is lower than for new products. This is not a valid reason unless capital is limited. Remember you should measure and compare cost, not price. However, if you do not have or cannot get the funds for new equipment, used equipment may be the answer even though the cost may be higher than new products. However, it is sometimes easier to get financing on new equipment than on used and even if you get the financing on the used equipment, the interest rate may be higher than on new equipment.

***Leadtime for New Product.*** New products may be in stock and have a relatively short leadtime, but much equipment is produced to order and can have extremely long leadtimes. Leadtimes of up to two years are not unheard of. Although it is more difficult to find the exact used equipment to meet your requirements, once found delivery is usually arranged immediately.

***Availability and Condition of Used.*** Some used equipment is simply not available or once found is in such poor condition that it has little life left. You may want to add the cost of your search when considering used equipment over new.

***Compare Time Required with Life of New or Used.*** By definition, used items have less life than new items, but if you only need the item for a short period, it may be sufficient for your needs. For example, if you want a machine immediately for long-term usage, but leadtime for the new product is 35 weeks, you could solve your problem as follows. Buy a cheap old machine with only a couple of years of life left and at the same time place your order for the new machine. By doing so, you can get up and running immediately and the life of the new machine will simply extend your capabilities further into the future.

## Buying Direct from the Manufacturer vs. Distributor

*Importance of Volume.* Don't always assume that you must have high volume to buy from the manufacturer. Inexperienced buyers and nonpurchasing people in particular source to local distributors or other middlemen without trying to buy directly from the manufacturer. That is not to say that there may be advantages and disadvantages in either channel, but your decision should be based on the proper consideration of each channel.

Generally it is true that manufacturers want to sell low value items in large volumes only and if your requirements are only for a few pieces or few pounds, you are probably better off with a wholesaler or distributor unless you buy other items from the same manufacturer.

*Need for Local Support.* A distributor or middleman may be a better choice for quick information or service than a distant manufacturer. If service is important, then consider the advantages of working with local people. There is also the possibility that middlemen will actually give you a lower price than the manufacturer. For example, we have experienced purchasing nickel for plating operations where we were able to obtain a significant discount from a distributor while the primary producer would not budge on price even though they very much wanted our business. We were constantly being threatened with being cut off by the producer in the event of a supply shortage and sales by allocation only. We continued to buy from the distributor at a lower price without a problem. In another case we found that we could obtain software cheaper from middlemen than we could from the producer.

## Determining Whether to Buy in Low or High Volume

*Type of Tooling.* Tooling is often needed for custom designed or proprietary products that you buy for use in production of components used by a manufacturing company. Your anticipated volume or usage of the products dictates the type of tooling that you should order. Engineering may specify what is called soft or hard tooling. Soft tooling is used to produce the first prototype product, and hard tooling is designed and manufactured to withstand thousands of operations. Therefore, should your requisitioner anticipate a short run requirement, soft tooling may save your company thousands of dollars. Even the design of hard tooling can vary and have a drastic effect on the cost of your product. For example, injection molding is one method of producing plastic components. The molds have an outside housing and cavities where the plastic is injected. The more cavities you have, the greater number of pieces produced by each shot or cycle of the injection molding machine. The bigger the mold, the bigger the machine necessary to produce the parts. With high volume the larger molds with more cavities produce the necessary volume cheaply. However, if you don't need so many pieces but you have a large mold, you are paying for the use of the larger machine in addition to paying more for the mold.

It is important to estimate your anticipated volume as accurately as possible because, once produced, it is difficult to change the tooling. Nevertheless, conditions change and an item that once was purchased in low volume can change to high or vice versa. When volumes significantly change, it is time to analyze the cost of changing tooling. The old tooling can be used as backup in case new tooling needs maintenance or repair.

*Sales and Administrative Cost.* Your analysis should try to isolate fixed cost including fixed expenses that are independent of volume. It is unfair to allocate the same cost to each piece purchased regardless of volume. Your unit cost should be lower when spread over larger volume orders or larger usage within a given time frame.

## Making the Final Purchase Decision

You will note that time is a repeated consideration in many of the six choices described. You must also compare product cost in the short term with the long term. Products needed for the short run need not last as long and therefore can be less durable. Consequently their price is lower. Products that are made to last for a long time have a higher price. Keep in mind we are talking about price being lower or higher, not cost. The lower priced product may cost you more if it wears out before your need is complete. In such a case the higher priced product may actually cost less in the long run.

For example, suppose you buy a stapling machine that is priced at $125 rather than buying another machine that is priced at $175. The first machine wears out and must be replaced when the work is only half done and you are forced to buy another machine. Therefore your total cost is $250 whereas the higher-priced heavy duty machine would have lasted until the job was complete at a cost of only $175. Conversely if your requirement was for a shorter period of time, it would have been a waste of money to buy the heavy-duty machine. As a buyer, you must know the intended use of the product. You cannot buy intelligently by accepting a requisition without question.

In summary, the analysis of information as it relates to your company's goals will become invaluable in providing the ingredients for a successful cost effective purchase. You will be able to satisfy not only your needs and the requisitioner's needs but those of management, finance, stockholders, and the ultimate consumer as well.

## —————— UNDERSTANDING THE SUPPLIER'S GOALS ————

Once you have met all the requirements of your company's needs it becomes necessary to find a suitable supplier, one that satisfies your criteria of price, quality, and delivery. You need to understand, however, that there is really only one criterion: COST. Disparaging remarks are frequently made about buyers who seem overly concerned about price, but we are not talking about price, we are talking about cost. Quality and delivery, if not properly managed, ultimately cost money. A late delivery can shut down your operations and substandard quality will cause rework, scrap, and customer dissatisfaction, all which become an intangible cost to you and should be considered a part of any buying decision.

To interpolate and extrapolate costs from the price is not an easy task. You must first understand what costs are included in the supplier's price, the meaning and importance to the supplier of those costs and the value of those costs to you as a part of your purchase price. The value of the time spent on investigating and negotiating cost must be more than covered by the savings result you obtain. A few cents saved for a week of effort is a loss unless those few cents are repeated thousands or millions of times over a year of purchases.

At the beginning of this chapter, we said that the price of an item includes an anticipation of return or profit on the sale of an item. Sometimes the demand is great, the volume of sales high and the margin of profit equally as rewarding for the supplier. However, if the conditions are reversed, the supplier may find himself selling his product below the cost of production just to unload it from his warehouse. Somewhere between these extremes is the price he is willing to accept at any instant in time. You need to determine the supplier's goals at that instant in time and the price from profits and costs.

## —————————— COSTING THE PRICE ——————————

In order to provide a detailed description of the costing structure and its relation to price, you first need to ensure that all possible value analysis has been done on the item, that the item or items have been approved by the necessary engineering functions and that we are comparing apples to apples. Value analysis will be covered later and a further discussion of relative value and quality will be covered in Chapter 11.

A simplified way to look at price is through the components of cost of materials, labor, overhead, and gross profit. These costs, generally referred to as the Cost of Goods Sold may be more easily visualized in Figure 6-2. The gross profit is further broken down into expenses attributable to selling, general and administrative costs, research and development, and net profit (see Figure 6-3).

## Calculating the Supplier's Profit Margin

One first approach in determining cost is to look at the margin of profit the supplier wishes to achieve. With the exception of government requirements, you rarely will be offered this information. You need to form your own cost model and decide if the figure is 5%, 10%, 30% or more. Is that his margin today? Will it be the same tomorrow? How much can you trim the profit portion of his price?

***Using Published Information to Calculate Profit Margins.*** You can obtain current company profits from the financial statements of public companies. You can sometimes obtain profit information from purchased Dun and Bradstreet reports. However, total profits for the company rarely are a good indicator of what profit is built in to a particular product produced by that company unless it is a one product company.

For example, consider a supplier who is a distributor of relays. The particular relay requested is manufactured by the XYZ Company. You establish that the relay is available in distributor quantities from the XYZ Company for $2.86. The distributor will take certain factors into account in

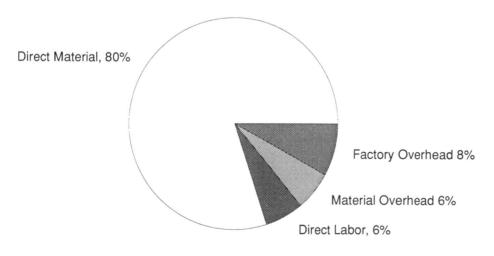

Direct Material, 80%

Factory Overhead 8%

Material Overhead 6%

Direct Labor, 6%

**Figure 6-2. Components of Costs of Goods Sold**

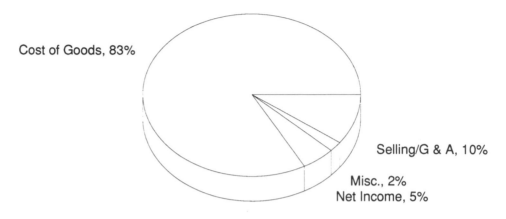

Cost of Goods, 83%

Selling/G & A, 10%

Misc., 2%
Net Income, 5%

**Figure 6-3. Components of the Earnings Statement**

determining his pricing schedule for this component. A typical pricing scheme, as published in the catalog, is as follows:

### CATALOG PRICE

| Quantity | 1-24 | 25-49 | 50-99 | 100-249 | 250-up | Cost* |
|---|---|---|---|---|---|---|
| Unit Price | 4.50 | 4.05 | 3.82 | 3.38 | 3.15 | 2.86 |
| Distributor's Profit | 43% | 35% | 30% | 16% | 10% | 0% |

*Distributor's cost from the manufacturer*

Keep in mind that the above price schedule is for a distributor and is a common format. That is, prices decline as you buy higher quantities. The justification for the price decline is that the fixed costs for any volume are spread over larger quantities as volume goes up and thus unit cost is lower. However, this assumption is more true for manufacturers that have fixed cost in tooling and set-up. The only cost that will tend to remain the same for each order is the order processing cost.

From the example, it is obvious that the supplier expects to make some profit (10%) even at the price of $3.15. Given that information, you can readily see that the 250-piece price is 30% less than the one-piece price. Since the 250-piece price will allow a minimum of 10% profit to the supplier, you now have a margin of at least 30% within which to negotiate. You now know that further reductions in price are available if you purchase the item direct from the manufacturer instead of the distributor.

You may be able to negotiate a volume contract (blanket purchase order) over a definite time period and obtain the lower unit cost. Let's say that you require several relays of different styles and ratings. The total number of pieces is 300 even though you may only need 50 of one and 125 of another. Since the total exceeds the maximum discount level in the catalog matrix, you have a good chance of receiving the lowest published pricing. Volume is usually the name of the game in sales.

Volume contracts may be your entry into ordering from the manufacturer direct, or the distributor may be willing to allow a lower unit cost on a volume order for a number of reasons:

- His need for your business, because:
  - He is a new supplier
  - This is the end of sales quota period
  - This is a slow market for the item
- Overstock of the item, due to:
  - Cancellations from customers
  - Speculation purchases
- Length of time in inventory, because of:
  - Out-of-date stock
  - Inventory turn problems
- His desire for a long-term contract, because of:
  - His sales goal
  - A need to reduce sales calls
  - A desire to prove supplier's performance

Additionally, groups of unrelated items may be offered at a certain discount of, say, 30%, as a buying incentive. The example here might include 100 relays, 200 transformers, 50 integrated circuits and 400 capacitors. The technique is called bundling, and if performed with skill, it can provide effective savings on certain commodities.

So, you see, there may be a myriad of reasons that the supplier may desire to offer a lower price for an item that appears to have a fixed or published price. Specific negotiation techniques on this point will be discussed in Chapter 8.

***Calculating Profit Margins Without Published Price Information.*** To deal with unpublished pricing, usually from manufacturers, is quite another matter. Much time and effort may be necessary to accomplish your goals. It is a good idea to set minimum guidelines before spending time and effort in analyzing prices or obtaining formal bids. Ideally such guidelines should be expressed in dollars, but exact dollar figures are not known. That is why you are considering the work in the first place. Possible guidelines are if you are buying:

- More than 100,000 pieces of a production item
- More than $25,000 commitment
- One year or longer delivery intervals
- A proprietary subcontract

Although pricing from competitive bidding is frequently accepted without negotiation, you can usually obtain the best results (i.e., the lowest cost) from negotiation after you receive the bids. Even when the price is acceptable, terms and conditions are often unfavorable and unfavorable terms are equivalent to added cost. However, before you can negotiate most successfully, you must plan. And to plan, you must seek out the facts and assumptions necessary to form a more detailed picture of the variable component costs of an item. See Figure 6-4 for some of the variables you should look for.

As you can see, most of the cost factors are variable and therefore negotiable. However, that is not to say that the fixed costs are not also negotiable. For example, salaries may be reduced by layoffs, buyouts, retirement, temporaries, and so on. The cost of leases may be affected by purchasing the building or machinery. Depreciation may be completed on a large area of the plant or machinery. If any of these events occur, there is a potential change in the supplier's costs and therefore a possible change in your price. If you do not know the specific details of the supplier's financial condition, these so-called "fixed costs" will be very difficult, if not impossible, to negotiate.

## DEFINING AND SEGREGATING
## FIXED COSTS

The economists will tell you that all costs are variable over the long run, but you as a buyer need not be overly concerned about such theory. Nevertheless, it is most important to separate certain fixed cost from variable costs, and you should attempt to do so right up front when you ask for bids. It is particularly important when ordering production items. When you know and separate the fixed charges, the cost for the balance should remain the same per unit regardless of the quantity.

The two largest fixed costs for production items are tooling and set-up. If the supplier owns the tooling and uses the same tooling for other customers, it will be difficult to obtain the portion of the tooling cost allocated to your order, but you should attempt to get such information.

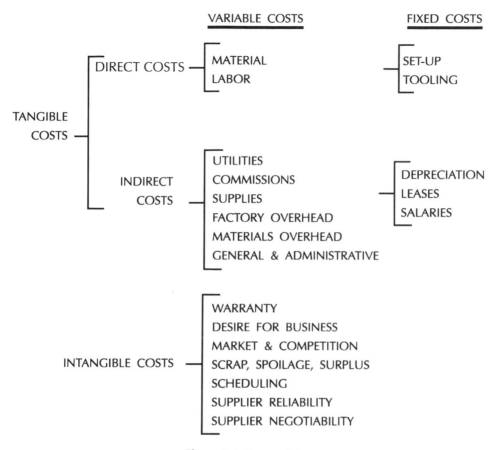

**Figure 6-4. Types of Costs**

You may not think that certain items involve tooling or set-up charges. For example, look at the printed forms you buy. Artwork, negatives, and plates are tools that must be made before the press is used. After you pay for those items, the cost of the material and press time should be the same per thousand copies regardless of quantity. When you look at a preprinted price sheet from a printer, it does not normally show such information and the prices are expressed in quantity ranges that will give you an unnecessarily higher cost per unit if your needs fall at the wrong point within the range. Figure 6-5 illustrates the prices that should be charged assuming the underlying costs are true and justified. Note that you

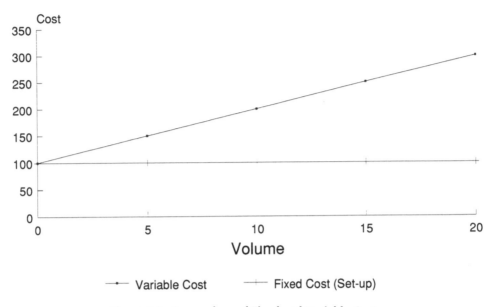

Figure 6-5. Comparison of Fixed and Variable Costs

can easily calculate the price for any quantity, $10 each plus $100 for set-up. Any different price for any quantity would be unjustified.

In most cases such an analysis will hold up. However, when your quantities radically change, different equipment or methods may require a different investment in tooling or a different type of set-up. In that event, both the fixed cost and the variable portion will change. It is still important to know the amount of the fixed portion for your calculations and negotiations. Suppose you know paper has gone up 5%, and you were told that paper accounts for 30% of the cost of the printing. You would multiply 30% times the $10 to determine how much of the cost is for paper. Then you would multiply 5% times the $3 paper cost to determine the amount of the expected increase. If your supplier asks for more than $0.15 additional you know he is trying to add something for profit. It would be impossible to do this calculation if the set-up charges were unknown and lumped together with the variable costs.

## _____ CALCULATING DIRECT COSTS _____

The most commonly contested costs are direct costs for material and labor. In the materials area, the government and many large corporations are able to secure a costed bill of materials from the supplier, especially on items that are the buyer's proprietary designs. If your company has made a make versus buy decision, you may have internal information at hand. In any event, the cost of the purchased material, as described in Chapter 1, will generally be the single largest item of cost in the price of the product.

The cost of material is affected by the following:

- specification and requirements
- sourcing pattern
- price escalation
- transportation
- storage
- supplier acquisition methods
- inventory levels and scrap

It is extremely important to understand the operations of the supplier and the methods he uses to purchase the items on your bill of materials. If such a bill of materials is not furnished by the supplier and your engineering staff cannot produce a workable replacement, try to single out the high expense items and find out what they should cost. Ask the supplier what he is paying for just those items. Most suppliers are quite surprised when they learn they have been paying an excessive price for their material. They are usually happy to pass along some (if not all) of the savings to you.

The following sections provide tips on how to evaluate your suppliers' costs in each of the areas listed above.

***Analyzing Specifications and Requirements.*** In dissecting the specifications and requirements you should look for items that may indicate excessive costs. Ask the supplier what items he feels are costly to him. Then do an analysis of these items for their value and determine if the results justify the cost.

***Assessing Sourcing Patterns.*** Single sourcing, called out by your specifications, may not be the best way to go. The source may be the only one known to your requesting engineer or your supplier. In asking questions and providing alternatives you may be able to save costs.

***Determining Price Escalations.*** Should you become involved in a long-term contract, invariably there will be changes in the pricing for parts, components, and subassemblies on the bill of materials. Any request from a supplier for a price escalation should be accompanied with documentation (copies of his vendor's invoices) showing his increased costs. You should stipulate this requirement in your contract along with guidelines for such cost relief such as when to implement, how often, and the share of the increase. When products have highly volatile prices, paperwork becomes burdensome unless some stipulation limits the frequency of price changes.

*Identifying Transportation Costs.* Transportation costs, although usually a small percentage of total cost, can become significant when expediting is needed. For example, should you anticipate a pattern of rush orders for components and the supplier's parts need to come from the Far East, the cost of transportation by air can be staggering. In one such case, a housewares company was forced to use air transportation for tableware in order to fill customer orders. The cost of the airfare exceeded the value of material to be sold. In another case a writing instrument company was losing customers because the Japanese supplier failed to deliver on schedule. The airfare amounted to over $12,000. Payment was negotiated so that each party to the transaction absorbed some of the added cost.

*Calculating Storage Costs.* Storage costs should not be significant. If you are using Just in Time (JIT) delivery at your end, this may cause the supplier to incur some storage of your product to satisfy your requirements. He should be able to manage his manufacturing to effectively minimize such expense.

*Determining the Supplier's Acquisition Methods.* Lack of knowledge of the supplier's acquisition methods may lead you to miss hidden costs within the supplier's quoted bill of materials. One example of how an acquisition method may effect your costs is typified in the following example.

Suppose you have contracted for a control unit that contains an expensive transformer. You receive a quote from the supplier that indicates that his cost for each transformer is $28.50. You check the price against your volume requirements and ascertain that the transformer, at a direct from the manufacturer discount is indeed about $28.50. However, in your study of the supplier's operations you know that he takes dozens of orders for similar control units for you as well as other customers. The supplier's "mix and match" volume purchase order from his supplier of transformers may qualify him for as much as a 20 percent additional discount from the manufacturer. His gross profit, previously an acceptable 12 percent, may now be 15 percent or more. Without a detailed analysis backed up with facts you may have to prove this to the supplier and his accounting department before you can effectively negotiate.

*Assessing Scrap and Inventory Carrying Costs.* Check the amount allocated to scrap, inventory carrying cost and stock shrinkage. Too much scrap means bad product, bad workmanship or bad purchasing. Spoilage results from improper storage, overordering dated material or improper handling. Surplus can occur from overordering and poor planning. In any of these cases you would be advised to be sure that these costs are not being passed on to you as hidden costs and look for other inefficiencies in the supplier's processes.

## CALCULATING LABOR AS COSTS

The direct labor costs can be a gold mine of cost savings. You can obtain labor costs statistics for specific operations from several sources including the Bureau of Labor statistics. Industrial (process or production) engineers can have a field day calculating the direct labor hours needed to produce a product. Factors such as time for machining, assembly, testing and packaging are merely estimates that are further adjusted by the learning curve factor (the more experience the higher the rate of production, hence the lower the cost).

The important fact to understand is that, on a new item, the supplier has had to estimate the labor times from paper calculations or at best, a pilot run of a few prototype products. By factoring volume, line loading, shift changes, rework (sometimes a little fat) and a myriad of other factors, he attempts to justify the time it will take to make a product. You must understand that usually a large amount of estimating and guesswork is involved in this process. Your job is to ferret out the most culpable areas that will be a significant benefit to reducing your costs.

All details are subject to cross examination and negotiation. You may need to engage the services of an engineer to help you estimate various manufacturing costs, or you might obtain the help of an accountant or financial analyst to check the costs of labor for each particular process.

During visits to a supplier's facility, ask "off-the-record" questions of the personnel you meet. How much do they pay their forklift drivers, secretaries, or maintenance people? On another visit ask what their average direct labor rate is and at what percentage do they figure the value of fringe benefits? Do they have a union contract and with which union? See if you can obtain a copy of the union contract. It will list the wages and rates for different positions. National contracts are often publicly available. You may not get any answers, but then again you may, depending on who you are talking with and how much they want to talk.

Compare the labor costs with statistical information available for the supplier's area. If his charges for labor are too far out of line, maybe it is time to look elsewhere.

*Case Study*

A case study of test times combined with rework times reveals a major flaw in the supplier's production process: A thorough evaluation of the supplier's process showed that he had not only an excessive number of inspection and test steps but an unusual number of rejects along the way that required rework. The buyer's quality engineer, while certifying the supplier's process, determined that the supplier was inspecting for quality rather than building for quality.

The supplier's answer to maintain the required number of finished products per daily rate was to increase the input at the front end of the line, exacerbating the amount of rework. The first pass line yield was only 70%, resulting in an inordinate amount of rework, a factor that was disguised in the quotation as a cost factor on labor.

Through a combined negotiation session between the buying team and the supplier's engineering staff, the process operator skills were upgraded. This allowed for several inspection stations to be eliminated and rework was reduced to less than 10%. Since rework was more costly in direct labor dollars than the original assembly, a savings of 12% was made on direct labor. The savings amounted to over $1 per piece. There was an enormous amount of time and effort required to obtain the savings, but with a possible 200,000 piece order, it was more than worthwhile.

### Case Study Analysis

Again you have seen costs disguised. The liability was transferred to an area where it was more difficult to detect. Even though direct labor costs may seem to be a small portion of a product price, in fact, they can be hidden and spread throughout the spectrum of costs. Your team analysis will be invaluable in providing a "sanity check" on these costs.

It would also be useful to determine if the supplier uses estimated costs, average costs, actual costs or a form of standard costs. Many companies use standards or averages as a means of simplifying accounting. You should inquire how the standard is established, when it was established and when and how often it is revised. Estimated costs are open to negotiation. See if you can induce the supplier to share the cost information with you. Many times even so-called actual costs are not really actual. They may have been calculated from orders for a small number of parts for prototypes. When production quantities are ordered, the price should drop.

A related cost factor that you should consider is machine times. By understanding the cost details of set-up time and the speeds and feeds of various types of machines used in your process, you are better prepared to assess the statements made by your supplier. By coordinating this information with your engineers, you will understand not only tooling requirements but be able to ascertain a supplier's ability to manufacture so many products within a certain time. Suppliers sometimes agree to deliver so many units when the requirement is clearly beyond their capabilities.

Having this detailed information available or using it during your analysis and later during negotiations will place you in a position of power. That power is what you need to achieve extraordinary results.

## ——— CALCULATING AND REDUCING INDIRECT COSTS ———

The cost to the product unit price of indirect factors generally takes more time to discover and it is even more difficult to negotiate. However, you may be able to benefit from some specific examples.

*The Cost of Electricity.* In many cases, this is the single most expensive utility cost. This cost may become an important factor in selecting the location for your source. The heat or air conditioning costs of maintaining a manufacturing line may be much greater in Minnesota or Florida than in Los Angeles.

*The Commission Schedule Related to Your Purchase.* This is naturally figured into the quoted pricing. By expanding, combining or changing the terms of one particular purchase, you may be able to redistribute commission costs throughout a greater product set. A long-term multiproduct type of contract will allow the supplier to redistribute some of the sales and marketing costs over a larger base and thereby grant reductions to each individual item.

*Supplies, Expendible Items, and Expense Tooling.* The effective use of these items is an important area of cost savings. The supplier's allocation of costs for these items may include insupportable amounts for theft, loss, damage, waste, and surplus. You should assess the extent of these items as a portion of factory overhead expense. If the supplier does not have the expertise to manage these items effectively, you may want to look for other deficiencies in the managerial process that were factored into costs.

*General and Administrative (G&A) Costs.* These are likely to be the most elusive to track. It has been said, as a rule of thumb, 10% of total factory costs may be used as a norm. Any great fluctuation to the high side of 10% may indicate over staffing or underutilization of the work force. Much less than 10% might indicate that some expenses are charged to or hidden within other areas or cost centers. In any event, the validity of a supplier's G&A figures may again reflect the efficiency of management.

One final note on tangible costs. Many accounting departments are understaffed and just too busy to coordinate with engineering and calculate all these costs for every item. Therefore, what you end up with is a grossly oversimplified percentage distribution of costs irrespective of the complexity of your product, the space involved or the skills required. Costing methods, unfairly applied to all products uniformly can substantially increase your real cost. Sales and marketing people are often unaware of this situation and will resist your attempts to obtain what they consider confidential cost information. Nevertheless, if you persist and convince them of your desire to work with them and to give them more business, they will be grateful for the improvements in their costing that you help achieve. After all, through your efforts you have made them more competitive with other customers.

## ——— WHEN TO QUESTION A SUPPLIER'S DEFERRED COST ———

Accounting sets up various accounts for anticipated costs. Any anticipated cost is usually based on averages from past experience but may be adjusted because a supplier expects to incur a higher cost than normal. For example, some amount is determined for the expected warranty expense. If the product has been sold for a long time and to many customers, the expected cost will probably be very close to the actual cost. If, however, the product is new or custom produced for you, or you have some reason to believe you will not require much service, the forecasted cost may be excessive. Nevertheless, a forecasted cost is usually included in the price of the product. It is an area for which you may be able to negotiate a more reasonable figure.

Furthermore, a high-average warranty cost indicates a low quality level. A high-estimated warranty cost indicates a lack of supplier's confidence in the quality of the product. An exceptionally low warranty cost might induce your own sales department to lower the price of your product or offer an extended warranty to your customers.

## HOW TO AVOID PROBLEMS BY UNDERSTANDING ——————— THE REASONS FOR LOW PRICES ———————

There are various reasons a new supplier may offer exceptionally low prices to obtain your business. Understanding the reasons is essential so you can prevent the wrong reasons causing you problems later. If the contract is large enough, he may be quite negotiable and willing to sacrifice profit on the first order in order to prove himself and be eligible for future orders. Or he may "low ball" the quote and apply for relief at a later date feigning ignorance of the extent of the work involved. Whereas the first case may provide an advantage for you, the second may cost you considerable expense in time and money.

If the product you required has many sources the competition may be fierce and margins traditionally cut to the bone; for example, in the personal computer market, prices dropped 10% per month on some items. On the other hand, with little or no competition, the supplier will have more negotiating leverage against cost cutting. When this happens you should attempt to increase your supplier base by developing and sourcing to one or more additional suppliers in order to increase the competition.

## PERFORMING VALUE ANALYSIS TO
## ———————— ALLOW THE BUYER TO DIVERSIFY ————————

There have been entire books written on the subject of value analysis. The important point to be aware of here is that value analysis is your key to becoming involved in other disciplines within the development, manufacturing and distribution processes. As a member of the purchasing function, you have the advantage of interfacing with virtually every aspect of the business. It is your participation and the overview that you command that has the greatest potential for suggesting changes that will result in product enhancement and cost advantages.

Because you may be in contact with many different engineering functions as the result of your planning for negotiating (see Chapter 8), you are a facilitator. One might question here just how much power you might wield as a purchasing agent. Let's examine a case study and evaluate the buyer's actions and the resultant savings.

### Case Study

The Quality Engineering specification required that a particular unit be burned-in (test operated under a heated environment) for 48 hours. In doing so the projected Mean Time Before Failure (MTBF) was at least 24 months. The Design Engineering Specification allowed for only a one-year warranty. The Product Manager did not desire to extend the warranty to 18 or 24 months. In order to maintain scheduled production levels in the heated chamber, the supplier needed to build a second chamber at a calculated cost per unit of $3 for the contracted 100,000 units.

On a suggestion from the buyer, a study was conducted by engineering to determine the effect of dropping the burn-in time to 24 hours. The resultant decision erased the requirement for additional chamber space and reduced the cost per unit by $3. The MTBF calculations only dropped to 18 months, satisfying the Design Engineer's one year warranty requirements.

### Case Study Analysis

The buyer uncovered a discrepancy in the specifications that would have resulted in additional cost. In effect, he simplified communication on a particular point, negotiated the issue internally, and left the final decision up to the Product Manager. The resultant $300,000 cost savings proved to be significant to the competitive pricing of the final product. The cost of additional burn-in did not provide an increase in value equal to the requirements.

## How to Analyze the Value of a Product

Purchasing Agents, as value analysis participants, do not take the place of engineers. However, engineers, in many instances, are not as predisposed to cost consciousness as purchasing agents. Nevertheless, the two working together as a team and communicating effectively become an invaluable asset to the effective manufacture of any product. It is this cooperative effort, this consensus management concept that has been a moving force in propelling Japan to such competitive heights in recent years.

Value analysis can be subjective in one sense and at the same time objective in another sense. Looking from the subjective side, "What is value to one has no value to another." On the objective front, "What saves cost here, may cause expense or inconvenience there." It is only with the best effort that value analysis will provide the lowest cost.

A formal value analysis program is usually conducted by a team. The team consists of one individual each from various departments within the organization. Those selected need not have technical training, nor do they all need to come from departments directly related to product design. The idea is to obtain unbiased suggestions from people who can make suggestions without being inhibited by past training or prohibitions.

The team member from the purchasing department is the ideal person to lead the value analysis committee, since he or she is usually involved with all departments within the organization as well as with outside sources. Once the team is established, the first step is to describe the product that will be analyzed in terms of what it will do or what function it is supposed to perform.

The next step is to use a brainstorming technique in which everyone on the committee makes suggestions on how the function may be accomplished. Each member of the team asks questions to get information about the product or to generate ideas from other members of the team. No suggestion or idea should be disqualified out-of-hand.

The VA technique considers alternative cost reduction ways of accomplishing the defined function, such as combining several products, reversing the design, or using an opposite approach. A recent example of using the opposite approach resulted from an exhaustive study of every conceivable conductor in search for a superconductor. The best material so far developed has been derived from ceramic, a nonconductor of electricity.

To determine the value of a product, ask the following questions:*

- Does its use contribute value?
- Is its cost proportionate to its usefulness?
- Does it need all its features?

---

* Stuart F. Heinritz, *Purchasing—Principles and Applications*, Prentice Hall, New York, 1981

- Is there anything better for the intended use?
- Can a usable part be made by a lower-cost method?
- Can a standard product be found which will be usable?
- Is it made in proper tooling, considering quantities?
- Do material, labor, overhead and profit total cost?
- Will another dependable supplier provide it for less?
- Is anyone buying it for less?

Value analysis need not end with product evaluation. The same process works with services. Or you can use value analysis to evaluate methods and procedures. As the following case study shows, the value of expedited delivery may not justify the cost.

### Case Study

The company was in the middle of a steep increase in production and the manufacture and delivery of components was just not fast enough to meet demand. On Friday at 1:00 PM, the production control analyst called the buyer requesting an expedited air shipment of 10,000 components to be used by overtime shifts on Saturday and Sunday. The buyer, through his knowledge of the operation, calculated that the logistics of such a delivery would not satisfy the requirement. The product would not be ready for shipment until 10:00 PM that night. By the time the truck arrived at the supplier's airport the last plane would have left; therefore a special plane would have to be chartered at a cost of $30,000. Even with this schedule the product would not arrive at the factory until 9:00 AM on Saturday.

The quality people required an incoming inspection of the component before use by manufacturing. The throughput at inspection was a maximum of 200 pieces per hour. To cover the needs of two double shifts on the weekend using 10,000 components at a rate of about 300 per hour the inspection team would have to be increased by 50 percent.

The product was shipped, however, and arrived at 10:00 AM. The first 200 pieces actually hit the line after lunch at 1:00 PM. The assembly line was idle for one half a shift with no components and then ran at 60% of capacity turning out less than 5000 completed assemblies at an additional cost of over $15.00 per unit. Since the planning people had projected $6.00 per unit in additional costs it became evident that the cost analysis had not been satisfactorily completed.

### Case Study Analysis

The lesson to be learned from this experience is that all the facts need to be presented to all the participants and the value of the decision thoroughly analyzed. A thorough analysis should have considered the probability that the shipment would arrive late and should have compared all the added cost to the expected return of such an investment.

## CONCLUSION: HOW TO REDUCE PRICES
## —————————— BY ANALYZING COSTS ——————————

Small individual savings on the various product components and from the cost inputs of labor, material, and overhead add up to high potential dollars. You can achieve many if not all these savings on your own but you improve your chances of large returns through a team effort. The following hypothetical example illustrates the cost savings of a typical team cost effectiveness effort:

| | | |
|---|---|---|
| Original Unit Price | $143.00 | |
| Cost Reductions | | |
| Fixed Costs | 3.45 | Eliminated leased plant |
| Direct Labor | 2.85 | Streamlined process |
| Purchased Materials | 22.45 | Reduced by 12% |
| Supplies | .45 | Consigned overstock |
| Materials Overhead | .25 | Combined supplier's P.O.s |
| Scrap Elimination | 3.10 | Upgraded rework skills |
| Test Labor | 3.00 | Reduced in-line inspections |
| | ——— | |
| Total unit savings | $35.55 | |
| Revised Unit Price | $107.45 | |
| Quantity | 100,000 | |
| Total Savings | $3,555,000.00 | |
| Percent Saved | 24.86 | |

Notice that there are a few unusual savings listed above. The smallest item, $.25 for materials overhead, amounts to $25,000 when quantity is considered. It is important to bargain for pennies when you are negotiating for production items. We have seen very serious discussions over the third and fourth decimal place. For example, if you can reduce a price from $0.0005 to $0.0003 on a quantity of ten million, the saving is $2000.

Buyers should gather cost data continually over a period of time. Information should be gathered from many sources to compare and verify costs. Wage rates, raw material pricing, speed and feed rates for various machinery, and geographic cost data are just some of the statistics necessary to analyze prices properly. See Appendix A for a list of price information sources.

The amount and type of probing that you attempt should depend on the size of your contract in quantity and dollars, the state of the industry and the economy, the type and location of your supplier, and the length and status of the business relationship. Obtaining the type information we discussed and then negotiating with that information require diplomacy and persistence. There are many ways to reduce costs. Only through asking will you be able to learn the facts necessary to calculate your savings.

**FIGURE 6.6  EFFECT OF FIXED AND VARIABLE COST ON UNIT COST (OR PRICE)**

| Volume | 1 | 5 | 10 | 15 |
|---|---|---|---|---|
| Variable Cost | 10 | 50 | 100 | 150 |
| Unit Contribution | 10* | 10* | 10* | 10* |
| Fixed Cost | 100 | 100 | 100 | 100 |
| Unit Contribution | 100 | 20 | 10 | 6.67 |
| Total Cost | 110 | 150 | 200 | 250 |
| Unit Cost | 110 | 30 | 20 | 16.67 |

*\* Note how this unit contribution stays the same regardless of volume. Therefore, if you know the fixed cost, you can calculate the price for any volume without negotiating each transaction.*

# CHAPTER SEVEN

# How to Find and Qualify Sources

Finding and qualifying sources is not that difficult, but there is more to it than you might suspect. None of us has trouble finding where to buy shoes or groceries so we all have experience in finding where to buy products. However, even in our personal shopping, we sometimes have to spend some extra effort to find the store that carries the size we want or that has reasonable prices or that provides the type of service we expect.

It is more complicated when buying for business. You are dealing with higher dollar volumes and because your purchase affects other aspects of the business, the risk of buying from the wrong source is much greater. The problems caused by purchasing from a poor source range from late deliveries to lawsuits because of product failure.

This chapter discusses 11 major factors you must consider when choosing a source. You will learn where to look to find domestic sources and where to look to find foreign sources and when to use each. You will learn why it is important to check sources and how to decide how much checking you should do. Then we will tell you the many ways to check a source. Finally you will learn the types of suppliers that are available to you and the advantages and disadvantages of each type.

## WHY YOU NEED NEW SOURCES

Some people might fear moving into a job as a buyer or purchasing manager because they have little or no knowledge of the product that they will be responsible for and do not know where to obtain the needed supplies.

Those of us who have accepted such positions without previous experience in the industry or particular type of business know that it is not a major problem to find most sources. New buyers and managers simply look at the records to see where the product was last purchased or they ask the requisitioner for advice or suggestions. As we indicated in our discussion about specifications, engineers sometimes recommend a source. However all of this is begging the question: professional buyers need to find new sources and are expected to know how to do so, better than any other specialist.

There are at least four reasons why you want to find a new source:

- New Businesses—A new firm has no records of previous purchases and must locate the suppliers that it is going to use.
- More Competitive Sources—Good buyers should always be looking for better sources. Without this effort you risk your competitors eventually obtaining their supplies at a lower cost than you. Then they will be able to increase their market share at your expense.
- New Products or Services—Not all purchases are for products and services that were previously used. Almost every buyer needs to obtain items that were never previously purchased. You need to find a source for new items. Although the selected supplier could be one that you use for other products you buy, that supplier may not necessarily be the best choice.
- Alternate Suppliers—One reason that it is necessary to find an alternate source is when your regular supplier is temporarily unable to deliver. Even though your regular supplier is normally excellent, problems occur that disrupt the flow of supply. Here are some examples:
  - Labor disputes, slow downs, strikes
  - Equipment failure
  - Natural disasters such as earthquakes, hurricanes
  - Fires
  - Illness or death of key employees

## WHAT YOU SHOULD KNOW ABOUT
## ———————— SOLE SOURCING ————————

In recent years, there has been much talk about sole sourcing, that is, using only one source. This method has been used by automotive companies in particular. It created news because automotive companies use very large volumes of the items they purchase and usually split sourced. In other words they would buy the same item from more than one source, giving each source a certain percentage of the business. The most competitive source would get the largest percentage. There could be as many as five sources for one item. Sole sourcing was a radical departure from this practice.

Sole sourcing has certain advantages as well as disadvantages.

Advantages of sole sourcing:

- Less paperwork and administrative cost.
- Higher volume with one source can reduce production cost.
- Higher volume with one source improves your negotiating ability with that source.
- Less tooling may be required.

Disadvantages of sole sourcing:

- Disruption of supply may result from the causes mentioned above (e.g., labor disputes or a natural disaster affecting your sole source)
- The supplier may be able to raise prices without restraint.
- It takes time to resource if quality or service slips.

Each advantage and disadvantage must be weighed carefully and compared with your own situation. In some cases you may find sole sourcing justifiable, but usually it is better to have a competitor waiting in the wings to handle your requirements if your regular supplier has a problem or his performance slips. Thus there is always a need to find better sources.

## WHERE TO LOOK FOR INFORMATION
## TO FIND SUPPLIERS

### Use Telephone Books to Find Suppliers

Telephone books are a good source for quick information on many products. The larger Yellow Pages from the major cities are much more useful than those of small towns or suburban areas. It is a good idea to purchase Yellow Pages directories for several cities, especially if you have branch locations near those cities and you are responsible for buying for those plants. The books can be ordered from your local telephone company.

The Yellow Pages have the advantage of listing companies by product category. Their use, however, is limited because they tell you nothing about the companies listed except giving an address and telephone number (unless there is an accompanying advertisement and those normally tell you very little). You must call each listing to find out the names of the people you need to talk to and a full description of the products they handle. Very little information appears about manufacturers. The addresses and telephone numbers listed are often for branch offices or local operations.

Nevertheless, the telephone books are useful in looking up retail businesses, service companies, distributors, and industrial supply companies. They have the added advantage of being inexpensive and up to date.

## Use Other Directories

*General Directories of Companies.* There are general directories of companies or organizations that list the names of the organizations across industry boundaries. The information contained in such directories differs depending on their intended use. Some contain names and addresses of companies, the names of the key executives, and data about their size and financial strength. They may also have a very general description of the products or services each company offers. These directories are used by financial specialists, marketing people, or anyone else who finds the information helpful. Some directories only list company names and give data on what is of interest to traders of stocks and bonds.

*General Buying Directories.* The general directories that are of most use to purchasing professionals describe the products in more detail and are indexed by product. Under the product category, they list the companies that sell the product. The most widely used directory of this type is the Thomas Register. It is on the shelf of purchasing departments more often than any other directory. The major drawback of the Thomas Register is the absence of key contacts and executives. You must call the companies and sometimes spend a lot of time trying to get hold of the proper person to give you what you want.

*Specialized Directories.* The third type of directory is the specialized directory. It is often published by a magazine or association. It lists companies in a particular industry or that sell particular products. For example, there are directories of graphics companies, steel suppliers, electronic suppliers, housewares companies to mention a few.

The following is a list of some directories. For addresses see "Where to Find a Source" in Appendix A.

- Appliance Industry Purchasing Directory
- California Manufacturers Register
- Directory of Hong Kong Industries
- Directory of Industrial Directories and Annual Buyers Guides
- Directory of Metal Suppliers
- Duns Middle Market

- Electronic Buyers' News Handbook & Directory
- Graphic Arts Trade Directory & Register
- Illinois Manufacturers Directory
- Italian Yellow Pages for the U.S.A.
- Japan Yellow Pages
- Kline Guide to the Paint Industry
- McRae's Blue Book
- Moody's
- National Job Shop Directory
- Official Directory and Buyers Guide of the National Houseware Show
- Official Directory and Buyers' Guide of the National Plant Engineering and Maintenance Show
- Packaging Buyers Guide
- Plastics Directory
- Popai Buyers Guide
- Sources for Iron Castings
- Standard and Poors
- Sweets
- Taiwan Buyers' Guide
- The Pocket List of Railroad Officials
- Thomas Register

There are hundreds of directories and you might wonder how much your investment needs to be to give you the information you need. Some directories cost over $500. Others you can obtain free. In practice, you can get along with very few of these directories, although it is best to have several. One should be a general directory that covers most products that you are likely to buy; the other can be a specialized directory for the product that represents your largest expenditure or the product that requires the most sources.

The best directories are revised every year so you can see your annual cost could be quite high if you purchase many. If you only use them for reference once or twice a year, the cost of the information seems excessive. There are two ways of getting around the high cost.

Although the good directories are constantly being revised, the number of changes per year is not high. Therefore, you need not buy new editions every year. Use the budget to buy another directory for the second year and perhaps still another for the third year. Then in the fourth year, go back and get a revised copy of your choice the first year. By doing this you will spend a fraction of what it would cost to buy all new directories every year and still you will have a wealth of information at your finger tips.

If you have multiple purchasing offices, you can send your old copies to other offices that need source information less frequently. However, this is not possible in all cases, as some of the directories are only obtainable on a lease basis and the old copy must be returned to the publisher when the revised edition is received.

The second economical way of obtaining source information is to use the public library or a university library. Most public libraries have more than one type of directory and the bigger the library the more directories they have. Public libraries usually carry Yellow Pages for many large cities.

## Attend Trade Shows and Conventions to Meet Suppliers

You find many sources gathered together, often from all parts of the world, at trade shows. What is better, exhibitors bring their goods which are displayed for your inspection. Trade shows can provide an economical way of shopping and comparing goods from many sources within a short period of time. You avoid the expense and time of traveling to distant locations and can often see many types of products at the same time. Exhibitors usually have brochures that give specifications of their products and sales representatives are there to answer the questions you have.

If you are located in a large city or are nearby and don't attend the trade shows available, you are missing a golden opportunity to see new products and learn more about the competition of products you already use.

Even suppliers who do not exhibit often attend major shows and conventions. It is their opportunity to see the competition and find out what is new in the industry. As a buyer, you should do the same. If you talk to various people at the show, they may refer you to other sources if they do not have exactly what you are looking for.

## Read Magazines and Trade Papers for Product Information and Supplier News

Many magazines print directories of their advertisers and others. Some have special issues devoted to directories. You should subscribe to the major magazines that address the industries that you buy from. They give you important information about the products, the companies, and personnel in the industry. They usually include information about price trends and problems that face the industry. As a buyer of the products sold by the industry, such information is essential if you wish to analyze cost and negotiate successfully.

News about the companies in the industry helps you evaluate their potential as new suppliers or forecast the performance of your existing suppliers. The story you get from sales representatives or your supplier's management may not be as revealing as what is brought to light by the news media.

Some magazines even help evaluate products for you. For example, the popular computer magazines compare software from the major sources. Business magazines, such as *Today's Office*, compare the features of office equipment. Printed articles discuss the advantages and disadvantages of particular products. A list of suppliers and their addresses is often included.

To you as a buyer of products for business, many industry magazines are free upon request. All you have to do to maintain your free subscription is to fill out a form periodically indicating that you are a buyer and then answer some questions about the size of your company and what you buy. Suppliers sometimes purchase the subscription list from the publishers to learn who is interested in the products they sell and who may be a potential customer.

You should not object to having your name or the name of your company used in this way. This makes your job much easier because suppliers then contact you rather than it being necessary for you to look for them. In addition to saving you the time of looking for suppliers, it gives you a negotiating advantage. It lets you know the supplier is looking for new business and may be willing to make concessions. On the other hand, when you approach the supplier first, he knows you need his product or service and you may be willing to pay more for it. If your purpose of looking for a new supplier is to improve on cost, you must make certain that this information is clearly conveyed to potential sources.

If you are having trouble finding a source, magazines and trade papers can be used in another way. You may advertise your wish to buy certain products. This method is seldom used by most private industry although certain industries and government buyers use it with success. For example, you will see ads by those wishing to purchase scrap metal and used machinery. You will see ads for antiques, works of art, and other collectable items. The government advertises for bids on construction projects and many other items that it wishes to buy.

## Contact Trade Associations

There are two directories of associations. One is the *Encyclopedia of Associations*, published by Gale Research, Inc. The other is the *National Trade & Professional Associations of the United States*, published by Columbia

Books, Inc. If you are looking for a source, there is probably a trade association for the product you need. Columbia Books says there are over 3,400 national trade associations.

Many trade associations publish a list of their member companies. Those that do not are usually happy to refer you to several of their members. Generally companies that are most concerned about their industry are the ones that belong to such trade associations. You therefore have some reason to believe the company could be a good source although we would not exclude any company simply because it does not belong to its trade association.

### Contact Consulates for Information on Foreign Sources

If time considerations and volume do not exclude the use of foreign sources, you may find what you need in a different country. Many buyers are reluctant to think about importing because they believe it is difficult to locate a source, because they believe it is difficult to communicate in a foreign language, and because they do not feel qualified to handle the complexity of import regulations. None of these things are necessarily true. You will note in the examples of directories listed above that several list sources for particular countries. In addition, you may contact the consulates of foreign countries to obtain source information. Major countries have consulate offices in the larger U.S. cities. Foreign consulates are always in Washington, D.C. and have their offices in the various embassies. Other cities that may have offices include New York, Chicago, and Los Angeles.

The job of the consul is to handle passports and visas and to help citizens from his or her country with their travel problems. However, often the more important responsibility is to promote foreign trade. Consuls are therefore happy to help you find a source in their country.

Sometimes, companies from their country ask them to find business for them in the United States. In other cases, they will contact companies in their country to see if those firms would be interested in doing business with you or supplying the product that you want.

### Obtain Referrals from Present Suppliers and Sales Representatives

You can often get referrals from people you are presently doing business with. Of course they are not likely to give you a source that sells a competing product, but they often are aware of good suppliers of related products. They are usually happy to help you and may even contact the potential source for you to let them know that you may be a customer. They do this because they feel that you will remember they helped you and because your new source may reciprocate and refer business to them if they get the opportunity to do so.

## Contact the American Purchasing Society

If all else fails or if you want the assistance of a third impartial party to help you find or develop sources, the American Purchasing Society is the organization to contact. The APS has many directories that they will check for you. In addition they have a large database of sources which they will check. There is no charge to members of the Society unless the type of supplier that you need is particularly difficult to find. In that case APS will conduct the search for a reasonable fee.

## 11 FACTORS TO CONSIDER WHEN CHOOSING A NEW SUPPLIER

Getting the names and addresses of potential new sources is just the beginning. Assuming there is more than one possibility, you need to consider eleven different things before making your preliminary decision. Here is a list of variables to think about—they are not necessarily in order of importance:

1. Location
2. Size
3. Facilities and Equipment
4. Product Knowledge and Experience
5. Type of Business
6. Employee Relations
7. Reputation
8. Long-Term Commitment
9. Length of Time in Business
10. Delivered Costs
11. Financial Strength

Not all these variables are of concern for every sourcing decision, but in each case you should evaluate their importance to be certain that a key item has not been overlooked. Now let's look at each item in more detail.

### 1. Location—Do Not Assume That Closer Is Better

It is easy to assume that suppliers that are close to us provide better service. It is only logical to believe that they can deliver faster and that the low cost of transportation on the average makes them a better choice. For that reason, many buyers do not bother looking very far away, let alone objectively evaluate any differences in delivery time or cost. Such a belief is easily refuted. For example, take two companies' delivery time in the same metropolitan area.

One company was 25 miles away and it took about 30 minutes to make deliveries. The other company was only 15 miles away, but it took almost one hour to make deliveries. Why? Simply because the former company could be reached by expressway whereas the latter could only be reached by going through stop-and-go city traffic.

Nevertheless, there may be times when it does make sense to favor a closer source especially when time is extremely important and one source is thousands of miles further away. For example, compare a source in your city with one overseas.

Here are a few factors that might dictate closer sources:

- extremely perishable goods where the difference in hours could be injurious.
- very bulky or heavy goods that are available locally at a low freight rate.
- the competitive source is in a remote area and has poor or costly inbound and outbound transportation choices.

## 2. Compare Supplier Size with Your Requirements

You should compare the size of the supplier to your requirements in various ways:

- Determine if the supplier has the capacity to produce your present needs and deliver on schedule.
- Consider your future needs.
- Find out how much added volume the supplier can handle.
- If the supplier claims that it will add equipment as needed, see if it has the space to do so.
- Consider how long it would take to obtain and install additional equipment.

Consider the size of your present and future needs compared with the size of the supplier. If you only want a few pieces or are only going to spend a few hundred dollars, your order may not get very much attention from a giant company that normally deals with million dollar orders. A small company may specialize in handling small orders and be happy to have you as a customer.

Large companies generally have better trained technicians and engineers. They devote more resources to research and development. On the other hand, they are not as flexible with schedules and pricing. It is more difficult to get the attention of top executives unless you are a major customer.

Smaller companies have a greater need for your business. On the average, they respond more quickly. You have the opportunity to deal with the top people who are frequently the owners of the company. However, smaller companies are more vulnerable to economic setbacks. They often have small staffs and find it difficult to perform satisfactorily if key people get sick or leave. You must weigh all these factors to take advantage of opportunities and minimize risks.

## 3. Match Supplier Facilities and Equipment to Your Requirements

Although facilities and equipment are related to size, you should consider them as a separate issue. For example, some large firms have many machines that are designed to produce small volume runs. If you need small volumes only, this type of supplier is what you are looking for. Other small firms may have a few machines that are designed to run high volumes.

When bids are made, they may be based on annual volumes rather than on the quantity run you need. If you order a small volume, the cost of the large machinery must be figured into your small volume. If you order a large quantity, multiple slower machines will be required or delivery time will be lengthened. In either case your cost will be higher. This consideration is reflected in the cost decision described below; however, the bid may not be based on your usual order volume for a single shipment.

## 4. Verify the Supplier Has the Proper Product Knowledge and Experience

Once in a while you may get a bid from a supplier that has had little experience producing the product you want. Sometimes the supplier simply does not have the education or background to know how to make a satisfactory product and underestimates the difficulty. He or she then submits a bid that beats the competition, either because bidding low is just to get established in the business, or because of ignorance about how to figure the cost properly. If you place business with such a source, you may run into a number of difficulties:

- late delivery because the supplier has to learn while doing or because the supplier did not realize how long various operations would take.

- the supplier returns to you trying to revise the contract with a higher

price. If you do not agree, the supplier cuts corners or slows shipments, or refuses outright to produce the goods. Although you may
win a legal battle, it may take years, and you still never got the goods
when you needed them.

Although you can take a chance with an inexperienced supplier, especially
if you have split sourced and have a backup supply, you should be aware of
the risk and decide if it is worth it or not.

## 5. Match the Supplier's Type of Business with Your Needs

Sometimes manufacturers with idle time for their regular products will
solicit business for other products. They may claim quite vehemently that
they are making a long-term commitment to the new business. It is ques-
tionable that they believe it.

If your needs are long term you should be very careful about sourcing
to a company that is in or has been in another kind of business. Perhaps
it has studied the market and is truly looking for ways to diversify. In that
case, fine, if it qualifies in all other respects, you may have a winner.

But beware of companies that are simply trying to cover their cost or
fill idle capacity. For example, companies in the auto industry often find
they can take in work during economic slow downs when auto sales are low.
When auto sales are booming they have trouble producing enough to meet
schedules. If you source to them during a slow period, they may dump you
when they need production capacity.

They can dump you indirectly by increasing the price an exorbitant
amount, by slowing delivery of your goods, or by making a number of other
excuses for not taking your business. Be very cautious when you must send
them tooling or have them make special tooling which will only fit their
machinery. You may have trouble finding another supplier that can fit the
tooling to their equipment unless you invest in having the tooling revised.

Therefore if your needs for the product you want to source are long
term, make sure the supplier you choose has a long-term commitment.

There are several clues to guide you:

- Has the supplier been selling the product you want for a long time,
  several years or more?
- Is the supplier expanding present capabilities of producing your
  item by investing large sums in plant and equipment?
- Is the supplier producing the same product for many other customers?
- Does the supplier make a satisfactory profit on the product?
- Is the profit as good as or better than the profit from other products
  produced by the supplier?

If the answer to one or more of these questions is yes, you have a good indication that the supplier is likely to continue producing the product.

## 6. Employee Relations—Pay Attention to Worker Satisfaction and Pride at Potential Suppliers

Although it is obvious that employee attitude affects supplier performance, few buyers pay much attention to this important factor in source selection. You will improve your sourcing decisions and reduce problems by being alert to the employee relations of potential sources. Ask about employee turnover rate. If people are constantly leaving and new people need to be trained, you may not get the quality you expect and delivery may be slow. High turn-over may add to the cost of the product.

Be alert to problems in labor relations:

- Is there one or more unions?
- What unions are they?
- When do the contracts expire?
- Have there been strikes or work stoppages?

Lack of a union does not necessarily mean you are safe. It could mean the company is ripe for an organizing effort.

If possible and you get the opportunity, question the employees to find out if they are loyal to the company. Find out their attitudes about management and the company's products. Ask them if they are happy working for their employer. Do they seem anxious to get you as a customer? Do they seem to be part of the team effort or do they complain about how the company is run or offer negative comments about the company?

For example, an important buyer was touring the plant of a major steel producer with key steel company executives when a union operator of a rolling mill made unsolicited disparaging comments about the company and its products. Although they could have been unjustified comments from a disgruntled employee, the buyer remembered these comments and weighed them against other evidence when making the sourcing decision. Those comments were very embarrassing to the company executives and psychologically helpful to the buyer during negotiations.

## 7. Check Suppliers' Reputations

If you don't check the reputation of the sources you are considering, sooner or later you will have a sourcing problem. You need to check the reputation for service, for product quality, for honesty, and for dependability. We will discuss the method and extent of source checking later in this chapter.

## 8. Ensure Suppliers' Long-Term Commitment to Your Product Needs

If a supplier devotes no efforts to product improvement or has nothing invested in research and development, you or your company must then be totally responsible to do so. The required investment may be prohibitive for your needs alone, whereas the supplier's cost would be spread over the requirements for many customers. A supplier that produces better products from its research activities can make those products available to you early and make you more competitive in the marketplace.

## 9. Check How Long the Supplier Has Been in Business

Most businesses fail within the first few years. Unless you are willing to take a high risk, it is better to avoid using new businesses. This is particularly true for products being placed with a job shop, or manufactured to your design, or where you are required to invest in tooling. If you are seriously considering a new business, make sure it has adequate financing and the principals have a reputation for honesty.

In some cases new businesses are partially owned by a large or well-established company. If the large or established company is willing to be responsible for proper delivery and that clause is built into your purchase contract, your risk is lowered.

## 10. Consider the Total Cost of Doing Business with Each Potential Source

As a buyer, you should be most concerned about costs. However, keep in mind that there are tangible and intangible costs. The stated price that is paid by your accounting department is only one component. It is the direct, out of pocket cost. Other costs include the level of quality and the service you receive. The risk you take by going to a new supplier or one with a poor reputation is a cost. That is why riskier investments in stocks or bonds pay higher returns than safer investments. If you are willing to take the risk, you may receive a higher profit or you may lose your money altogether.

Understand that there are short-term and long-term costs. For example, if after one year or less it is necessary to find another supplier because of poor supplier delivery and you end up paying a higher price, the actual original cost was much higher than assumed.

Good purchasing management requires buyers to source to the lowest cost supplier or explain why they are not doing so. Valid reasons for not choosing the lowest *apparent cost* are selected from the above 9 factors. Given the same set of facts, there may be differences of opinion. The only sure way to know if expected performance materializes is through experience.

## 11. Verify A Supplier's Financial Strength

You may obtain the lowest possible bid and have the most technically qualified and willing supplier, but if it is not financially sound, you still could have a host of problems. If a supplier is financially weak, it may have trouble getting raw material. It may have trouble obtaining and keeping qualified personnel. Or, plant and equipment repairs may be neglected.

Consequently, deliveries could fall behind and quality could be lower. In the worse case scenario, it could declare Chapter 11 status or go bankrupt. Bankruptcies can be a major problem for you, if you need a steady source of supply. When a bankruptcy happens, the courts sometimes lock up the facilities and you need to get a court order to release tooling or inventory that you legally own.

You should make some type of financial check of all new suppliers involved with all but the smallest of purchases (for example, where annual purchases are expected to exceed $1,000). A minimum requirement might be a request for a D&B report to see if the supplier is paying his bills on time and to evaluate its net worth.

We have seen a case where orders were being given out by a major corporation to a supplier whose net worth was less than the value of the order. What is worse, the supplier demanded 50% down with the order. See Appendix B for a more detailed discussion of financial analysis.

## HOW TO DECIDE THE EXTENT OF SOURCE INVESTIGATIONS

As implied in the previous section, you should investigate a source before placing large orders or before using a source for long-term requirements. In practice, many suppliers are used with minimum checking. This may account for the high rate of supplier failures. If suppliers find it more difficult to get new business because they know that their past performance is being checked, they may pay more attention to their existing customers.

One of the stated reasons for lack of checking is the constraints on buyers' time. Another is the failure to recognize the risk of making the wrong sourcing decision. Still another is the lack of confidence in references. All these objections to source reviews are easy to answer.

### Save Time Investigating Suppliers Selectively

As in all other aspects of management use the Pareto Principle to investigate sources; a very small percentage of new sources require thorough investigation. You need not spend more than a few minutes checking a source that is only going to be used infrequently for small expenditures. Ask the seller how long he has been in business. Ask the seller for the amount of his sales volume. Ask for a bank reference and the names of several customers. If you use a standard form, the supplier can simply fill out the form and you or a clerk can check one or two of the key items. See Figure 7-1 for a sample questionnaire.

Most of the time allocated to investigations should be reserved for your major sourcing decisions. If you simply do not have the time or skills in-house, you can always hire an investigating service.

## Calculating the Risk of Supplier Failure

Ask yourself some key questions to evaluate the cost of supplier failure. Here is a list of things that will help you decide if it is worthwhile to check before using a supplier:

- Will the supplier be paid before we find out that we received bad material? How much money will we lose if the supplier cannot be found?

- Will our production be slowed or stopped because the goods are not satisfactory? How much will that cost us? Will we lose our customers? What is the value of that business?

- If the purchased item malfunctions, can it cause an accident or is it possible that someone will be harmed? Will we be responsible for product liability? Could we be sued for a million dollars because of the failure of a 25-cent bolt?

- Will the supplier be around to provide repair parts when we need them? Will we be able to get needed supplies to run the machine we are buying? How much will it cost us if we have to scrap the machine because we cannot get the repair part or the supplies?

## Believe Your Suppliers' References

It is always amazing to us how candid references are. Some people say that you would not be given the name of a reference if you were going to get a bad one. What surprises us still more is that references usually provide you with a fairly accurate picture of their experience with a supplier even though the supplier gave the name of the reference. However, it does take some skill to ask the right questions and evaluate the answers. The following section of this chapter explains how to investigate suppliers. Investigations for small or unimportant sourcing decisions require a minimum of checking. Sourcing for major purchases is another matter. You need to do a great deal more than just check references.

## CONFIDENTIAL SUPPLIER INFORMATION

The following information should be submitted to the X company for evaluation and consideration for future business. It is the responsibility of the supplier to submit accurate and complete data and to notify the X company of any significant changes to the information submitted.

Company Name (full legal name including division name if applicable).

Address of corporate or home office (Please supply 10 digit zip code).

Addresses of local offices and shipping locations if applicable

Officers Names and Titles

Names and Titles of Local Representatives (Indicate if employee or type of agent)

**Company History**

    Number of Years in Business

    Ownership History

**Financial Data** (If major sales volume is to be considered, please submit financial reports for three years. Include balance sheet, profit and loss statement, and uses of funds reports).

    Annual Sales Revenue

**References**
Please submit three or more credit references plus a bank reference. Include contact names and titles, addresses, and telephone numbers.

Please submit three or more customer references including names of the organizations, contact names and titles, addresses, and telephone numbers.

**Products Sold** (Indicate if each product is manufactured or purchased in whole or in part.)

**Facilities and Equipment List** (Attach a description of plants, offices, and type of equipment. Useful information includes age and number of feet of facilities, storage space available, age and capacity of machinery if applicable. List testing equipment and quality control methods used. Indicate if you have your own delivery trucks).

**Union Affiliations**
Names of Labor Unions and Contract Expiration Dates (Provide history of labor relations including the dates of strikes).

**Pending Law Suits** (Please describe).

Date Submitted                     Submitted by

                                      Title (must be company officer)

**Figure 7-1. A Sample Supplier Information Form**

# HOW TO INVESTIGATE A SUPPLIER AND
## ─────────── WHAT TO CHECK ───────────

You can do investigations by telephone, by written requests, and by physical interviews and inspection. Information from the news media is also helpful. Several telephone calls may be all that is necessary for a simple check. Thorough investigations usually require the use of all methods. Your investigation should be aimed at answering the 11 factors to consider when choosing a new supplier. Let's look at each method.

### Checking Supplier's References by Phone

Call the references given. If a particular name was furnished, talk to that person. Verify the person's position in the company. If the reference is not in the purchasing department, it is a good idea to talk to the purchasing agent as well as the user. You may get an entirely different rating. Simply tell them that their company has been given as a reference and that anything they tell you will be strictly confidential. Ask them:

- Do they buy from the company that you are checking on?
- How long have they been buying from the company?
- How much do they buy?
- Are they satisfied with the service?
- Are they satisfied with the quality?

Answers will vary from a brief yes to much longer replies. If they say the service was satisfactory, you can probe a little deeper, by then asking if the supplier was ever late on delivery. If they say that the quality was good, you can then ask if there ever was a rejection.

Not infrequently people who say that everything was fine, will begin to tell you about a number of problems when you ask a few more rephrased questions on the same topic. We are not implying that you should disqualify a supplier because of one reported bad delivery, but it is grounds for digging deeper. References tend to gloss over minor failures because they do not want to be held responsible for a supplier losing business. That is why you must attempt to dig a little deeper, but without seeming to question the person's veracity.

Furthermore, your interpretation of satisfactory performance may be different from that of the reference. Learn to interpret the hidden meaning behind certain words. Listen carefully to the tone of the voice. Note how rapidly the reference gives his or her answers. Long pauses may mean the reference is being careful what to tell you and is hiding certain bad experiences with the supplier.

Ask about other suppliers furnishing the same product. This will help you evaluate how the reference judges. We encountered a reference that said that all suppliers of our product need were bad, but the one we were calling about was as good or better than the lot.

Make sure you write down your questions and the answers given. Record the date, the persons you talked to and their titles, and the company name. File the information for future reference to avoid duplicating the effort, to add to additional data received, and to provide documented evidence that references have been checked.

## Checking References By Written Requests

Written requests for references have advantages and disadvantages over telephone checks. Written requests can be standardized on a form and sent out routinely and quickly by any clerk or secretary. Figure 7-2 provides a sample form. The planned standardized form contains all the questions that you would like answered. This avoids neglecting to ask for important information (however, the same form can be used as a checklist when telephoning). Standardized reference forms save the buyer time and effort. Telephone calls are more costly and it sometimes is difficult to reach the person that needs to give the reference.

The major problem with written references is that the reference does not always return the form and follow-up letters or telephone calls are therefore necessary. Many references do not want to put anything in writing (you can get around this problem by not requiring a signature). Written requests also take longer. It takes a few days for the reference to receive your requests and they are not always answered promptly. If you can wait and you want a thorough check, sending a written request followed by a telephone call is an effective way to get information.

Additional written information can also be obtained directly from the supplier. Again a standardized form is recommended. (See Figure 7-2.)

## Inspect The Supplier's Plant Yourself

You can verify much of the stated or written information by a physical inspection of the supplier's facilities. It is extremely advantageous for you to visit a supplier's office and production operation. Not only will you be able to verify data that has been given to you, but you will be able to evaluate the supplier's performance better than any other way.

Here are some things you should observe during a physical inspection.

- See if the supplier has a clutter-free operation with everything in its place. More efficient operations are neat and clean.
- See how many production people are being used and if they are busy.

**X COMPANY, INC.**
1 Main St.
Anytown, NJ 00000
(515) 555-5555

Date

Mr. R. S. Green
Sales Manager
ABC Company

Reference: Ajax Manufacturing Company

Dear Mr. Green:

You have been given as a customer reference by the Ajax Manufacturing Company. It will be much appreciated if you would candidly answer the following questions about your experience with this supplier. Simply write your answer beside each question. No signature is needed. If you feel you cannot give out certain information, please answer the questions you can. If you prefer to respond by telephone, please give us a call at your convenience or return this form checking the space at the bottom of the form and we will contact you.

How long have you been doing business with Ajax?

What is your overall rating of the supplier? Excellent, good, average, fair, or poor?

How do you rate the supplier in the following areas? Please indicate excellent, good, average, fair, or poor.

Meets delivery promised (If percentage of early or late shipments are known, please specify)

Meets specifications

Someone can always be reached and handles requests promptly

Flexible in policies and procedures

Invoices and statements are always accurate

Personnel have high ethical standards

Personnel are highly trained and competent

Personnel are always courteous

How do you rate the supplier's prices or cost to you? Please indicate if very high, high, average, low, very low.

What annual dollar volume do you buy from this supplier?

Please return this form in the enclosed envelope or if you wish you may call me to answer by telephone or give the time if you want me to call you.

Thank you for your help.

Sincerely yours,

A. C. Jones
Purchasing Manager

**Figure 7-2. Sample Form Letter for Checking a Supplier's References**

- Note the age, condition, and type of equipment and how much of it is running.

- Meet and talk to the key people at the top as well as the production workers. Ask them as many questions about their work as time permits.

- Ask to see the Quality Control areas. Find out what type of measuring and test equipment is available. Ask for a demonstration of the checking procedures used.

- Look at cartons and shipping containers to see the names of the suppliers they use. You can contact these suppliers later to see how promptly bills are paid. You can also obtain bids for the raw material to learn about the cost of components. This will help you refine your cost estimates of the total product.

- Keep your eyes peeled for containers of finished products for customers. This information will help you in several ways. If they are not your competitors, you may wish to contact such customers to obtain additional information on performance.

  If they are your competitors, you may be reluctant to buy from the supplier for fear proprietary information would get back to your competition from this supplier. Or you can discuss this with the supplier and negotiate security measures. **CAUTION:** If you are sourcing a major item for resale to the same supplier as your competitor, find out what happens when you both want to get into the supplier's schedule at the same time. Who comes first? If you are the biggest customer or the strongest negotiator you may have the edge. But how can you be sure? Discuss this issue with the supplier and if you are not satisfied with the answer make plans to protect yourself. Either source elsewhere, or plan your requirements well in advance.

- If the business normally requires the purchase of special tooling by the customer, ask to see where it is stored. Note how it is protected.

## Obtain Information from the News Media

As a professional buyer, you should be receiving and reading various business publications. Most business news publications include news about companies, products, and personnel. Start a clipping file of articles about suppliers that you use or might use in the future.

Be aware of news on the following regarding your suppliers:

- Union negotiations, work stoppages, contract terminations, and strikes or possible strikes.

- Personnel changes and background of the new people. This could mean a change in policy. For example, products may be continued or discontinued or prices may be raised or lowered.
- New products or changes in products.
- Changes in location or plant closings.
- Hirings or layoffs.
- Finances and profits.
- The economic status of the industry.
- New equipment purchased or planned.

The sources for such information include local and national newspapers, newsletters, business magazines, and trade magazines. There are hundreds of such publications and you cannot possibly read them all, so you must be selective. For information about large suppliers, you can use the business section of most major city newspapers. *The Wall Street Journal* has wider and better coverage. Pick one or two trade magazines for each industry of interest to you. Still you probably will not be able to keep up or read every issue, so get a clerk or your secretary to skim the periodicals and either cut out the articles for your attention or mark the areas you should read.

## SOURCING TO THE RIGHT CHANNEL—WHEN TO DEAL WITH MANUFACTURER'S AGENTS, MIDDLEMEN, OR DIRECTLY WITH THE SUPPLIER

Marketers must decide which channel to use when selling their product. They can sell direct to consumers, or direct to retailers or they can go through middlemen such as wholesalers. Manufacturers can hire their own sales force or work through manufacturer's agents. If you are trying to sell used equipment you can sell to a second hand dealer or sell at an auction.

As a buyer, you often need to make a similar decision. Each channel has a purpose to the buyer as well as the seller. Retailers sell in small quantities and are conveniently located, but the unit price is high. Wholesalers sell in higher volumes, but they markup the price they receive from the manufacturer.

If you have sufficient volume, it is usually to your advantage to purchase directly from the manufacturer. However, many manufacturers have no sales force. They work through manufacturer's agents who receive commissions for the products they sell rather than a salary. The agent may carry more than one type of product and from more than one manufacturer.

Agents do not normally carry competing products although the products may be related.

Purchasing from a manufacturer's agent has several advantages:

- The agent can be a conduit for information between the buyer and the manufacturer.
- The agent can look after your interest by getting your order scheduled properly to meet your needs.
- The agent can follow your order to make sure it is delivered on time or expediting it if necessary.
- The agent can provide technical advice about the product and its use.
- The agent can suggest ways to improve the usefulness of the product for you or help you design your product to sell better.

In most cases, the agent does none of these things. We have known cases where all the agent does is sit in an office and take the order, send it to the manufacturer and then collect the commission. When this happens, you should make every effort to buy directly from the manufacturer and eliminate the three to five percent commission that is normally given to the agent.

Manufacturers seldom want to keep goods in inventory. Therefore, if you do not have room to store large quantities, you may be forced to buy from distributors or wholesalers. They sell the material from stock in warehouses. There is a cost connected with receiving the goods, keeping the inventory, and then reshipping it. Consequently, you will pay a higher price than if you received it directly from the manufacturer.

## CONCLUSION: YOU NOW KNOW HOW TO ———— FIND AND QUALIFY THE BEST SOURCE ————

We discussed some of the advantages and disadvantages of sole sourcing and the need to look for new sources. We discussed where to look to find suppliers and the 11 factors you must consider when choosing a new supplier. You now know how to decide on the extent of source investigation and how to conduct that investigation. Finally, you learned the importance of buying from the right channel. After all of this you might assume you are ready to place your order. Perhaps, but not necessarily. Now is the time to sit down and begin serious negotiations. The next chapter will discuss negotiating methods with your old suppliers as well as your new ones.

# CHAPTER EIGHT

# How to Negotiate the Best Deal

Negotiations go on all the time. People negotiate everywhere and everyday to get what they want without having to give too much in return. There is usually a compromise. One side to the negotiation may win most of the concessions but as long as everyone is content with the settlement, you will probably agree that the negotiation was a success.

Our object in this chapter is to make you aware of the various types of negotiations and how to conduct them to obtain the results that you want. You will learn when to negotiate, how to prepare for negotiations, and what tactics to use.

By negotiating you can reduce your cost by as much or more than obtaining bids from many suppliers. Suppliers submit bids that have prices with a 50% difference. At other times there may only be 5% to 10% differences in the bids, but serious negotiations can double the percentages. Just recently, we asked suppliers to bid on printing. There was a 27.3% difference between the lowest and highest bid. Because of other factors we wanted the business to go to the supplier with the highest bid but we still wanted to pay the lowest price. Through negotiation, we managed to have the highest bidder reduce his price by over 30%.

## —— NECESSARY SKILLS FOR SUCCESSFUL NEGOTIATION ——

Whether you are negotiating for a box of hardware or to change a supplier's payment policy, you must be prepared by knowing what you want. Perhaps the most important personality trait is confidence. The most important skill is the ability to communicate. The skills of a good salesperson are the skills needed for a good negotiator. In addition, a good negotiator must be cost conscious and not be embarrassed by asking for the moon.

The best negotiators have highly developed imaginations. You must be able to look for different possible ways of giving people what they want. That is right, giving people what they want. For you only succeed in negotiating when both you and the other party get what you both want.

If you extend the sales skills comparison further, success can be interpreted in either the short term or in the long run. A buyer can obtain an exceptionally good one-time purchase but lose the supplier because the supplier was selling without making a profit, just as a sales person can take advantage of you with a high price. If your company survives and you discover that you have been paying too much, you probably will never buy from that supplier again.

The successful negotiator looks for ways of giving the seller a better deal while at the same time getting a better deal for himself. That is possible because standard prices, terms, and conditions normally include cost factors and legal clauses for many contingencies. In addition, the usual offer, even if it is allegedly customized for you, is normally a combination of averages and protection from worse case situations. It is the average offer of what the market will bear. It contains an average figure for overhead. It contains a figure for profit within an arbitrary acceptable range. It contains clauses that protect the supplier for risks with the worse customers and risks that are unlikely to occur.

Your job is to ferret out the true cost and the real risks, and to provide the seller with the proper incentives to put a higher value on your business. To be a pro you must have a thorough knowledge of the product and a thorough knowledge of the marketplace. You must have a thorough knowledge of "buymanship." That is, you must know how to purchase including how to communicate. You should know all the rules and regulations that you must follow. Most importantly you must have a thorough knowledge of human nature.

## KNOWING WHEN TO NEGOTIATE

As a purchasing professional you should always be negotiating. The way you conduct yourself every day and in every casual contact with your suppliers and your colleagues affects the success of your purchases. Your image is of paramount importance in dealing with suppliers. If a supplier feels you are not knowledgeable about the market, he will bid higher. If the supplier feels you don't really mean what you say, he may delay shipment past the scheduled delivery date. If a supplier thinks you tell untruths or exaggerate, it influences his decision to offer the lowest cost or give the best terms. If the supplier hears that your company is slow in paying its bills, (whether or not this is true), it affects his willingness to give you the best possible deal.

If you seem too friendly, if you are too willing to accept gifts or entertainment, if you engage in excessive frivolity, the supplier may not offer you as much as he would if you were more reserved and serious. Your image is important for all types of transactions.

Therefore, for successful negotiations:

- Don't be too friendly.
- Don't accept gratuities or entertainment.
- Be serious.
- Be businesslike.

In addition to these general negotiation guidelines, you should negotiate in the following specific situations:

**When You Purchase a New Item.** You should negotiate whenever you make a purchase for a new item. Some negotiations take only seconds. Others may take a year or longer. Some are over the telephone, one on one. Others require large team efforts.

**When the Potential Rewards in the Long Run Are Higher Than Accepting the Original Offer.** If you really need material or service at once and any delay will cost you more than any possible savings by shopping or negotiating, you have little choice. Nevertheless, you can always point out to the supplier that if he treats you fairly and gives you a low cost on this order you will favor him with future orders.

**When You Have Been Buying from a Supplier for a Long Time.** If you have been giving orders for the same item to the same supplier for a long time and the volume has been increasing, you may be over paying. The prices you are receiving are probably based on a much lower volume. It is time to negotiate. Here is where you use the learning curve to advantage.

**When Competitors Are Trying to Win Your Business Away from Your Present Supplier.** In this situation, you may be in a very powerful negotiating position. It has been proven that suppliers provide less service with higher prices to long-time customers than they do to new customers that they are trying to win. Even if you are satisfied with your present source, it doesn't hurt to mention that the competition is doing everything possible to get you as a customer. Ask your existing source if he can't improve on what he is doing for you. He may be able to lower prices, but possibly you want better delivery or improved quality or better payment terms. You are not likely to get any of these things unless you ask.

***When You Are Not Rushed.*** Plan a block of time to negotiate your major purchases. It doesn't have to be done all at once either. It may require many meetings spread over months. One of our major successes took almost a year negotiating with a half dozen steel companies that refused to budge. When one company finally made us a small concession, it was like a break in the dike; then the other suppliers kept lowering prices to get some of the business. The annual savings amounted to over three million dollars.

***When Businesses Are Looking for Orders.*** It is always easier to negotiate under these circumstances. You should be aware of the marketplace. If it is a declining market and you need material, you are in a strong position.

***When Prices Are Dropping.*** Read the trade magazines and the newspapers. If the news indicates that prices are dropping and you have not received a reduction, start negotiation proceedings at once. You also might inform your suppliers that you don't want to hear about such reductions through the media. Tell them that you want to know before it is publicly announced.

***When Prices Are Increasing.*** You should always negotiate when a supplier announces a general price increase or a supplier tells you he must increase prices.

***When You Are Well Informed and Know Your Product.*** This is always a good time to negotiate. You need to know about whom you are dealing with and the state of the marketplace. The supplier may be in a hurry to make an agreement because he wants to make a quota or show a high sales figure for the month or the year. If so, he will make concessions that he might not make at other times. It is your time to act.

## HOW TO ADJUST YOUR NEGOTIATING STYLE
## ————————— TO FIT THE SITUATION —————————

Today there are many books that explain various negotiating theories. Most of them approach negotiating from a rather narrow point of view. They talk about planning, strategies, team efforts, meeting sites, and about establishing long-term personal relationships. We intend to mention those things also, but they are most involved with high level purchases and contracts for large companies. What about the purchases that buyers make everyday for items that will only be bought every twenty years? What about purchases that only amount to $10 rather than ten million dollars? Many of these are bought at the price that the buyer is willing to pay.

## Use Different Negotiating Methods for Different Purposes

You cannot be successful at negotiating if you treat all sources the same way. For example, very small companies may not wish to sell to you if mountains of paperwork are required to do business with you. Conversely large companies may require documentation and detailed specifications to give you their best offer. Or, if your normal style is to deal one-on-one, you will find it difficult to do business in Asia, for example, where they traditionally use the team approach. Still, entrepreneurs and some high level corporate moguls often like to deal privately and quickly.

## How to Negotiate When Placing Rush Orders

Maximum negotiating results are obtained when you have plenty of time, but what if you don't? Should you simply accept whatever the seller asks? Buyers in the typical purchasing department need to place rush orders often. Many rush requirements can be better planned and avoided, but that does not excuse you. You must get the material to keep the business running.

When placing orders for rush items or items that are rarely purchased and do not amount to large sums (and if you are concerned about cost), never give the impression that you must place the order at once regardless of price or terms. Never give the impression that you must have the product immediately even if that is so. Get the price and terms before you discuss the delivery schedule.

Sometimes you will run into a seller that is a little smarter than many. He will ask you when you need the goods before he gives you his quotation. At that point, you have a choice. You may flatly state that you need it now and accept what probably will be an inflated price, or you may answer his inquiry with a question. When he asks when you need it, you ask if that will make a difference. Ask him what his normal leadtime is. Most suppliers like to claim very short leadtimes and many don't want to admit that they are going to charge you a premium for quick delivery. If in the end the supplier insists on a premium charge for quick delivery, at least you know what the premium is and can negotiate a compromise. Furthermore, perhaps your requisitioner will be willing to wait if he knows the added cost and if normal leadtime is not that much different from the early delivery.

After the offer is made always ask the seller if he can't do better or ask if that is his best possible offer. You will be amazed at how frequently lower prices are quickly offered. If that doesn't work ask what you have to do to get the price down. It is sometimes helpful if you give the seller a target. For example, if the seller says he cannot possibly go lower than $20, you might indicate that he has a deal if he could accept $18. After the price and terms are agreed upon, you then can say fine, you can have the order if you can deliver by Wednesday.

### How to Negotiate for Repetitive Purchases

Items that are purchased repeatedly require periodic shopping, competitive bidding, and planned negotiating. Consider making long-term agreements to avoid time-consuming constant renegotiation. The length of time for these agreements or the need for renegotiation depends on the potential savings that can be obtained.

For example, most buyers like to make annual agreements. If you buy a product every month, an annual agreement saves 11 negotiating sessions. In practice the annual agreement may take much longer than a single monthly negotiating session, since much more is at stake, but even if it takes three times as long, you still have saved the time of 9 sessions.

The changing costs that suppliers may incur through inflation or unforeseen and uncontrollable cost increases are the biggest stumbling block to long-term agreements. This is particularly true with companies that are not accustomed to such agreements. Your way around this is to allow adjustments in the price because of what is called "escalation." A formula is developed based on impartial published figures such as the consumer price index or the producer price index. Adjustments based on one of these indices may be allowed every three months or any other agreed upon time interval. Although you do not have total control over the price, you will maintain your relative position in the marketplace and you save the time of having to renegotiate every requirement.

## HOW TO USE ALL AVAILABLE SKILLS AND RESOURCES ———————— TO NEGOTIATE SUCCESSFULLY ————————

Many smaller operations do not have large enough staffs to help you negotiate every purchase. However, whenever you need to negotiate a major purchase or need technical assistance you should utilize the available people. In addition, get the people involved who have a vested interest in your success with the purchase. This team approach gives you the benefit of specialized knowledge that you may not have.

The buyer or purchasing manager must retain control and be the leader of the team; otherwise, your company may lose credibility with the supplier. The buyer coordinates activities and sometimes acts as a liaison between the various departments of the buying and selling company. Some members of the team are behind the scenes and act as advisers only. They provide you with the information to conduct your negotiations successfully. Other members take a more active part and may meet with their counterparts at the seller's or may sit in during the negotiating session. The following sections describe some possible resources to consult if you need information or specialized assistance.

## Use Your Engineering Specialists if You Need Technical Information

There are many types of engineers and it is conceivable that any of them can supply you with technical help during negotiations. Design engineers can modify designs to reduce cost or can explain why a certain design is essential. Plant engineers and plant management can contribute suggestions that will improve productivity. Packaging engineers can suggest other methods of protecting the product or of reducing packaging cost.

**CAUTION:** Make sure your engineering department does not contact suppliers first, however, for an estimate or a bid unless it is going to do all the negotiating and approve the contract. The official buyer must make the initial contact and engineering's contacts should be closely supervised by purchasing if cost is a serious consideration.

Engineers often work so closely with suppliers over a long period that the specifications tend to be oriented toward one supplier. When this happens, successful negotiations become very difficult if not impossible.

## Use the Traffic Department to Determine the Best Delivery Terms

Many purchasing departments are also responsible for traffic and have their own specialist, but if your company has its own traffic personnel, consult them to determine the lowest cost routing. If you have no expertise in this area either within purchasing or with a separate traffic department, it may be worth while to contact an outside traffic service for its advice.

You must weigh the transportation cost against the time and fees involved. If you expect to buy the product over a long period of time and if the size of the shipments is significant, you may save a substantial sum by seeking help. Keep in mind that if your company has no traffic expertise, neither do many suppliers. Often sellers pick a carrier and choose routing without much study. In addition, the best choice for shipments to your location may require an entirely different selection.

## Check with Your Legal Department for Special Contracts

It has been said that the best way to kill a deal is to get the lawyers involved. Many sellers will shy away from formal contracts. Also as a professional buyer or purchasing manager you should have enough knowledge of the law to handle 98% of your transactions, especially if they are similar to previous transactions that your legal counsel has approved.

Nevertheless, you should still have your legal department review high-value contracts or contracts or clauses that are unusual or different from what you have previously encountered.

You should develop a standard set of clauses that are recommended by your counsel. Each state or government jurisdiction has certain rules that need to be considered. Many of these terms can be or should be printed right on the purchase order. Others should be typed in when special circumstances require them.

You can compare these standard terms with any terms that the supplier wishes to incorporate into the agreement. If the supplier insists on his clause or on removing your clause, you can then consult with your attorney on possible compromises or course of action.

## Check with Your Sales/Marketing Management to Determine the Need for Some Products

If the product you need is for resale or is a component of a product for resale, input from your sales or marketing department may be helpful. Marketing may be able to approve elimination of some product requirement. The product manager may agree to a less expensive material substitute. We have found the buyer's own sales and marketing people often have a high degree of rapport with outside salespeople. Their opinions about the need to keep cost at a certain level are taken more seriously than they are from others.

## Find Out What Payment Terms Accounting/Finance Want

Many buyers take payment terms too lightly. Appropriate payment terms can save your company many dollars. If your company is cash rich, it can afford to pay quickly. In such case, you can negotiate to get a discount by paying the bill in 10 days rather than the usual 30-day business terms. If the supplier is paying a high price to buy working capital, he may be willing to give you a good discount for paying early. If the supplier needs funds badly, he may be willing to cut the price if you give him a large downpayment with the order, or if you pay for the raw material he needs to make your product.

Conversely, if your company is paying a high price for funds, you can negotiate extended payment terms such as net 60 or net 90 days. The supplier may even be willing to finance payments over one or two years. In most cases, the supplier will want to work through a bank or other financial institution, but some companies do their own financing. Sometimes the rates and terms of these financial arrangements are not particularly favorable, whereas at other times, there is little or no charge and in effect it is like obtaining a price reduction.

But even without unusual payment terms, the buyer and seller should agree on which terms will be used. In practice, payment terms are probably abused more than any other portion of business agreements. Even though net 30 is the most common payment term offered, the average company takes 45 days. Other companies take payment discounts long after the period for discounting has passed. After the salesperson and buyer agree on terms, suppliers frequently ignore the terms and send invoices and second notices demanding payment before the agreement calls for payment. To eliminate such abuses both buyer and seller must make sure that everyone is informed of the terms of the agreement.

Obviously, you cannot evaluate offers or negotiate for the one you want without full knowledge of your company's financial situation. Your financial officers should be able to give you this information and let you know what you should be aiming for.

## HOW TO PREPARE FOR EACH STEP
## IN THE NEGOTIATING PROCESS

We have said that you must always negotiate. If that is the case, how can you prepare for negotiating? First, you must separate the day-to-day requirements from the major purchases. Prepare for routine everyday transactions by learning all you can about your company, the requisitioners that you work with, and the suppliers that you will deal with most of the time. It helps if you have a good background in psychology, economics, marketing, and business law. A technical knowledge of the products you buy is a great asset. The more you know, the better you will do. Obviously, no one can be an expert in all these subjects, but you should never stop learning even though you can call on specialists for advice.

Get to know your requisitioners because part of your negotiation is with them. By knowing them you will learn their strengths and their deficiencies. You will know when you can rely on what they tell you. You will be able to communicate your needs to them. One of your needs is learning what they want. You must be able to help them define their real requirements. You must be able to influence them to restrict their purchases to items that help the company meet its goals rather than to satisfy their own egos or whims. You need to influence them to be specific and put their requirements in a standardized format that is easy to interpret. (See chapter 2 for details on the requisitioning process.)

Most purchasing departments are so busy that they have little time to reflect on what they are doing or how. You need to take the time to organize your work and your records. Look for ways of reducing paperwork without sacrificing information needed to do the job properly. If you seem to have extra time, use it productively by learning more about the products you buy as well as the products your company sells. Learning is a never-ending process, and the knowledge you gain is the tool that will make you a better negotiator.

Here are the steps to take to prepare for the negotiating process—before you even call the supplier:

1. Get to know your requisitioner.
2. Learn about the products your company sells and what your company buys.
3. Learn the marketplace from magazines, newspapers, trade shows, and interviews with salespeople.
4. Make sure the requisition is properly filled out and includes all information required to make the purchase.
5. Make sure the purchase has been approved by the authorized person. If your responsibility, make sure there is budget for the requested purchase.
6. Check purchasing records to see where and when the item was previously purchased.
7. Check purchasing records and buying directories to see who supplies the item.
8. Estimate the price. The method for doing this varies depending on whether or not you have bought the item before.

   If the item was previously purchased, update the previous price quotes by using the producer price index or other estimating techniques. Make sure you are using similar quantities or making allowances for differences in quantities.

   On the other hand, if you are purchasing the item for the first time, prepare a written request for quotation form, allowing sufficient time for each supplier to send in a reply. (See Chapter 4 for a typical RFQ form.) You may wish to call suppliers to expedite the process, but submitting your request in writing and getting the quotation in writing gives assurance that each company is quoting with the same information. Using this method assumes you have a policy stating that all bids are subject to negotiation.

   If you have never purchased the item before and it is only available from one source, you can still try to estimate its cost. Calculate the cost by multiplying each material by the unit cost for that material. Add the estimated value of labor. Add an estimated amount for overhead and profit. This may be a rough figure, but it can be refined when you begin discussions with the supplier.

9. Prepare a list of questions to use as a guide so you will not forget to ask for important information. A good negotiator always asks questions. See Appendix C for a list of questions you might ask.

10. Plan your negotiating schedule. You may want to do this before you send out requests for quotations to see if you have the time you need to negotiate on this particular purchase.

11. If your negotiation is going to be for an existing item or with an existing supplier, gather all the information on supplier performance that is available. For example, try to obtain the following information about your suppliers:

    • Dates of shipments arriving late or too early.
    • Items received with quantity discrepancies, by date and type of discrepancy.
    • Number of price increases and percentage amount of increase for the past 18 months. Compare this with the inflation rate.
    • Number of invoice errors.
    • Length of time to respond to service calls.
    • Cost cutting ideas submitted.
    • Product improvement ideas submitted.

12. Prepare a list of concessions that you can make in return for concessions by the supplier. List them in increasing order of value.

## HOW TO DECIDE WHICH NEGOTIATION TACTICS ARE BEST

By this time you know if you are making a routine quick purchase or a major agreement. You know if you are only going to spend a few minutes placing an order or if you might need to have many meetings spread over several months. In the latter case the pressure is off in making a commitment. You can decide on a tactic that gives the impression that you are going to check the market thoroughly because making the right selection of a supplier is very important. You can legitimately put off making a commitment because you need to check facts or because you need more information. However, be careful that the supplier does not lose interest because of delays or thinks that you are not really serious about placing an order. In such case, you will either receive no concessions whatsoever or ones of little consequence.

You must make certain that the supplier realizes you are serious about making an agreement. If the volume that you intend to purchase is high, make sure the supplier knows that. We are amazed at the number of times suppliers walk away from business because they refuse to believe the size of the orders that will follow.

If the volume of your intended order is low but there are chances that it will grow, make sure the supplier understands the potential. He will sometimes give you lower costs hoping that you will grow and stay with him when your needs are greater.

If yours is a new company, you must sell the potential. You must point out the advantages of youth and new ideas. If you are with an old, well-established firm, you should point out the advantages of maturity and stability.

You need to use tactics that are appropriate for both your company and the supplier's. You need to use tactics that are appropriate for your personality and for the personality of the people you are dealing with.

For example, divide negotiating methods into three styles; the hard sell, the soft sell, and objective oriented. The hard sell may be effective for temporary relationships or if your company is significantly larger than the supplier. It is doubtful if it works when your company is small and is trying to buy from a giant organization. Big companies involve many people in the decision process and much structure needs to be overcome in changing established policies and procedures. When concessions are made, they are usually discussed and approved by more than one individual and with much of the hard sell emotional language removed. The same for the soft sell approach. More and more large companies are looking at buy-sell agreements unemotionally. The seller wants facts and figures the same as you the buyer. Compare the differences between the soft, hard, and objective or principled methods as shown on the chart from *Getting to Yes* by Roger Fisher and William Ury (see Figure 8-1).

Look at some of the differences between these methods. The hard sell negotiator, whether he be salesperson or buyer, makes demands and looks at the buy-sell relationship as an adversarial one. Demands are made. Threats are made either obviously or subtly. For example, a salesperson may say, "If you don't buy from me now, we won't be able to help you if the product goes on allocation." The hard-sell negotiator may look at negotiating as a game or as a war which must be won.

Soft sellers want to be friendly. They do not want conflict. Soft sellers trust others. They want to be liked and their purpose is to get agreement even if they have to give up a lot to get it.

The objective oriented negotiator tries to eliminate emotions from the transaction. Roger Fisher and William Ury in their book *Getting to Yes*[1]

---

[1] *Getting to Yes* by Roger Fisher and William Ury Copyright© 1981 Houghton Mifflin Co.

| PROBLEM<br>Positional Bargaining:<br>Which Game Should You Play? | | SOLUTION<br>Change the Game-<br>Negotiate on the Merits |
|---|---|---|
| **SOFT**<br>Participants are friends | **HARD**<br>Participants are adversaries. | **PRINCIPLED**<br>Participants are problem-solvers. |
| The goal is agreement. | The goal is victory. | The goal is a wise outcome reached efficiently and amicably. |
| Make concessions to cultivate relationship. | Demand concessions as a condition of the relationship. | **Separate the people from the problem.** |
| Be soft on the people and the problem. | Be hard on the problem and the people. | Be soft on the people, hard on the problem. |
| Trust others. | Distrust others. | Proceed independent of trust. |
| Change your position easily. | Dig in to your position. | **Focus on interests, not positions.** |
| Make offers. | Make threats. | Explore interests. |
| Disclose your bottom line. | Mislead as to your bottom line. | Avoid having a bottom line. |
| Accept one-sided losses to reach agreement. | Demand one-sided gains as the price of agreement. | **Invent options for mutual gain.** |
| Search for the single answer: the one they will accept. | Search for the single answer: the one you will accept. | Develop multiple options to choose from; decide later. |
| Insist on agreement. | Insist on your position. | Insist on using objective criteria. |
| Try to avoid a contest of will. | Try to win a contest of will. | Try to reach a result based on standards independent of will. |
| Yield to pressure. | Apply pressure | Reason and be open to reasons; yield to principle, not pressure. |

From GETTING TO YES by Roger Fisher and William Ury. Copyright© 1981 by Roger Fisher and William Ury. Reprinted by permission of Houghton Mifflin Co.

**Figure 8-1. Three Styles of Negotiating Methods**

referred to the objective oriented method as the principled method. When you use this method you look at the facts about the product or service you want to buy and to the things associated with those items which will bring about a satisfactory transaction for both parties. You are not interested per se in the people involved but rather in the cost of designing, producing, and delivering a satisfactory product. Objective oriented negotiators use objective criteria rather than subjective criteria to evaluate products and to evaluate the benefits of the sale or purchase for each party to the transaction.

## Determining Where to Negotiate

You should think about where you are going to hold negotiating sessions and the advantages or disadvantages of each. Most industrial buyers negotiate their agreements at their own office, but that may not always be the best place. You have three choices: your facilities, the supplier's offices, or neutral ground.

You must weigh the pros and cons of each location. There may be good reason to pick your own turf. You may want to get input from your chief executive. You may want to hold the meeting at the supplier's to get approval for an important concession from its president.

*Negotiating at Your Own Facility.* If you want your own negotiating team to sit in on discussions, it is less costly and more convenient to hold the meetings at your location unless the supplier is close. In addition all your records are easily available. One disadvantage is the possibility of having your own people present who do more harm than good during negotiations. Another disadvantage is that you can be interrupted by company executives that might not realize the importance of your need to concentrate. However, interruptions sometimes are useful as an excuse to break away from an awkward point in the discussions.

*Negotiating at the Supplier's Facility.* If you travel alone to the supplier's facilities, you may find yourself outnumbered. If you alone try to negotiate with a team you are at a decided disadvantage since members of the supplier's team have more time to think and observe your actions. Yet, you can see the supplier's facilities and learn more about the way it operates. You probably can meet more of the employees and can assess their capabilities. You can gracefully break off the discussions by leaving any time you wish.

If you want to negotiate with a small foreign supplier, it is more usual for you to travel there than to have them visit the U.S. Sometimes you have no choice if you want to buy from such a company. Buyers get around this problem somewhat by seeing the supplier at the hotel where they stay. Even so, the supplier often shows up with two or three companions. You are at a double disadvantage if you are inexperienced and don't know the customs or the language. You can get around this by hiring a neutral local interpreter and by being well prepared before you take your trip. Furthermore, when traveling so far you most certainly will want to see the supplier's facilities.

## NINE WAYS TO NEGOTIATE FROM A POSITION
——————————— OF STRENGTH ———————————

Your negotiating ability is strongest when you plan well, have superior knowledge in all relevant areas, and do not hurry. You can capitalize on that strength by using the tools available to everyone who negotiates.

*1. Ask Questions.* Asking the right questions at the right time is probably the most useful negotiating technique. It provides you with information. It keeps you in control of the session. It allows you to give information in a somewhat subtle way by the questions you ask. For example, if you ask if the company is an Equal Opportunity Employer (required for federal government contracts), you are implying that it is important to you. If you ask if the company has ever been shut down because of labor disputes, you are implying that stability and a continuous flow of material are important.

*2. Listen Carefully for the Answers.* When salespeople avoid answering your questions by changing the subject or giving a vague answer, there can be several reasons. They may simply not know the answers. They may not have heard you. Or the answers may be embarrassing. Don't be timid about clarifying the issue. Ask, "Did you hear my questions?" If the answer is vague, say that you want more specifics. If the subject is changed, repeat the question.

*3. Listen to the Words Used.* There are hidden meanings behind words. Learn what they really mean. Why should someone constantly say, "honestly" or "believe me"? When someone says, "incidentally," listen carefully, for what is said next is very important.

*4. Listen to the Tone of Voice and Enunciation.* If someone mumbles, he or she may not want you to hear what he or she is obliged to tell you.

*5. Remain Silent, Encourage the Seller to Say More.* When you ask a question, wait until the other party answers before you speak. Long pauses encourage the seller to tell you more and to offer suggestions. Even when you are asked a question, take plenty of time to answer. Don't be rushed into a reply that may not be well thought out.

*6. Watch for Mannerisms and Gestures.* Movements of the face, head, shoulders, hands, or any part of the body are often forms of nonverbal communication. Pay attention to these movements and you may be able to establish a pattern that reveals what the person is thinking. Some gestures indicate insecurity or fear. Others indicate confidence. Others indicate that someone may be lying. As a buyer you should study this subject thoroughly.

There are various books on the subject that you can find in the library. See the bibliography for suggestions.

But be careful when reading these signs from people with a different cultural background. They have different mannerisms and use different gestures that mean different things. The common handshake is not universally the same. For example, the Japanese have a habit of continually nodding the head in seeming agreement and saying "Hi," while you are talking. It does not mean they accept what you say and are agreeing with you even though "Hi" means yes. They simple mean, I hear what you say or I understand what you say.

***7. Keep Careful Notes; Record What Has Been Said.*** You may think you will remember at the time, but after much conversation, you may forget an important detail. Make sure you record the date, time, location site, and names and titles of everyone present at the meeting. Go over your notes after the meetings and expand on what was said in the places where your notes are too sketchy or unclear.

Sometimes it is advisable to send a copy of your notes to the supplier to verify your understanding of what was said. You cannot always do this without editing since the notes may contain your own embarrassing thoughts. Still, it is always good to clear up misunderstandings so if you wish to include your interpretation of what was said, so much the better.

***8. Be Skeptical of All Alleged Facts and Figures.*** For example, if a sales rep says that something is the law in this state, make sure that it is really true. We have often found that those types of statements are either half-truths, not true at all, or misinterpretations of the law.

Also, question averages and performance figures. Ask for demonstrations and do your own testing. In one case, we were told that a machine was to produce 7,500 pieces per hour. We later found out that it only produced near that quantity when a very special, seldom-used material was used. Our best efforts could get no more than 2,000 pieces per hour.

***9. Rehearse and Coach Your Negotiation Technique.*** Rehearsal and coaching are part of the planning process. It helps you discover things that you may have forgotten to list in your objectives. It helps you prepare arguments to persuade the other negotiators.

Rehearsal and coaching are especially important when using a team. You may prefer that certain individuals of your team remain silent. It is just as important to tell members of the team what not to say as what to say. We have heard engineers and others make statements that almost sabotaged our discussions. For example, one individual began telling the group what a poor product and what poor service we were receiving from our present source. The supplier must have then realized that we needed him and any concessions were much less than what they might have been.

# HOW TO NEGOTIATE WHEN YOUR SUPPLIER
## ──────── INSISTS ON "STANDARD" TERMS ────────

Companies make policies and procedures to make running a business easier. Employees do not have to rethink similar situations when they arise. They just follow the procedure. They just use the established form. The trouble with those established policies and procedures is they get people into the habit of not thinking. They discourage the use of imagination and creativity and those are just the things you need to negotiate successfully.

To confound your negotiating efforts, salespeople will often rely on the so-called fixed policies and procedures of their company. Here are 6 tips on how to avoid "deal killers"—i.e., so-called standard terms that your supplier may use to end negotiations.

**1. *Don't Be Intimidated by Printed Price Lists.*** These just make it easier for the salesperson to give you a price. Someone must have approved the prices on the list. That may be the person you should be talking to. The excuse will sometimes be made that they can't change the prices for you because that would be price discrimination and a restraint of trade. This is nonsense, unless your purchases are significant enough to restrict competition.

**2. *Ignore Printed Discount Sheets.*** You should compare prices, not discounts, but beside the fact that you should not pay much attention to discount percentages, be careful which list you are given. For example, a salesperson may tell you that you are getting the maximum discount: you are receiving the discount in the far right column. What he doesn't tell you is that you are getting the discounts off of the green sheet. The discounts on the pink sheet or some other color are significantly better.

Many companies have different price structures for different industries. If a company can sell to one industry for less then there is no reason why it can't sell to you for less.

**3. *Question "Standard" Leadtimes.*** Companies often quote an average leadtime or a maximum leadtime. These leadtimes are usually negotiable if you need material delivered earlier. Be careful however, that the seller does not simply agree to ship earlier to get the business but really has no intention of delivering on time. It may even be impossible to meet your schedule.

To avoid being disappointed, carefully question suppliers to learn what facilities are available to produce what you want. Ask them how they are going to deliver sooner than their normal time. If they are going to reschedule other customers to meet your needs, you may suspect that they will do the same to you later when they have an opportunity to get business from a new customer.

*4. Inquire if Changes Can Be Made to the Fixed Product Design.* If a company has a line of standard products it may not seem willing at first to change the product for your particular needs, but if you have sufficient volume or if you are willing to pay additional cost changes can sometimes be made. You may be able to pay less if your suggested change reduces the cost. For example, take bulk packs rather than individually wrapped or boxed items. If you can accept looser tolerances and still meet your requirements, the supplier may be able to reduce the cost.

For example, one company purchased rail car wheels at 15% less than the going price because it accepted wheels that did not meet the supplier's tight tolerances (even though they were within the tolerances specified by the American Association of Railroad and the Department of Transportation guidelines).

A supplier may be willing to give you a lower cost if it leaves its name off the product. Many manufacturers of standard products also will produce products to meet your specifications and with your private label.

*5. Don't Be Intimidated by Published Credit Terms.* Payment terms are often standardized by the seller. The credit terms seem inflexible because they are preprinted on standardized sales agreements, in catalogs, and on invoices. When making the sale depends on revision of payment terms, the terms are frequently changed to agree with what you need.

*6. Don't Feel Restricted by Standard Contract Forms.* Standard contract forms are written and printed to make it easier and quicker to sell. When you are presented with a standard contract form prepared by the seller, remember that such forms are always written in his favor. There is nothing to prevent you from crossing out unfavorable terms and adding your own clauses. The supplier will think twice before rejecting your changes. Don't give up even if he objects. He may say, "Our lawyers won't allow us to make the changes you want." If you insist on the changes you want and the sale depends on it, the seller's management may overrule the advice of attorneys.

## DISCLOSING INFORMATION DURING NEGOTIATIONS: KNOWING WHAT HELPS AND WHAT HURTS YOUR POSITION

When you negotiate you want to promote communication with the supplier, but that does not mean that you have to disclose everything about your business. There is no point in telling the seller things that will only hurt your chance of making a profitable purchase. That is not to say that you want to mislead the supplier or tell an untruth. If it is important to warn the supplier about potential problems, then you are obligated to divulge the information. If the knowledge does nothing more than provide the supplier with reasons to increase your cost, then you should prevent such information from being disclosed.

Here is a list of things that the supplier may find out that may hurt your negotiating efforts:

- If the buyer has had any bad experiences with the competition.
- If a competitor cannot make delivery on time.
- If a competitor is on strike.
- If a competitor has a bad reputation.
- If the competition has poor service.
- If a competitor cannot make a product.
- If your company has financial problems.
- If your company has legal problems.
- If your company has a poor payment record.
- If your company has poor ethical practices.
- If you plan to buy one time only.
- If you plan to buy in low volume.
- If you expect low usage.
- If you have future plans to make the product yourself.
- If your company is young or new.
- If others at your company already have favorable opinions about the seller's product.
- If others at your company have unfavorable opinions about the competition.

On the other hand, the following is a list of information that a buyer should disclose because it will improve his or her negotiating position:

- If your company is in a position of financial strength. For example, the fact that your company is cash rich.
- If your company has a good payment record.
- If your company has a good reputation.
- If your company uses the supplier's product in high volume.
- If you plan to buy in high volume order quantities.
- If you are satisfied with the competition.

- If you are open to discussion and the possibility of accepting a better offer elsewhere.
- How you are going to use the product or service, what the end product is, your market.
- If the supplier's competitors have excellent performance, an excellent product, or excellent service.
- If the supplier's competitor is stable, or efficient, or provides goods at low cost.

**CAUTION:** if you make it seem that you are so satisfied with your present sources that there is little possibility that the supplier has a chance for the business unless it gives the product away, it may lose interest and give you no concessions at all. Negotiating is an art. You must assess the situation and divulge or withhold information depending on the players and the circumstance. You will not always be right. If you conduct enough transactions, you will at times misjudge. In the long run—with proper planning and care—you will obtain material and supplies at a much reduced cost. Remember, savings of from 10% to 30% are not uncommon. That means millions of dollars added to profits for even small companies.

## CONCLUSION: PROFESSIONAL PURCHASING ————— MEANS EFFECTIVE NEGOTIATING —————

Anyone can place an order. It takes no special training. Obtaining the proper material when you need it, and at a cost that permits a profit, demands the skills of a professional negotiator. That is what buyers should be. And buyers should negotiate at all times, even though it is not sitting down at a formal long session. Your negotiating may only take a few minutes.

To be good at negotiating you need knowledge of the supplier, of the people involved in the negotiation, both within your own organization and with the suppliers. You need knowledge of the product. You need knowledge of the law.

For major negotiations you must plan your negotiating strategy, you must use all the tools at your disposal, you must use specialists when you don't have the in-depth knowledge needed, and you must communicate your needs and understand the needs of the supplier.

# CHAPTER NINE

# How to Establish Policies and Procedures That Will Maintain Control

The three most critical problems in the purchasing department are lack of time, insufficient communication and conflict. There never seems to be enough time to accomplish all the things necessary to eliminate all the problems. A breakdown of effective communication inside your company or with outside entities can cause misunderstandings and backtracking to re-establish the accuracy of information. Conflicts and frustrations that can result from any of the above further erode productivity and morale. Therefore you must institute some form of organized requirements as you grow.

Organizations have alternately embraced and shunned the formal documentation of requirements. Most smaller companies choose to rely on broad outlines of policy and on-the-job solutions to problems as they arise. Some businesses prefer to operate solely from a position of honesty and trust (common in the Far East). Larger corporations tend to publish volumes of procedural requirements. The U.S. Government, with its Defense Acquisition and Federal Acquisition Regulations (DAR and FAR) totaling thousands of pages, is probably the best example of over regulation.

Some foresighted corporations have reduced the volume of their procedures in an attempt to centralize control only to discover that ambiguities prevented the effective communication of those requirements. Even IBM, noted for its detailed purchasing procedures, attempted once to reduce its purchasing procedures to the size of a suit pocket booklet, only to return to more detailed requirements shortly thereafter.

In today's ever changing business and industrial environment you need to provide continuity, responsibility and consistency in handling your day-to-day operations. Therefore, some form of controls, regulations, procedures or guidelines must be compiled to ensure this goal.

## DEVELOPING A BUSINESS PLAN
## FOR THE PURCHASING DEPARTMENT

Figure 9-1 illustrates a business plan for the purchasing department, which outlines the steps necessary to provide adequate controls for your operation. Using the chart in Figure 9-1, your action plan might be something like this:

I define my *strategy*,

by setting of *goals and objectives*,

that are *communicated* to my employees,

through the use of *policies and procedures*,

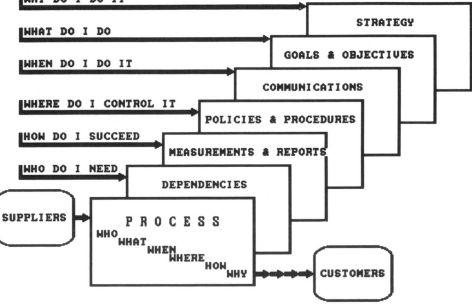

**Figure 9-1. Sample Business Plan for the Purchasing Department**

that I *measure with reports* that are,

coordinated with all *dependent* organizations,

that make up my business *process.*

## How to Determine What You Want To Accomplish

Most organizations have little trouble determining their strategy (where they want to go with their business). Statements like "Provide high quality products to the public at bargain prices," or "Increase revenue by 20% per year," may be reasonable motivation for upper management, but have little meaning to an entry level employee.

**REMEMBER:** *Goals and Objectives must explain your business aspirations.*

Most problems with strategic goals arise when specific goals and objectives must be communicated from the CEO to the Purchasing Manager and then on down to the buyer. More layers of management like a plant manager, operations manager, materials manager and so on, greatly complicate the communication. The Purchasing Manager must translate the company's strategic goals into operational goals and objectives that relate specifically to each purchasing operation.

For example, a company's strategic goal might be "to provide on-time deliveries of competitive, quality products to its customers." That's a fine statement for the board room, but may carry little weight when communicated directly to an associate buyer, new to your organization. Your buyers need to understand the impact of timely processing of purchase requisitions, the negotiation procedure and how to ensure quality when placing a purchase order. These are operational objectives that buyers can understand, because they relate directly to their daily activities.

Long-range objectives (more strategic in nature) tend to transcend immediate realities and are sometimes difficult to quantify and document at a buyer level. Therefore, operational objectives designed to meet those strategic goals need to be put in place and modified periodically as the business progresses. It is these purchasing-oriented objectives that are the foundation for the formulation of objective control mechanisms that will help you define actual targets for achievement.

When establishing objectives, you must also consider their impact on interdependent departments. Sometimes what is a productive objective for one department is counterproductive for another.

One example of a counterproductive objective is one that requires the lowest possible price, without adequately addressing the quality and delivery issues. An objective of manufacturing to produce a set number of parts in a particular time frame would not be satisfied if parts were not on time or were rejected before reaching production. Therefore strict adherence to a purchasing objective (always get the lowest price) is counter-productive to the objective of manufacturing.

Once you have considered the potential points of conflict and have assessed potential bottlenecks to productivity you will have a better understanding of the process, as a whole operation. Now you can progress to the next step, putting in place those policies and procedures that will assure the accomplishment of your objectives.

## HOW TO TRANSLATE OBJECTIVES INTO POLICY AND PROCEDURES

Let's take a moment to differentiate between the terms policy and procedure:

- A policy is a general rule or governing principle that establishes basic *philosophies* and determines major values upon which the company must operate.
- A procedure is a prescribed *method* or specific course of action which will accomplish the requirements of a policy.

Once you have grasped this distinction, you can establish policies that will ensure the procedures to support those policies make sense.

### What a Policy Statement Should Look Like

A policy statement should be reasonably brief but include enough information to cover what you are trying to accomplish. A good policy statement is, "All communications with suppliers will be done by, or with the knowledge of, the Purchasing department." It is clear from that statement that anyone who contacts a supplier without the knowledge of purchasing is in violation of company policy. Now it is necessary to set procedures that will be followed in carrying out that policy.

Another policy statement says that "No specification changes will be made by purchasing without the approval of the requisitioner." Again, certain procedures will be necessary to administer this policy.

### How to Turn a Policy into a Procedure

To define the operational requirements necessary to carry out a policy you must first look at the task from a point of view of all parties involved and how that procedure will effect each department. Points to include in formulating your procedure are:

1. Define the mission
2. Assign ownership of the information or item
3. Assign ownership of the process, task or operation
4. Develop mutual goals
5. Explain in detail what happens and how
6. Name originator of the policy

*Step 1. Define the Mission.* Any mission statement must relate to and include an overview of the activities necessary to accomplish your strategic goals. An example of a general purchasing mission is:

> The mission of the Procurement organization is to procure parts, materials and services for all plant operations.

More specifically, a mission statement would read,

> The mission of the Procurement organization is to provide the *timely delivery* of *quality* parts, *appropriate* materials, and services at *competitive prices.*

You can see that the second statement more specifically defines the goals of the company.

*Step 2. Assign Ownership of the Data (Information).* Ownership can be defined as that person (or department) ultimately responsible for the validity, expense, productivity or management of the physical information on a document. You must first assign ownership of the data (such as the information on a purchase requisition) and then ownership of the process steps (the activity of obtaining pricing and placing orders).

An example of data is the description and specifications placed on a purchase requisition by a requisitioner. That requisitioner owns the data, whereas the purchasing department owns the physical paper on which it is written. This may seem quite detailed but when you are required to be responsible for the validity of a set of specifications given to you by a requisitioner you may decide that it is not your responsibility. For example, you might establish the following system of ownership for the following items:

| Data/item | Owner |
|---|---|
| Requisition Form | Purchasing Dept. (buyer) |
| Part Specifications | Requisitioner (engineer) |
| Account Code | Accounts Payable Dept. |
| Shipping Routing | Transportation Dept. |
| Price, Delivery Date | Supplier (salesperson) |

Be aware that the process or task involved in obtaining data may have a different ownership than the data itself. For example the price and delivery date is owned by the supplier who gave the buyer that information but the task of obtaining the information is owned by the buyer.

The following case study describes a situation when ownership of certain portions of the process and the data involved was not firmly established.

*Case Study*

The company was a fairly new but profitable midsized electronic assembly house. The buyers, while completing the data on the Purchase Requisition, would enter the name (sometimes abbreviated) of the supplier with whom they placed the order.

Later the data entry clerk who processed the requisition typed in this supplier information to the system Purchase Order entry screen. Various suppliers' "order-from" and "remit-to" addresses would appear on the screen. The *clerk* then attempted to match the supplier name with the addresses. Many times there were multiple choices and many times the clerk entered the wrong address. The accounts payable department, though concerned for the error, attempted to provide the correct information resulting in further confusion.

A consultant, during an audit of the process, discovered this irregularity. During a meeting with purchasing personnel, he established that the "ownership" of the validity of the data (order-from and remit-to) fell on the buyer. The buyer, after all, is the one on the telephone with that supplier and the only person qualified to ascertain the correct addresses.

After establishing ownership, the next step was to institute a policy that required the buyer to be responsible for the supplier's address information. The ensuing procedure directed the buyer, while on the telephone, to enter the actual supplier number that matched the supplier name.

This change of the "ownership" of the data from the data entry clerk to the buyer virtually eliminated billing errors in the accounts payable department and the mailing of confirming purchase orders was more accurate.

By establishing a policy of ownership of data, that owner is in a much more favorable position to delegate responsibilities which will provide a basis for effective management of problems before they occur.

**Step 3. Assign Ownership of the Process (Tasks).** It is not enough to assign ownership of the data; you must also establish ownership of what is done with the data. It's not unlike taking home a bicycle from the store marked "Some assembly required". First you are instructed to identify and inventory the parts and then you are told how to put them together. As simple as this analogy is, many businesses do not follow such simple rules and as a result are not as efficient as they could be.

There are many processes and subprocesses in any purchasing operation. In essence, the processes are the everyday tasks necessary to prepare and execute a purchase order. Some of these are locating a supplier, and establishing price, delivery, and terms. However, the list does not stop there. A buyer may be required to write letters, prepare contracts, expedite late orders, report on progress or establish long-term arrangements with suppliers. All these activities combine to form the purchasing process and you need to have well-defined procedures for them in order to maintain consistency and continuity of operations.

***Step 4. Develop Mutual Goals.*** These are essential for effective operations. When you establish your objectives you must also consider their impact on interdependent departments. What may be a productive procedure for handling a receiving problem from a buyer's viewpoint may be counterproductive from the receiving clerk's standpoint. You should solidify and emphasize the importance of those goals for all parties when setting your objectives.

Another example of a counterproductive objective is one that requires the lowest possible price, without adequately addressing the quality and delivery issues. The goal of manufacturing—to produce a set number of parts in a particular time frame—would not be satisfied if parts were not on time or were rejected before reaching production. Therefore, strict adherence to such a purchasing goal would be counterproductive to the goal of manufacturing.

A procedure that would address such an issue would have to emanate from a level of management that combines both of these departments. A Plant Manager would be one such possibility. The origination of a procedure must be, not only at a level necessary to provide adequate control of the impact of that policy, but approved by each dependent organization.

So you need to share your purchasing objectives with all of your interdependent departments to ensure continuity of purpose.

***Step 5. Explain the Procedure.*** Now you can explain what happens, what tasks are involved and the step by step flow of operations that will accomplish the task. A diagram or flowchart of some procedures that have multiple steps may surprise you as to just how involved the process is.

***Step 6. Identify the Originator of the Policy or Procedure.*** Blanket policies and procedures can be generic enough that no one pays much attention to them and when changes are necessary, you may not be sure who is responsible.

All requirements must include the name of the person or department responsible for maintaining, evaluating and altering that requirement.

Since we have said that it is necessary to document any policy or procedure, it therefore is necessary to include in that documentation the name of the entity to contact for questions or changes.

## TYPICAL PROBLEM AREAS THAT REQUIRE PROCEDURES TO HELP MAINTAIN CONTROL OVER PURCHASING FUNCTIONS

### Setting Buyer Commitment Limits to Help Regulate Ownership

Probably the most important control is that of the level of dollar value a buyer is allowed to commit. You certainly would not allow a new buyer with a few weeks' experience to commit the company to a million-dollar contract without some form of review by higher authority. Nevertheless, such situations exist.

One way that commitment authorizations may be determined is by the number of years of buying experience or according to position title. The following matrix of commitment levels may be used as a guideline:

| POSITION | EXPERIENCE | COMMIT UP TO: |
| --- | --- | --- |
| Purchasing Trainee | 2 to 26 wks | $ 5,000.00 |
| Purchasing Specialist | 1 to 2 yrs | $ 10,000.00 |
| Junior Buyer | 2 to 3 yrs | $ 25,000.00 |
| Senior Buyer | 3 to 5 yrs | $ 50,000.00 |
| Purchasing Manager | | $100,000.00 |
| Materials Manager | | $250,000.00 |
| Plant Manager | | Unlimited |

Note: The purchasing manager reports to the materials manager who reports to the plant manager. Other echelons of management may or may not exist but the idea is to provide a level of checks and balances for approval of the expenditure of funds.

The authority to commit is usually given by the next higher authorized individual by obtaining his signature on the purchase requisition prior to the buyer giving the order to the supplier.

This brings up another interesting commitment requirement, that of the requesting department. It would not be prudent to allow a new engineer to request a piece of test equipment costing over $100,000 without some authorization from those who maintain that department's budget. You need a procedure to require that a department manager review and approve the purchase requisition prior to sending it to purchasing. Therefore, you should also establish a matrix of these *requisitioner commitment limits*, similar to the purchasing department matrix, and the authority of the signature should be reviewed by the buyer who orders the material.

In some larger organizations the Finance or Accounting Departments may also become involved in the commitment level requirement. As a check and balance requirement, the purchase requisition may be short-stopped between the requisitioner and purchasing in order to formally have a third party confirm the availability of funds in the requesting department's budget.

As a further note to the commitment level subject, the approval levels obtained by the requisitioner and finance are generally based upon the *estimated commitment* or cost suggested by the requisitioner. Should the buyer determine that the actual purchase price or total commitment is far greater than the estimate, the requisition must be sent back for further authorization prior to placing the order. As a form of policy, purchasing management should make buyers aware of these limitations in requisitioner authorization and instruct buyers to return underauthorized requisitions to the requisitioner for the required approval. The purchasing manager may set a percentage variance (over or under the estimate) to improve efficiency.

## How to Decide When Just a Purchase Order Is Not Enough Protection

In order to protect the company's interests, define a policy that limits expenditures (covered solely by a routine purchase order). The terms and conditions you may have included with your purchase order may not be adequate protection when large expenditures are made. If a purchased part is to be specially manufactured, the supplier may require more terms to protect his company. In any event, you should establish a policy that covers the limits of routine purchase order terms and conditions.

The general criterion most companies use is the dollar value of the commitment. One company may require a separate contract for all purchases over $100,000. Another may use a custom contract for any "Build to print" items to ensure the exactness of the specifications. A third criterion for a contract is when proprietary design or patents are involved. In these instances, the standard terms and conditions on a purchase order may be inadequate to define the intellectual property rights involved in patent issues.

### Ensuring That All Company Employees Understand Vendor Relations and Ethical Purchasings Practices

The purchasing department's contact with the outside world, the vendor, requires policy direction. Issues such as vendor visits, back-door selling (to nonpurchasing personnel), and gifts and gratuities can have a major impact on the integrity of the business and cause legal implications as well. These policies should be spelled out in a booklet, distributed to all purchasing personnel, all plant personnel who deal with vendors, and to the vendors themselves. Many companies have such booklets available in the lobby designated for vendor visits. Procedures to cover special circumstances might be: escorting visiting vendors, gifts and gratuities, conduct on visits to vendor locations, and so on.

The maintenance of sound ethical principles during the conduct of business is probably the most essential reason for a policy in any business. The National Association of Realtors thought enough of the ethical relationship between buyers, sellers, and agents to publish a 200-page *Code of Ethics* with interpretations.

Gone are the days when the golden rule was all that was needed to ensure a fiduciary business relationship. Today we must manage our business under the scrutiny from many fronts. What may appear usual and customary for one person may be labeled flagrant misconduct by another. In the United States, bribes are illegal and buyers are told to maintain an *arm's length* relationship with their suppliers. As we become increasingly involved in the global marketplace the handling of variances in ethical behavior must be addressed. Guidelines must be written down and discussions made to prevent misunderstandings.

### How To Develop Operating Procedures

The military has a common term for operating procedures called Standard Operating Procedures (SOPs). Possibly due to this origin, SOPs, as such, have never been popular with business organizations, especially smaller operations. Nevertheless, the advantage of a printed reference document is invaluable in setting limits, maintaining control and resolving disputes.

A buyer asks, "What do I do in case of . . . ?" That buyer should be able to pick up the manual and resolve the problem rather than asking his coworkers who may offer several conflicting answers. Certain procedures tend to be easy to document while others may be more subjective. The following is a recommended list of subjects that might be included in your operating procedure:

- Purchasing Commitment Levels
- Supplier Selection and Certification
- Supplier Surveys and Audits
- Requisition Processing
- Purchase Order Processing
- Blanket Purchase Order Processing
- Request for Quotation processing
- Economic Ordering Quantity
- Purchase Order Alterations and Cancellations
- Expediting
- Emergency P.O. Processing
- Billed Not Received/Received Not Billed Procedure
- Repair Order Procedure
- Return To Vendor Procedure
- Invoice processing
- Price/Quantity Variance Procedure
- Expedited Transportation Procedure
- Minority Supplier Handling
- Contract Administration
- Contract Negotiations
- International Purchasing
- Cost Savings Reporting

Sample procedures relating to the above list may be found in the *Policy and Procedures Manual for Purchasing and Materials Control* by Prentice Hall.

One important fact to keep in mind is that the people actually performing the work are probably the most effective resource in formulating and updating any procedure. In addition to the obvious benefits of consulting with your employees on matters of operations is the added benefit of *consensus* which facilitates the implementation of any resulting procedure. Figure 9-2 provides a form that you can use as a guideline for preparing the final copy of your procedure.

| Title: | | POP # | Rev# |
|---|---|---|---|
| Primary Area: | | Effective Date: | |
| Supercedes POP # | Rev# | Page: | |
| Submitted by: | Approved By: | | |

PURPOSE: The purpose of this procedure is to.........

SCOPE:  This procedure applies to [ persons, functions, groups]

INTER-DEPENDENCIES: [ What other entities enter into this process]

RESPONSIBILITIES: [ List for each organization]

PROCESS: [ Describe what happens, step by step, include a flow

ohart if neoessary.]

Figure 9-2. Sample Form for Defining Procurement Operating Procedures

It is also beneficial to route any draft procedure through those dependent organizations that will interface with purchasing during the application of the procedure. Obtain their signature of approval before you implement the procedure. Again, involvement and consensus are important in ensuring the smooth operation of the final product.

## How to Accept or Reject Purchase Requisitions to Help Control Rework

You should provide a purchasing procedure which deals with the acceptance of a requisition in purchasing. The word acceptance implies that purchasing, in fact, has provided some policy, some criteria for that acceptance (or rejection) of a requisition. Some pertinent items included in that procedure should be:

- Requisitioner must complete all items.
- Requisitioner must provide sufficient item description and sourcing advice.
- Requisitioner's management approval (proper level) must be completed.

By shading required requisitioner blocks, both the requisitioner and the buyer are able to see at a glance if all pertinent areas are completed. The sufficiency of the completed information is a somewhat more subjective criterion. Familiarity and communication between buyers and requisitioners are needed to determine how much descriptive product and sourcing information is necessary. Sourcing advice or suggestions by the requisitioner can further aid you in determining from which source the item may be available. The sourcing, in most cases, should be generic enough to allow room for you to provide alternative sourcing suggestions subject to the requisitioner's approval.

An example of an insufficient suggested source might be a request for a "binomial rear actuating recilitator" with a suggested source of "distributor." This type of request would surely necessitate a call to the requisitioner for further information. Requisitioners are not always available and days of phone-tag cause delays in processing the requisition. A policy that would aid the buyer in resolving this problem would be simply to return the requisition and pass the responsibility for delay back to the requisitioner. Naturally this will delay the delivery of the parts but not cause a delay chargeable to purchasing. After repeated returns due to insufficient information the requisitioner should "get the message." If not, a management meeting between the departments to ascertain requirements would be indicated.

Approvals by management on accounting should be required for all requisitions. Some companies prefer to allow nonmanagement employees to submit requisitions that do not exceed a nominal amount, possibly $200 for exempt employees and $1000 for supervisors or foremen.

An alternative policy is to delegate to some central departmental authority (a requisition analyst perhaps), approved by management to maintain departmental expenditures. This is advisable in organizations with large ordering requirements such as production requirements, parts cribs, or administrative stores. By submitting daily reports of requisition expenditures, the requisitioning manager then may approve the daily "requisition summary" with one signature. That summary would accompany that day's requisitions to purchasing and serve as the authorizing signature.

### How to Control Requests for Information

The Request for Information (RFI), in its formal written form, is rarely used by small companies or for standard items. Required information is rather obtained by telephone or from sales representatives. The reasoning behind the RFI is to gather detailed comparative product and/or market information from a number of suppliers in a short time.

While resembling the format of a Request for Quotation, Bid, or Proposal (RFQ, RFB, RFP), the RFI must include a definite statement that the RFI is not to be construed as a formal request for pricing, that no purchase orders will be placed relating to the supplier's response and that you are seeking only information at this time.

Many companies use the RFI to gather information which will assist them in a "make versus buy" decision. If you choose to use this method for gathering information you will generally save valuable time on the part of both the requisitioners and purchasing. You must obtain sufficient parameters describing the requisitioner's need. Also you should set a policy establishing a dollar limit for the use of the RFI in order to minimize its over use on small projects.

### How to Become Involved in Make versus Buy Decisions

The sourcing information known to purchasing can become a valuable asset to requisitioners and management considering a *make versus buy* decision. The procedure recommendation here is to establish a purchasing representative who attends the meeting where such decisions are made. This person would coordinate documentation, such as the gathering of RFI specifications, between the decision makers and purchasing.

### Using Requests for Quotation to Ensure Consistent Bidding Procedures

When to quote and when not to quote should be covered by a policy that is in the best interest of time and the protection of the company's assets. For example, the practice of compiling a written Request for Quotation (RFQ) for a handful of resistors totaling $100 may not be advantageous to your goals. Some purchasing departments, however, require written quotes on all items, although this is not cost effective.

Most companies would agree that an RFQ would be helpful for defining pricing and terms on a $100,000 purchase. The decision to set policy for formal (written) RFQs might contain the following criteria:

- Total annual commitment for an item
- Complexity of the item to be purchased
- Prior experience in purchasing the item
- Unit prices exceeding $X
- Line item extensions exceeding $X
- Purchase order totals exceeding $X
- Term of commitment exceeding X weeks
- Term of delivery exceeding X weeks
- Proprietary materials involved
- Engineering specifications involved

In addition to the above criteria, set a level of ownership or responsibility to the information. For example, engineering must own the specifications and their validity. Production planning must own the quantities and dates of deliveries. The product manager must own the pricing decisions and set targets related to negotiation and acceptance of pricing and terms. The purchasing manager owns the process by which the items are ordered.

Procedures like the following will help the flow of information from suppliers by setting limits on when to use a:

- Telephone request—Written response
- Telephone request—FAX response
- Written request—Written response
- Next-day-air request—Next-day-air response
- Fax request—Fax response

The procedure should include definitions of the amount and type of information required related to the feasibility of transmittal and limitations of the media. For example, detailed engineering specifications are not easily transmitted by telephone and 20-page responses including drawings and charts transmitted by FAX can be unreadable. Needless expense and/or delay may be caused by not predetermining procedures related to the management of this part of the RFQ process.

The number of suppliers to quote is another issue that may be facilitated by a predetermined procedure. If you quote just a few suppliers you may not have enough information to make an effective decision to buy. Too many suppliers quoted can cause unnecessary work in analyzing the responses. Some criteria relating to the number of sources to quote are:

- Did you get enough information through the RFI process?
- Are the suppliers selected to bid knowledgeable?
- Is the technology new?
- Does the high-dollar value purchase cause you to be more cautious?
- What is the time available for processing the RFQ?
- Do you desire to expand your supplier base?

Procedures established to spell out these directions will enhance consistency in your organization and will result in less exposure to a hit-or-miss approach to managing high dollar purchases.

### Making Sure Your Source Selection Is Consistent

In most organizations the responsibility for source selection is assigned to purchasing. However, in the case of contract manufacturing or development projects other departments or even your customers may become involved. Requisitioners and customers sometimes insist on a single source or the use of an Approved Vendor List (AVL) when purchasing parts. However, since there are many factors other than price or quality involved in any source selection, purchasing, through company policy, should be allowed a significant amount of authority in this area.

The purchasing department's view of the performance of any supplier includes the supplier's ability to deliver, provide appropriate documentation and invoices, and generally maintain effective communication with buyers (see Chapter 6 for other cost considerations).

### Defining How Contracts Are Administered

Based on the procedures in Chapter 8 relating to negotiations, you will need to provide approved guidelines for the activities of the buyer and the other departments or individuals involved in contract negotiations. The procedures used to form the negotiating team, formulate the strategy, approve changes and concession points must be documented. Identify in detail the responsibilities of each person and organization in order to maintain integrity and continuity of purpose in these matters. (The Prentice Hall *Policies and Procedures Manual for Purchasing and Materials Control* provides some effective guidelines for this purpose.)

When it comes time for all internal organizations to approve a negotiated contract the problems usually arise due to a lack of a preapproved *standard contract*. The procedure of establishing such a vehicle greatly reduces time and conflict and enhances communication. The necessity for all dependent organizations to understand and support standard terms and conditions also facilitates supplier relations.

The following case study illustrates an instance where the absence of a well-defined procedure caused undue delay in establishing a contract.

### Case Study

With contract draft in hand, the buyer proceeded to negotiate with the supplier. Terms and conditions were addressed, specifications for assembly and test were sorted out and agreements made between the parties. The buyer returned home and prepared the results in *final draft* form. The next step was to obtain the signatures of all internal parties related to the contract. When the buyer circulated the final draft for internal approval he was aghast at the response.

Engineering decided that it now wanted an engineering change prior to the signing. Planning requested a change in the delivery dates and quantities. Finance became embroiled in a controversy with warranty terms. The legal department insisted on "word-smithing" the language in no less than six succeeding re-drafts.

In each of the above instances, the buyer was obliged to contact the supplier to get his concurrence on the changes. The exercise spanned 18 months, during which the product was already being manufactured on authority of a one page *letter of intent.* As each succeeding month wore on the buyer's leverage with the supplier was eroded due to the fact that the supplier now was so deep into the process of manufacturing the part that he now had the power to dictate his own terms.

There was no calculation of the dollars lost due to the delays caused by the lack of firm decisions by the parties and absence of a preapproved contract.

The company's contracting procedure was corrected to require that a standard contract would be approved and sent with the initial RFQ to the supplier. After the supplier and the company decided on the language from the original negotiation, no further changes were to be requested without upper management approval.

The prior existence of a procedure for handling such matters would have eliminated the misunderstandings and resulting conflict in the case study above. Your credibility with suppliers will be greatly improved as well.

## HOW TO USE CONTROLS TO MONITOR ———————— YOUR PURCHASING PROCEDURES ————————

One of the most difficult operations to manage in any business is formation of the mechanisms necessary to monitor conditions and rate performance under your existing procedures. Purchasing management must have accurate and timely feedback in order to be able to measure buyer achievement, workload administration, supplier performance, costs, burdens, efficiencies, effectiveness, and so on. Purchasing must know when it is in control.

Therefore, it is paramount that a system of measurements and audits be established that will:

- Be understandable
- Require the minimum of maintenance and review
- Provide ready access to pertinent information
- Allow for qualitative as well as quantitative perspectives. The quality (lack of errors) of requisitions processed is just as important as the quantity of requisitions processed.

It is helpful to provide periodic graphs of a supplier's performance and view them like the familiar "sales chart" with the trend either going up or down. Some samples of these types of graphs are provided on pages 227 to 232. Of course you may make them by hand if you have obtained the required data.

## Use a Purchase Order History to Measure Purchasing Activities

A data base should include some means of analyzing purchase order statistics. These records are referred to as purchase order histories. (Although this information can be calculated without a computer, the process is very time consuming.) Included in such a data base might be the following purchase order information:

- Activity by buyer
- Activity by supplier
- Activity by department ordered
- Activity by department placed
- Number of requisitions vs. number of P.O.s
- Total supplier commitments

In reviewing such a database, purchasing management will be able to justify actions to improve the flow of work. Trends that may appear are:

| Problem Area | Possible Solution |
|---|---|
| 1. Too many orders placed by a particular buyer | Additional resources needed in that area |
| 2. Too many suppliers | Consolidate order placement with a smaller supplier base. |
| 3. Difficulty in judging buyer appraisals | Dollar commitments by a buyer may be used as criteria |
| 4. High total supplier commitment for the year compared with a report of that supplier's total revenue | Reduce dependence on that supplier to preserve his solvency should you have no more requirements for him. |

This valuable tool, the P.O. History application, although used primarily by larger companies, can be custom designed for your needs or purchased outright through a number of sources. (See Chapter 10 for information on software sources.)

## Develop a Supplier History to Measure Supplier Performance

The formation of a database solely related to suppliers may be included as a part of the P.O. History program. The object is to design a means for a detailed evaluation of a supplier based on the following information:

- Quality performance
- Delivery performance
- Billed Not Received/Received Not Billed activity
- Invoice referral activity (wrong price, terms and so on)
- Pricing competitiveness comparisons
- Receiving referral (no packing slip, wrong information, no part number)

The ability to statistically measure the performance characteristics of a supplier is too often disregarded by many companies. It is not unusual to find two buyers, responsible for the same commodity, having totally opposite opinions of the performance characteristics of the same supplier. A formal evaluation is essential, and will allow you to step back and review the supplier's performance from a totally statistical and objective point of view. We will expand on this area later in the section on "Effectiveness Reports."

## Use Commodity Codes to Group Purchases

The finance and accounting areas will probably be the first to suggest the use of commodity codes. These codes are used to track particular product groups, sort them for depreciable capital items and further identify specific areas within purchased materials. Commodity codes, unlike internal part numbers, can more accurately facilitate data sort capabilities, a necessity in today's computer environment.

Most companies use a four-digit numbering system such as "9062" for grouping like products. The following example is just one possible method used to classify your commodities:

| | | |
|---|---|---|
| 1000 | Administrative Supplies | |
| | 1100 | Services |
| | 1200 | Repairs |
| 2000 | Production | |
| | 2100 | Services |
| | 2200 | Repairs |
| | 2300 | Packaging |
| | 2400 | Components |
| | | 2410 Semiconductors |
| | | 2420 Resistors |
| | | 2430 Capacitors |
| | | 2440 Printed circuit boards |
| | 2500 | Sub Assemblies |
| | | 2510 Power supplies |
| | | 2520 Card Assemblies |
| 3000 | Non-production | |
| | 3100 | Services |
| | 3200 | Repairs |
| 4000 | Capital Assets | |
| 5000 | Facilities | |
| | 5100 | Services |
| | 5210 | Lighting |
| | | 5211 Lamps, fluorescent |
| | | 5212 Lamps, incandescent |
| | | 5213 Lamps, instrument |

The only limitation in selecting the categories to classify and/or track is in the time you wish to spend analyzing this information. The proper code should be entered on each purchase requisition by the requisitioner or accounting.

The benefits of such a system are many. Using a database program (or simply Lotus 1-2-3), anyone will be able to analyze the flow of materials through your system. Some principal benefits are:

- Combining of similar orders to one vendor
- Establishing average market pricing
- Selecting areas for cost reduction
- Managing department budgets

If your small company does not employ a commodity code system you should at least provide some means, for tax purposes, of identifying those depreciable versus expense items and production versus nonproduction expenses.

## HOW TO USE MEASUREMENTS AND REPORTS
## ——————— TO TELL HOW YOU'RE DOING ———————

Without some means of determining the status and effectiveness of the controls you have installed to manage your business, you will never be quite sure whether you are, in fact, operating in the mode you have designed. Those people who have to keep track of measurements and produce reports say that they are cumbersome and time consuming, but for management they are indispensable. You must know when you are succeeding or deviating from the prescribed path.

Categorize your measurements into two activity classifications, *efficiency* and *effectiveness*. The basic difference between these ratings is that the efficiency ratings generally involve productivity or the time to do something and the effectiveness ratings relate to cost savings. Peter Drucker would look at this as efficiency is getting the right work done; effectiveness is getting the work done right.

For example efficiency measurements are those designed to monitor the flow of operations, manage workload and resource distribution (equipment and personnel) and assess or appraise the activities of your employees. Effectiveness measurements, on the other hand, relate to the accomplishment of the company's strategic goals. A measurement of effectiveness would be the cost savings accumulated in relation to the pricing objectives of the marketing and planning areas. Another such effectiveness measurement would be a decrease in the number of buyer's errors when completing a purchase requisition.

In the area of efficiency, the number of requisitions placed by a buyer is a measurement of his relative capability compared to buyers with similar commodities. You must note, however, that a buyer required to negotiate large dollar purchases will most likely have a lower requisition volume processed than an MRO buyer. Therefore, the measurement may have to be weighted in relation to the complexity of the job.

## Efficiency Reports That Help You Manage Time

*The Open Requisition Report.* This report helps purchasing manage the distribution of requisitions. This report tracks a requisition in and out of the purchasing function and tabulates the number of days between its receipt in purchasing and the placement of a P.O. from that requisition. The number of days in purchasing will monitor the efficiency of individual buyers by monitoring their expeditious handling of the paper. Again, a requisition that requires several months of quotations and negotiations will be rated differently than one for $100 worth of secretarial supplies.

*The Burden Report.* This report helps track your costs of doing the business of purchasing. It tracks the expenditures of certain areas of purchasing in relation to the cost of maintaining that area in terms of personnel and overhead. As an example, the MRO area may purchase a total of $2,000,000 worth of products with a budgetary staffing cost of $60,000. That is a purchasing burden rate which is 3% of expenditures. On the other hand, a capital equipment area may spend $12,000,000 with a staff cost of only $30,000 and a burden rate of only .0025%.

This points up the fact that it costs more to manage the large volume of paper required for small orders than it does to negotiate a small volume of large purchases. You need to monitor the trends of these expenses over time to help distribute the workload.

## Effectiveness Reports Grade Your Thoroughness

*Invoice Variance Report.* Invoice referrals can point out a lack of communication. An Invoice Variance Report covers the number of discrepancies between the information received on the supplier's invoice and what was agreed to when the Purchase Order was placed with that supplier. A discrepancy in the quantity, price, payment terms, or other information will require you to contact the supplier in order to resolve the issue.

A great amount of such variances may indicate a less than communicative relationship between the buyer and the supplier. By measuring a supplier's accurate handling of an order it focuses on that supplier's effectiveness. On the other hand, the buyer may not be totally accurate in filling out the information. Either way, the end result of such miscommunication is rework and extra costs in time and effort.

*Receiving Variance Report.* A report on receiving variances tests the supplier's accuracy. Receiving must match the quantity of each item on the actual Purchase Order, the vendor's packing slip quantity and the actual count made by receiving. Any discrepancy in the numbers must be reported to the responsible buyer for resolution. This report is another measurement of a supplier's effectiveness.

However, your own receiving department may cause an error in the counting, inventorying or otherwise documenting the material received. This proverbial "search for the blame" is the nemesis of many buyers. Nevertheless, the buyer is ultimately responsible for the supplier's performance to the requirements of the Purchase Order.

Other problems relating to incoming shipments can be:

- Purchase order number is not on the packing slip
- Your required internal part number is missing
- Manufacturer identification or part number is missing
- Items are counted by bags or rolls on invoice versus pieces on purchase orders
- Required data sheets (e.g., for chemicals) are missing

All of the above can cause the receiving clerk to have difficulty in identifying or counting the items, to be confused about where to send the items, and be unsure of any special storage or handling requirements. Again, communication is the key and this report measures the effectiveness of this communication.

***On-time Delivery Reports.*** Another rating is a supplier's *On-time Delivery Report* which measures the percentage of deliveries from that supplier that arrived on the promised date. Many buyers think they can keep these figures in their head. What they tend to remember is the complaints of their requisitioners and not the actual delivery performance of a supplier.

The arrival of a shipment from a supplier may be contingent on several outside factors such as delays by the carrier (trucking company, ship, air cargo, and so on), customs delays for foreign shipments or even weather delays. There is little excuse, however, for early shipments which can also be detrimental to your inventory costs.

You need to establish a *window* for delivery that will allow for normal fluctuations in the above criteria while at the same time protecting your requirements. A possible solution is to consider as *on-time* any shipment that is one week early or two weeks late, forming a three week window. By informing your inventory and production control areas of this criterion they will be better able to plan accordingly.

The measurement criteria must also be communicated to your suppliers. They will want to know how they are being judged in this area, compared to other suppliers.

***Rejection Reports.*** These help monitor the supplier's quality. The number of "quality rejects" is a good measurement of the buyer's selection of a supplier as well as the effectiveness of a supplier. You must have adequate communication of your specifications to a supplier in order to perform this measurement effectively.

Many times the specifications will be the supplier's own published specifications that you are using for a measurement. Naturally if the supplier is not meeting his own requirements, yours will suffer as well.

***Audits and Surveys.*** The term *audit* generally implies something other than a pleasant experience, as when one receives a notice from the Internal Revenue Service that his income tax will be audited. So, for those interfaces with a supplier, we will refer to *surveys* instead of audits. Audits (of your own purchasing function) will also be addressed.

In purchasing, the most common survey is a trip to a supplier to ascertain his capabilities. Generally some dollar commitment limit is placed upon the necessity of this type of survey due to the time and expense to travel to suppliers. The survey is sometimes conducted by a buyer alone, but often the buyer may be accompanied by an engineer knowledgeable about the anticipated purchase or the manufacturing process to be used. (Figure 9-3 provides a sample form for a supplier survey.)

Another type of survey is one conducted at that supplier who maintains a file of your confidential information or proprietary materials. It will be necessary for the buyer and/or a security person to check that file at least annually to ensure the proper safeguarding of your information.

Some guidelines for inspecting the material are contained in the audit form in Figure 9-4.

Forms such as these shown in Figures 9-3 and 9-4 should be modified in accordance with your particular business or requirements. These forms are valuable reference tools for others in your company who will not have the opportunity to see first hand what conditions prevail at your supplier.

A type of *audit* performed in your own purchasing area is one used to cross check compliance with controls and procedures. Purchase orders and requisitions should be reviewed periodically by a person not directly associated with the controlled process to check compliance on the following:

1. Proper dollar commitment signatures (requisitioner/buyer)
2. Quotation documentation
3. Single source justifications
4. Coding requirements

For example, mechanical parts buyers might audit electrical parts buyers, senior buyers audit junior buyers, managers audit senior buyers and so forth.

## SUPPLIER SURVEY

Company _____

Address _____

City _____ State _____ Zip ____

Contact Person _____ Phone _____

Describe the location and condition of the facility _____

_____

Type of business _____

Approximate size of facility _____

Office area _____ % manufacturing _____ %. whse _____ %.

General appearance _____

_____

Total employees _____ administrative _____ production _____

Describe manufacturing operation; automation, organization, cleanliness, workers, supervision, morale: _____

_____

_____

_____

Describe purchasing operation; # personnel, organization, efficiency, reports:

_____

_____

_____

Surveyor's general opinion of supplier, the facility and operation:

_____

_____

_____

_____

Recommendation: Pass _____ Fail _____

Signed: _____ Date: _____

     Surveyor

**Figure 9-3. Sample Supplier Survey**

# SECURITY SURVEY

Company _____

Address _____

City _____ State _____ Zip ___

Contact Person _____ Phone _____

Describe the location of the facility _____

_____

Entry facility controlled by: (Yes/No)

|  | Business hours | After hours |
| --- | --- | --- |
| Receptionist | _____ | _____ |
| Guard | _____ | _____ |
| Controlled Access System | _____ | _____ |
| Visitor Log | _____ | _____ |
| Contractor Log | _____ | _____ |
| Escort Required | _____ | _____ |

Security Guard employee of company (Yes/No) _____

Contract Guard company: _____

Bonded (Yes/No) _____

Janitorial service by company (Yes/No) _____

Contract janitorial service company: _____

Bonded (Yes/No) _____

Confidential Material stored in:

Room _____

Cabinet _____

Access to confidential material controlled by: _____

_____

Inventory of transmitted material results: _____

_____

_____

_____

Other comments by surveyor: ⸺⸺⸺⸺⸺⸺⸺⸺⸺⸺⸺

⸺⸺⸺⸺⸺⸺⸺⸺⸺⸺⸺⸺⸺⸺⸺⸺⸺⸺⸺⸺⸺

⸺⸺⸺⸺⸺⸺⸺⸺⸺⸺⸺⸺⸺⸺⸺⸺⸺⸺⸺⸺⸺

Recommendation: Pass ⸺⸺⸺⸺⸺⸺⸺ Fail ⸺⸺⸺⸺⸺

Signed: ⸺⸺⸺⸺⸺⸺⸺⸺⸺ Date: ⸺⸺⸺⸺⸺
         Surveyor

**Figure 9-4. Sample Security Survey**

Though time consuming, such an audit is necessary to ensure that policies and procedures are being followed.

## How to Interpret Reports to Maximize Their Usefulness

To effectively manage a purchasing function you must be able to recognize, at a glance, when problems appear. Indicators of problem areas in a manufacturing environment are called *defect criteria*. By using this available term and the process of correcting the problem, you will greatly improve your management skills.

There are two types of measurements *quantitative* and *qualitative*. Quantitative measurements (the *number* of things) are the easiest to measure because they are objective. If, for instance, you decide that all purchase requisitions should be converted to a purchase order within 15 days, then the number of open purchase requisitions still not placed by the buyer after that time can be measured as a percentage of the total. The buyer received 100 requisitions during the month of June and, of those received, 95 were placed as orders. The buyer receives a measurement of 95%.

As a defect criteria you may wish to set a 10% limit. With this workload management indicator, if one-half of your buyers continually fall below 90% of requisitions placed, you may need to make a decision to increase personnel, redistribute work, or institute training to resolve the problem of not meeting your goals.

Similarly, a divergence in a supplier's "on-time delivery" will indicate the necessity for corrective action. The date agreed to by the supplier and the buyer for delivery on your dock will become the benchmark. You may allow a grace period of five days late or 10 days early. If the delivery does not fall within this window, the supplier needs to be contacted. However, you need to establish a percentage of "not-on-time delivery."

This percentage will become your defect criteria, a quantitative measurement.

A qualitative measurement is a more subjective criterion to determine. The quality of something is generally considered in terms of how long it will last, how well it was done or how much rework was required.

These criteria could be used to evaluate the thoroughness of internal procedures and how often they need to be revised. Quality in communication with the supplier means the buyer makes the most effective use of time and resolves problems efficiently without undue delay. Quality measures the *effectiveness* of a buyer just as quantity measures the efficiency.

Quality is important in the accuracy of transferring information from a purchase requisition to a purchase order. Quality is the efficient management of time and the accomplishment of activities without excess overtime. Quality may be simply getting to work on time, not hanging around talking about the ballgame, or too many trips to the break area.

Many of these qualitative measurements appear to fall into the category of employee appraisal. So do the quantitative measurements. Both must be considered as important criteria for the successful management of purchasing personnel and operations.

## CORRECTING PROBLEM AREAS TO IMPROVE PURCHASING EFFICIENCY AND EFFECTIVENESS

When and if you determine that you are out of control it is necessary to make adjustments to bring the operation back on course. Before you can make any determination, you must first understand the deviations and what factors came to bear in causing the deviation. You must determine also what organizations and persons have impact on the measurement.

For example, consider a late delivery. If a delivery is not received on time there are several organizations involved:

- the supplier
- the buyer
- the carrier
- the receiving area
- the inspection area

Did the buyer communicate the required delivery date to the supplier and did the supplier acknowledge that date in writing? Was the product shipped by the supplier in plenty of time to arrive at your company on time? Did the *proof-of-delivery* report show the actual date the shipment was signed for at your receiving dock? Was there a delay in passing the product through inspection because of a lack of specifications, test equipment, trained personnel? Was the product rejected and reshipped by the supplier?

There are many reasons why the product may not be *officially* received. Before you can begin to cast stones you must be in possession of all the facts. Then you will be in a good position to begin to correct recurring problems.

New procedures may be necessary. Training of personnel in various areas could be indicated. Better communication with the supplier, a change in carriers, better specifications, a change of supplier, all are possible solutions. You may find that the buyers do not fully understand the commodities they have been assigned.

Measurements and reports are of little value if they do not point out areas that need improvement. And if corrective action resulting in an improved situation does not follow, the time and effort required to generate such reports is wasted.

## RECOGNIZING AND REWARDING THE PURCHASING STAFF FOR COMPLIANCE WITH POLICIES AND PROCEDURES

Admonishments and adjustments for noncompliance should be balanced with recognition of employees who meet requirements as well as for those who exhibit superior effort. The subject of recognition, although ever present, needs to be formalized and become a major item of visibility to upper management.

Industry today has made a significant movement to reduce middle management, increase worker to management ratios and enhance the responsibilities of nonmanagement personnel. Coupled with this are the constraints put on "real salary" enhancements in order to manage the rising costs of benefits and reduce the exposure to inflation.

If employees are asked to excel, within the guidelines of the aforementioned controls and measurements, you must have well-designed programs to recognize individual and group efforts that are realizable as a direct result of those efforts.

Awards of a material and monetary nature are just a few of the options. Additional responsibility coupled with enhanced position and title can lead to an expansion of the job description and result in an expanded career path.

When individual effort results in the resolution of a difficult mission, a "dinner-for-two" is an effective reward. Awarded as soon after the completion of the project as possible, the effect of the hard work will be forgotten and the joy of completion remembered.

If, through personal effort, a buyer is able to save your company $100,000, don't pass it off as "it's just the buyer's job." That buyer may not be so eager in the future to offer his personal time and effort to that great extent the next time. Ensure that there is financial support from top management in the form of meaningful recognition for exceptional circumstances. An "achievement award" of $500 or $1,000 will be a great incentive for that individual to continue to excel.

Not to be overlooked are the intrinsic values that are linked to publicity. It is a rare occurrence for purchasing to be lauded in the company newspaper or interviewed for an article in a national periodical. The local daily and weekly newspapers are also good sources for publicity.

By applying a concerted effort toward communications and public relations, you can increase the prestige value of not only your employees but of the overall purchasing function as well.

These recognition methods have been proven to increase worker satisfaction and productivity. Tracking and reporting them in conjunction with planned target requirements can serve to motivate management and supervisors to encourage high performance from employees.

## CONCLUSION

As the business changes, so do the controls. As the purchasing manager, you must continually modify your policy, update your procedures, adapt your controls, adjust your measurements, and redefine your reports. As goals are reached, set new and higher ones. As missions are accomplished, make new ones. As employees succeed, give them new challenges. Such continual attention to these areas will ensure the efficiency and effectiveness of your organization is maintained as well as the inner vitality of your company.

# CHAPTER TEN

# How to Use Computers to Increase Purchasing Productivity

A computer is not the answer to all of purchasing's problems, as some sales reps promise. Purchasing's problems, however, in today's fast-paced, shrinking, global business world, can become unmanageable if computer technology is not brought on the scene. Manufacturing operations have adopted what they call Computer Aided Manufacturing (CAM). Engineers have sought the use of the computer for Computed Aided Design (CAD). The latest offering from IBM is called Computer Integrated Manufacturing (CIM). Why not, then, Computer Aided Purchasing (CAP) to enhance the efficiency of the internal purchasing operation and Computer Integrated Purchasing (CIP) to provide more effective communication between purchasing and requisitioners, accounts payable, production, and inventory control?

Many large purchasing operations already use Electronic Data Interchange (EDI), a computer link with their suppliers to expedite the placement of orders. But even with this technological enhancement, internal communications may not be as efficient as they can be.

Many purchasing processes create an overabundance of manual operations in many so-called modern purchasing departments. Nevertheless, many purchasing managers resist automation and computerization. Some say they want to "feel the paper," don't trust computers, feel technologically incompetent, or make any excuse to stay manual while the rest of the business world passes them by.

Because of this attitude, and the marginal demand for specific purchasing applications, the variety of purchasing applications for computers has fallen behind that for other business functions. Since purchasing interfaces with virtually every department and requires timely and accurate information from most, this must change to meet the competitive challenges ahead. You must have computers in purchasing to be competitive.

Computers have been around for 50 years, PCs for over a decade. It is surprising that many small-and medium-sized companies are not making full use of the technological advantages of the computer. They fall into three categories:

- companies that have no computer access at all
- companies who have computers, but do not utilize them to full advantage
- companies who over-rely on the computer to the exclusion of thinking

As this chapter shows, the computer is a tool, a resource upon which the purchasing department can rely to reduce work, enhance transaction accuracy, decrease processing times and increase cost savings.

## ___ EIGHT WAYS COMPUTERS CAN IMPROVE EFFICIENCY ___

The complexities of today's material specifications coupled with the push toward even greater productivity by each buyer dictate that the mechanical operations buyers perform must be made more manageable if not eliminated altogether. Adding computers to handle the mechanical tasks will give buyers more time to manage the more important jobs of selecting suppliers, analyzing quotations, developing a negotiation strategy, and managing long-term contracts. A computer is one indispensible tool that can enhance the efficiency and effectiveness of any purchasing department.

### How to Reduce Errors in the Purchase Requisition Process

Paper purchase requisition forms usually have several copies: one for the requisitioner to keep, one for purchasing, one for accounting, and one to return to the requisitioner as evidence order was placed. Even with carbonless forms the bottom copies tend to be unreadable in certain areas. A computerized requisition will allow you unlimited, first copy, clarity for everyone's records. Each required copy of the requisition can be printed individually from the computer input. Additional copies may be printed in seconds without a trip to a copy machine.

Calculator tasks required when completing a purchase can be handled instantaneously by a computer. The computations of unit quantity × unit price to get the extended price, plus the totaling of all extended prices are typical areas for buyer error. If a buyer is entering the unit quantity and price into a computer the extension prices and total price can be automatically calculated. In this case the only possibility for error is having the wrong price or quantity entered in the first place, a problem that exists even without a computer. If an error is encountered, only the error need be reentered on a computer; the recalculation of totals is instantaneous.

A computer is more reliable in checking various codes used by many purchasing departments. Buyers may need to look up codes (see Chapter 9), message codes, and supplier numbers in a reference book—just one more book to clutter a buyer's desk. If the lists are available on a computer data base, a buyer can check these numbers (on screen) while filling out the requisition, without searching through other reference material.

How often you update that reference material and print copies for all interested parties can be another reason for error, not to mention the expense. With a networked computer data base all that is required is one change for all to have access to the updated information (networks are covered later in this chapter).

## How Buyers Can Save Time, Space, and Paper

Filing and retrieving requisitions and purchase orders in paper form require substantial storage space. The periodic destruction of files no longer needed is a time-consuming job for a clerk. An active purchasing department with 25 buyers may generate up to 20 file drawers of data in one year and require two or three file clerks to maintain order. Computers allow for instantaneous retrieval of data. Modern electronic storage technology can handle purchasing's most ambitious requirements with minimal floor space.

## How to Generate Purchase Orders Almost Automatically

Most suppliers require that a confirming purchase order be sent to them. Since a requisition form is rarely adequate or may contain internal information you do not want the supplier to see, you are required to generate a separate document for the confirming purchase order. In most purchasing departments this requires a separate person to retype the buyer's notes on a requisition onto another form.

An advanced computer application, used by a buyer, can accept online requirements from requisitioners, resort the information, accept necessary coded information from other data bases and generate the confirming purchase order automatically. Instead of penciling in the information on paper, the buyer makes entries directly into the computer thereby bypassing the extra person's task.

## How to Duplicate and Split Requisitions with Ease

Manufacturing planning favors multiple sourcing by purchasing to protect the continuity of supply of parts. This necessitates extra requisitions for parts that normally could be obtained from a single supplier.

Conversely, requisitioners are specifying more Approved Vendor Lists (AVL) sources for specialty items (single sourcing, by manufacturer) for components that must adhere to exacting quality specifications. Requisitions may have to be split or duplicated because parts that may be available from one distributor-supplier are now ordered from several due to any one distributor's inability to provide all AVL manufacturers. This may require the buyer to duplicate requisitions for each supplier or require requisitioners to use a different requisition for each line item. Either choice dictates extra paperwork.

Splitting a purchase requisition into several purchase orders is a simple task via computer which eliminates the retyping of information from the original requisition.

## How to Generate RFQ Forms Online

To ensure competitive costs, some companies require more quoting (RFQ) activity. An RFQ to several suppliers is time consuming to prepare and analyze and must be typed individually to each supplier (unless a special RFQ form is used as described in Chapter 4. See Figure 4-11). Much RFQ information is standard such as the wording of response times and terms and conditions. This can all be stored in computer memory. Then the buyer merely calls up the form on the computer, adds addresses, dates and specifications, and a printer automatically generates the documents. This function of most word processors is called *merge* and can also be used to customize mass mailings of letters.

Quote analysis and the calculations and recalculations that are necessary can certainly be more accurate and efficient by using a computer. A spreadsheet application allows a buyer to instantly add, subtract, multiply, and so on, all pricing information from all suppliers. (Some popular spreadsheet applications are Lotus 1-2-3, Quattro, Excel, and Supercalc.) With these programs the buyer can perform unlimited "what-if" exercises to provide price comparisons or formulate negotiation strategy. Unlike a calculator, all this is performed by entering the original figures only once.

## How to Quickly Produce Purchasing Contracts

Long-term ordering requirements should be accompanied by some form of contract. Written contracts, including engineering and quality specifications, may contain 100 pages or more. Without some form of automation these requirements may create a full-time typing job for an administrative person and many hours at the copy machine.

*Case Study: How One Company Reduced the Contract Workload by Using Word Processing*

Before computerization, one large Southeastern office products company employed one typist for each of three contract administrators. Each contract was made up by editing an old contract or cutting out pieces of text from various sources and taping them together before sending to the typist.

Then the engineers, buyers, accountants, and lawyers all added their notes in the margins. The final draft that was submitted to the typist was almost impossible to follow, let alone understand.

After the introduction of computers and a versatile word processing application, all standard contract clauses were entered into a master file by number. The contract person would enter a list of numbers (usually 15 or 20) into the computer and press the appropriate key. Within a few minutes, thirty pages had been printed while the administrator was attending to other duties.

Now all that was left was some fine tuning and the document was ready to send to the supplier. The company estimated that this one function of the computer had saved them several labor-years in costs.

Most contracts have many standard clauses but a specific contract may only use certain of those clauses. Keeping a computer file of your standards and using a variable-merge function on a good word processor virtually eliminates the cut-and-paste routine still used by many companies. This feature allows you to store as many standard clauses as you choose, name them for reference and you merely list the clauses you choose for inclusion on your contract. The computer will compile each stored clause you have chosen into a final document and print the contract for you, eliminating re-typing of standard information.

## How to Dispense with Manual Logs, Journals, and Records

Most companies require all paperwork to be logged-in to purchasing, logged to a buyer, logged in a buyer's log, logged out of purchasing . . . log, log, log. It is surprising that even today some large companies require purchasing personnel to maintain handwritten MANUAL logs. It is not unusual for a busy buyer to spend over one hour per day just filling in the daily log of requisitions placed. In today's computer environment, this is unnecessary, redundant, and wasteful.

Once you have committed your requisitions and purchase orders to a computer file, the tracking of daily activity is automatic. The numbers, dates, and descriptions can be retrieved and printed daily to provide a record for each buyer. Some applications even produce weekly, monthly, or quarterly reports of activity by buyer, supplier, commodity, department ordered, costs—the possibilities are endless.

### How to Create Valuable Reports in Much Less Time

The reports referred to in Chapter 9 are all available by using high-level purchasing applications software. The time saved is enormous; the informational advantages considerable.

Supplier history and performance, traditionally kept as a mental record by individual buyers, tends to be subjective because it is modified by individual personalities and assumptions. With a computer to more effectively track supplier performance measurements, the record is more objective. This can be accomplished by programming purchase order line item due dates into a data base and entering the received date of that line item. The computer can provide a mathematical comparison of those dates measured against your *delivery window* criteria.

Other applications allow you to track the number of orders to a supplier, dollars committed, progression of pricing by part number, performance at incoming quality inspection, and so on.

## HOW TO JUSTIFY USING
## —————— COMPUTERS IN PURCHASING ——————

The easiest way to present the advantages of computers is by drawing up a presentation which will show the cost savings in personnel and individual productivity. Here are some salient points you can present to your manager or CEO that show how computers can benefit the company strategic goals:

- Productivity—We can do more work with smaller staff
- Efficiency—Buyers will spend less time writing and placing orders, more time for selecting better suppliers
- Effectiveness—Increased time will be available for negotiating better quality, pricing, delivery

- Accuracy—Errors reduced and data reliability enhanced
- Retrievability—Time will be saved in looking for information
- Visibility—Greater buyer awareness of facts, figures, and trends

The following sections describe these benefits in greater detail.

## How to Increase Productivity and Do More Work with a Smaller Staff

Executive management is more conscious than ever of worker productivity and the streamlining of the workforce. The difficulty of hiring quality people, training expense, increased benefits, employee turnover, and space costs has put a premium on the hiring of additional human resources. We constantly hear of trying to do more with less and when a company needs to reduce expenditures, it seems to first make cuts in personnel. Obviously, to maintain status quo operations those remaining employees must increase their productivity.

Someone once said that a computer can replace hundreds of people. That may be overstated when you focus on just the purchasing department but the following case study will illustrate how the computer can eliminate those jobs that are mechanical, boring, and thankless.

*Case Study: How IBM integrated computers in purchasing*

In the spring of 1982 an **IBM** facility decided that, because of the large increase in the volume of requisitions, computerization was preferable to expanding the number of buyers and support personnel. Terminals were installed at each buyer's desk and connected to a System 36 minicomputer. Buyers were not altogether in favor of this new twist in their daily routine. Trainers circulated among the buyers teaching them how to enter data online instead of marking blocks on a purchase requisition.

Soon the computer fright disappeared and it was readily apparent that there was a marked time savings at the buyer's desk:

- There were no more manual logs; the system took care of the tracking.
- Stacks of production requisitions were greatly reduced because all production requirements were online.
- Data entry clerks no longer had to spend many overtime hours converting the requisitions to purchase orders; the buyer already had entered the data which the computer translated into a purchase order.

- Trips to the file to check some bit of information were eliminated; the buyer now could call up the information on his terminal.
- Two data entry clerks and one file clerk were promoted to other areas. Tiresome mechanical tasks were now replaced with more productive pursuits.

Computerization reduced the number of administrative personnel required to run the purchasing operation and diverted resources to other purchasing disciplines. Shortly thereafter nonproduction requisitioners were put "online" and nearly all incoming paper disappeared. The buyer could now concentrate on other matters: specifically, buying.

## How to Reduce Overtime and Increase Efficiency

The business of buying takes lots of time. Buyers who are constantly burdened with paperwork cannot effectively manage the other more important tasks in purchasing, cannot do all the right things and are, therefore, not efficient. Automation, through the use of computers, is essential to the elimination of such paperwork tasks.

Within the plethora of tasks required of any buyer are those that, according to one buyer, are "Just busy work." Tasks such as filling out activity logs, filing, retrieving files, and writing RFQs always seem to take more time than they should, valuable time that buyers should be using for sourcing, evaluating suppliers, negotiating and making buying decisions.

The computer is able to provide rapid retrievability of records, data, and files. Open requisition logs and open purchase order logs that are stored on a computer database will eliminate the trips to the files and time-consuming manual logs of daily activity. In addition, the computer is a highly efficient replacement for the calculator. A spreadsheet application is a super calculator that facilitates:

- changes to costs on bills of material
- comparison of different suppliers' pricing
- re-entry of numbers
- what-if scenarios
- merging and copying of data
- making charts and graphs

All this reduction of tasks and speeding up of tasks leave more time for buying.

## How to Increase Effectiveness by Using Computers

There are several categories of effectiveness in purchasing. The first has to do with managing suppliers. Ensuring on-time delivery, getting what you ordered (in terms of both quantity and quality), using accurate packing slips and flawless invoices all result in the elimination of rework time, hence they save money. The computer can be not only a valuable tool in assisting the buyer with managing a supplier in these areas, but tracking the supplier's performance as well. A detailed database that measures the supplier's performance from many standpoints eliminates the guess work.

When comparing quotes, the computer is able to make instant changes and provides a tool to make "what if" comparisons without a lot of paperwork. This visibility reduces subjective reasoning and promotes more knowledgeable buying decisions.

In the area of cost effectiveness, the computer can store vast amounts of historical data in a form readily retrievable by the buyer. Price history, lead times, return on investment all can be available at a buyer's fingertips.

## How to Increase Accuracy and Reduce Rework

The computer spreadsheet is the greatest asset to mathematical calculations since the calculator. If you have ever used a calculator to add the same column of numbers more than once, and the totals do not match, you will understand rework. Having to re-enter the same numbers again and again is history when you use a computer.

The *copy, move, combine, import, export* and *merge* functions of software programs reduce the amount of errors in transposing numbers from one area to another. All these functions do is take data that is already available and place it somewhere else. The advantage is in not having to re-enter the same data again, whether the data is numbers or words.

Word processors can send the same letter to many addresses through the *mail merge* function. One list contains the addresses and the other list, the letters. Even the letters can be customized in many ways with different names, different figures, or different values.

## Retrievability Reduces File Trauma

"File this, retrieve that. Where is that file? We need more file cabinets. There just aren't enough people to handle all this and the stacks are backing up." Sound familiar?

The purchasing department is one of the biggest filers in business. This is because purchasing not only has to maintain its own paper but paper from requisitioners, engineers, and accounting as well as from its suppliers. By reducing internal files to computer memory, most of the trips to the files can be eliminated. This paper filing dilemma has been realized by the US Government:

*Case Study: How the DoD Automated Purchasing to Facilitate Information Retrieval*

The Department of Defense declared in 1989 that it has just too much paper, too many files, too many manuals. Recently the DOD instituted a program called CALS (Computer Aided Logistics Support). As the story goes . . . if all the documentation were removed from an aircraft carrier, the ship would rise three inches in the water—if all the aircraft were removed, the ship would only rise one inch.

The real need, the Defense Department realized, is to have access to the information, not the information itself in the form of thousands of pages of documentation, much of which may never be accessed. Further the task of updating individual printed pages of technical and operational information coupled with the indexes and cross references is a never ending process and a full time job for the government printing office.

The CALS (online) system will contain every manual, technical reference, operating guide, and repair documentation for every piece of military equipment. Every supplier to the DOD will provide a uniform computer file of the necessary information that will be kept in a central computer. The information can be accessed via satellite from this computer or downloaded to smaller systems where needed. The reduction of the paper and the sheer weight of the documentation will be a great savings for the military.

Some buyers tend to hoard paper. In order to have easy access to P.O.s, they make copies of every purchase order and keep them in a personal file in their office. A copy is also kept in the receiving department, incoming inspection, the requisitioner's file and accounts payable. Many purchase order printouts contain five copies just for this purpose. From the sublime to the ridiculous we continue to duplicate paper when all we really desire is *access to the data*—quickly, accurately, and completely. The computer can do this better, cheaper and quicker.

## How to Increase Visibility and Buyer Awareness

In addition to all the above benefits of effective use of the computer, a computer can provide graphs and charts to enhance the visibility and understanding of information without having a draftsman close by. A chart comparing the performance of your suppliers will readily show which ones excel. A graph of one supplier, over time, will show the progression of performance and whether he is heading for problems.

Buyer presentations to management or suppliers will be greatly enhanced by the use of computer generated graphics. Reports might include:

- financial summaries (see Figure 10-1)
- status of "make vs. buy" decisions
- number of requisitions/purchase orders processed
- total value of purchases
- purchases by supplier

See also Figures 10-2 through 10-6. The added benefit is the professional look of such presentation material when generated by computer. Gone are the days when a few hand written remarks on blue-lined paper would suffice.

If all of the above fails to impress management of the need to computerize the purchasing department, try researching the competition. Those companies who automate, whether it be the manufacturing line or administration, always seem to be on the cutting edge of productivity and therefore are more competitive in the marketplace. They will survive; the others must struggle.

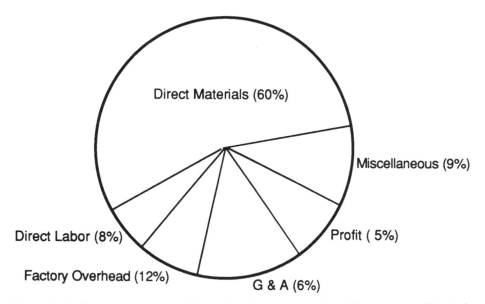

**Figure 10-1. Financial Summary (Note: This pie chart of a financial statement effectively shows that the direct materials category is the largest single category of expense to a company.)**

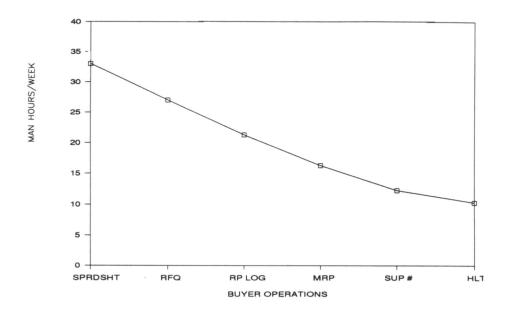

The X axis shows time savings by using:

SPRDSHT - Computer spreadsheet applications instead of calculators
RFQ - Standardizing of RFQ requirements on a word processor
RPLOG - Replacing hand-written daily requisition logs with automatic computer tabulation of daily activities
MRP - Part numbers and descriptions entered on a Materials Requirements Planning application instead of a reference book
SUP# - Referencing a specific supplier number (from on-line list) instead of using just supplier name
HLT - Elimination of manual highlighting of requisitions for data entry clerk.

**Figure 10-2. Procurement Efficiency (Note: This line chart portrays the declining labor-hours needed to perform various functions at a buyer's desk. Times savings were calculated by Lotus 123 and are a cumulative result of the savings by a total of five buyers. The enhancements were designed to increase efficiency by a factor of one buyer/week [40 hours])**

# HOW TO DETERMINE
# IF YOU ARE OPTIMIZING
# THE USE OF YOUR COMPUTER

By looking at the applications described in the preceding section you may find that you are not using some of them. Another way to determine if there is a process or task that is "dragging down" your productivity is to circulate a written survey to all purchasing people, not just the buyers.

Some questions you may want to ask are:

- What do you consider the most time-consuming part of your job? Why?

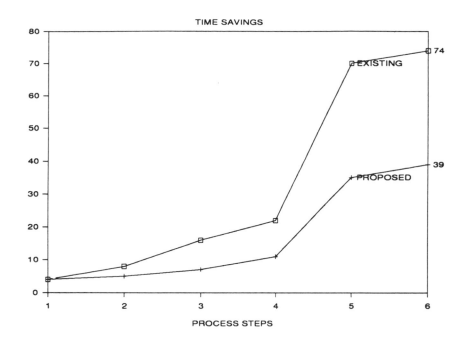

The steps are:

1. Assembly of documents needed for RFQ

2. Copy of data for each department

3. Typing of RFQ and transmittal to suppliers

4. Analysis of RFQ responses from suppliers

5. Retrieval of price history information

**Figure 10-3. RFQ Enhancements/Time Savings (Note: This graph illustrates the before and after time factors used to process a Request for Quotation. The various steps in placing an RFQ are automated via the computer, and it is evident by the use of the graph that step number 5 saves the most time.)**

- Do you have sufficient data to make daily decisions? If not, what data do you need?
- What other departments furnish data to you? Is it timely and accurate?
- What is your opinion of the amount of time you have to spend on: (too much - about right - not enough - none)
  — shopping for new suppliers
  — obtaining second-source price queries

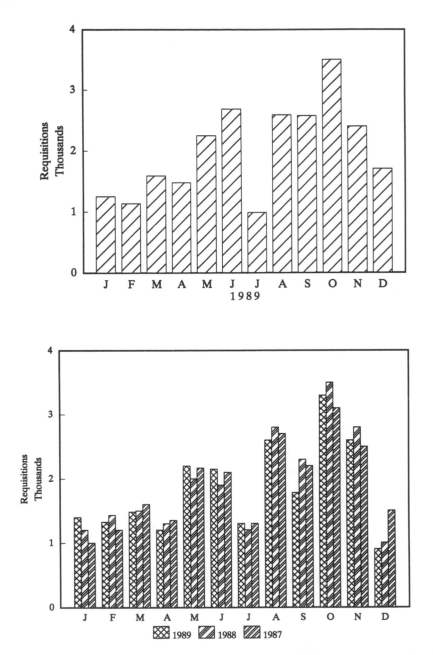

**Figure 10-4. Requisitions Process (Note: The top bar graph illustrates the periods of peak buyer activity. With this information in hand management can provide more effective workload management. Vacations and education time can be more effectively scheduled, as well as any part-time or supplementary help requirements. The second chart shows the same information over a three-year period.)**

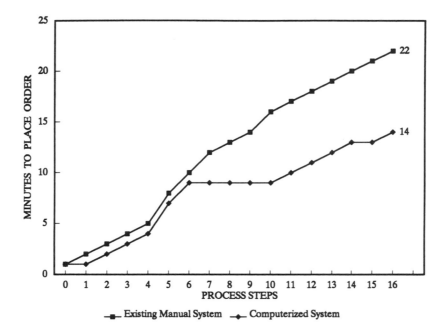

Process Steps

1. Document control requisition log-in
2. Assignment of requisition to buyer
3. Sort requisitions by buyer
4. Distribute requisitions to buyers
5. Buyer sort requisitions by vendor/priority/quote requirement, etc.
6. Buyer calls vendor and receives information
7. Buyer completes information on requisitions
8. Buyer completes daily activity log
9. Buyer highlights important information on requisition
10. Document control logs-in completed requisition
11. Document control types confirming purchase order
12. Document control prints confirming purchase order
13. Document control sorts completed purchase orders by buyer
14. Purchase orders distributed to buyers for signature
15. Buyers sign purchase orders
16. Purchase orders mailed to suppliers

**Figure 10-5. On-Line PO Placement by Buyer/Time Savings (Note: This chart illustrates the average time to place a single purchase requisition. Time saved in this case is 8 minutes each or a 36% time savings in labor minutes.)**

— consolidating orders for quantity discounts

— negotiating with requisitioners

— negotiating with suppliers

— monitoring suppliers with respect to deliveries, quality, costs

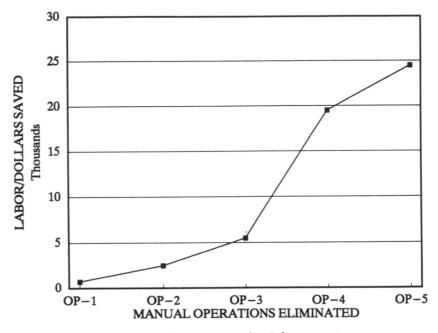

**Figure 10-6. System Integration Enhancement**

- recordkeeping and maintaining logs, journals, notes
- generating reports for management
- gaining knowledge of the products you buy
- keeping up to date on buyer education in general

*Case Study*
*How One Company Was Too Busy To Try To Save Time*

A consultant found that a purchasing department that was perceived to be smooth-running was totally out of control. Employee responses to a questionnaire revealed the true situation. Only a small percentage of purchasing functions were accessed on the mini computer because, as the purchasing manager admitted, "They are too busy placing orders to learn how to use the computer."

After determining that there was a marginal effort to negotiate prices or seek volume discounts the consultant found that, indeed, time would be found to train the buyers on the use of the computer. Time was also found to evaluate department enhancements for education and general morale issues through the computer taking care of manual and time consuming tasks.

If you are not a computer expert, engaging one from within your company or from outside may be the answer. However, since purchasing functions are not generally well understood by many computer people, a consultant versed in purchasing applications and programming possibilities is recommended. Just having a third party survey your operation, without any predetermined limitations, can greatly improve the objectivity of any recommendations.

## HOW TO PREVENT OVERRELIANCE
## ON THE COMPUTER

The old saying "garbage-in-garbage-out" certainly applies here. The accuracy of the data you store in a computer is only as good as you make it. An audit or "sanity check" is necessary for all data, whether it is computerized or not. This refers not only to the input of data but to the functionality of the application program itself. Like anything mechanical there is always room for error and computers are no exception. The myth is that because it came from the computer, it must be correct. The reality is oftentimes quite the opposite.

Generally a periodic sampling of data from each group of stored information will be sufficient to maintain accuracy. Assign specific individuals to be responsible for data base input and changes such as supplier addresses, commodity codes, receiving information, accounting records, quality numbers and such. You can provide special security locks within each application that will restrict access to certain areas of the data and provide for:

- View only (no entries or changes can be made)
- Enter only (no changes can be made)
- Change capability

This additional security will enhance the accuracy and reliability of your data. You may also wish to define an internal policy that any information that appears out of line or unusual should be double-checked before decisions are made or the information distributed outside purchasing.

## HOW TO DECIDE ON THE COMPUTER
## FUNCTIONS YOU NEED

When you have convinced management of the need to computerize or upgrade an existing system you should think first of the software. Software may only run on certain systems; therefore you need to think first of what you want to do before you decide what (hardware) you are going to do it on.

The key here is to evaluate your needs first, then decide on a software application that fits those needs, (whether it be a standard package or a custom program), then decide on the hardware needed to run that application. The three steps are:

1. Analyze your needs
2. Select your software application
3. Install the hardware

Too many times the order of priorities is reversed. Either your needs are not fulfilled or the total installation is not conducive to improving an existing situation. One such predicament can arise in a PC environment. For example, the database used for suppliers' addresses may be stored in one program used to merge (add) those addresses into a different program but may require that you translate or convert the information before the application will run. Compatibility of systems and software is an important point to consider.

In order to obtain an efficient computerized purchasing system, you will need a checklist of tasks you want the computer to handle.

For data entry, the system should be able to accomplish the following functions:

- Generate requisitions (i.e., for requisitioners)
- Generate purchase orders
- Revise purchase orders (e.g., for alterations)
- Prioritize purchase orders
- Provide standard messages (e.g., redelivery, terms, notes)
- Input receiving data
- Input accounts payable data

For data inquiry, the system should be able to provide the following information:

- Item master file (part descriptions)
- Requisition master file (open requisitions)
- Purchase order master file (open P.O.s)
- Vendor master file (vendor data)
- Invoice master file (accounts payable information)
- Purchase order history (prior purchases)
- Supplier performance statistics

The system should also be able to print the following forms and reports:

- Purchase orders
- Logs (requisition, PO, RFQ, supplier)
- Performance reports (supplier, buyer activity)
- Requests for quotation
- Correspondence
- Charts and graphs
- Presentations

NOTE: You may not desire all of the above functions during an initial installation, but it certainly pays to anticipate future needs and allow for upgradability.

Many times you will hear the phrase "dock-to-stock" which refers to the handling of material from the receiving dock to inventory (stock room). A computerized system should be able to not only handle all transactions in this area, but every transaction from "requisition-to-payment."

One tell-tale key to identifying a task that needs computerization is to find someone sorting a large stack of paper for distribution or filing or making extra copies for another department. These activities are usually an indication that some automated system should be implemented to reduce or eliminate such tasks.

## How to Select Software to Match Your Needs

In selecting the application program best suited to your *prioritized* list of needs, there are several points you will want to address:

- Availability of applications
- Cost versus versatility
- Compatibility with existing computer systems
- Ease of use
- Training and technical support
- Modification and upgrade availability
- Vendor reliability

***Availability of Applications.*** Your first priority should be to eliminate day-to-day manual tasks. Many times the software promotional material highlights esoteric added functions that will not necessarily provide you with the basics. The software package should, at least, effectively address over 50% of your basic needs. The fewer applications you purchase, the less training time you will need.

***Compatibility with Existing Systems.*** Incompatibility is a problem that must be faced when there is more than one operating system resident within your business. Remember that the operating system tells the computer how to perform tasks. The buyers may be operating on a PC network under PC DOS, the accounting department in an APPLE environment and the rest of the facility using a mini-computer. At best, translation will be required for any transference of information; at worst, there will be no communications at all.

An analogy to this situation might be like trying to build a custom automobile with a General Motors engine, a Ford transmission, and on a Honda wheel base. It will not be easy to match the parts and some may just not work at all.

***Ease of Use.*** Implementation of a software application is often an arduous task. Irrespective of sales claims of "user-friendliness" or "ease of use," there will be resistance from the users. Something new always requires patience and persistence. There will, no doubt, be an air of stress during any implementation phase. The transition period required for bringing your system online may take a few weeks or even a few months. Be prepared for unforeseen breakdowns and information loss. It would be wise to operate under a dual system (manual/automated) for a time in order to eliminate a "line-down" in the purchasing function.

***Training and Technical Support.*** The availability of training and technical support cannot be overstressed. Seemingly simple glitches in operations can sometimes be impossible to fix in a reasonable time without expert support. Many software companies offer regional support teams, agents or representatives. If you operate in a large city this service may be close at hand.

Some individual should be assigned within your company as the technical interface. If you are a large company this individual may be located in your Data Processing (DP) department or Management Information Systems (MIS) area. You should also have someone within purchasing trained to a reasonable level of computer knowledge as an internal, quick response, trouble shooter. Many software vendors provide special training courses for this purpose.

Advanced technical support to coordinate the hardware and software is quite another matter. The mysterious world of computers has special requirements that even the most knowledgeable internal person may not understand. An information "Hot Line" to the hardware and software provider is a necessity to adequately protect yourself against breakdown. Just as a good mechanic is periodically required for your automobile, a good technician is required for your computer system.

***Modification and Upgrade Availability.*** Software vendors are generally eager to modify their applications for individual users. This, of course, will cost extra money. However, when it comes to compatibility and functionality, the benefits of upgrading existing software, over changing to a different application, can be many. It will not be necessary for operators to learn new access keys, learn new menus or functions.

The progressive posture of a software provider will be indicated by the number and frequency of revisions and upgrades to existing applications. Check the history of the application you select. If there have been too few changes, the vendor may not be on the cutting edge of technology; too many changes might indicate continual faults in the application. Your standard supplier evaluation skills will come in handy here.

Also important is the *language* the software is written in, both system software and application software. Many microcomputers operate with programs written in BASIC. There must be some form of translation before the information from this type of program can be merged into a minicomputer environment.

Some languages found in the minicomputer environment with versions available for PCs are COBOL and FORTRAN. It is not important here that you understand these differences, but that you are aware that system and application programmers will generally have definite ideas related to which language they prefer to use. System language too may become an important factor in choosing your hardware. Ask your expert.

***Vendor Reliability.*** Throughout the criteria for selecting a software supplier you have seen many instances that refer to vendor reliability. Purchasing tends to rely on engineers to evaluate the technical issues related to a particular purchase. If you do not have experienced software programmers in your company you may wish to engage the services of a reputable consultant to assist you in selecting a software supplier. In any event, the recommendation is to hire the best first; don't scrimp here or the consequences may be very costly.

## Selecting Computer Hardware

There are three basic categories of computers: mainframe, minicomputer, and microcomputer. In years past most business thought of a mainframe when computers were mentioned. A mainframe computer is a very large system usually found in the largest companies in such industries as insurance, automobile, government, and the like. Costing millions of dollars, these multiprocessing giants can handle every conceivable task from launching a space craft to processing electronic (computer) mail.

The minicomputer made its debut about 30 years ago and revolutionized most mid-sized companies' financial and manufacturing operations. The minicomputer systems allow interface with a vast storehouse of data that would not be accessible on a desktop unit. (We will cover the different types of installations later in this chapter).

***Using Microcomputers for Purchasing Applications.*** The latest addition to the computer age is the microcomputer or Personal Computer (PC) as it has come to be known. These versatile machines can be used in the home as well as in business and are fast approaching the calculating and storage capabilities of what the minicomputer could do just a few short years ago.

Costing from $1,000 to over $10,000, these PCs bring computerized applications to a level affordable by every business. Many PC software applications are being written for purchasing by a number of software providers (see listing at the end of this chapter). Automated ordering, inventory, costing and vendor performance are just a few of the tasks that can now be performed with a high degree of automation on a PC.

One benchmark for deciding which system to use may be based on your revenue. Most companies under $10 million dollars in revenue may not feel the need for the expense of a minicomputer. A few PCs, with or without a small network (a connection that allows them to communicate with each other), may suffice. By networking your PCs with manufacturing, accounts payable, receiving and inventory control, you will, in effect, approach the basic capabilities of a minicomputer without the expense. Engage a computer networking consultant who specializes in this area. One can be found in most Yellow Pages under the heading of "Computers, System Designers and Consultants."

Even a stand-alone desktop PC for every buyer will greatly enhance productivity and efficiency by eliminating many manual operations, speeding up calculations, and increasing accuracy and visibility. For instance, a PC with a spreadsheet application can be used to compare quotations, cost models and vendor performance. Prefiled standard written communications can be retrieved and modified quickly, eliminating the retyping of letters. A simple listing of vendors, commodities and telephone numbers will eliminate the necessity for a rotary file on the desk, a savings of space and time (have you ever tried to calculate the amount of time a buyer spends searching through this file?)

There are Material Requirements Planning (MRP) type software packages available now for the PC environment. (See the end of this chapter for applications packages.) Now even the smallest company can provide planning, production, and inventory information to purchasing in a timely and accurate manner. Applications have the ability to store over 60,000 suppliers, write purchase orders, automate receiving, and interface with accounts payable.

The mini and mainframe environment are best suited to the maintenance of a full function MRP system. However there are a few MRP applications available for the micro environment such as PC/MRP available from Power Up Software. (See the list at the end of the chapter.)

***Using Minicomputers.*** If a minicomputer is available in your business, does the purchasing function have access to it? Have you purchased all of the available application packages for that system that relate to purchasing? It is surprising how many companies have not taken full advantage of their own computers. A meeting with the data processing or MIS department should be a priority in defining your needs and determining the applications available to fulfill those needs. Smaller companies may have to rely on a product representative from the manufacturer of the equipment.

Production and inventory control is enhanced by such applications as Manufacturing Accounting and Production Information Control System (MAPICS) and Communications Oriented Production Information System (COPICS). These large software programs provide an application for practically every function of materials management. They can also be customized to your particular requirements.

***Accessing the Mainframe.*** Due to the power of present day minicomputers it is unlikely that you will find yourself attempting to justify a mainframe computer acquisition. The chances are that you may find yourself in a company that already has one of these systems and it will be your job to access the power of the mainframe for the purchasing function. When and if this happens, you will use most of the same requirements for applications that you would for any other size system. The difference will be that you may need to engage the services of a consultant and/or programmer in order to fulfill your needs.

The mainframe environment, although not unlike any other computer, tends to be esoteric to most and specialty applications for purchasing may have to be specially written for your needs. Further, customizing even a seemingly minute function may take thousands of lines of computer code to accomplish and cost hundreds of hours of programming time. In the long run it may be more appropriate to install a smaller system that can interface with the mainframe for the information you need.

## How to Enhance Internal Communication by Computer

Eventually you will find that you want your computers to communicate with each other or with the outside world in order to further reduce the duplication of documentation and speed up processes. One way to do this is by using a *modem* and standard telephone lines. A computer operates on a *digital* signal whereas the telephone only accepts an *analog* signal. These differences are not important here except to understand that the word

MODEM merely stands for MOdulation of a signal, then DEModulation of the signal at the computer on the other end of the line so it can be read by the computer.

Another way computers can communicate within your company is via a special cable. This system is called a *network*. With the advent of high powered microcomputers networks of microcomputers are replacing mini-computers in many instances. A central computer, such as an IBM Model 80, has the ability to store over 600 MB of information, applications and files. Called a *server* this large CPU then is connected via cables to other smaller computers or workstations. This ability to communicate is especially valuable in purchasing to tie receiving, inventory and accounts payable into a materials system. All departments then have access to the same information. The amount of paperwork and additional copies of paperwork can be substantially reduced and productivity enhanced through such a system.

An internal network of computers that can link all departments to purchasing will allow you to completely automate the requisition and purchasing functions. Paperless purchasing or CIP (Computer Integrated Purchasing) is now possible. Requisitioners complete on-line requisition forms and send them to purchasing over the cable. Purchasing completes the form while talking with the supplier. The finished confirming purchase order is then printed and mailed to the supplier. Any data that is required to be filed is already in the computer memory and no paper copies need be saved in the file cabinets.

Receiving, quality, and accounting can access the original purchase information and complete their own notations on the same computer document. This system, according to one midwestern firm, saved 10 labor-years of administrative time.

***Electronic Data Interchange.*** Further enhancements to communication are being made now between purchasing and its suppliers. The confirming purchase order, in this case, is transmitted electronically to the supplier (via a modem) instead of being mailed. The supplier may make an electronic acknowledgement or adjustment to the information and transmit it back to the buyer. All this without a postage stamp—truly a cost savings.

## SUMMARY

In the realm of computers there is almost always more than one right answer. You will receive opinions and ultimatums from dealers, sales reps, programmers, and consultants. Always get a demonstration before you buy and ask for references of other companies that are using the same system. Negotiate a trial period as well as six months of "FREE" technical assistance.

Most importantly, have the utmost patience with the computer supplier and your employees.

Since the field of computerization is moving in quantum leaps, there is practically no one person who has all the answers. Actually you will find, after a short time, that it may take several people to solve just one problem. Learn who these people are and take them under your wing. They will be your Red Cross and you will need them.

---

### Purchasing Software For Minicomputers

| | |
|---|---|
| Purchasing Management | ShawWare<br>1552 Hertel Avenue<br>Buffalo, NY 14216 |
| Purchase Order & Receiving | MCBA<br>425 West Broadway<br>Glendale, CA 91204-1269 |
| MAPICS | IBM Corporation<br>Dept A79<br>P.O. Box 28331<br>Atlanta, GA 30358-0331 |

---

## Canned Purchasing Systems for Microcomputers

1. BUY THE NUMBERS

   Buy the Numbers
   P.O. Box 27046
   Pittsburgh, PA 15235
   (412) 795-8011

   1. A "Computerized Line Card Program." Shows what products your distributors carry or what distributors carry the products. You must input the data. $49.95.

2. fisCAL

   The Halcyon Group
   447 Fleming Road
   Charleston, SC 29412-9904
   (803) 798-7336

   2. Business analysis software to ensure stable suppliers by analyzing their financial statements. Predicts chance of bankruptcy. Single machine $495, site $1095. Discounts available to purchasing through American Purchasing Society.

3. PC PROCUREMENT GATEWAY

   Technical Services Associates, Inc.
   5002 Lenker Street
   Mechanicsburg, PA 17055
   (715) 975-0513

   3. Single user $1175 to $2495, multiple users $3750 to $4750. Add on modules available. Check for latest pricing.

4. P.O. WRITER PLUS

   American Tech
   Colonial Commons
   670 N. Beers Street
   Holmdel, NJ 07733
   (908) 946-8844

   4. Thirteen modules ranging in price from $695 to $3495 for a single user or $795 to $5495 for multiple users.

5. POWER 1000

   Purchasing Systems Technologies, Inc.
   4268 South Biscay Cir.
   Aurora, CO 80013
   (303) 693-8711

   5. $4995 includes a 3-day training session. Annual support/maintenance agreement, $1200/year.

| | | |
|---|---|---|
| 6. PURCHASING INFORMATION CENTER | Kehlbeck & Associates<br>7812 Cedar Ridge Court<br>Prospect, KY 40059<br>(502) 228-3636 | 6. $595 for a single user, $1595 for a local area network. A new inventory module will be $995. |
| 7. PURCHASING MANAGEMENT EXTRA | Bellwether Software Corporation<br>9900 Shelbyville Road, Suit 6B<br>Louisville, KY 40223<br>(502) 426-5463 | 7. Five modules ranging in price from $416 to $1295 per module for a single user or $700 to $2500 per module for multiple users. |
| 8. PURCHASING MOD. | Fourth Shift Corporation<br>International Plaza<br>7900 International Drive<br>Minneapolis, MN 55425<br>(612) 851-1500 | 8. Request quotation for manufacturing system. |
| 9. PURCHASING PRO | American Purchasing Society<br>11910 Oak Trail Way<br>Port Richey, FL 34668<br>(813) 862-7998 | 9. Tools for buyers and managers including a work load analyzer and staffing calculator. Single user $99. Free to seminar participants who submit questionnaire. |
| 10. QPII PURCHASING MANAGEMENT SYS. | Dynamic Software<br>109 S. Main Street<br>Greer, SC 29650<br>(803) 877-1122 | 10. Single User $725, multiple users $1448 to $2175. |
| 11. REALITY | Structured Computer Systems, Inc.<br>302 West Main Street<br>Avon, CT 06001<br>(203) 677-0222 | 11. Request quotation. |

# CHAPTER ELEVEN

# What the Buyer Needs to Know About Quality

As founder of The Quality College and author of several books on the subject of quality, Philip Crosby has helped business focus on the real issues in quality. Crosby's first best seller, *Quality Is Free*, sums up the issue in simple terms:

"Quality is getting people to do *better*, all the worthwhile things they ought to be doing." Quality is an integral part, not just in the products a buyer receives from his supplier, but of all areas of what everyone in a company does every day. The purchasing department is no exception. Quality is measured by customer satisfaction, internal customers as well as external ones. Evidence of quality is in the paperwork you process. Quality, or the lack of, is shown by your communications conducted day to day. Some degree of quality can be measured in all things. Most commonly it is thought of in terms of a tangible product, but it is just as much exhibited in service performance.

## HOW TO GET MANAGEMENT COMMITMENT TO QUALITY

Does your company have a written, documented, approved, and disseminated quality policy? Those are the first steps. The policy may be as simple as "We will deliver defect-free products to all our customers." That's nice, but you will have to have written, documented, approved, and disseminated details on how to attain that goal if you want your program to succeed.

Whatever your policy may be, it must be well defined and communicated to your managers, your employees, *and* your suppliers. The content of the policy must convince all that you are determined and will accept nothing less than what your policy describes.

Once a policy and procedure is in place it will be everyone's responsibility from the chairman of the board to the janitor to uphold that policy and everything it stands for. Deviations must not be ignored. Off-spec products must not be approved except in the rarest of instances. If it is decided that the specification is in need of alteration, change the specification first, then approve the product.

## HOW TO DECIDE
## ————— WHO IS RESPONSIBLE FOR QUALITY —————

The buyer of a product is responsible for the supplier's adherence to the agreed upon quality standards. However, if quality performance is needed everywhere, then everyone should be responsible for it. The buyer, the supplier, receiving, accounts payable, inventory control—everyone shares the responsibility for the many inputs that make the total quality of the product. Any deviation from the agreed standard by anyone has the potential of causing a degradation of total quality. Anyone who accepts a deviation from the standard causes an *assumed* dual standard and total quality will suffer.

Quality is everyone's business but there may be specialists in your firm that have more detailed knowledge of certain products and have the technical knowledge required to measure performance. To assure product quality your company may have an engineer or technician that can be very helpful to purchasing. Purchasing people rarely have the time to become quality engineering specialists. If you already have specialists in your organization, encourage an internal partnership between purchasing and those specialists. They can make your job and the job of the supplier much easier. It may be wise to ask for advice and recommendations from engineers or quality specialists when you are involved in:

- supplier selection
- supplier qualification
- supplier certification
- incoming inspection
- rejecting material

- engineering changes
- failure analysis

By facilitating the communication between the persons responsible for quality in your company and those responsible for quality at the supplier, you gain knowledge as well as become a mediating and expediting force for the resolution of disagreements arising out of quality issues. There can be many such disagreements.

Other department specialists are invaluable to you in defining and maintaining the various aspects of quality. In addition to the departments described in the following sections, accounts payable, receiving, traffic, in particular, are your allies in the search for the best quality level.

***Supplier Selection, Qualification, and Certification.*** When selecting, qualifying, or certifying a supplier,[1] purchasing must assess every aspect of that supplier's operation. Few buyers are qualified to evaluate electronic test equipment, manufacturing process controls or statistical process data. A *qualified* engineer should be able to give you the assistance you need. A thorough evaluation of the supplier's capabilities is important to assure the required quality level you need.

***Inspection and Rejection of Incoming Goods.*** Quality Control personnel such as inspectors and engineers are frequently able to offer suggestions to remedy rejected goods problems. Their suggestions may range from changing the specifications of the goods to changing the manufacturing process. They may even suggest changing the supplier. Great care should be exercised before such drastic action. You must assess the motives and impartiality of everyone involved. Even though you may not have an ideal supplier, it may not be easy to find another that is better.

***Engineering Changes to Product Specifications.*** Purchasing should always be consulted by engineers or other technical people before changes in specifications are made. Such changes may raise or lower the cost of the product and purchasing needs to be brought into the discussions before any final decision is made. Cost increases are difficult to negotiate or avoid if the supplier has been authorized to make the changes and purchasing has not been consulted. It is also going to be difficult to obtain a price reduction if the change results in a lower cost if purchasing has not been involved at the start of the discussions.

Some product changes may require resourcing to another supplier. It

---

[1] The American Purchasing Society provides third party certification of suppliers, but does not evaluate the accuracy of test equipment or the competence of nonpurchasing technical personnel.

could take considerable time to find a qualified new supplier. Additional tooling cost may be involved.

*Failure Analysis.* Failure analysis is probably the most overlooked function of the manufacture of a product. Many companies merely replace the product and trash the defective one. Certainly this is not in the best interests of the customer, you or the end-user. If your supplier will not or cannot provide effective, documented failure analysis, you will have to rely on your own resources. Technical people regardless of their actual title can help determine the causes of product failure. They may be quality engineers, process engineers, manufacturing engineers, or lab technicians.

## HOW TO DETERMINE
## WHEN QUALITY IS AN ISSUE

Specifications, measurements, and corrective actions are the "what" in quality performance. Let's take a look at the "when" in quality. Quality begins before the selection of a supplier. Through the use of a detailed supplier selection and/or certification process, purchasing can eliminate many potential problems. Before deciding on a manufacturing source you should ask for the quality plan for manufacturing the product. If the supplier has given no consideration to produce your desired quality level you should be skeptical of what result you will obtain. Another supplier with a detailed plan to assure your quality requirements may give you more confidence that actual performance will be what you need.

Ask the supplier the following questions to determine his commitment to quality:

- What criteria do his inspectors use?
- What quality assurance is built into packaging?
- If the packaging is not of your design, has the supplier developed a package that adequately protects the product?
- If the package design is yours, what measures are being taken to assure that the package conforms to your specification?
- What measures are being taken by the shipping department, the traffic department, and the billing department to assure conformance to your requirements accurately?
- What is the supplier's method of processing claims for rejected material?
- How quickly will rejected items be replaced?

- What are the supplier's procedures to investigate problems and take action to prevent future occurrences?
- Does the supplier have an ongoing research and development function to provide upgrades to the product?

If you look at quality as an all encompassing concept, you will also delve into areas that are often separated from quality considerations:

- Are the supplier's salespeople and order department employees easy to deal with?
- What is the turn-around time for orders?
- What is normal leadtime?
- How quickly can the supplier respond to emergency requirements?
- What is the supplier's record of delivery schedule compliance?
- Does the supplier have a disaster plan in case of a work stoppage?

Your buyers should consider all these criteria as a part of the total quality package.

## HOW TO QUALIFY
## ——————————— AND CERTIFY A SUPPLIER ———————————

Evaluation of a potential supplier is not easy. Too frequently the process is done quickly and poorly. The result is usually a continual problem in getting the kind of material you want or in getting the material delivered on time or in some other type of poor vendor performance.

The process of checking a supplier before hand is time consuming, and buyers normally do not have sufficient time to do a good job investigating every supplier. For this reason, they will continue to stay with less-than-satisfactory suppliers because they prefer to accept what they have rather than risk getting something worse.

In practice the problem is minimized by spending the most time checking suppliers that will be used for major purchases and not bothering to check on suppliers that are used infrequently or for small volumes. Nevertheless, using a poor supplier for an infrequent or small dollar purchase can still cause enormous headaches and consume much time straightening out errors.

Proper evaluation of a supplier can take from a few steps to many. A supplier used for a small volume or infrequently may only require a minor investigation. Those used for major purchases or for key items should be checked thoroughly.

Here are the steps to take when evaluating a potential supplier.

*Check the Financial Condition of the Supplier.* You want to know if the supplier will remain stable and stay in business. Some buyers have gotten into difficulties because the supplier they were using went out of business and the material ordered was never delivered. Ordering from a new supplier caused serious delays that resulted in lost production and possibly lost sales. Most suppliers do not go out of business without some warning, but if they are having financial difficulties, they may have trouble getting raw material because of slow payment practices or their cost may be higher because they cannot order in economical quantities. Chapter 7 provides suggestions on how to evaluate suppliers.

*Find Out How Long the Supplier Has Been in Business.* Most companies fail within the first few years of going in business. While young companies should not necessarily be ruled out, care should be taken in properly evaluating their capabilities and resources.

*Check References.* This is the area that should be given most attention. Usually the supplier will give you the most satisfied customers as references. Nevertheless, a close questioning of these references often reveals a true picture. When a reference avoids answering your questions directly or is vague with answers, you should become suspicious.

*Obtain Answers to Your Questionnaire, Which Should Request a Description of Facilities.* (See Figure 7.1 for a sample questionnaire.) The facilities list should include a description of the plant and offices. It should list major equipment or machinery as well as test equipment and measuring devices to check quality.

*Request a List of Key Personnel with a Description of Their Background.* This may sometimes be obtained from annual reports or ordered through a financial services organization such as Dun and Bradstreet. Knowing the education and experience of the key people helps you assess their capability.

*Conduct a Physical Inspection of the Supplier's Facilities.* Although this is not always possible for the buyer, it is highly recommended if any significant amount of business is to be awarded. It allows you to see things and hear things that may not be evident in written reports. Getting to know the people that will be making your product helps you determine where problems might exist and helps you obtain better performance.

## How to Make Supplier Evaluations Easy

The solution to the time constraint is to use third party supplier evaluations. The American Purchasing Society has a supplier evaluation program that does all of the things mentioned above and at no cost to the buyer. The buyer should simply indicate to potential suppliers that they require supplier certification by the American Purchasing Society. The buyer may obtain the application forms and give them to interested suppliers or the seller may request the forms directly from the Society. They should write to American Purchasing Society, 11910 Oak Trail Way, Port Richey, FL 34668 or telephone (813) 862-7998.

There are significant advantages to both buyer and seller in using the American Purchasing Society's supplier certification program. The buyer saves time and gets a thorough and nonpartial report at no expense. The seller gets qualified for a small fee and the rating and report can be used with other potential customers. It saves time for the seller by not having to do the same thing over and over for different customers.

*Case Study: How One Company Obtained Quality Improvement from its Suppliers*

Keep in mind that proper quality is getting what you want. The following example illustrates the value in visiting a supplier's facilities and the importance of asking questions and communicating what you want.

Suppliers of bulk wire charge for what they call "standard industry variance" in the amount they ship to customers. For example, a buyer orders 1,000 feet of wire and the supplier measures and ships 1,090 feet. The extra 90 feet is charged to the buyer because it is within the normal plus or minus 10% factor for this commodity (the buyer recognized that the supplier never shipped quantities that were less than what was ordered).[2]

During a visit to this supplier, the buyer asked to see the wire repackaging area. The operation was accomplished by taking the wire end from a 10,000-foot reel and passing it through a footage counter and spooling it onto a motorized smaller reel. As the counter reached the prescribed footage the spooler motor was turned off and the wire cut to length, usually at some figure longer than the ordered amount.

The buyer asked the operator what happens if he manually pulls the wire backwards or forwards through the counter. "No problem," he answered, "the counter just moves in the direction you pull the wire. I have to

---

[2] This same practice appears in other industries as well. It is common in the castings business and the printing industry, but negotiations can get you closer to what you want. For example you may change the percentages from 10% to 5%.

do that sometimes to stay within the 10% overage limit." Noting this, and the fact that *exactly* 1,000 feet could be measured, the buyer later made a requirement of the salesperson that only exact measurements would be accepted; all overshipments would be returned. Repeated returns would cause the buyer to seek alternate sources that could deliver the exact amount.

As a result, the "standard industry variance" disappeared at this supplier and a calculated cost savings of several thousand dollars was achieved. That's quality performance from a supplier.

W. Edwards Deming was quoted in *Purchasing: Principles and Applications,* "It is up to (the purchasing manager) to discard the old philosophy that accepts common defects in purchased items." Overcharges and overshipments are quality defects. The total elimination of overshipments produced a 100% quality rating for that category. That was the goal.

### Documenting Results of Supplier Quality Evaluations

Not only must you evaluate a supplier's performance but you must do it in a systematic and routine way and it must be documented in writing. To do otherwise introduces the possibility of unintentional bias.

Companies prepare forms of various sizes and shapes that do the job to varying degrees. It pays to take time when developing your guidelines and forms. Figures 11-1, 11-2, and 11-3 provide examples of supplier evaluation reports.

## DEVELOPING A PARTNERSHIP WITH YOUR SUPPLIERS
## ———————— TO ENSURE PRODUCT QUALITY ————————

In today's intercompany business relationships we hear statements such as "Core Supplier," "Base Supplier," "Strategic Alliance," and "Business Partner." These terms may seem enigmatic or at least vague, but they all denote a similar idea. That idea is the importance of quality and the goal of constant quality improvement for the profit of all parties.

The concept of a close alliance between any two companies equates to a partnership. *Black's Law Dictionary* defines a *partnership* as "a voluntary contract between two or more competent parties to place their money, effects, labor and skill . . . in lawful commerce or business . . ." Therefore, in essence, a partnership is based on *quid pro quo*, a sharing something for something or the mutual consideration which passes between the parties to a contract. Buyers must share information with suppliers and vice versa—especially information on:

SUPPLIER EVALUATION FORM

SUPPLIER _____ DATE _____

PRODUCTS _____ BY _____

| | Always | | Usually | | Seldom | | Never |
|---|---|---|---|---|---|---|---|
| | 6 | 5 | 4 | 3 | 2 | 1 | 0 |
| Is experienced in our standards | | | | | | | |
| Delivers quality materials | | | | | | | |
| Is sincere in desire to serve | | | | | | | |
| Has competitive prices | | | | | | | |
| Delivers at quoted prices | | | | | | | |
| Has technical ability | | | | | | | |
| Anticipates our requirements | | | | | | | |
| Will stock special items | | | | | | | |
| Supplies catalogues & technical data | | | | | | | |
| Is helpful in emergencies | | | | | | | |
| Regularly solicits our business | | | | | | | |
| Supplies quotations promptly | | | | | | | |
| Has 24-hour availability | | | | | | | |
| Handles rejections promptly | | | | | | | |
| Keeps promises | | | | | | | |
| Delivers on schedule | | | | | | | |
| Delivers per instructions | | | | | | | |
| Has adequate delivery service | | | | | | | |
| Maintains good records | | | | | | | |
| Closes order quantities accurately | | | | | | | |
| Packages properly | | | | | | | |
| Invoices correctly | | | | | | | |
| Total Number of Checks | | | | | | | |
| No. Checks X Point Value | | | | | | | |
| TOTAL SCORE | | | | | | | |

Instructions:
1. Evaluate supplier on each question and check appropriate answer
2. Count up the number of checks in each colums.
3. Multiply number of checks in each column by the column value.
4. Add together the point values to arrive at the total score.

**Figure 11-1. Supplier Evaluation Report—Equal Weight Questions**

VENDOR EVALUATION REPORT

COMPANY _____     COMMODITY _____

| OFFICERS   Local | (5)_____ | Manager |
| | _____ | Assistant Manager |
| | _____ | Sales Representative |
| | _____ | Other |
| | | |
| (1) Financial Reports | (5)_____ | Dun  & Bradstreet |
| | _____ | Bank Report |
| | | |
| (2) Inventory Value | (6)_____ | Local |
| | _____ | Backup Branches |
| | | |
| (3) Inventory Turn-Over | (3)_____ | Frequency |
| | | |
| (4) Inventory Control | (5)_____ | Perpetual |
| | _____ | Minimum/Maximum |
| | _____ | Other |
| | | |
| (5) Stocking Capabilities | (10)_____ | Coverage of Overall Requirements |
| | | |
| (6) Historical Performance | (15)_____ | Buyer |
| | _____ | Expediter |
| | _____ | Requisitioner |
| | _____ A. | Outside Companies |
| | _____ B. | |
| | _____ C. | |
| | _____ | On-Time Deliveries |
| | _____ | Quality |
| | _____ | Engineering Ability |
| | | |
| (7) Personal Observations-- Plant Visits | (15)_____ | Order Processing |
| | _____ | Purchasing |
| | _____ | Invoicing |
| | _____ | Equipment |
| | _____ | Delivery Proximity |
| | _____ | Housekeeping Warehouse |

**Figure 11-2. Supplier Evaluation Report—Weighted Questions**

VENDOR EVALUATION REPORT (Continued)

COMPANY _____     COMMODITY _____

(7) Personal Observations          _____  Building:  a. Wood
    (Continued)                     _____             b. Brick
                                    _____             c. Multifloor
                                    _____             d. Single Floor
                                    _____             e. Fire Protection

(8) Systems Contracting       (10)_____    A. _ Existing Contracts
    Concept                       _____    B. _ Interest
                                  _____    C. _ Capability
                                  _____    D. _ Understanding

(9) Expansion Potential of    (10)_____    A. _ Broadening of Lines
    Systems Contracting           _____    B. _ Services, Other

(10) Pricing                   (5)_____

(11) Funding Participation     (6)_____

(12) Distribution of           (5)_____
     Spending--Equal Service,
     Cost, and Quality

**Figure 11-2. Continued**

<u>TECHNICAL EVALUATION</u>

| | Max. Score | Vendor #1 | Vendor #2 | Vendor #3 |
|---|---|---|---|---|
| General Engineering Requirements | (90) | | | |
| 1. Understanding of the design requirements | 15 | 15 | 12 | 10 |
| 2. Ability to solve potential problems | 18 | 18 | 10 | 12 |
| 3. Cooperation | 21 | 12 | 12 | 12 |
| 4. Positive impact on the following resulting from a relaxation in the specs: | | | | |
| a. Performance | 12 | 8 | 8 | 8 |
| b. Schedule | 12 | 9 | 3 | 6 |
| c. Quality | 12 | 7 | 5 | 1 |
| Inherent Problems Proposed Design (high score means less problem) | (90) | | | |
| 1. Binding | 9 | 6 | 6 | 9 |
| 2. Adjustment | 6 | 6 | 4 | 6 |
| 3. Compensation | 12 | 8 | 3 | 8 |
| 4. Contamination | 6 | 4 | 4 | 6 |
| 5. Impact loading | 6 | 4 | 3 | 4 |
| 6. Susceptibility to impact | 9 | 6 | 6 | 9 |
| 7. Alignment | 9 | 6 | 6 | 6 |
| 8. Susceptibility to leakage | 9 | 6 | 6 | 7 |
| 9. Assembly | 9 | 7 | 3 | 5 |
| 10. Insulation breakdown | 3 | 2 | 1 | 2 |
| 11. Dielectric breakdown | 3 | 2 | 2 | 2 |
| 12. Switch interface | 9 | 5 | 7 | 6 |
| Compliance to Construction Requirements | (60) | | | |
| 1. Compatibility | 6 | 6 | 4 | 4 |
| 2. Ability to meet weight | 9 | 4 | 6 | 4 |
| 3. Ease of interface | 6 | 4 | 4 | 6 |
| 4. Ability to achieve | 9 | 6 | 6 | 9 |
| 5. Construction | 3 | 3 | 3 | 3 |
| 6. Terminals | 3 | 3 | 2 | 1 |
| 7. Filter | 3 | 3 | 2 | 2 |
| 8. Compatibility of materials | 3 | 1 | 3 | 2 |
| 9. Wire construction | 3 | 3 | 1 | 1 |
| 10. Plating and Finish | 3 | 3 | 2 | 2 |
| 11. Braze ability | 3 | 3 | 2 | 2 |
| 12. Solderability | 3 | 3 | 3 | 2 |
| 13. Weldability | 6 | 6 | 4 | 4 |
| All Design Features | (60) | | | |
| 1. Simplicity | 6 | 4 | 4 | 4 |
| 2. Commonality | 18 | 12 | 12 | 12 |
| 3. Reproducibility | 18 | 12 | 6 | 9 |
| 4. Reliability | 18 | 12 | 6 | 12 |
| Total | 300 | 219 | 171 | 205 |

The Buyer develops the weighting factors in advance of the actual vendor evaluation. Items that may impair success are usually given relatively higher weights than items that pose no implementation problem. The weighting factor values are open to review by management prior to the actual vendor evaluation.

Figure 11-3. Technical Evaluation Report

- objectives
- planning
- scheduling
- resources
- risks
- cost savings

Furthermore, buyer and seller must share the desire for profit and the relationship must be profitable to both parties for it to be successful.

In a partnership, the relationship is based upon trust (a fiduciary relationship) so that you must ensure that there are no surprises. Your marketing and product strategies, the objectives and goals that you wish to attain, all must be shared with your partner. Advance notice of any planning and scheduling changes needs to be coordinated first with your partner to fit them into his capabilities and resources.

You must also share the risks as well as the rewards. If you should ask a partner to "build ahead" or maintain a protective inventory, you need to be willing to share in the disposition of that inventory if it becomes unusable.

Jim Morgan, Editor of *Purchasing* magazine, provides three important insights into the partnering exercise. He states that instead of easing a buyer's job, partnering " . . . demands greater vigilance on the part of purchasing." Three important areas according to Morgan are:

- Buyers need to know more than ever about their suppliers' labor, material, and overhead costs.
- Buyers must have greater understanding of market forces to establish target costs early in the planning cycle.
- Buyers may have to "go to bat" for their partners, using their larger buying clout in price and delivery.

A leader in the partnering field is Bendix-King Air Transport Avionics Division in Ft. Lauderdale, Florida. As manufacturer of highly sophisticated electronics for commercial aircraft, the failure of a component or assembly can have catastrophic results. Bendix-King's ground rules for partnering embrace the following:

- An exchange of ideas
- Sound stock agreements
- Safety stock agreements
- Contingency plans

- Improvements in design and reliability
- Mutual trust through open communications

In the area of engineering change requests (ECRs), whether initiated by you or the partner, a prearranged sharing of the cost increase or cost savings must be established. If your company initiates a cost increase ECR, you should bear all the expense incurred. As for a cost savings ECR, if it is initiated by the supplier, you should allow a greater percentage of sharing by the partner as an incentive to continue to improve the product and cost structure. If such an ECR is initiated by you it would be appropriate to share some of the savings with the supplier.

## HOW TO HELP YOUR SUPPLIER
## —————— ACHIEVE WHAT YOU WANT ——————

If you expect suppliers to perform to high quality standards you must respond in kind. The expression, "Do as I say, not as I do" does not work effectively in most business situations. First, make sure your buyers set the example of a high level of quality if you expect the same from your suppliers. This should be evidenced in all things that you do, especially those that are visible to the supplier. Salespeople see your concern for quality when they see your offices, when they are greeted by your receptionist, when they receive requests for bids or purchase orders.

If you want to convey an impression that you are concerned about quality, typographical or misspelling errors should not be tolerated. Engineering drawings should have accurate and complete information. They should be properly dated and approved. These standards will help you establish the impression of demanding high quality by having error-free administration.

Before you demand 100% from a supplier you need to show the supplier that you too are operating at 100%. Some of the things you do toward that end help the supplier do the same. Here are some guidelines.

***Provide Accurate Product Specifications.*** Errors of omission or commission slow progress until clarifications are made or the errors are corrected. Sometimes the errors result in high unnecessary cost. For example, when nonfitting parts are manufactured. Make sure it is right the first time.

***Ensure Ease of Communication With Your Suppliers.*** That is, make sure they can reach you easily and promptly to clarify information if necessary.

***Ensure On-time Payments.*** Make sure that your finance department or your accounts payable honors the agreement you made. If terms are net 30, then the supplier should be paid in 30 days, not 40.

***Keep Engineering Changes to a Minimum.*** Changes are costly. Even when you are paying for them, changes disrupt plans and slow down the flow of work.

***Minimize the Number of Delivery Schedule Changes.*** The cost of delivery changes is usually much higher than estimated. Many departments are affected.

***Allow Sufficient Leadtime.*** Sufficient leadtime permits planning. It permits the supplier to shop and negotiate for the lowest cost raw material. It also permits the supplier to schedule work efficiently. Insufficient leadtime does the reverse.

***Avoid Unnecessary Harassment or Follow-ups.*** This is especially important if the supplier is meeting schedules and shipping high quality goods. These contacts waste time and are costly. Your objective should be to help the supplier, not to slow him down. Same goes for extra paperwork.

***Work With Your Suppliers.*** Offer the supplier any help you can provide and that he needs. For example, you may offer the assistance of an engineer or a packaging expert or you may offer assistance in locating better sources for raw material. You may help in negotiating the supplier's source or in guaranteeing payment for the material.

## Communicating with Your Suppliers

Purchasing is the funnel for communication between your internal departments and the supplier. You must act as a sort of editor or critic for all your company's information that will be sent to the supplier. Wherever practical, you should review all things before they are sent to the supplier. If a specification is not complete or in error you should try to have it corrected before it is sent to the supplier. If you get notice from the sales department or production control to change a schedule, you should investigate if the change is absolutely necessary and make sure the people in charge of those departments understand the costly effects of changes. Too many companies accept unreasonable delivery requests from customers, when the customer would have been perfectly happy to wait an extra week for normal delivery. That is not to say that we should not try to satisfy the customer. After all that should be a paramount concern, but some requests are only made because the customer did not know the normal ordering method.

## Responding to Your Suppliers

You expect your supplier to communicate promptly with all the facts and in a way that you can understand. You want him to respond quickly to requests for price and delivery. You want his company to provide accurate invoices and packing slips. You require on-time delivery and exact quantities ordered. Likewise, the supplier expects equivalent treatment from you and your company.

You need to return telephone calls promptly. Be patient, cordial, helpful, but firm when asking for expedited service or delivery. Be aware of the limitations of his organization and do not demand unreasonable performance. A breakdown in communications will signal future quality problems and a possible change in supplier.

Since suppliers are interested in selling, they tend to possess infinite restraint in their dealing with customers. If they do not possess this characteristic, they usually do not last long in the business. However, it is not uncommon for those on the buying side to slip into a demanding mode. A confrontational posture with a supplier rarely produces good results.

"Doing it right the first time" does not only refer to manufacturing processes. Suppliers do not like to make changes, accept returned product or cancel orders. Changes cost time and money. Suppliers consider the type of demands you are likely to make and the way you conduct business before submitting bids. If your business is a lot of trouble compared with other companies, you are likely to be quoted a higher price—a price reflecting the supplier's anticipated higher cost in handling your account.

To minimize the burden placed on your suppliers, ask lots of questions of your requisitioner. Know what you need to order, try to make sure that it is the correct item, the correct quantity, and that your requested delivery date is when the material is really needed. Try to reduce changes of any kind once the order has been placed. Both parties lose when changes are made. If your company is known to a supplier as "one that can never make up its mind" you will not be considered a quality customer regardless of how much you buy. Suppliers do make such judgments.

## WHEN AND HOW
## —————— TO NEGOTIATE FOR QUALITY ——————

Remember the saying, "You can't teach an old dog new tricks"? The same can be said for suppliers. It is much harder to improve on the quality produced by long-time suppliers than to start a new supplier off right.

Your buyers should instill potential suppliers with the importance of quality before any business is placed. A detailed discussion of what you expect should be given to the suppliers so they will not be surprised if material is rejected. It is not always easy to get the message across. Some suppliers will not take you seriously. Others will test you to see what they can get away with. Thus, to assure good quality from the beginning you must convince the supplier that you mean what you say and you start this when the supplier walks in the door. Many purchasers discuss quality issues in their "welcome to" brochures or "Suppliers' Guides to Purchasing" which are given to all suppliers wishing to do business with them.[3] Appendix F provides tips on preparing a supplier's guide. It is a good idea to give written quality guidelines to potential suppliers. By having it in writing you can be certain all points are covered and everyone has the same guidelines.

Yes, quality is negotiable. More precisely, the specifications are negotiable and the specifications determine the quality level that you want or need. If a supplier tells you that its product is better because it lasts five years but you only need the product to last two, there is a good possibility you can reduce the cost by reducing the durability. On the other hand if the product is only supposed to last two, you can have the specifications changed to make the product last five years. After that your discussion will only revolve around cost and price.

Sometimes the aspirations of the engineer need to be modified in order to make the product manufacturable. The buyer can help resolve these issues. Many times a supplier can suggest an alteration in the process or the material or the source of supply that will fulfill the quality expectations of the requisitioner. Specifications locking the buyer into a single source may be altered to permit competition. Required testing procedures may be revised to make more material acceptable. Inspection criteria may be changed to loosen or to tighten quality requirements.

None of this is to condone or encourage deviations from specifications. Changing specifications are not the same as allowing deviations. A deviation is a temporary suspension of a requirement to allow goods that do not meet the requirement to pass inspection. Changing a specification is changing the requirement for a longer period of time and can be thought of as permanent. In practice, few things are permanent although they may last for many years.

## —— DETERMINING ACCEPTABLE QUALITY LEVELS ——

Using an engineer's definition of "quality" you first think of adherence to specifications. So in order to determine whether or not you have high-quality products, you need a well-defined set of specifications. Many purchasing managers understand and rely on engineering specifications but take administrative specifications for granted, don't commit to them, and don't measure performance.

When you order product quality you will need specifications from an engineer. When describing purchasing administration quality the specifi-

---

[3] See "How A Supplier's Guide to Purchasing Helps You" in *Professional Purchasing*, published by the American Purchasing Society, Port Richey, FL, Report Number 8, September 1991.

cation could be your operating procedures outlined in Chapter 6. Other administrative specifications may be found in company policy, directives or performance plans, and in any document or set of expectations related to how any task or operation should perform.

To find out whether or not you are conforming to the quality specifications you must have measurements. You also will need numerical goals and targets to strive for. Quality should be 100%, but many purchasing people hear of Acceptable Quality Levels (AQLs) quoted in engineering specifications such as 97.2% or 98.7%. This of course assumes that there is a margin for error and an expectation that errors will occur, as well as bland acceptance when they do occur.

Another quality program that has been around for over 25 years is called "zero defects." We can assume as the name implies that the quality level is to be 100% all the time. Of course that rarely happens. But as Tom Peters says in *In Search of Excellence,* "If you don't shoot for 100% you are tolerating mistakes." "You'll get what you ask for." Another way of looking at "Zero Defects" is that it's better to shoot for 100% and miss it a little than to shoot for 95% and just make it.

The secret to managing quality specifications in purchased material is to set limits that, when reached, signal the insertion of some corrective action to turn around an unacceptable situation. Since quality expectations can change, corrective action is an on-going process; it never stops.

What was acceptable yesterday may not be acceptable tomorrow. The influx of high-quality Japanese products into the U.S. in the last decade or so has raised consumers' expectations of the level of quality they will accept. Automobiles are a good example. Quality is perceived as acceptable form, fit, and function. The car must look good, be user-friendly, and operate well over a long period of time. The availability of parts and efficient service also are requirements of today's consumer. While it may be presumptuous to assume that any automobile will operate for 20 years or 500,000 miles without service or a breakdown, the Japanese have surpassed, in many areas, the quality specifications of U.S. automakers. Consumers have noticed this shift and the resultant increase in the percentage of Japanese cars sold in the United States reflects that. What was acceptable transportation 20 years ago is no longer appropriate today. The bar has been raised.

## Tools for Measuring Quality and Verifying Conformance to Specifications

When evaluating a supplier's ability to deliver the quality level you want you should see what equipment they have available to measure the finished products they produced. Lacking such equipment, they either need to buy and learn how to use it or give you an adequate explanation of how they will know if the product meets your standards. For example, if they do not have adequate testing equipment, they may say they will send the product out to an independent laboratory for testing. In some cases this may be completely satisfactory, while in others it will be costly and impractical.

Your technical people, consultants, and other suppliers can tell you the type of instruments or equipment needed to test various products. Although there are many pieces of equipment needed to conduct special tests or conduct an analysis of material, here are some examples of common testing or measuring devices found in laboratories of many manufacturers.

- Calipers—Instruments resembling compasses usually with curved legs used for measuring inside or outside diameters.
- Gauges—Instruments that come in various shapes and sizes to accurately measure holes or openings. They may be bought in sets off the shelf or custom made for a particular purpose.
- Hardness testers—Brinell, Rockwell, and Scleroscope hardness testers are instruments to measure the hardness of various materials, usually metal.
- Micrometer—Used to accurately measure distances, particularly thicknesses, threads, or depths.
- Microscope—A magnifying device used in laboratories and by manufacturing companies to detect flaws in a product.
- Pantone color chips—One of various methods to check the color of paint or ink to see if it matches the specifications.
- Rulers—Used to measure distances.
- Scales or balances—Used to measure the weight of material.
- Spectroscope—An expensive laboratory instrument to test for the chemical constituents or elements in a material.
- Ultrasonic devices—Used to test for voids in metals.
- Universal testing machines—Used to measure tensile strength, elasticity, and other characteristics of material.
- Visual display units—Used to detect flaws which are shown on CRT screens.
- X-ray—Used to reveal the internal structure of materials.

You should not only look for this type of equipment when you visit a potential or existing supplier, you should observe if it is being used. I have often seen fancy laboratories and test equipment completely dormant. That is, no samples were being tested and no QC personnel were anywhere in the vicinity. Sometimes the equipment is covered with protective coverings or has an accumulation of dust. If you see this condition, you may well wonder if any testing is ever really conducted. It would be a fair assumption to make that testing is not done on a routine basis.

## How to Determine How Many Samples to Test or Measure

Some management people advocate that no testing or checking should be necessary by the buying company. They say that if the supplier is producing and shipping proper quality, it just adds unnecessary cost to have goods checked. We believe this is a rather extreme point of view and not realistic. After all, people do make errors and machines do fail or wear over time. Although you may want to depend on your supplier to check the goods to make certain it is to specifications, you cannot expect all suppliers to do as you would like every time.

Other management people feel that everything should be checked 100% of the time. This is the other extreme. Actually, it all depends on your industry and objectives. If you are purchasing pharmaceuticals or instruments that may determine someone's life or death, you will no doubt want very strict quality controls and a great deal of checking. If you are in a low tech industry that is selling a harmless inexpensive product you may not need much checking.

Today the choice is somewhat easier because there are many automatic devices and on-line systems that measure and control the manufacturing process without costly labor. But some of this equipment can be expensive also, especially if tight tolerances are necessary and the product is complicated.

For most products, random sampling and checking do the job. Using a true mathematically correct random checking method, statistical quality control will let you know what percentage of items are incorrect. All you have to do then is determine what level of accuracy you want and then build in methods and procedures to make sure you get that accuracy. Continual random sampling will tell you when you have a problem that needs correction. Some types of products require random sampling because testing them requires their destruction. For example, you might strike a match to see if it will light. If it does, you know you had a good product, but you destroyed the product. If you tested ten matches and only nine would light, you might conclude that 10% of the total shipment was defective (the actual probability of 10% being defective would depend on the size of the shipment in relation to your sample and assumes that your sample is truly random).

Any buyer who insists on 100% accuracy must realize that there is a cost involved in obtaining such accuracy. Some quality assurance people are claiming otherwise, but we believe that this is an unsophisticated and unrealistic idea. It neglects to consider that some products are much easier to make than others. Less complicated, easy-to-make parts may achieve 100% accuracy most of the time. Complex items are much more difficult to control. The probability for errors increases as more steps, more components, and more people are involved in the manufacture of an item. The quality of an automobile, with thousands of parts, is much harder to control than the quality of a simple bolt. We hope that most of the quality control going into an automobile or airplane goes toward achieving 100% accuracy on the items that control steering and safety. While we want the trim and decorative items to look good, we should realize that there may be some flaws if we want our cost to be within reach.

## HOW TO CONTROL PRODUCT DEFECTS
## AND HANDLE REJECTED GOODS

Most of what you read about quality tells you how to improve your quality or how to avoid quality problems. Very little is mentioned about resolving the problems that every business encounters, and that is what a buyer spends most of the time doing. In spite of all the efforts that you and your colleagues take to minimize quality problems, some will happen. There will be shipments received with shortages. There will be instances when you receive the incorrect item. There will be products received that are broken or mismanufactured. If you build proper quality control measures into your system and make sure the supplier understands the importance of quality from the beginning of your relationship, you will minimize these problems but you will still need to have a method of handling the few that inevitably will crop up.

The first thing you need to do is to establish clear procedures to record the errors. Proper documentation goes a long way toward solving the problem. Without proper documentation, you will waste time arguing over who is responsible and disputes could result in ill will that would break down the buyer-seller relationship that you may have taken weeks, months, or even years to establish.

Documentation of the error should be done at the moment the error is detected and must include all pertinent facts. You need to establish who is responsible for such record keeping and make sure it is done with care so that accuracy is assured. Companies may appoint inspectors or supervisors to prepare the paperwork. It is best to discover the error at the time and place that you take ownership of the goods. This may be at the supplier's shipping dock, at a port of entry, or at your receiving dock. If the goods are received without detecting the error, it may be necessary to report the problem at the using department. The sooner the problem is discovered and reported the more likely an easy solution will be attained. Claims against a carrier may be very difficult to settle if they are not discovered when the goods are received.

If goods are received damaged it is a good idea to take a photograph of crushed or broken packaging.

Here are some of the things that a good receiving clerk or receiving inspector (or both) should record.

- Date received
- Name of carrier
- Bill of lading number, airbill number, or waybill number
- Number of packages, pallets, and so on
- Items and quantities actually received
- Items and quantities described on packing list
- Description of damage to containers or packages
- Description of damage to product or error
- Weight of cartons
- Name of inspector and/or supervisor

Notify the carrier and the supplier promptly of any problems found. Depending on the severity of the problem, it may be wise to telephone the supplier first, but always send a written notice. Make sure that damaged or defective goods are kept in a segregated place, preferably in or with the packaging that it came in. Normally you will have little trouble getting most suppliers to correct a problem on a particular shipment if:

- It is clear that the error was caused by them.
- You report the problem quickly.
- You have evidence of damaged packaging or damaged goods.

The third item requires attention. Once in a while foremen or supervisors will use goods that are off-standard because they need them to complete a job or satisfy one of your customers. This is a mistake if you want to get credit for the goods or even if you want to convince the supplier that the goods were below standard. Although some suppliers will honor your claim to retain your good will, many will not be willing to pay for goods or give you credit for material that you have used.

Sometimes it takes special negotiating efforts to get compensated for defective goods. In most cases you will find it very difficult to be reimbursed for consequential damages or for anything but the material cost. You can obtain compensation for labor that you spent in trying to use poor quality goods or in trying to repair or process it in some way, but this is not usually given without a good effort on your part.

Many companies consider the matter closed once you have been paid for a claim or once the error has been corrected for the shipment in question. Then the problem occurs again and more time must be spent negotiating a settlement. The key to improving quality is to solve the initial cause of the problem. Were directions misinterpreted? If a machine needed recalibration or maintenance, why was it not done? Were the goods checked before they were shipped? The supplier should get to the root cause of the problem and see that that cause is corrected. The quality level will not be improved simply by curing the symptoms.

## CONCLUSION

Quality begins when you first see a potential supplier. You must spell out what you expect before you place an order and you should make sure that specifications or descriptions of the products you want are detailed and complete. Then it becomes an easy matter to compare what you ordered with what you get.

Whenever a major purchase commitment is contemplated, visit the supplier's facilities if practical and find out what quality policies and procedures are in place. Observe what measuring devices are available and if they are being used.

Make sure you document errors and notify the supplier of all problems that occur. Keep damaged or defective goods in a segregated area and make sure they are not used. Negotiate with the supplier to reach an amiable solution to the problems.

Get to the cause of quality deficiencies and make the changes necessary to eliminate those causes rather than only fixing each error as it happens.

# CHAPTER TWELVE

# Obtain Delivery When You Want It

Getting prompt delivery has often been a problem for both small and large companies. Larger companies with mass production requirements exert more effort in solving the problem and because of their economic clout achieve a high degree of success in obtaining prompt deliveries. But all companies, large and small alike, experience occasional delays. To solve the problem you need to know the causes of off schedule deliveries. Then you can take steps toward minimizing, if not entirely eliminating, the problem.

First, prompt delivery is here defined as delivery on a specific date required. That means not early or late. Late delivery can disrupt production schedules and produce customer dissatisfaction. Early delivery can cause congestion and increase the need for costly warehouse space. Paid for early shipments are a needless drain on cash because of too much inventory.

How serious is the problem? Firms which live "hand to mouth" experience many late deliveries because of poor planning and inadequate allowances for leadtime. Other firms avoid the problem by keeping excessive inventories; however, high inventories alone will not eliminate late deliveries. In fact, some firms have excessive inventories and late deliveries. A good inventory control system or Material Requirements Planning (MRP) will help solve both situations. When combined with efforts made by the purchasing department, late deliveries will be rare.

## MEASURING THE PROBLEM OF
## ———— SUPPLIERS' DELIVERY PERFORMANCE ————

To determine how serious the problem of off-schedule deliveries is to a company, some statistics need to be developed. The figures obtained in measuring delivery performance can be grossly distorted by making false assumptions or using the wrong base. An easy and fairly effective method is to count items off schedule for a given time period and divide by the total number of items received for the same period:

$$\% \text{ OFF SCHEDULE} = \text{NUMBER OF ITEMS OFF SCHEDULE/}$$
$$\text{TOTAL ITEMS RECEIVED}$$

The percentage figure so derived will be used to compare performance in future time periods. This method can be applied to each supplier, a group of suppliers furnishing a similar product, or to the purchasing department to measure the effect of a particular strategy.

If you are in a position to demand tight delivery schedules, any delivery not made on the date specified should be counted as "off schedule." If you are not as demanding or you feel that long distances preclude most suppliers' shipping to arrive on a specific date, then you may only count shipments arriving two days before or after the due date as being off schedule. Thus you may modify the formula to fit your particular criteria.

### Calculating the Cost of Late Delivery

The precise costs of off schedule delivery are very difficult to measure. General management may not even be aware of the problem or its cause if there has been no change in method or shifts in results. With either an improvement or a deterioration of performance, the importance of prompt delivery becomes clear. If a company is growing rapidly, most members of management realize that things could be better. If the productivity levels are difficult to maintain, production management may try to point to purchasing or the suppliers as the cause of the problem. This is usually a half truth at best. Production, in-house scheduling, or purchasing may then become defensive and begin to build excessive inventories to eliminate production shut downs. Soon accounting will realize that costs are getting out of hand and begin to exert pressure to reduce inventories. At this point purchasing often becomes caught in the middle between production management and the accounting management. Too often purchasing is in a weaker political position and the game of revolving chairs begins. If you see a company where the purchasing manager has been replaced three or four times within several years, there is a very good chance that this has been the problem. Rarely is a purchasing manager terminated because he cannot negotiate or does not know where to obtain the necessary product.

But putting politics aside, how many companies analyze the consequences of poor delivery? For example, does the sales department keep records to determine how many sales are probably lost because of delivery promises that have not been kept? What is this estimated cost to profits versus the cost to remedy the situation?

## Quantifying Lost Sales as a Result of Poor Delivery

Companies lose existing customers for a variety of reasons. High price and poor quality are two which are not related to this discussion. However, sales reps calling on previous customers can often learn why the customer has left. Having each sales rep submit a standardized report form will help quantify the reasons for the lost sale. You can then use the figures obtained to evaluate the cost of corrective action. For example, if a demand for quality improvement will take an investment of $100,000 for a return of only $4,000, it may be advisable to continue with the present level of quality. If these reports indicate that a half million dollars in business is lost because of poor delivery, an investment in curing the problem is likely called for.

Obviously the figures are only guidelines since many factors are usually involved in making a customer leave. For this reason, you should carefully analyze the data and realize that the figures are estimates. Before assigning specific responsibility for the lost customer, check your records to see if shipments were really late to the former customer. Check the extent and frequency of lateness. For instance, you may find shipments were made on schedule as promised. This may indicate that your own salesperson made a different promise than that which scheduling agreed to.

Even if sales are not actually lost, what is the loss to profits because of reduced efficiency which is caused by shortages or by aisles cluttered with excess inventory? The production department may not actually shut down but may change plans and produce other items which have the raw material available for processing. These changes involve costly extra set-ups. Sometimes production fits in short runs until stock arrives and then returns to previous scheduled work which needs to be completed for a customer. Or production may use substitute stock which is more costly or which was intended for another job and another customer (Although this example obviously refers to manufacturing companies, the ideas apply equally well to hospitals, financial institutions, or other service industries.) The sophisticated company may keep records of all these added costs and charge the excess to the responsible area, but that may serve no real purpose and in itself is a cost. If all concerned realize the extent of the problem and develop a system to minimize off schedule conditions, more elaborate controls may not be needed.

Excessive off schedule conditions also cause morale problems. Tempers become short and chaos reigns. Turnover may be higher than necessary. Production shutdowns cause layoffs. Higher costs because of excessive inventory may make the company unprofitable, uncompetitive, and a candidate for failure. While this may seem an exaggeration since companies seldom fail from one cause, poor deliveries may be a significant contributing factor.

## DETERMINING RESPONSIBILITY
## FOR LATE DELIVERY

Responsibility for off-schedule deliveries is divided between buyer and seller. Usually more than one individual is responsible for off schedule conditions. A lack of understanding of the nature and complexity of the problem is often a major cause. This may be reflected in general management's attitude at the highest level.

Establishing unrealistic or conflicting objectives in various departments or even in the same department can also contribute to off schedule conditions. For example, suppose your staff budget constraint prevents hiring additional help for expediting or does not permit overtime. If available hours do not permit expediting which must be done to obtain timely delivery, then there will be shortages.

More often the responsibility and difficulty are not so apparent. The general manager may be demanding more sales. To get added sales, sales management may in turn make promises to potential customers which are impossible to keep. The sales department feels it has done its job; it got the order as instructed. The production department is now under pressure to deliver the product as promised. The job must be given high priority and bump other jobs later in the schedule. Production is ready to go. Now it begins pushing purchasing to obtain the necessary parts. Purchasing may even demand impossible deliveries from suppliers. With this scenario continued, some vendor will be found who will promise the delivery to get the order. In the final analysis, he cannot deliver as promised, but few realize why or what caused the problem in the first place. Multiply this case by hundreds of transactions for the company which operates in this mode and you can be sure there will be many late shipments or much added cost. The best suppliers will tire of changed schedules and constant panic buying. They will begin to turn a deaf ear to reasonable requests, most likely charge higher prices, and respond to their more reasonable, better organized customers first.

Responsibility may be isolated or shared by general management, production, sales, accounting, production control, and purchasing. Purchasing can do a lot to help solve the problem, but it cannot work in a vacuum. It must have support and cooperation from all departments.

The aforesaid is not to forget the responsibility of the supplier, but a good purchasing manager has more control over supplier performance than he or she has over conditions within his or her own company. Suppliers must compete with other suppliers for business and there is usually more than one to choose from. The management of each function within the company has many vested interests to protect but is not concerned about outside competition.

## UNDERSTANDING THE CAUSES OF A SUPPLIER'S LATE DELIVERIES

*Lack of Communication Regarding the Delivery Date.* A major cause of off-schedule deliveries is poor communication between buyer and seller and poor internal communications at both the buyer's company and the seller's company. Salespeople from the supplier may make promises that are not passed along to the people who are responsible to produce and ship the goods. Production management of the supplier may not advise the sales department of manufacturing problems or capacity problems that affect delivery schedules. One major steel company was in just that type of situation: to the amazement of the supplier's sales personnel, the buyer was the one who discovered where the delivery problem was.

*Poor Capacity Planning.* In other cases suppliers do not properly calculate what their capacity is and make promises that are impossible to keep even if they worked 24 hours a day. They simply do not have sufficient tooling to produce enough of the product.

It is important to consider previous experience producing the product when planning delivery schedules. Repeat orders or orders for existing products usually encounter fewer problems and require less work. New products require more time for administration, planning, costing, engineering, tool development, and resolution of a multitude of unforeseen difficulties. Prototypes may have to be made. Quality Control will have to check specifications. There may even be legal problems connected with government regulations.

*Rejected Orders Because of Poor Quality.* If the required specifications are difficult to meet, delays may be caused by rejections of stock received. Quality Control may be forced to have products reworked or scrapped and produced from scratch.

*Unrealistic Delivery Commitments.* The real cause of poor delivery can be internal. Neither plant management nor sales management should dictate delivery schedules unilaterally. With manufacturing-oriented general management, leadtimes become too inflexible, regardless of the size of the order and regardless of the extra costs that the customer is willing to pay. When the sales department sets the schedule, it most likely will promise deliveries early to assure getting the sale. It is in the sales department's own best interest (short term) to do so. Even though Production Management and Purchasing have pointed out that the schedule is unrealistic and that leadtimes are all too short, somehow the work may get done and the goods are actually produced as promised. With this result, the sales department is pleased and Production Management and Purchasing are proud that they did a good job. Few realize that the foundation of solid management practice has begun to decay.

Two unfavorable consequences have occurred while filling this order. First, in the eyes of the sales department, Production Management and Purchasing have both lost credibility. Even though they made the schedule they said it could not be done. In the future, Sales will use its own judgment more often. Second, even though the schedule was made, what has been the cost to the entire company? Companies with sophisticated cost accounting systems will know the cost of each job. They will know if the particular order in question was profitable or not, but the adverse effect of this particular order on all other orders is exceedingly difficult to measure.

***Changing Order Quantities.*** The above scenario implies a new customer or at least a new order, but suppose quantities on an existing order are substantially changed. In fact, delays because of changes are even more likely to occur because, though the original order had been planned and scheduled correctly, no one realizes the potential harm of changing the quantity. The results, however, are the same as the situation with no planning. If you can only make 100 widgets a day and someone changes the order to 500, you are going to be behind 400 widgets. Somebody is going to have to wait four extra days.

***Supplier Failure or Bankruptcy.*** Serious delays may be caused by supplier failure (i.e., business failure). Before a firm actually goes bankrupt one of the symptoms may be delays in shipments. A firm with major financial problems may have difficulty getting raw material to produce the product when needed. Employee turnover may be high as workers see the handwriting on the wall and leave before the end comes. Even when Purchasing sees this problem in time some disruption in service may still take place. It can take a long time for your buyers to obtain a well-qualified new source. If the failing company were of substantial size, other customers will be looking for a new source also. Consequently, the new supplier could well be overloaded with new customers all clamoring for immediate attention. If the new source plans carefully and gives a realistic delivery promise, lead times may seem excessive and sourcing may then be placed with a less qualified source or one that quotes a delivery schedule which cannot really be met.

***Misunderstandings or Miscalculations.*** What could be categorized under miscellaneous causes of delays are simple misunderstandings or miscalculations. For instance, take the example of certain industries which traditionally deliver quantities within certain percentage ranges from the quantity specified in the order. Even if the buyer is aware of this practice, he or she may not wish to negotiate further or is unable to do so. At that point an add-on to the original quantity requested may be suggested by the supplier. If a minimum quantity of 200 is needed and the supplier's terms indicate shipments will be made within plus or minus 10% ordered, the supplier may suggest ordering 220 to make sure the buyer gets what he needs. Unfortunately if it is critical that 200 be received, the supplier could ship only 198 and still be meeting the terms of the agreement. The simplest way around this problem is to specify in writing that a minimum of 200 must be shipped. (See the appendix for a formula to determine the economic order quantity for this example and in general.)

## HOW TO OPTIMIZE THE PERFORMANCE
## OF SUPPLIERS' DELIVERY

Just as management must determine a desired service level before adequate inventory levels can be calculated, so too a service level must be determined to produce the machinery or procedures to assure on-time delivery. If you are ordering material for a hospital it would seem to be more important to get drugs and surgical tools delivered on time (to a short schedule if necessary), than to get soda or pencils. Likewise, in a manufacturing environment, production supplies take precedence over office equipment. There are usually planned schedules for production jobs; not so for the office equipment. This is not to say that planning for office equipment may not be beneficial, especially for a major replacement or remodeling program. Nevertheless, if management expects the same kind of delivery performance for everything, either disappointment will result or the cost of such performance will become extremely high.

The problem of determining the service levels that should be expected and setting objectives for delivery is a difficult one. In theory we can show that the optimum point is where the marginal cost curve for shortages intersects the marginal cost curve for follow-up activity. This is the point where dollars will be wasted if the added cost of shortages exceeds the added cost of follow-up, and likewise dollars will be wasted if the added cost of follow-up exceeds the added costs of shortages. While the cost of follow-up activity is fairly easy to calculate, determining the exact cost of shortages is more of a problem. The service level obtained at this point should be our ideal objective even though in practice it will be difficult to achieve. To apply the above theory, you must determine the cost of follow-up activity and the cost of shortages.

You can determine the cost of follow-up or expediting efforts by adding the products of the wage rates of all those performing such functions multiplied by the number of hours spent on these activities. Make certain that the time of supervision is included as well as the time of anyone—regardless of actual title—whose duties are involved in improving delivery. These persons may be working internally only or involved in supplier contacts. A factor for fringes and overhead should also be included.

Placing dollar figures on the cost of shortages may require some arbitrary judgments but at least there will be some needed quantification and if you carefully estimate as many factors as possible, you should obtain a reasonable approximation. (For example, you may want to estimate costs on the items shown in Figure 12-1.) Setting up good records will permit better statistics to be developed and the estimates can be improved over time. As the costs change, the minimum point will shift up or down indicating a need for more or less follow-up activity.

To determine the present off schedule condition and equate this to present follow-up activity, now use the formula suggested earlier:

$$\% \text{ off schedule} = \text{number items off schedule/total items received}$$

Then compare present follow-up activity to that suggested at the determined minimum cost point. If follow-up cost is substantially below shortage cost, you can improve off-schedule conditions with a cost saving by investing in more follow-up. You can estimate the extent of the improvement from the figures obtained; however, the accuracy of the estimate will depend on the true cost, skill of the expediters, and real shape of the curves. You can ascertain the shape of the curves through experimentation. The true cost will be more closely approached through experience and time. Skills of the expediter will be improved through experience and possibly using some of the suggestions offered later in this chapter.

The effectiveness of the individuals doing the follow-up work will shift the curves and change costs, therefore changing the target. The individuals' effectiveness will depend on the methods they use, the persuasiveness in their voices and the particular company environment in which they work. A company which shops and negotiates well may be a less profitable customer and therefore may require greater follow-up effort, especially if the purchase volume is very low. A company which is slow in paying or a bad credit risk may not get the attention of a company which pays early.

For these reasons, the slopes and relationships of the curves will vary from person to person and from company to company. In fact, they will probably vary from time to time within the same company if for no other reason than because of general economic conditions. For example, when

### Cost of Shortages

Customer dissatisfaction—lost sales

Lost efficiency because of rescheduling

Substitution of material

Resourcing premium (higher prices or costs to an alternate supplier)

Premium transportation

Management time diverted from other problems and opportunities

Unused resources—idle facilities or equipment

Delayed billing causes cash flow problems which in turn causes lost payment discounts

Overtime required to make up schedule

Extra set-up cost

Contract penalty by customer

Delay causes holding inventory of other items longer than necessary

Need to lower prices to recapture business or get more business because reputation has suffered

### Cost of Follow-up

Wages and fringes of labor necessary

Office space and equipment of follow-up personnel or extra purchasing personnel needed

Telephone expenses

Mail expenses

Travel expenses

**Figure 12-1. Shortage and Follow-up Items for Costing**


business is booming, suppliers may not be able to keep up with schedules (the reverse also occurs; that is, as business slows down, companies cut back the work force and deliveries are again delayed).

It is suggested that several service level objectives be developed rather than a single figure (note: although service level is here used synonymously with percent-off schedule, strictly speaking they would be reciprocals). Use one figure for important or high priority items (some firms may call these critical items) and another figure for less important items. Keeping in mind that these are not absolutes, targets can then be agreed upon based on a given degree of improvement over the present service level. As time passes, a minimum service level can be established.

Using a hospital as an example it may be found that critical items are 3% off schedule, whereas other items are 12% off schedule. (Keep in mind that "off schedule" does not necessarily imply that any staff or personnel were out of material. It simply means that the goods or services were not delivered as agreed.) The target may be to reduce the off schedule condition for the critical items to 2% and reduce the off schedule conditions for all other items to no more than 8%. As these targets are met and maintained for a time, the minimum allowed may be somewhat lowered.

## MINIMIZING THE PROBLEM
## OF OFF-SCHEDULE DELIVERIES

Various steps can be taken by Purchasing Management to keep the problem of shortages at reasonable levels.

*Evaluate New Suppliers.* When selecting new suppliers, buyers should get the names of three or more customers (the number of references will depend on the importance of the item purchased). The buyer should prepare a list of well-planned questions before calling the references and then should contact each reference for an opinion on delivery performance. Of course, at the same time, the buyer should obtain information on quality performance and other factors of interest to the buyer. In fact this helps in providing more honest responses since references will avoid giving excellent ratings on many questions. (See Chapter 7 for details on how to evaluate suppliers.)

Verbal reference checks over the telephone will provide better data than written replies. In person interviews are even better. Much can be learned from the tone of the voice, facial expressions, and body language (nonverbal communication).

To handle a high volume of reference checks and provide uniformity of format, a written questionnaire to be returned anonymously may provide useful information. This system can be particularly helpful when comparing many suppliers. Refer to books on the methods of conducting marketing surveys for the appropriate methods to use. If you wish to have a third party do the checking, the American Purchasing Society has a supplier evaluation program which is most helpful to buyers.

One side benefit of the survey, when older suppliers are included, may be to provide valuable data in assessing internal operations. If many responses indicate that a given supplier is excellent and never late, but your experience is different, you have a clue that the problem may be within your own company.

*Consider Supplier Location.* The location of the new supplier is a factor in making a sourcing decision. Although inexperienced or less capable buyers are too reluctant to source out of their local area, distant shipping points must be considered. Parts coming from Asia or Europe will require larger safety stocks if single sourced. Careful planning will overcome longer transit time and may provide cost savings and superior sources. Nevertheless, if items are purchased "hand to mouth", local suppliers most likely will provide better assurance of on time delivery. This would be particularly true of MRO items (Maintenance, Repair, and Operating Supplies) if they are shelf items.

*Assess the Supplier's Financial Stability.* The financial strength of the new supplier is of major importance and is frequently overlooked or given very little consideration. Large companies with high production volume, such as Ford Motor Company, do a detailed financial analysis on a continuing basis of suppliers of production parts. It would be very costly indeed to shut down an assembly line because parts are not available. However, there is more than that to consider. Cash flow problems make it difficult and costly for the supplier to buy material and get timely delivery. A poor financial picture may indicate weak or incompetent management, prevent the company from obtaining the best and latest equipment, and may even handicap the company in attracting qualified managerial talent. All these factors can affect delivery either directly or indirectly.

*Consider Employee Attitude at the Supplier Company.* The employee relations of the supplier are also important. If you can find out the employee attitude and morale which exists within a supplier's operation, it may provide you with an advance warning of trouble. Nonunion suppliers always are potential targets for organizing. Union shops obviously present the possibility of strikes. The unionized company in many cases may be more predictable than the nonunion company. Some purchasing managers keep a record of each supplier which shows the union affiliations, the contract expiration date, and wage adjustment dates. Using this data you are alerted to potential delivery problems as well as timing of pricing adjustment requests.

*Buy from More than One Supplier.* Potential delivery problems can be reduced by split sourcing. There are well-recognized advantages as well as disadvantages to this strategy. Single sourcing increases the volume of purchases to the supplier and provides more incentive to obtain and keep the business. Dealing with fewer sources reduces administrative costs for Purchasing and Accounting. As volume builds, the buyer has more and more negotiating leverage if the threat of changing sources is believed (regardless of how subtly implied) and is relatively easy to accomplish.

On the other hand, split sourcing provides supply protection. Each supplier can be measured against the other and the percentage of business can be adjusted to one or the other depending upon performance. Where many sources exist for the same product, a conservative policy of using as few suppliers as possible without single sourcing would seem to be the wisest policy. This will keep volume per supplier relatively high, minimize administrative cost and provide supply protection.

***Monitor the Delivery Performance of Existing Suppliers.*** Records will reveal when performance is slipping or improving, and this information can be used advantageously when negotiating. Reward your good performers with a larger percentage of business, and penalize poor performers by giving them less business.

As in most other business statistics, the Pareto Principle is applicable here. A small percentage of the suppliers accounts for a large percentage of the delivery problems. Effort concentrated on these few suppliers will yield the greatest gains. However, there are always some suppliers who, for one reason or another, are intractable. It is probably necessary to re-source in these cases. Since good Purchasing Management is constantly shopping, there are usually suppliers hungrily awaiting the opportunity to prove their extravagant claims of superior performance. The prudent buyer will carefully check references before making the change. There is the possibility that off schedule performance is prevalent throughout the industry.

## —————— PREVENTING SUPPLIER DELIVERY PROBLEMS ——————

### Planning and Forecasting

To prevent shortages or assure on time delivery it is necessary to plan for material needs. Many companies delegate this job directly or through omission of assignment to the lowest level within the organization. That in itself may not be so bad, but the problem is accentuated by dispersing the responsibility. No one in particular is accountable to see that supply needs are planned. Under this system a foreman, first line supervisor, or laborer must determine his or her needs. Because his major concern is in producing the product or service, the need for supplies is determined in a haphazard method and often too late.

If the supplies are requisitioned before available stock is exhausted, the responsibility has been answered. He may only allow purchasing and the supplier a day or two to process the order and get it delivered. When the shipment is late, the failure of the purchasing department or the supplier is the reason stated. In fact, both Purchasing and the supplier may have achieved wonders getting delivery in two weeks when normal delivery takes four. Of course, faster delivery is costly to the supplier, and these costs will inevitably be passed on to the buyer sooner or later.

All of this can be avoided by delegating authority to a central individual or department. This function will plan for supply needs. When a good job is being done, inventory will be kept low and shortages will be very few.

Planning will be more or less sophisticated depending on the size of the company, the importance of supply to operations, and the objectives of management. At minimum, make sure manual records are maintained, information is obtained freely from various departments (i.e., cost, sales data, production schedules, product plans, etc.), and that decisions are made based on good judgment. At the other extreme, you can use statistical forecasting with the aid of a computer. Bills of material may be time phased to provide a complete material requirements planning system (MRP) if the business warrants.

Planning and forecasting are primarily for company requirements but may also consider industry demand versus supply. If a forecast indicates scarce supply, you can take various actions to prevent problems. Obviously, you can obtain additional inventory to avoid stock-outs and to avoid later price increases. But this is a temporary measure and can also be costly. Another solution is to look for an alternative product. The company may decide to make the product, or to buy a supplier's company, or to develop another supplier either domestically or overseas. Through proper planning, management becomes aware of the potential problem while there is still sufficient time to handle it.

## Determining True Leadtime

A most common problem in many operations is misinformation about true leadtime and confusion between *purchasing* leadtime and *sales* leadtime. Purchasing leadtime should be measured from the point where the requisition is delivered to purchasing to delivery of the material. Sales leadtime includes order processing and in-house manufacturing.

Allowance must be made for proper paper processing, contacting the supplier, and transit time. Transit time, which is often overlooked, may take several weeks.

Leadtime will vary among vendors. Some suppliers pride themselves on short delivery time but charge higher prices. Good planning will help avoid paying this unnecessary premium.

Since leadtime varies from supplier to supplier, the person responsible for material control must decide which leadtime figure to use. If the shortest figure is used, stock-outs may develop. Even if an average is used, there may be some, albeit fewer, stock-outs. Choosing the longest leadtime may be costly to sales and unrealistic. Coordination between the various departments and Purchasing will help solve this dilemma. The person responsible for the planning function is the most logical candidate for this assignment. Perhaps the suppliers normally used have leadtimes within a narrow range, differing from each other by only a few days. The maximum figure for these suppliers can be used as the planning leadtime. When it is necessary to use a supplier who has a leadtime well outside this range, the planner will be advised as quickly as possible and adjustments made accordingly.

*Leadtime Depends on Product Design.* Leadtime for a particular product will also depend on the design of the product. Standard products usually require shorter leadtimes. Often they are "shelf" items available immediately at a local distributor or dealer. Even if the product falls in the category of items which are always manufactured to order, the more standard or usual the item is, the shorter the leadtime will be. The reason for this is that manufacturers run high usage items more often than seldom used products.

If one of your company objectives is to service the customer quickly, you then should instruct Engineering to design your product using standard components and sizes wherever possible. The additional advantage gained is a lower priced item. These advantages must be carefully weighed against the advantages of a "special" or a custom designed product. There are certain advantages of non-standard items to Materials Management and Purchasing, but generally they do not outweigh the disadvantages.

*Leadtime Depends on Order Quantity.* The quantity ordered also affects leadtime. If a manufacturer is 75% booked up and you place more than 25% additional business with him, you are going to have to wait until he solves his capacity problem one way or another. He can do so by adding to leadtime, by stalling other customers, or by adding capacity. Part of the problem to the buyer is that many managements do not have a clear idea of what their capacity levels are. For this reason, the supplier will continue to accept orders until serious delays are encountered. It is up to the buyer to ask enough probing questions to find out what real capacity is. The buyer may need to find out which machines will produce the product and what speeds and feeds are on those machines. How many hours does the plant work? What is the backlog?

Knowing the industry and the market is very helpful. Is business down generally? Is the industry in a boom or a slump? How many competitors are there? Are similar businesses expanding or contracting? Visiting the supplier's facilities is invaluable for the smart buyer to really learn about the supplier. Ask to see the schedule. Surprisingly, most suppliers are willing to oblige.

When you are ordering quantities similar to most other buyers, you will affect leadtime least. If, however, you are ordering very small quantities, you may run into trouble. If the supplier normally transacts business in millions of pieces and you only want a few hundred, be prepared for special action, for you have a potential problem.

*Leadtime Is Affected by Previous Orders.* Repeat orders for the same product or with the same supplier take less leadtime. The administrative leadtime with an existing source is shorter because you save time looking for a source, investigating that source, and qualifying the source. The supplier does not have to run a new credit check and he has experience with your requirements. Even though items may be custom-made, repeat orders mean that tooling is available, and engineering and initial production problems have been solved.

Conversely, new products require time for design, tooling, approval of prototypes, quality approval, and elimination of production problems. Experience with a product helps the buyer reduce the price through application of the "learning curve," but it also helps shorten leadtime.

Leadtime with established suppliers is affected by your company's relationship with the supplier. Do you pay your bills on time? Do you require exceptionally tight tolerances, and are your inspectors inflexible? Does the buyer look for every opportunity to take advantage of the seller's mistakes while never giving an inch on those of his own company? Although the buyer's job is to obtain the lowest cost, does anyone doubt that the more profitable customers are in a better position to negotiate shorter leadtimes?

***Leadtime Depends on Shipping Routes.*** Routing of the shipment from the supplier is another variable to consider when determining true leadtime. A change in carrier may mean a two- or three-day difference in delivery. Smaller companies may not have a specialized traffic staff to study this variable, but if records of shipping dates and receiving dates are kept with the name of the corresponding carrier, an analyst can determine the best delivery based on past experience. Do not overlook carrier-caused damages when recommending a particular carrier to be used in the future.

A shorter transit time may also involve a cost penalty. You should weigh the disadvantages of the extra cost against the speedier delivery. Perhaps the normal routing would use the slower, but less expensive, carrier and the more expensive carrier could be reserved for emergency situations. In some cases "premium transportation" (air freight, air express) will be used to meet schedules. These methods do not refer to the name of the carrier, but the method of shipment. For most goods these methods are cost prohibitive and are not considered as normal means of shipping. An exception might be fresh flowers or fresh fruit moving from the Orient to the United States.

***Leadtime Is Affected by a Supplier's Plant Shutdowns.*** A few caveats are in order. Obviously leadtime is affected by strikes. A record of union contract expiration dates will help the buyer to prepare for potential problems. Higher inventory may be advisable as these termination dates draw near. This is especially important for major items or where items are single sourced.

More and more suppliers are notifying customers of plant shutdowns because of vacation, but buyers should still prepare for possible delays during the vacation season. Even though companies do not close, they may be working with a substantially reduced work force which will affect the delivery schedule. Again, an analyst referring to good records may be able to show a clear pattern of problems with particular suppliers during vacation season. Corrective action may require larger shipments prior to inventory or negotiating with the supplier to hire additional help during these periods. Other times of similar problems include holidays and periods of bad weather. Allowances for these problems can be made by applying probability forecasting, but no method will assure total protection. There are bound to be some shortages in a sufficient time span.

## NEGOTIATING THE DELIVERY SCHEDULE

The time to think about delivery is before the buyer places the order. As elementary as this may seem, it is an aspect of buying that is frequently overlooked unless the item in question is to cover a shortage or emergency situation. Even where very long leadtime is acceptable and normal, the delivery schedule calls for special attention. When businesses order capital equipment with schedules months or even years away, it is common practice to neglect discussing delivery performance in detail. Later these businesses often experience hardships because of delays. Do not assume that long leadtimes can be relied upon any better than shorter ones. Sellers sometimes feel that if you waited six months for an item, you certainly will wait seven months without a serious complaint.

Here is a checklist of tips for negotiating successfully for the delivery date you need:

- To keep your negotiating hand strong, you may want to reserve discussing the schedule until last—That is, you should agree on minor points first or on those points where you know there will be no dispute so that an agreeable atmosphere is established. Some sellers try to find out how urgently the material is needed and will then base their price on meeting an early requirement. This price may be exorbitantly inflated.
- Beware of the seller who too quickly offers to meet schedules which seem very difficult for the competition—His offer may be based on wishful thinking and on his determination to get the sale first and worry about the problems later. Consider the following issues:
  — Is the delivery promise realistic?
  — What is the normal leadtime for this supplier?
  — Are raw materials available?

- — What is the manufacturing cycle time?
- — When will work begin?
- — How much open capacity does the supplier have?
- — What is the backlog?
- — After getting answers to these questions, do all the answers agree?
- — What is the probability of success in meeting the schedule?
- — Should the sales rep obtain approval from others within his company?

• Even Sales Managers or company officers may offer unrealistic delivery if the business is badly needed. A buyer who visits his suppliers on a regular basis and gets to know the schedulers will be able to determine normal and unrealistic delivery promises. If previous experience indicates that you can trust the supplier's judgment, you now have solid ground for negotiating.

• Build performance incentives into the agreement—Such incentives may be actual cash bonuses. For example, you might pay $5000 extra if delivery is one week earlier than scheduled. Or you might pay 1% above the selling price for each day the shipment is early. Penalties for lateness are more difficult to negotiate or enforce but are worth trying. A 1% reduction in price for every day behind schedule can be a tremendous motivator. Large incentives provide the best motivator, but even a very small penalty can produce favorable results and is more likely to be accepted. The objective of these motivators and penalties is not to produce income but to obtain timely delivery.

Occasionally, finished goods are held up on shipping docks waiting for the credit department to release the shipment. You can avoid this by making certain that credit has been approved. The Purchasing Manager should make certain that Accounts Payable is up to date and no invoices are being held. If there is a cash flow problem, make special arrangements with your accounting department or with the supplier to assure that shipments will not be held up.

The buyer should try to determine the areas which will cause supplier delays. Perhaps the purchasing company can help solve the problem. Certain tools can be either lent or given to the supplier. The purchasing company may help by doing a portion of the processing or by obtaining a subcontractor who will help. The purchaser can provide raw material (extremely helpful during general shortages). Perhaps the supplier is restricted by limited cash and cannot obtain credit to buy material. The purchaser may help by buying the material, lending cash, underwriting a loan, or by providing a copy of the purchase order to the bank or lending institution. Sometimes, a telephone call to a bank, investor, or supplying company is all that is needed to get credit approval.

The buyer may need to pay for set-up cost to get the supplier to make a short run before his regular schedule. Good purchasing, like good selling, requires imagination. If the seller does not provide the ideas to achieve the buyer's objective, it is up to the buyer to do so.

Buying is a selling job. Taking an adversary position will not provide a long-term relationship or help the buyer in obtaining purchasing objectives such as on time delivery. The buyer should promote cooperation and make an effort to open lines of communication. This is not to imply weakness in any way. The buyer can still be firm when certain limits are reached, but he should be willing to compromise prior to those limits and should strive to understand the other person's point of view and problems. The idea is to discover what the real obstacles are so that solutions can be worked out.

After determining that normal leadtime is unsatisfactory, the buyer must find out what can be done to improve on the schedule. Can overtime help? Will extra staff solve the problem? Although the supplier may not state his objection out loud, he may not want to add to staff or work overtime because he feels the buyer will expect him to absorb the extra costs. If costs are not as critical as delivery, the buyer may offer to pay for a portion or all these costs.

- Be as specific as possible when writing the contract (purchase order)—Avoid using vague delivery dates indicating only the month or week. Avoid using the words "approximate" or "estimated delivery date." Your objective should be a particular date, such as January 7, 19__. Even if your own company schedules are not that refined, it will assign responsibility clearly and minimize future argument. In addition, inventory levels will be much better controlled. If you specify only the month, material needed near the end of the month could arrive on the first of that month. On an annualized basis this amounts to over 8% additional inventory.

- Make certain that any incentives or penalties are carefully and clearly written into the agreement—If delivery is for production, emphasize it in the agreement. You might want to include a clause for revisions of schedule, although the supplier may counter with a need for compensation when schedules are changed (or changed by more than a certain amount). The same suggestions apply to quantity as well as to date.

- Check, and double check, to make sure that all attachments to the order such as drawings, materials lists, separate schedules, and specifications sheets agree with the order. Make certain that the drawings are the latest revisions.

- Specify that you do not want the shipment early and spell out any penalties for early delivery. Such penalties may be as mild as measuring payment terms from the date of scheduled delivery to deducting storage charges from the invoice when submitted.

- Make certain that the supplier understands the difference between ship date and delivery date.

- Require signed acknowledgment of the order and written notification of shipment being made. The former is a basic good practice for important purchases; the latter will give you notice of delays if the form is not received. In addition, expediting effort can be concentrated on the problem or potential problem areas rather than on shipments moving smoothly.

- Require written notices indicating any delay or potential delay. Indicate to the supplier that this will help you take action to avoid a shortage. Emphasize that absence of delay notices will be considered a serious omission.

After several shipments have been made, you will be able to forecast future delivery performance. By comparing the delivery promise with actual receipt of the goods, you can make a statistical forecast of how many shipments will be late.

Untrained and inexperienced employees can damage a good contract relationship by not understanding the problems and objectives of buyer and seller. You can minimize this problem by instructing employees before they contact suppliers. Expediters, engineers, production personnel, and accounting personnel are those who frequently contact suppliers. Company executives and sales personnel may also contact suppliers. All discourteous occurrences cannot be prevented, but you can minimize them by conducting individual preliminary briefings or group instruction sessions.

## IMPROVING A SUPPLIER'S DELIVERY PERFORMANCE

If your company has accepted poor delivery performance, you will need to implement an extensive educational program in order to get the suppliers to understand a shift in your policy and to have them change their habits. In some cases it will probably be necessary to change suppliers.

Inform each supplier of what is expected. However, if this is a radical departure from previous policy, your suppliers may not believe you. The farther away your expectations are from the supplier's normal practice, the less he will believe in your sincerity. A formal presentation giving all of the reasons for timely delivery will help make your new policy credible. Follow up this presentation with subsequent meetings to determine the supplier's true capabilities to meet your new requirements. After the buyer has presented the new policy, it will help to have the Purchasing Manager, Vice President, or President of the company speak to the supplier about the importance of the new policy.

To achieve the new objective, the buyer may have to offer overtime pay, price concessions, more business, advice and information, help in obtaining raw material, or help in expediting with those who supply your supplier.

Occasional minor lateness by an old supplier can be handled by the buyer. Again, if the problem persists, the Purchasing Manager and eventually upper management may need to contact the supplier. As a last resort, legal action can be used before changing suppliers. At first this could take the form of a letter from the legal department or outside law firm. Finally a suit would be entered. The buyer can probably dismiss any supplier if this stage is reached. At this point serious shortages would have probably developed so the remedies offer little help in preventing problems and may only partially compensate the buyer for the cost incurred.

You can reduce shortages and long leadtimes by using *blanket orders* and *stockless purchasing* techniques. Blanket orders allow the supplier to forecast the buyer's quantities well in advance of actual need. The seller may decide to produce all of the goods at once or run off economical batches well ahead of schedule. Blanket orders are frequently given out to reduce paperwork, but the buyer should require some concession from the supplier in exchange for the benefit of a blanket order. The seller saves costs by reducing selling costs, has the opportunity to make or buy in more economical quantities, and can schedule work with a more even volume. The buyer should be able to obtain better regulated deliveries and possibly other benefits (i.e., price concessions, firm prices, special packaging, and so on).

In stockless purchasing, the seller holds the goods on his shelf until the buyer needs stock, or they may be held by the buyer, who is not billed by his supplier until the goods are used. Under the former method, leadtime is short; essentially it consists of order processing and transit time. When supplier and buyer are geographically close to each other, this may only be one day. With the latter system, the stock is on premises and leadtime is zero.

## ROUTINE FOLLOW-UP
## TO ENSURE ON-TIME DELIVERY

Most purchase order forms have an acknowledgement copy which is sent to the supplier with the original. The supplier is supposed to sign the acknowledgement copy, indicating agreement to all terms and conditions including the delivery schedule specified, and return it to the buyer. If the supplier disagrees with any portion of the order he may revise that portion on the acknowledgement form, which legally constitutes nonacceptance of the order as written and is interpreted as a counter offer. (However, Section 2-207 of the Uniform Commercial Code states that additional or different terms from those offered or agreed upon constitute acceptance ". . . unless acceptance is expressly made conditional on assent to the additional or different terms." See Chapter 3 and the UCC, page 419.)

If the buyer in turn disagrees, action must be taken immediately. Such action may be a letter of protest, a telephone call, or a counteroffer. Oral action should be confirmed in writing. If the buyer does nothing, he is indicating acceptance of the revised order as submitted by the supplier in the form of the returned acknowledgement copy.

In practice only a small percentage of acknowledgements are received. Those received consist of the acknowledgement copy of the buyer's purchase order or the seller's sales acknowledgement form. A small percentage of the buyer's form is received. Receiving the seller's form places some burden on the buyer since the document must be carefully checked for differences in the agreement. All terms and conditions should be compared with the previous agreement to evaluate any changes or difference. Here, however, we are only concerned with the scheduling portion.

Because of the difficulty in receiving acknowledgements, there are two prevalent policies used in purchasing operations. One is to constantly work and struggle to obtain acknowledgements; the other is not to worry about them at all. A more prudent approach seems to lie between these extremes, using the Pareto Principle—assuring receipt of a small percentage of acknowledgements (for example 20%) will protect the buyer's interest. The buyer need not worry about shipments which are to be sent within one or two days time after the order is placed. Nor is it necessary to require acknowledgements on orders of very small dollar value which do not affect production schedules. Non-submission of an acknowledgement by the seller implies acceptance of the order as written.

With all of the above said, it is still to the buyer's advantage to get written agreement on the schedule of shipment, especially when the supplier cannot be relied upon to ship on schedule. Purchasing managers or buyers may find it a burden to monitor acknowledgements. To ease the workload, the records may be assigned to a clerk or secretary with instructions to pass acknowledgements with revisions back to the buyer. An expediter may be assigned the task of assuring that certain types of acknowledgements are received.

It is important to keep records and keep them in such a manner that information can be retrieved readily. One method is to attach acknowledgements to the Purchasing file copy of the purchase orders. (All paperwork regarding a given contract or purchase order is kept stapled together. This includes documents such as engineering drawings, specification sheets, requests for quotations, bids, bid analysis sheets, purchase orders, changes, correspondence, and acknowledgements.) Later if litigation on the order develops, the Purchasing Manager will be very glad that these documents were kept together.

Small organizations may of necessity require the buyer or purchasing agent to handle routine follow-up. Medium-size and large organizations have a choice. Specialists may be assigned to do all follow-up and expediting, and there may be fewer buyers than the usual number for that size organization. Or there may be more buyers than normal, who also have the responsibility of follow-up and expediting. Both systems have advantages. The buyer who has both buying and follow-up responsibility will be fully informed about all of the details of the order and how it is progressing. However, he will be constantly diverted from his shopping and negotiating duties and will tend to slough off the activities that he likes least.

Using specialists will reserve the buyer's time and energy for the more difficult problems. The buyer's voice will be more respected by the supplier if he is not involved in routine matters that can be handled by someone with less authority. The primary disadvantage of taking the specialist approach is that communication of data may be delayed or not conveyed at all. The follow-up person or expediter and buyer must be on good terms and work closely together as a team.

**CAUTION:** When following up with suppliers, don't overdo it. Although it is important to keep informed about schedules and shipments, excessive follow-up action is possible. Harassing the supplier with repeated telephone calls on a routine basis can be compared to the story of the boy who cried wolf once too often. When a real shortage situation develops, the overzealous buyer or expediter may find it difficult to get the supplier's attention. In this case extreme action may be required before he is believed. Such a situation also develops when the buyer's company cannot forecast or control its own schedule in a reasonable fashion.

Proper contract negotiations and complete forceful instructions from the buyer to the supplier should alert the seller to delivery requirements and the advance notices of delivery which are required. Routine follow-up should then be handled easily and quickly without the need for frequently repeated contacts. If the buyer can really count on a supplier's prompt delivery, advance notice of shipment may not be necessary. Why generate unnecessary paperwork routinely? As in all business activities, management by exception is a cost effective guideline. Keep in mind that many businesses operate successfully with little or no routine follow-up.

### Obtaining Necessary Follow-up Information

The scheduled date of the shipment is usually about all the information that can be obtained prior to shipment. More sophisticated or larger companies, which are accustomed to careful materials planning on their own part or on the part of the selling company, can determine more details prior to shipment. These details may include number of packages, method of packaging (such as carton, drums, skids, pallets), the name of the carrier, and routing. After the shipment has been made, all of the above mentioned information should be available in addition to the following:

- either a waybill, bill of lading, or air bill number.
- a car number, for full carload rail shipments
- a trailer number, for truckload shipments
- the flight number, for air shipments
- the date the shipment was picked up by the carrier and the expected or estimated time of arrival (ETA).
- how many items are in the shipment as well as the quantities and a description of each item.

If the above information is obtained by telephone, make sure the name and title of the person giving the information are recorded. The availability of all this information indicates that the shipment really has been made. If tracing the shipment in transit is necessary, the buyer or expediter will have the data to do the job.

The objective of routine follow-up is to assure that shipments will be made on schedule or have been made on schedule. Often the follow-up activity breaks down because the sheer volume of work overwhelms the staff available to handle it. What results is attention to real shortages only. If policy calls for maintenance of a routine follow-up system, you can employ a number of work saving techniques to reduce the labor-hours required. For example, mail form letters and postcards routinely to obtain delivery schedules or remind shippers of due dates (see Figure 12-2). If the responses to these communications are unsatisfactory, telephone contacts can then be made. Using the telephone to get information for a large number of items from many suppliers is very time consuming and costly. Recording data from acknowledgements eliminates some of the calls necessary, but a great many others can be eliminated by the use of the mails.

It is important to develop a detailed system to handle the volume and to monitor that volume and its related activity to assure coverage and effective results. A record of all contacts should be kept and compared with hours expended and results obtained by each different method.

## EXPEDITING REAL AND POTENTIAL SHORTAGES

The purpose of routine follow-up is to obtain information and avoid problems. When the expediting function is employed, a problem already exists. The problem may be an unreliable source, an unpredictable schedule, a

**COMPANY NAME**

**ORDER SCHEDULE INQUIRY**

To:

Date of this inquiry:

**Please refer to the Purchase Order or Request for Quotation Numbers shown in column 5.**

| 1 | 2 | 3 | 4 | 5 | 6 | 7 |
|---|---|---|---|---|---|---|
| Items or Item | Description | Quantities Ordered | Quantities Received | Purchase Order Or Quotation Number | Order Dated | Scheduled or Promised Delivery |
|  |  |  |  |  |  |  |
|  |  |  |  |  |  |  |
|  |  |  |  |  |  |  |
|  |  |  |  |  |  |  |
|  |  |  |  |  |  |  |
|  |  |  |  |  |  |  |

☐ Please confirm in writing immediately that ordered items and quantities will be shipped in accordance with the scheduled or promised delivery shown in column 7 above. For your convenience you may use the attached copy of this form when replying.

☐ In accordance with your promised schedule and delivery shown in column 7 above, YOUR SHIPMENT IS NOW LATE. If the item(s) have been shipped, please immediately advise us the Bill of Lading or Waybill number, date shipped, name of carrier, number of pallets, skids, cartons or packages, weight and routing. If shipment has not been made, advise reason for delay and when shipment will be made. Immediately after shipment, advise us full shipping details as spelled out in the second sentence of this paragraph.

☐ Items marked * are urgently needed. ☐Use premium transportation, ☐ Take steps necessary to make delivery to us by _____

☐ Your delivery schedule or promise date is too vague. Please give us a specific date when the item(s) can be expected to arrive.

☐ Only partial quantities of the above items have been received. When will we receive the balance of the entire order. Please supply details on each item and on total quantities.

☐ Please mail all required information immediately.       ☐ Please FAX all required information immediately to 555-5551

☐ Please phone requested information to 555-5552 and confirm in writing.

Requested by _____

Title: _____

**SUPPLIER'S REPLY**

_____

_____

_____

_____

Submitted by _____

Title: _____

**Figure 12-2. Order Schedule Inquiry**

potential strike. The point is that expediting should not normally be necessary.

If you decide that expediting is necessary, take action at the earliest possible time to achieve the best results. The expediter should contact the persons who are best able to supply reliable information and who have the authority to get the action required. These people may be at the top of the company echelon or at the bottom. For example, officers, managers, and supervisors of one company in a major mid-west city could not be relied upon to give truthful information about production schedules or shipments. The expediter of the buying company got to know the shipping and receiving clerks of the supplier and obtained accurate information. Needless to say, the buyer was earnestly searching for a better source, but in two years still had not found another company that could produce the product competitively. Meanwhile, the resourceful expediter was keeping the buyer out of trouble.

It does not matter who supplies information for routine follow-up as long as the data is complete and accurate. With potential or real shortages, someone in authority should be the contact. The level of authority depends on the importance of the item and the urgency of the situation. Since the status of some buyers is relatively low within their own companies, they are often reluctant to contact top executives in other companies. This is particularly true when they are contacting very large organizations which intimidate the caller and attempt to block the call or shield the executive from trivial matters. Nevertheless, the attempt should be made because it pays off.

Some buyers have failed to get through to the President but reach his secretary who offers to help and get action. With a giant corporation that has many divisions and plants, a call coming from the President's Office has almost as much effect as a call from the person who holds the TITLE. Sometimes, the secretary will give the message to a Vice President or Division Manager to handle. This has the same effect.

## Solving Delivery Problems

When contacting suppliers for expediting purposes, the expediter should keep in mind the objectives of the contact. First, there is an immediate problem to be solved: to eliminate the shortage or potential shortage. Less urgent for the short run, but perhaps more important over an extended period, is how to avoid similar difficulties in the future. The supplier will tend to forget about the long-term problem while he concentrates his efforts on curing the immediate difficulty. The expediter or buyer may allow this lapse to happen temporarily but should set up a meeting soon after the crisis is over to discuss permanent measures to prevent reoccurrences.

Part of the expediter's or buyer's responsibility is to determine the real reason for the shortage. The stated reason frequently is a cover-up of some of the problems previously discussed, or the underlying cause of the problem may not even be known. The former case sometimes can be solved by the buyer when he finds out what the problem is. The latter situation is more serious and may mean the buyer should find a new source as quickly as possible.

Delays can sometimes be solved by overtime work. The supplier is usually reluctant to incur this extra expense unless pressured to do so. The buyer should realize that all extra cost will ultimately be reflected in price. This is not to imply that the buyer should not occasionally take a firm stand and insist on the supplier absorbing the extra cost if the responsibility is clearly that of the supplier. Doing so on a regular basis will either weaken the vendor as a source or cause prices to be raised. To get delivery without these future problems, the buyer may have to authorize payment of overtime. But when you ask a supplier to work on Sunday or a holiday and tell him you will assume responsibility for the charges, it is amazing how delivery, which was previously impossible to make before, suddenly becomes possible. Few people want to tell employees to work on holidays. Offer to fly 3,000 miles to your supplier's plant so you can watch your parts being completed. Or better yet, simply say you will be there, and then take the trip if you are willing to spend so much time and money.

Delivery of goods can sometimes be speeded up by using premium transportation methods, such as air freight. Ford Motor Company has used a private plane, with the back seats temporarily removed, to ship some small sheet metal parts from one assembly plant to another to keep the lines moving.

On one occasion a sufficient number of laborers did not show up to complete the installation of a new crane and hoist at a Chicago metal stamping company. The job was to be completed over the weekend so that regular production would not be affected. The contractor said that he simply could not complete the job as scheduled. The buyer solved the problem by giving the supplier three of the company's maintenance workers to help. The supplier was still held responsible, and the job was finished as scheduled.

The buying company can provide various things to the seller to help him directly to meet the schedule or help him indirectly with his business. The latter method may provide sufficient motivation to solve the problem permanently. Consider offering various services such as maintenance, data processing (MIS), marketing, advertising, personnel, consulting. Tools or equipment may be of use in solving the problem. Extra capital may be needed for raw material. Expediting effort with the supplier's source may help.

Ford Motor Company used to have a purchasing department representative practically live with suppliers who were having difficulty meeting "Job 1" commitments for the new model year. They called this their Production Assurance Program. Each year a number of representatives were sent to certain suppliers and stayed with them for a month or two until a continual supply of acceptable quality parts was available. The same supplier might be making parts for both GM and Ford. In one case the Ford representative stepped out of the supplier's plant for a few hours. When he returned, he found the Ford parts' production had been stopped and the GM parts' production started. He learned quickly that he could not be gone for very long until production levels were adequate for both customers.

For smaller companies with smaller expediting budgets there are services available which will handle expediting in distant cities. Retired purchasing agents and other executives can produce effective results at a low cost. Many would be glad to keep busy and contribute.

## REPORTING AND ANALYZING
### DELIVERY PROBLEMS

Keeping all of the recommended records will not do management much good unless periodic reports are prepared, read, and analyzed. After analysis, informed decisions on whether or not to take action and what kind of action to take will then be made to remedy the problems.

Personnel may exaggerate the severity of the shortage situation. This is particularly true of production people who depend on every item being available to meet their own schedules. If they are missing a half dozen items, it may seem to them like everything is short. Reporting will clarify the extent of the problem and allow you to concentrate your effort on eliminating the areas of difficulty. Comparing reports will permit a systematic method of determining if the same items or suppliers are repeat offenders, or if the troublesome items or suppliers are always different.

Comparing reports for different periods of time will enable you to measure performance improvement or lack of improvement. You can compare the volume of shortages to the sales volume and output to help measure company efficiency at various levels. Analysis of the reports can reveal causes of customer dissatisfaction, decline in sales, or other areas which require management attention.

Buyers or expediters may issue various types of reports. These may be automatically generated by the computer but certain input data will probably come from either the buyer or expediter. Other data may come from receiving, quality control, and production control. The computer can be left to do the tedious work of analyzing the data and producing the report. Nevertheless, interpreting the results and taking corrective action is ultimately a job for human skills.

Some of the reports which have been used include the following:

- Leadtime report—A report listing leadtimes by product category, part number, or supplier. General reports covering wide categories are often published in various purchasing periodicals. These reports usually indicate changes in leadtimes since the previous report was issued.
- Shortage report—A list of items which are either behind schedule from the supplier or which are out of stock. Note the difference: out-of-stock items do not necessarily mean that the supplier is behind schedule.
- AUTHORIZATION FOR EXCESS TRANSPORTATION REPORT (AETC)—A list of items which require the use of premium transportation to meet the schedule requirements or to eliminate a shortage. This report shows the excess cost of using premium transportation (such as air freight) over the normal or least costly method. It may also summarize the number of uses and total the excess cost by area of responsibility (i.e., supplier, sales, schedule change).
- Analysis of service level—This report shows the rate of on-time deliveries compared to those off schedule.
- Analysis of leadtimes—This report shows the predicted or stated leadtime by the supplier compared with the actual performance.

## SUMMARY

We have discussed the extent of delivery problems and how costly they are to any organization. Suggestions were made on how to measure the cost. We have indicated who may be responsible and what the causes may be. Methods of minimizing the problem and preventive measures were covered in some depth.

The importance of determining true leadtime was covered as well as certain problems which affect leadtime.

It was demonstrated that buyers play a key role in minimizing delivery problems by placing scheduling on their agenda of items to be negotiated prior to the purchase.

Routine follow-up was differentiated from expediting of shortages. Effect performance requires difference in the method used. In either case detailed forwarding information should be obtained.

And, finally, we showed that it is necessary to keep records and report activities; in this way management can make informed decisions on solving the problems which are either causing the off-schedule deliveries or which result from them.

# CHAPTER THIRTEEN

# How to Use Different Buying Techniques for Different Products

New buyers sometimes believe that all products and services are purchased in the same way. While this has an element of truth many products require special knowledge of those products and the way they are sold. An experienced buyer knows that many things need to be considered for one type of purchase which do not apply to another. Specification requirements vary widely and no one is expected to know them all, but a well-informed buyer will attempt to learn the essential characteristics of the items purchased most frequently.

The American Society For Testing and Materials publishes volumes on most types of products and services that you buy. It is expensive to buy all of them, especially since you most likely will not need most. A compromise is for you or your engineering department to buy the complete specifications for the major items you buy. In addition, we suggest you purchase *Selected ASTM Standards for the Purchasing Community*[1] which contains 200 standards taken from 31 different volumes of the *Annual Book of ASTM Standards*. The buyer should scan this book to see what is included with most specs. You will obtain better quotations if you use accepted nomenclature. A knowledge of specs will go a long way to help you make better purchases, but the ASTM books do not give you other important

---

[1] *Selected ASTM Standards for the Purchasing Community*, Second Edition 1990, ASTM, Philadelphia

information about the products. They also don't tell you how the products are made or what substitutes you may use. Most importantly, they do not tell you how prices are established or price formulas that are used. You must go elsewhere for this information.

To simplify the types of purchases that are made, they are usually divided into three or more broad categories:

- production material used in products being manufactured (sometimes misleadingly referred to as commodities)
- maintenance, repair, and operating supplies items (MRO)
- capital equipment.

Depending on the type of business, sometimes other categories are used such as services, construction contracts, finished goods for resale, and office supplies. In manufacturing organizations all of these except goods for resale are usually included within the MRO category. Depending on the size of the company, work volume, and the organization structure, MRO and Capital Equipment Purchasing may be assigned to one section, department, or person. This chapter provides different purchasing techniques that are used for each of these categories. The chapter also discusses unique features of various products that you should know before attempting to purchase them.

## ⎯⎯ BUYING PRODUCTION MATERIAL (RAW MATERIAL) ⎯⎯

Although not spelled out as such, much of the writing about purchasing concentrates on production material. Perhaps this is so because purchasing has received most attention in the manufacturing area where a very high percentage of the sales dollar is spent. Production material normally has the following characteristics:

- The product is purchased in large quantities.
- The product is purchased repeatedly over an extended period of time.
- Particular specifications are important and frequently are unique.
- Specifications are often furnished by the buyer and may be proprietary.
- The unit price may be very small, even in fractions of a cent, but the high volume translates into a large annual expenditure.
- The products usually are not shelf items. That is, they are not available out of stock. Consequently, leadtimes are relatively longer.
- The accounting department charges production items to inventory accounts.

Since production material (or raw material) accounts for a large percentage of the purchase volume in a manufacturing company, most of the negotiating effort should be spent on getting the lowest possible cost. Buyers need to learn everything they can about the product, the industry, the suppliers, and the people they are dealing with. Good buyers make sure they visit the facilities of their production suppliers to learn how the products are made and to get to know the key people that are involved in making the product.

Buyers should try to negotiate long-term agreements for production items that are used on a continual basis over an extended period rather than negotiate for each shipment. Although many companies use a new purchase order form to release every shipment, it is better to have a release form or to schedule the shipments in advance on the original purchase order. It is often impractical to schedule the shipments on the original form because of inaccurate forecasts; therefore in those cases a separate schedule form or release form is preferred.

Negotiating for every shipment or requirement when an item is continually purchased is wasteful of time. In addition, it is a poor method of obtaining the best agreement. It puts the buyer under undue time pressure to conclude the purchase without obtaining the best terms. By negotiating in advance, the buyer has time to schedule the negotiations and plan a strategy to achieve desired goals.

The buyer should negotiate when there is minimum need to conclude the agreement quickly. Renegotiation of the same item can be planned for a specific time of the year when other activities are at a low level. Although it is to your advantage to postpone any price increases until the annual (or other time interval) discussions take place, allowing price changes during the term of the agreement may be necessary. However, price changes alone need not be the criteria for issuing a new purchase order. The price may be allowed to fluctuate according to a formula spelled out in the initial order. The fluctuations may be limited as to frequency or amount and depend on actual additional cost incurred by the supplier.

Because of the usual higher dollar amounts in production purchases, it is often worthwhile to spend time in doing value analysis, cost analysis, and more comparison shopping.

## MAKING MRO PURCHASES

The unit cost and volume of maintenance, repair, and operating supplies is usually low. However, the purchase price of the item may only be a small fraction of the cost involved with the need for the item. For example, a small gasket costing only fifty cents may be needed to repair a machine that is worth $100,000 and the machine produces products to fill customer orders worth millions. Some items that usually fall under the MRO classification for most companies include stationery supplies, janitorial supplies, first aid items, plumbing supplies, electrical supplies, and safety supplies. The accounting department charges MRO items to expense accounts.

Because the unit cost of the items is normally low, management and requisitioners alike fail to appreciate the MRO buying function and its difficulties. For this reason, junior people, trainees, and sometimes the less capable buyers are given this responsibility.

The MRO buyer must deal with all levels of employees. Requisitioners, regardless of their level or their function, feel their needs are most important and should be served first. When they don't get the service they believe they should have they complain loud and clear. It takes a special person to be able to handle this criticism and pressure. When the MRO buyer is very likable, any delays or problems may be directed at the purchasing department in general rather than at the buyer involved.

Again, because of the low value of MRO purchases, the purchasing manager, even in large organizations, often neglects this specialized area. This is especially so when complaints or problems are at a minimum. But because complaints are at a minimum does not mean that a good purchasing job is being done. The reverse may be true. Products may be of the proper quality and be delivered on time which eliminates most complaints, but the price for the products may be highly inflated. A buyer or purchasing manager who plays politics and tries to please everybody regardless of costs does the company little good.

Without using time-saving methods it is often difficult if not impossible for the MRO buyer to handle the work volume and satisfy the needs of requisitioners. One solution is to add more people to the function, but it is usually a costly solution. Time-saving methods include the use of efficient well-designed forms, electronic data interchange, blanket orders, and systems contracts. Standardization of products is also an important aid to efficient MRO purchases. A buyer who shops the market for the best price on every item may be desirable when the items have an extremely high purchase cost, but it is not a cost effective or efficient way to handle low price and low volume items. For example, one MRO buyer shopped every item relentlessly. He called six suppliers to get the best offer. No doubt about it, on a single item basis, he got a price difficult to beat. However, he had great difficulty in keeping up with the work volume and thus many of the requisitioners complained about the poor service. This same problem buyer refused to take the time to negotiate long-term agreements or to build up the volume with the best suppliers so that he would receive better discounts based on the higher purchase volume of all items. You know the results. The company was forced to dismiss him.

When MRO buyers are so busy placing orders for individual items that they fail to look at the bigger picture, they overlook cost saving opportunities. For example, in another situation, management cared little about

MRO purchases except that the products needed were delivered on time. When blanket orders and systems contracts were instituted, statistics could be accumulated and reports generated. The result was that it was discovered that there were three times as many prescription safety glasses ordered every year as there were employees and that there were a hundred times as many work gloves ordered as there were employees. Controls were established and cost reduced significantly.

Here are some guidelines to help you do a better job with your MRO purchases; they will make the job easier too:

- Negotiate long-term agreements and issue blanket orders or system contracts with general line distributors for most of the products you buy repeatedly. Most companies use many standard products which are purchased from distributors. For example, you might have one agreement with an office supply source, another with a janitorial supply source, another with an electrical supply source, and so on.

- Insist that your requisitioners give specific dates when material is needed rather than vague statements such as "rush" or "ASAP." Through personal contact and written instructions, teach requisitioners the advantages of planning their needs and giving sufficient leadtime. Use diplomacy with your requisitioners.

- Insist on proper documentation of all requirements. Make sure that all requests are put in legible writing and signed. Preferably, such documentation should precede any action you take, but in emergencies make sure that a requisition is submitted to record the authorized transaction.

- Maintain a log of incoming requisitions by date and record the date action was taken and the date that the order was placed.

- Keep your requisitioners informed about progress on placing their orders and the expected date of delivery. Doing this in writing usually saves time in the long run.

- Code the products purchased by category so that you can see how much is spent in each category. This helps negotiate agreements for those categories and lets you know which areas to concentrate your efforts for the largest rewards.

- Develop EDI (Electronic Data Interchange) systems with your suppliers to eliminate paperwork and save labor.

## BUYING CAPITAL EQUIPMENT

Capital equipment items are usually purchased in low volume but have relatively high price tags. The accounting function differentiates between MRO and capital equipment by what account they are charged to. As indicated, MRO items are charged to an expense account within the month they are purchased, whereas capital items are charged to an asset account and are depreciated over time as allowed by the IRS.

The amount of time you spend shopping and negotiating for a capital equipment item should depend on the total expenditure you plan to spend for that item within a given period of time. For example, if you are going to buy a computer display and do not expect to buy another for several years, you might only want to look at three or four sources. If you expect to buy several hundred in the next few years, it is prudent to spend much more time considering the purchase and doing much more shopping. Or suppose you are going to buy an airplane for your company and never expect to buy another. Even though you are only going to buy one, the value of a single airplane is so high you will certainly want to do a thorough job shopping and analyzing the facts before you make the purchase.

In many cases, purchasing isn't given much room to shop or negotiate. The requisitioner and frequently higher level management select the product and even the source. We can say unequivocally that such practice is usually detrimental to the interest of the company.

Many companies use good budgeting techniques and strict controls on expenditures only to give the game away when a purchase is approved. Management of these companies must have the belief that they are controlling purchases. No, not really. They are only controlling the authorization to purchase, not the amount that will be spent on a particular item. This mistaken notion may be because higher level management believes that the purchasing department will control the purchase, but buyers are often prevented from doing so by the budget control system. When preparing the request for budget, the user obtains one or more quotations from outside suppliers to use as a guide or cost estimate in requesting the budget. When the budget is approved, the approval is misconstrued as approval to purchase the product as specified in the quotation used for the estimate. **NOTE:** The budgeting procedure must be divorced from the purchasing operation to obtain good purchasing results. Ideally all quotations should be obtained by the purchasing department rather than users who are going to establish specifications that lock purchasing in to a single source. When purchasing is given this responsibility, allowances must be made for the additional work volume. The number of hours budgeted to other departments for this function should be transferred to purchasing.

Capital equipment purchasing is complicated by the fact that products differ among suppliers. Each supplier usually has its own specifications and each product may have slightly different characteristics to perform the same function (unlike items used in production which are often specified by the buyer and may be proprietary with the buyer). For example, the engineering department of an automobile manufacturer specified the length of forks on forklift trucks. The user at the plant level preferred another brand which was less costly but the purchasing department was mandated to buy the specifications established by the engineering department (See Chapter 5). This forced the purchasing department to buy from a particular source since that was the only supplier to offer trucks with forks of that length.

Good purchasers evaluate the available products on features as well as cost. Costs are measured in the long run and compared with the plans and objectives of the organization. For example, let us say brand "A" is expected to last for 20 years versus brand "B" that will last for 10 years. Even if the *cost* per year for brand "A" is lower, brand "B" may be a better choice if the *price* is lower and if your company only expects to use the product for the next few years.

## BUYING SERVICES

Purchases of many services frequently fall on the MRO buyer although a special buyer for services may be appointed, especially with larger organizations. The average MRO buyer handles many purchases of repair services, such as repair of typewriters, computer hardware, other office machines, plant equipment, automobiles and trucks, motors, and maintenance of fire extinguishers, to mention the most common. Some of these repairs are done at the suppliers' facilities and some are conducted on the buyer's premises.

There are some areas of caution when purchasing services:

- If the work is on your premises, obtain proof of workmen's compensation insurance, and attempt to limit your liability for injury.

- If you are sending an item out for repair, determine if the supplier is reliable, obtain a receipt for delivery, and determine if the supplier has insurance to cover your material.

- Obtain references and check them out.

- Keep records of all service calls. Measure the cost of paying for service as you need it versus service contracts. Remember companies would not sell service contracts if they were not making a profit on them. Scare tactics are frequently used to get the buyer to take the service contract. "We service our customers with service contracts first; we may not be able to service you for a long time if you don't have a contract." However, I have experienced no such delay and actually achieved a sizable saving by eliminating many service contracts.

- Make sure quotes and invoices separate material and labor costs. Some states impose a sales tax on material but not labor. If they are lumped together, you pay the sales tax on the full amount.

- Establish the cost for the service before you allow the supplier to do any work.

Buyers agree that the first three items mentioned above are good purchasing practice, but they tend to neglect making sure they are accomplished. You should insist that the job should be done properly. Once in a while, an emergency repair is needed and this is used as an excuse for not covering the necessary steps. Of course, it is too late to do some of these things if you need immediate action. This is especially true if the repair is necessary on a weekend or holiday when the buyer is not available. Good purchasing anticipates the need for repair sources. Check your sources before you need them and notify your requisitioners as to which sources are qualified and approved.

### Negotiating Prices for Services

Buyers have the most trouble establishing costs prior to awarding purchase orders for service. Service-oriented businesses say they cannot give an exact price because they don't know how much work needs to be done or what parts they will need to do the repair. This same argument is sometimes even used by professional services such as lawyers and public accountants.

There are various ways of handling pricing on services. You may insist on an absolute maximum that the job will run. You then place this on the purchase order: "Price not to exceed $xxx.xx." The problem with this approach is that the invoice price will tend to be very close if not actually at the "not to exceed" price. Nevertheless, using this approach is better than a nonpriced order. It helps avoid arguments and unpleasant surprises.

Another approach is to obtain the hourly labor rate and possibly an estimate of the number of hours to repair the item or do the service. When the work is performed on your premises, this allows the buyer or a designated company employee to observe how many workers were used and how long they worked. If the work is done off premises, the buyer should ask for details about what will be done and how. Some of the steps may not be required.

The buyer should try to get some type of guarantee about how long the repair will last and negotiate payment terms as in any other purchase.

## BUYING SPECIAL PRODUCTS—WHAT YOU SHOULD KNOW
## ————————— BEFORE YOU BUY —————————

A buyer should learn as much about the products purchased as time permits. The more you know, the better your chance of making a wise purchase and keeping cost at a minimum. While information about some products is readily available and knowledge about those products is widespread, you will occasionally run into items that few people know about and even less information is available from the libraries. In those cases, a buyer needs to be somewhat of a detective. You need to ask probing questions from the supplier and perhaps contact buyers with other companies who have experience with the same item. The following sections give some information about various items or categories of items that are often purchased. Some of this information is available in reference sources and some of it is based on experience.

## Buying Chemicals

Many organizations buy chemicals in various forms for various purposes. They may be purchased by an MRO buyer to use as solvents or cleaning agents. Sometimes they are purchased to use in the manufacturing process or to be used as raw material. The word "chemicals" is somewhat vague. Normally, we are referring to compounds. That is, two or more elements are chemically combined to form a different material. Various compounds are widely used in business and industry. Some of the most common are benzene, caustic soda, ethanol, methanol, and sulphuric acid. Sulphuric acid ($H_2SO_4$) is a colorless, heavy, oily inorganic compound made up of hydrogen, sulphur, and oxygen. The concentrated acid is sometimes called oil of vitriol. It is used as a dehydrating and oxidizing agent. It is used in making dyes, drugs, explosives, fertilizers, batteries, and the metal industries.

*Quality Control.* Chemical specifications often include percentages of concentration and filtration of the solution. Unless you have total confidence in your source of supply, it may be necessary to have your own testing laboratory to make sure you get the quality you need. If your requirements are not that strict, you may want to take random samples and have them checked by an outside testing service. Some suppliers will get this done for you and will provide you with documents that certify the product meets a particular specification.

*Shelf Life.* This is an important consideration when buying chemicals. Some deteriorate quickly. You should ascertain how long the material will remain stable and compare this with your usage to make certain your stock is fresh and will give the quality level you need.

*Price.* Many chemicals are particularly vulnerable to the law of supply and demand and therefore have high price volatility. A buyer heavily involved in the purchase of chemicals or any other raw material should keep abreast of price movements by checking trade journals, magazines, business newspapers. *Purchasing* magazine publishes price information on selected chemicals on a regular basis. You should be familiar with price

movements and try to forecast future prices. If the product you buy traditionally has a higher price during certain seasons, you should try to avoid
buying during those seasons and increase the quantities of your purchase
when prices are lower. However, before you increase the quantity, you
must make certain that you will use the material before it begins to deteriorate.

*Quantity and Container Size.* Some chemical products are not particularly susceptible to spoilage and therefore maintain a comparatively long
storage life. If such is the case, you should investigate your usage and see
what size containers the product may be purchased in. Generally the larger
the container, the lower the per unit cost. For example, sulphuric acid may
be obtained in pints, quarts, one-gallon containers, two gallon containers,
50-gallon drums, and in rail tank cars. If you are purchasing the product in
large capacities, the containers may be purchased or leased. Just make sure
you have the facilities to store the product on your property in a safe manner.

*Disposal of Waste or Scrap.* An especially important consideration for
the chemical buyer is the effect of the product on the environment. All
buyers need to be aware of the environmental impact of the products
purchased but this is particularly true for the chemical buyer. Waste or
scrap generated from chemical processes must be disposed of in a safe and
legal fashion. When you buy products you should be careful to obtain
information on disposal. You should be concerned that disposal is made
using the most economical method, but your primary concern should be
the health and safety of everyone that could be exposed to hazardous
products.

*Checklist for Buying Chemicals.* When buying chemical products
consider the following:

- Do you know all the facts about the product and your intended use
  of it?
- What volume will you be using over a period of time?
- What storage facilities do you have?
- How do you plan to dispose of scrap or waste?
- What is the price history of the product? Is there seasonal variation?
  Can you see a pattern and forecast future price movements?

## Buying Electronic Components

Electronic components tend to be subject to wide price swings and are
especially subject to the law of supply and demand. During the mid-1980s
when personal computer clones required mountains of memory modules

(chips), the price of a 64K DRAM (Dynamic Random Access Memory) reached a peak of nearly $15 each. When Korea entered the market just a year later, the market became saturated and the price dropped as low as $.59 (a price so low, in fact, that most U.S. manufacturers were driven out of the memory chip business). Some buyers are still trying to understand what happened.

Semiconductors, unlike most other electronic products, are subject to a variety of idiosyncrasies. Since the contact pins commonly contain gold, when the price of gold rises steeply, *gold adders* are attached to the pricing. These adders, at times exceed the individual price of the chip. (The contacts for PC boards also are made of gold and their price is also affected by the price of gold.)

The cost of electronic components is affected by the practice of using off-shore sources for assembly operations. For example, chips manufactured in the United States are exported to Asian subcontractors to have them encapsulated into the final substrates. Inherent in shipping the material back and forth across the Pacific are many pitfalls such as delays in delivery, lost and damaged shipments, tariffs, duties, and taxes. Suppliers pass these extra costs along to the customer.

In order to minimize problems with price and delivery, it is wise to negotiate long-term contracts and/or blanket purchase orders for items purchased repetitively. Such contracts encourage suppliers to grant lower prices. It reduces their cost of sales, allows them to plan schedules, and obtain needed raw material inventory at a favorable cost. By stocking inventory, they can ensure on time delivery.

Periodically the supply of certain chips becomes restricted. In order to satisfy all customers, suppliers institute *allocation*. This practice allows only a certain quantity of a particular item to be sold to each customer, usually based upon the customer's past purchase quantities or sometimes based on the amount the supplier has available in stock. Allocation generally occurs when the buyer's needs are increasing. During these periods the buyer usually can obtain material from brokers, reclamation houses or other nonstandard sources, albeit at inflated prices.

Although you may maintain supply for your company during these periods, the quality is often less than desired and therefore extra receiving inspection and testing is recommended. Extra caution should be exercised when selecting new or untried sources. When supply is tight and prices are very high, the unscrupulous and dishonest become active. You may be approached by "fly-by-night" dealers who work out of a hotel room or the trunk of a car.

The goods may be below acceptable quality levels. If the goods are of high quality they may be stolen and you will not receive legal title to any purchase you make. Even though you pay for the material, it may later be confiscated.

## Buying Metal and Metal Products

If you are buying for a manufacturing company, at one time or another you will probably have to buy a metal product. It may only be a small piece of steel to make a repair or build a protective rail. If your company uses metal in the products you manufacture you will be buying larger quantities.

The term *metal* covers a wide range of products. Although many of these products are normally classified as raw material, most of them are to some extent fabricated goods. For example, let's look at the purchase of steel. The most basic raw material is iron ore. The ore is used to produce ingot which in turn is raw material used to produce other products such as iron castings or various types of steel. The steel is produced in various standard shapes and sizes and grades to suit the needs of the customer. Some may go into bars and plates which in turn are used by machine tool builders and other industries. Some goes into architectural shapes for use in the construction trade. Some is made into flat, rolled carbon steel coils. Some is used to make stainless which is produced in a wide variety of forms for different purposes.

*Buying Fabricated Metal Products.* You may buy fabricated metal products in the form of castings, forgings, or stampings. Each of these is produced by various methods to produce products with different specifications to meet the needs of the customer. You may wonder why it is important for the buyer to know all this and more about the availability of different types of products. While it is true that the end users or requisitioners should specify what they want, you cannot assume that they are as familiar with all products as they could be. It is the metal buyer's responsibility to learn as much as possible about the availability of products, how they are made, and what they will do. The buyer can sometimes save significant cost by recommending a switch from a metal assembly made from two or more pieces to a one-piece casting. Or an expensive casting may be replaced by a simple metal stamping.

*Getting the Best Value.* The engineer or user does not always request the most economical product. The engineer's primary concern is to get the finished product to work. The buyer's primary concern is to obtain the best value for the funds spent. In most cases the buyer will not be able to decide unilaterally if another type of product is acceptable, but the facts should be gathered to determine possibilities and suggestions made. In some cases, the change will affect other items and will be rejected. Therefore, changes in design should be a team effort.

The buyer cannot expect suppliers to reveal alternative types of products which are not within the realm of their expertise or within their interest. Different types of metal working are not usually performed by the same supplier. Casting manufacturers do not make stampings or forgings.

Forging manufacturers do not produce castings or stampings. The technology required to do so is different and the equipment needed is completely different.

*Choosing Where to Buy Metal Products.* In addition to deciding what type of product is best for your need, you need to decide where to buy the product. If you are buying steel for processing in your own operation, you must decide on which channel of distribution is your best choice. You have the option of going to a mill or a distributor (commonly referred to as a "warehouse" in the metal industry). It used to be clear-cut. For large quantities with sufficient leadtime you purchased from the mill to obtain the best price. Small quantities or requirements needed quickly were purchased from a warehouse.

In recent years, the decision has not been as easy. Some warehouses are offering prices at or below the price quoted by mills. In addition, some warehouses will stock the particular type of material and quantities you need. When you calculate the reduction in your inventory cost, you may find that the warehouse is a better choice. But don't assume anything. Check and double check your figures and do not use the published list prices. Use the figures you obtain after a conscientious negotiating effort with both types of sources. As always, you have to shop, compare, and analyze to make sure you are obtaining the best cost.

*Checking Prices.* To find out if you are getting a good price for raw material, you can check various publications to see what has recently been paid. *The American Metal Market*, a newspaper published Monday through Friday gives prices of selected products. You will also find prices of certain products published in *Purchasing Magazine*. However, the prices you find will probably not be for the exact products purchased or for the quantities you buy. As in most products price is to a large extent based on the quantity you buy. In addition you pay extra for different grades, finish, and the shape of the product you want. The base price is quoted in pounds or tons. Steel companies and other metal producers have the habit of quoting with the proviso that prices are those that are in effect at time of shipment. This is unacceptable for a professional buyer unless leadtime is into the distant future (for example, over six months). Even then, any change in price should be at least negotiable. Normally, when you issue an order, make sure that you indicate that prices are firm.

Obviously published prices cannot be used directly when you are buying castings or forgings or even pieces of stock shapes. You need to add labor and other factors to the base price of the material.

If you purchase copper, gold, lead, zinc, or various other products that exhibit volatile prices it may be to your advantage to use hedge techniques. Hedging is used to reduce the risk of price fluctuations. To reduce the risk of future price changes, a buyer might make a futures contract to sell an extra quantity of the commodity being purchased for use now at a future time based on today's price. If the price then falls, the buyer can "cover" by buying at the reduced price and selling at the higher contract price. Purchases of this type are made through commodity brokers and are only good for a limited number of items. In addition brokerage fees and other costs are incurred. Buyers using these techniques are aware of prices worldwide and may check daily prices on the London Metal Exchange and elsewhere.

The purchase of castings, forgings, and stampings designed for your particular needs also involves an investment in tooling. You need patterns and dies to make these items. Although the tooling will last for thousands of pieces, it will eventually have to be replaced. It is the responsibility of the supplier to maintain the tooling and sometimes even replacement can be negotiated or amortized in the price over a specified number of pieces.

***Reducing Costs by Changing Specifications.*** I have saved millions of dollars by changing the specifications of products. For example, a major cost reduction was obtained when buying tinplate (coils of steel with a thin coating of tin electrolytically applied). Engineering and marketing agreed that the plating was only necessary as a protective feature before we applied a silicon coating for non-stick cookware. Reducing the amount of the expensive tin saved several millions of dollars in the first year, and no reduction in quality was evident.

In another situation, I was buying an expensive high grade of tool steel which was being used in the manufacture of machine tools. The design engineers had established the specification many years earlier and the higher grade had been used ever since without questioning its necessity. A slightly lower grade saved a half million dollars per year and gave the same performance characteristics.

In still another case, the cast steel wheels for rail cars were purchased with dimensions near the edge of acceptable tolerance levels. The wheels were still within tolerance, but not up to the standards of the wheel manufacturer. The supplier made a certain number of these wheels on a continual basis, but did not wish to deliver them to some railroads who were overly fussy. The buyer obtained agreement from management to accept the wheels at a saving of 10% off the normal price. The saving again amounted to millions of dollars per year.

## Buying Office Supplies or Stationery

Office supply purchases is one of the areas that are frequently neglected by general management as well as purchasing management. Concentration on the high dollar expenditures relegates the control of office supplies to the lowest priority level. Although this seems to make sense, ignoring cost control in any area is a mistake and it can be a costly mistake even in the purchase of office supplies.

Included in the cost of office supplies are the purchase price, the cost of inventory, stock shrinkage, and the order processing cost. Let's look at each of these cost factors separately.

**Containing or Reducing Price.** The unit price for most consumable office products is very low. Pencils, paper clips, scratch pads, erasers, and many other items are only a few cents each. In addition, it is assumed the volumes of these items are relatively low for any one organization. All this is true, and although you can obtain a 50% reduction in price by shopping and negotiating, the total dollars saved remains relatively small. However, there are other items that fall in the realm of office supply purchases that are not so inexpensive. For example, look at accounting books, high quality pens, electric pencil sharpeners, hole punchers, paper cutters, desk sets, lamps, calculators, and typewriters. These items can cost several hundred dollars or more.

To make sure you have a low price, you need to periodically shop. You need to keep records of how much you spend in total and calculate how much you are spending per year per office employee. If that figure seems unreasonable, then you need to look closer to find out why. If your business is office intensive, you will spend more per employee. For example, insurance companies, banks, and legal and accounting services normally on the average spend more per employee than manufacturing organizations. Check the figures for your business and then compare the ratios to see if you are spending much more than the average.

### Assign Office Supplies to a Single Buyer

To obtain the best prices, make sure that all purchase agreements are made at one central point, preferably by one buyer in the purchasing department. Buy from one source for an extended period (a minimum of one year) so that you have negotiating strength with the supplier. By buying from one source, the small value of many items adds up to a significant purchase and gives the supplier the opportunity for a sizable profit from your business.

### Establish Approved Products.

Most office supply companies are able to supply many different brands of the same product. They all have different prices but don't necessarily perform differently. When you allow the supplier to choose the brand, he will supply the one with the highest profit margin. When you allow the requisitioner to pick the brand, you may pay a higher price than necessary, and sometimes you may be forced to place the order with another supplier which will dilute your negotiating strength.

### Establish Cost Guidelines

You can obtain writing instruments that cost twenty cents each or ones that cost several hundred dollars each. You can obtain a calculator that costs $10 or one that costs $200. Unless you have established a policy, you will find everyone wants the two hundred dollar item. They will have more than one reason to justify the purchase of the more expensive item for them to do their jobs.

That is not to say that all such purchases will be excluded, but guidelines should be established ahead of time so that only legitimate reasons for paying more are acceptable. Luxury items that provide no advantage to the company should be limited. Perhaps they can be justified for the highest ranking executives, but you should not let other employees expect to receive anything they order. Unless guidelines are established before requisitions are submitted, you will either be spending excessively to honor the requisitions or you will get disgruntled employees who expected their request to be honored.

### Consider Buying Direct From the Manufacturers

Most companies that are not in the office supply business order their supplies from distributors or retail businesses. This is usually necessary because of the low volume of each item used. However, if you keep records of your usage, you may find certain items that are better obtained directly from the manufacturer. Of course, if you are a distributor of office supplies, you must buy from manufacturers if you hope to be competitive. As in all other products, you obtain the names and addresses of manufacturers by checking directories such as *Thomas Register of American Manufacturers* or *McRae's Blue Book.* Or you can find the names of suppliers in business magazines or magazines aimed at the office supply buyer. Magazines offer the additional advantage of reviewing new products and sometimes giving the buyer a list of suppliers and the list price of their products. One such magazine is *Today's Office.*

Keep in mind that even retailers buy from the major distributors, such as Boise Cascade. Nevertheless, if you feel you may have a sufficient volume to interest a manufacturer, it doesn't hurt to ask for a quotation. One reason that buyers often neglect to contact manufacturers is because they lack the time to do so on every item. They feel it is easier and cost effective to make all their purchases from one source. This is normally true, but a good buyer never takes things for granted. There may be exceptions. Look at those items that you buy the most, even in office supplies. Shop them as time permits for the best deal. There are many distributors for specific products, such as paper. However, there are only a few general line office supply distributors. Boise Cascade Office Products and United Stationers, Inc. are leading examples.

Other possibilities for sources are in foreign countries. International suppliers may be more willing to ship small quantities than domestic sources and there is usually a big price advantage in using a foreign source. Nevertheless, there is more risk; it is sometimes difficult to communicate your needs, and the leadtimes are considerably longer.

***Controlling Inventory Levels.*** The larger companies usually have some type of office supply stores function, although not always. If your company is large enough, and busy enough, you may even have a full-time attendant that handles the stock. Properly done, the inventory level is controlled. Stock is ordered for replenishment before it runs out. The material received is checked and counted for accuracy and the stock is stored in its proper assigned location in a systematic fashion.

Some large companies and most smaller companies do not have a central stores area for office supplies. Rather each department and sometimes each user keeps what they believe is a reasonable supply on hand. Even when there is a separate company stationery stores area, other departments may keep an inventory of what they believe they will need. Individuals also keep a small inventory of what they will need. Thus, a great deal of money is often tied up in inventory and subinventories.

The solution to the problem lies in keeping records of what is ordered and establishing budgets. Then the actual usage should be compared with the budgets and discussed with the individuals to motivate them to keep inventory low.

***Controlling Stock Shrinkage.*** Beside the requirements for business, employees have a tendency to take low cost items for their use at home. It is well documented in the stationery supply industry that *orders and quantities increase from business* at the beginning of the school year. Although a business will find it very difficult, if not impossible, to control stock shrinkage of office supplies, record keeping, budgets, and central control will go a long way in keeping the problem at a minimum.

Some office supply companies offer to help you solve the problem. They advise you to get rid of your stores area, and offer to stop at the desk of every employee to take their orders. They sometimes say they will only provide the brands that management approves. That way, they claim, your inventory and cost will be at a minimum.

The fallacy in this proposal is that the supplier conducts a selling effort, either subtly or overtly, with each employee. The employees will tend to order more than they need and will often become very loyal to the supplier. The official buyer will then find it difficult to negotiate or change supplier without much commotion.

*Reducing Order Processing Costs.* The last item to consider when buying stationery supplies is that they generally fall into the category of low value items. This means that the cost of ordering frequently exceeds the value of the item. Therefore, you should make every effort to reduce ordering cost. The buyer should use any or all of the techniques previously discussed to keep administrative cost at a minimum, including annual blanket orders, systems contracts, and EDI. While it may sometimes be difficult (especially for small companies) to obtain firm prices for an extended period, percentage discounts are commonly used. Those discounts may be as low as 5% to 10% or as high as 30% or more. Whatever the percentage, don't accept a high discount as evidence of a low price or a low cost. Actual prices must be compared. Expenditures per employee and total annual expenditures compared with previous periods should be looked at to determine the direction and extent of cost changes.

## Buying Packaging Materials

Packaging material includes many different types of products:

- metal containers such as tin cans.
- bottles made of glass or plastic.
- corrugated paper used for shipping containers.
- pallets made from wood or plastic.
- metal or plastic strapping used to bind the containers together.
- display cartons or shelf cartons.
- polyethylene film and rolls of other types of plastic, which are used for wrapping or shrink wrapping.
- plastic pellets available in various shapes (sometimes called peanuts) which are used as filler and to protect products.
- urethane foam, which is molded for bracing to protect fragile items.
- lumber, used for heavy duty crates, particularly for overseas shipments or for large products.
- many types of adhesive tapes used to seal packages.
- padded envelopes.
- associated packaging material, such as bags, marking devices, twine, labels, and staples.

With so many different items, it can be a full time job learning about them and knowing where the most competitive sources are. Most companies do not buy all the items mentioned above, but if your company sells tangible products you surely use packaging material. Packaging material is used by manufacturers, but is is also used by distributors and retail establishments.

If packing material accounts for enough volume, it is a good idea to have a buyer specialize in this area. If the volume is somewhat less, still give one buyer the responsibility for packaging material along with some other category of items to fill the workload.

Here are some points to remember when buying packaging:

- Avoid custom designs wherever possible and use stock sizes instead. Special sizes for corrugated may require cutting dies.

- Remember printing on boxes is a cost. Avoid using it if it is not necessary or the volume is low. If printing is required, make it simple. Avoid special colors, bleeds, and multi-colors.

- Keep in mind that corrugated prices are based on linerboard prices which are published in trade magazines. Try to relate your pricing to the price of linerboard.

- Stock as much corrugated as you can if you have space and if your inventory cost does not exceed the saving from a higher volume purchase. Low-quantity runs of corrugated skyrocket your cost, especially for custom designs or nonstandard sizes. The set-up cost can be large and will be spread over the smaller quantity.

- Buy directly from a mill if you have a high-volume need for a particular size of corrugated. This will probably be the lowest price. Otherwise, your lowest price may be from a sheet plant.

- Check prices and cost of corrugated at locations a good distance away from your using destination, even though the cost of freight may seem to make it uneconomical. You may find your local supplier is asking an unfair price.

- When buying corrugated, do not buy more strength than you need. Different flute shapes and higher-wall thickness increase the price dramatically.

- Be alert to special designs that save money, but be careful to measure any alleged savings. For example, self-seal flaps save tape and the labor to apply the tape, but the cartons cost more. Be sure the extra cost of the carton is more than offset by the saving in tape and labor expense.

- Remember that all price formulas are subject to negotiation regardless of standard practice in the industry. Corrugated is normally priced per hundred or per thousand cartons when purchased from a sheet plant. For example, you may receive a price of $494.94 per thousand for a certain size carton. However, some buyers obtain prices per square foot of material. This makes it easier for you to have a long-term agreement with a supplier. You then can calculate the price on a box with any dimensions without having to telephone the supplier.

- When getting display cartons printed, see if you can get a price reduction by letting them gang run with your supplier's other customers.

- If you or your marketing department are not too concerned about image, look around for used cartons. For example, one Ford Motor Company parts depot obtained used boxes free of charge from a supermarket. They were used for parts being shipped to dealers. The final customers never knew the difference because they received the parts in good looking shelf boxes.

- If you need many wooden pallets for shipments, consider used ones. They are much less expensive and in most cases do the job just as well as new ones.

- If you use pallets internally only, consider higher-priced pallets made of plastic or metal. They last many times longer and could reduce your cost. Just make sure that they are not used to ship material out of your plant.

## Buying Paint and Other Coatings

Paint, lacquers, and varnishes are used by consumers as well as businesses. They are used to protect and decorate the interior and exterior of houses and buildings. They are used to cover automobiles and trucks. They are used for a multitude of products. When purchased for the home or for fix-up of a small item in business, they are purchased by the gallon or in smaller containers. Consumers therefore frequently shop by comparing the price per gallon. They may assume that a higher price per gallon means a better grade of paint. As any professional buyer knows, this is not necessarily so. The cost is often based on a perception of the product. A highly advertised brand name can demand a higher price because it is a recognized name and is therefore perceived as a better product.

That is not to say that the nationally advertised brand name doesn't cost the seller more. A higher price is needed to cover the cost of the advertising. However, the higher price may exceed the additional cost of the extra marketing effort.

The true cost of the paint cannot be measured from the price alone. We need more facts about the product. We need to know what area the paint will cover per unit of measure (usually a gallon). The consumer will find it very difficult to obtain this information accurately. On the other hand the buyer for business can insist on obtaining information which will help reveal the true cost. The answer is not in simply asking the salesperson to tell you how many square feet the paint will cover, although asking the question may tell you about the candor and knowledge of the salesperson.

***Composition of the Paint.*** You need to know the composition of the paint. Paint is made up of three components, a binder, a dispersion medium, and pigment. The binder and medium are usually referred to as the vehicle. In other words they carry the pigment. The dispersion medium is a solvent such as water. When the paint is applied the volatile solvent evaporates leaving the pigment and the binder on the surface to which it was applied. Now the important thing to remember as a buyer is, you should be interested in how much is going to remain on the surface, not how much is going to evaporate into the air. Therefore, you should be interested in how much binder and pigment solids are contained in the paint rather than the cost per gallon alone.

***Ease of Application and Durability.*** You should also be interested in ease of application and durability if you want to estimate the true cost. These variables may not be compatible. A more durable paint may require more labor to apply. You must add the cost of labor to apply the paint if you really want to compare the value of each product offered. You should consider using a lesser quality paint if it is not necessary for it to last very long. For example, if you expect to replace the item to be painted within the next year or two, the cost of a high quality paint may be a waste. You should weigh the advantages of using various types of paints for your particular application.

***Choosing a Supplier.*** Shop for paint as you would any other product. The nationally advertised brands may cost a little more to cover the advertising expense but the larger companies that do so may have research facilities that can provide you with a specific product that meets your needs better than a standard product. The larger company may also have better quality control procedures that assure uniformity and product reliability—but you must check it out. Some highly advertised products are brand names sold by marketing-oriented companies that do little or no manufacturing themselves. They simply buy their products from other manufacturers and have their proprietary brand label applied. In fact, many paint manufacturers are nothing more than packaging operations. They buy products in bulk and sometimes mix them and then repackage the paint in smaller quantities.

There are over 1,000 paint manufacturers in the United States. Make an effort to select the ones that serve your needs the best. Determine if your purchase is for a one-time need or will be for a continuing requirement. Determine if you need a product with tight specifications that must meet a high level of quality. Determine if you need a common shelf type item or an item that is specially formulated to meet unusual requirements. Huge sums are wasted by the purchase of the wrong product. If you use a significant volume of paint, you will achieve large savings by selecting the right product from the right source.

## How to Buy Software Without Wasting Your Money

As in all purchasing, you are better off if you know the technical aspects of the product or service you are going to buy, but most buyers buy so many products it is impossible for them to know enough about all of them. Therefore, you must depend on the user, engineers, or technicians to help with the specifications. This is especially true when buying software for mainframe computers. However, in today's highly advanced business environment, every buyer should have some knowledge of the computer through working with personal computer systems. If not, you should start learning as it won't be long until you are considered incompetent.

Much mainframe software is developed in-house, so you do not have to worry about that. When shopping for canned software, your first concern should be about the functions you want accomplished. Then you should be interested in the speed and efficiency with which those functions will be accomplished. The software supplier should give you the data you need. When your questions are not answered or answers are incomplete, you should be alerted and either insist on a complete answer or get the answer elsewhere. In any event you should check the answers out with third parties where possible. Above all, get references. Interview other users of the product and obtain demonstrations.

When you buy software you need to take a slightly different approach if you already have hardware than if you are purchasing new hardware. Software will only work on the type of machines for which it was designed. So , if you intend to use the equipment you have, you must make certain that the software works on that machine. You should find out what operating system is needed. Find out what computer language the program is written in if your own people might want to revise the program. If they are unfamiliar with the language, they may find it difficult if not impossible to do so.

When buying a new system, some computer consultants say you should look at the software first before you select the hardware. The software is very important. It is actually a big project to buy a new system. You need to make a list of all the things you want it to do and then calculate what equipment you will need to do all those things. Then add a big percentage factor because most people discover many more things they want to do after they have their computers. Then it is difficult and costly to change the hardware.

Above all, if you are not familiar with the equipment and software get demonstrations and make sure the demonstrations are complete. You need to set aside a considerable amount of time to make sure that the system works the way you want and does all the things you want it to do. If possible, the buyer should sit down at the keyboard and work with the system rather than let the salesperson push all the keys.

Read as much of the sales literature as you possibly can fit into your time schedule. Read the specifications and when you do not understand the terms used, ask the salesperson for an explanation. If that person cannot explain, or is evasive, insist on an answer. Don't be intimidated because you don't know. Chances are he or she doesn't know either or an explanation would be forthcoming.

For example, I was once buying a system and the word *modem* came into the conversation. In response to a question on what it meant, the salesperson simply said not to worry about it. Actually, it is a piece of hardware that is needed to send computer information over telephone lines from one computer to another. The speed of the transmission is measured by baud rate, which typically can be 1200, 2400, 4800, and 9600 baud. Is that so difficult to understand? If you were comparing two computers with internal modems (as opposed to external stand-alone hardware), and the price was exactly the same except on one the modem could only send at 1200 and on the other it could send at 4800, you would know which was the best buy (assuming everything else was equal). If you really didn't need to use the faster equipment or didn't need to send messages over the telephone, you could use this information to negotiate with the supplier of the slower equipment. You might be able to reduce the price more than the cost of the modem if you used the proper tactics.

As in all purchasing, remember you need to look at more than the direct cost of the items you are buying. Consider the labor of the user. Consider the warranty behind the products. Consider the stability, reliability, and reputation of the suppliers.

Don't be hasty to buy new software that has rave revues in all the magazines. New software often has "bugs" in it that have not been fixed. Let some other people try out the new things a while before making your purchase. Incidentally, purchase is not technically the right word. Most software is not purchased. When you pay for software, you are leasing the program for use on one machine only. You are asked to sign an agreement or a registration card that includes an agreement that you will not copy the software to give or sell to anyone else.

# CHAPTER FOURTEEN

# What You Need to Know to Manage and Control Purchases

Job titles are often given out today with little regard for what people really do. Many people have the title of this kind or that kind of manager, but do little or no managing. This is particularly true in the purchasing function. Many have the title of "Purchasing Manager," but they function as a buyer only. You might say they manage the purchases rather than people and that makes them managers. If that is the interpretation, then we can agree that they are managers. However, that is not the usual interpretation and often they do have a supervisory responsibility over buyers or clerks within the department.

The traditional functions of management are decision making, organizing, staffing, planning, controlling, communicating, and directing.[1] A buyer does most of these things in one way or another, but a true manager does much more of them. In fact, that is the real difference regardless of the title. When you put on your manager's hat you should be managing. Buyers spend much of their time doing administrative tasks. When purchasing managers spend all their time with paperwork or placing orders or even negotiating they are not managing. In small companies with only a one or two person department it is expected that much of the time will be devoted to buying and administrative tasks. When the departments are larger, a

---

[1] *Essentials of Management*, by Joseph L. Massie, Prentice-Hall, Inc. Englewood Cliffs, NJ 1979

greater percentage of time must be spent managing the department if optimum results are expected.

# HOW TO DELEGATE BUYING DECISIONS
# —————— AND STILL CONTROL PURCHASES ——————

As a manager, you can delegate some of the decision-making functions although you are ultimately responsible for the results. You can start out and cover much ground at the same time by assigning buying authority guidelines to the buyers who report to you. Give the buyers the authority to sign the purchase orders to the dollar level of commitment that you believe they can handle or that you are willing to risk that they can handle. If buyers do some work involved with a purchase even though they don't have the authority to make a commitment, they still should sign the purchase orders before presenting them to a higher level for signature. Such a procedure provides an incentive to perform at their best. It holds the buyer partially responsible so that a sincere effort will be made to eliminate errors before presenting the form for approval. It gives the manager some confidence that the transaction is proper without having to spend undue time checking every detail. In larger companies many signatures are sometimes required on purchase orders involving large expenditures.

The smart manager spot checks purchase orders submitted for approval. You should look to see if the important clauses are included. You should look at the reasonableness of the prices. See if the units of measure of quantities agree with the units of measure of price (they should). Make sure that vague terms such as ASAP or "best way" are avoided. Spend a proportionally greater length of time on high-dollar orders than on low-dollar orders.

## How Questioning Buyers Reveals Problems and
## Improves Performance

Question the buyers about the order. If documentation of activity concerning the purchase is not routine, request supporting evidence of shopping, price analysis, quotation analysis, previous purchase history, and results of supplier reference checks. This need not be done with every purchase. Even though it is done randomly, the buyers will never know when to expect such questioning and will therefore get into the habit of doing the job properly. Insist that written documentation of all discussions and analyses of most purchases be made and placed in the file. Exceptions may be made for low value purchases of stock items not used in products for manufacturing or resale. (Such documentation may be needed to enforce warranty claims.)

As you become more confident about a given buyer's ability and reliability, the amount of questioning and checking should be less although it should never be too rare or totally eliminated. Such checking keeps both the buyer and the manager alert. It helps the manager know what is going on in the department. Naturally, younger or less experienced buyers need to be checked more frequently and questioned in greater depth.

## How to Make Sure Your Buyers Are Honest

Ultimate responsibility for honest dealing rests with the company's chief executives, but a large portion of responsibility involved with purchases is with the purchasing manager. Every buyer is required to be honest, but any unethical or dishonest dealings reflect on the purchasing manager's performance and the manager can be held accountable. The purchasing manager may even lose his or her job if a subordinate's activity compromises the company even though the manager was not involved or knew nothing about the misdeed. It is therefore very important for the purchasing manager to make every effort not only to be 100% honest and ethical in his own dealings but to make certain that all persons in the purchasing operation are honest and ethical.

Responsibility to protect the company goes even beyond personnel within the purchasing department. If influence is exerted to misdirect the purchasing decision, the purchasing manager must take steps to counteract such influence. For example, when salespeople are calling on and entertaining engineers or quality control personnel, it is the duty of the purchasing manager to instruct the individuals involved about their obligations to their employer and, if necessary, inform general management of violations in policies and procedures set up to deter unethical activities. This is not an easy task. If not done diplomatically, you can earn the enmity of the people you are trying to improve. When this happens you may be subtly undermined in all that you attempt and criticism will be heaped upon you for minor mistakes that everyone is bound to make.

You can help make sure that buyers are honest by following these twelve tips:

1. Make sure that requests for quotations are put in writing for purchases of significant value. This will assure you that all suppliers are given the same information.

2. Make sure that contracts are awarded (that is, purchases are made) to the lowest *COST* bidder. When the lowest *PRICE* bidder is not selected, an adequate explanation should be written and placed in the file so that the manager or an auditor will know the reason for the sourcing decision. Valid reasons might include, the supplier has a bad reputation for quality as revealed by the sup-

plier investigation or the supplier could not deliver to meet the required delivery schedule.

3. If the same item is purchased again and again over a long time, make sure that new quotations are obtained periodically. See if the same high priced suppliers are always given the chance to bid again without giving an opportunity to other suppliers.

4. Be aware of the living style of your buyers. If they seem to be living beyond their income, you may wonder where the source of those additional funds is coming from. Be especially alert to buyers that like to gamble or drink heavily.

5. Be cautious of buyers that seem to praise particular suppliers excessively or criticize the competition too much.

6. Randomly check competitive prices yourself or have them checked confidentially by a third party. Outside auditors or consultants can do this better. When done internally the fact that you are checking often gets back to the supplier being used. This may undermine the supplier's confidence in your buyer and cast an unfair light on an honest buyer.

7. Make sure that you have a policy of keeping all prices confidential. Keep files and papers that contain supplier information or prices out of sight from outside suppliers and from employees that have no need for the information. Even though someone works in the purchasing department he or she should not be given free access to all cost and sourcing information.

8. Analyze the reasonableness of costs. If they seem out of line, find out why.

9. Investigate candidates for buyer positions before hiring them. See if they have certification from the American Purchasing Society. The Society investigates the background of each applicant before certification is granted.

10. Keep an open door. Encourage employees and suppliers to stop in to see you and discuss what is going on. Get to know the top executives in the companies you do business with. When you get to know them, they often will tell you about the buying techniques used by your buyers. They sometimes innocently tell you about the fishing trip they took your buyer on or how your buyer was entertained at a party they had.

11. Have a strict ethics policy and enforce it. If the buyers know that a violation makes them subject to termination, they will be more cautious in what they do. If a buyer is treated to lunch or dinner in the course of business make sure that it is not habitual and the buyer reciprocates by paying for the supplier the next time. Make

sure that buyers disclose conflicting interests. Remove them from transactions where they could be biased or would tend to favor any supplier.

12. Check the components of costs and all aspects of purchases. Checking price alone is not enough. Business can be awarded to a low bidder, but the price may still be exorbitant for the quality of the goods received. Or a buyer may order excessive inventory to please a supplier. Or a buyer may neglect to insist that a supplier make good on a claim for defective goods.

Keep in mind that some of these errors of omission or commission are just that—errors or oversights. As a manager you need to sort out what are legitimate mistakes from dishonesty. Those working in purchasing should know required proper behavior but those outside of purchasing who come in contact with suppliers may not know. It is the purchasing manager's duty to either instruct those people or alert general management of the need to have all employees made aware of correct business ethics when dealing with suppliers.

## FOUR TYPES OF
## ———————— BUDGETS TO CONTROL COST ————————

All managers should be concerned about budgets, but purchasing managers have a double role with budgets. As a purchasing manager you are concerned that requisitioners do not exceed their budgets and as a manager you need to make sure that your own department is properly included in the budgeting process and that you control your departmental expenditures within those budget guidelines.

Most well-run businesses except the very smallest use budgets to help with financial planning and to see to it those plans are realized. Period results are compared to the planned budget to evaluate performance. Some companies go through elaborate and time consuming procedures to prepare the budgets and then fail to properly monitor them so their value is realized. Other companies are so strict in their enforcement of established budgets that no expenditures are permitted that exceed the approved budget except for extreme emergency requirements. Most companies fall between these extremes.

Buyers and purchasing managers are sometimes given the responsibility of helping to control budgets. They are not permitted to purchase items that exceed the approved purchases or capital equipment budget. Usually, it is left to the requisitioner to obtain approval from an authorized supervisor or an accounting function to make the purchase. Quite frequently, department managers are left to control their own budgets and they are only criticized when they far exceed the amount for the particular item or when they exceed their total budget allotment.

There are many different types of budgets (and similar types of budgets are called by different names), but four types of budgets that the purchasing manager needs to be aware of are the capital equipment budget, the expense budget (or so-called operating budget), the inventory budget, and a headcount or personnel budget. Any particular company may use one or more of these types of budgets. The purchasing manager is directly and primarily concerned with all but the inventory budget. Levels of inventory are normally determined by other departments, although the purchasing manager has an indirect effect because of leadtimes, supply protection policy, and quantity price breaks. Properly defined inventory budgets are variable or flexible and depend on sales volume. Such budgets, at least in part, are developed from forecasts usually made by the sales departments.

Although all budgets are variable in the long run, capital, expense, and personnel budgets tend to be fixed for a year period even though actual quantities may vary from month to month. Established time frames are arbitrarily chosen but normally fit in with the company's fiscal year.

The purchasing manager can help control company expenditures by obtaining the authority to see that requisitions have been cleared through a budget monitoring function. But beware, many requisitioners obtain budgetary approval long in advance of any actual purchase. The estimated cost of the expenditure is frequently obtained from suppliers selling a particular brand of the product. Then when the time comes that the requisitioner wants the product, he feels there is no need to get further approval or justify the purchase or shop for the best product to fill the need. Keep in mind that the original quoted price is only an estimate. It may have been made low or high. The requisitioner may have even obtained more than one quotation and discussed the purchase with the suppliers, but chances are that the product was not shopped thoroughly and very few if any negotiating efforts were made.

Add to this the long time that has elapsed between the cost estimate and when you are ready to place the order and you realize that the market may have changed drastically. Take computers or software, for example. In three months, prices may drop as much as 25% and the lower price is for an improved product as well. Figures for planned purchases obtained and used to prepare budgets should not be blindly accepted by a conscientious buyer. It is up to the purchasing manager to inform management and requisitioners of the need to reshop and negotiate when bids have been obtained long in advance of the actual purchase. The lowest bidding supplier, who had a bid much lower than present cost, will not necessarily be the most competitive when his price is adjusted for present conditions.

## Purchasing Should Provide Budget Input For Purchasing Operations

Many purchasing managers help control expenditures that are made by other departments but they neglect to budget for their own expenses. As a purchasing manager, you should learn about the budgeting procedures within your organization and make sure you provide the input necessary to run your department efficiently, especially in the following areas:

- expenditure planning, so that you can buy the furnishing and equipment you need.
- salaries—you need to know which budget includes salary data and make sure that you are included so that the people in your department are paid according to their worth and responsibility.
- training for purchasing people—you need to provide for funds for seminars or courses at local colleges.
- travel—you need to have input into the travel budget so you can visit suppliers and attend conventions.

Table 14-1 provides a list of budget items that a typical purchasing department needs to operate properly. Note that the list does not include any

**TABLE 14-1. SAMPLE PURCHASING DEPARTMENT BUDGETARY ITEMS**

| Item | Type of Budget | Cost |
|------|----------------|------|
| Personnel | Administrative Salaries | $150,000 |
| Headcount | Personnel | 5 |
| Desks, File Cabinets | Capital Equipment | 2,000 |
| Microcomputers | Capital | 9,000 |
| Printers | Capital | 4,000 |
| Travel Costs | Expense | 5,000 |
| Seminars | Expense | 2,000 |
| Department Forms | Expense | 5,000 |
| Stationery Supplies | Expense | 800 |
| Subscriptions | Expense | 700 |
| Memberships | Expense | 500 |
| Telephone Costs | Expense | 3,000 |
| Heat, Light | Expense (usually pro-rated) | 1,500 |

amount for the amortization of existing equipment. That figure is usually supplied by the accounting function.

Also note that a separate budget is established for salaries and head-count. Some companies have both. Management may restrict hiring additional people or may sometimes require across-the-board reductions in the number of employees, yet will still allow salary increases if you are within the salary budget. Make sure you understand how your company operates. It is much easier to get approval for additional help when you need it, when it has been included in the budget. It is much easier to get raises for your employees when they deserve them if the additional cost is in the budget. In some companies, it is next to impossible to get someone a raise if it is not planned in the budget. The time to get approval is when the budgets are being prepared.

## HOW TO MEASURE PURCHASING WORKLOAD

You should be concerned about purchasing workload for several reasons:

- To maintain adequate workforce to get timely delivery.
- To distribute assignments equitably.
- To minimize administrative cost.
- To evaluate buyer productivity and performance.

### Maintaining Adequate Workforce

It is important to get requisitions processed and material ordered promptly to satisfy your requisitioner and to allow enough time for the supplier to produce and ship the goods to make your schedule. If you have insufficient staff to do so all the time, you will be in trouble and your company may not be able to satisfy customer requirements.

You also must be aware of the impression that other departments and managers have of your activities. If business slows to the point that layoffs are being made in other departments, you must have the facts and figures necessary to justify retaining your workforce. In addition, you need those same statistics to alert you to the need to reduce your headcount. It may be better to take the lead when such action is required rather than have someone order you to reduce by some arbitrary amount. In this age of consolidations, mergers, and divestitures it is wise to be prepared.

More often than not, purchasing departments are understaffed. Those that claim otherwise are usually neglecting some of the important functions of purchasing operations. Even so, it is normally difficult to request additional help and get it simply by looking busy or claiming that your people are unable to keep up. Unfortunately, this is an all too common complaint from employees. To get the help you need, you must prove your case. To prove your case you must plan ahead and do some homework.

If you wait until the time to cut arrives or the time when you are so swamped with work that orders won't be placed promptly, you may be too late to gather the necessary information. To be properly prepared, you must continually gather statistics. If your purchasing operation is computerized, it is relatively easy since it is a byproduct of your routine data entry process. If you are still using a manual system, you need to keep a log and count the various types of transactions that are handled.

## Assigning Work Equitably

If you have more than one buyer, you need to allocate work assignments equitably so that each buyer has the amount of work necessary to be kept busy without being overburdened. Gross inequality in assigned work volume among buyers creates dissension in the department and leads to poor performance from all parties.

You need to measure the volume of work produced by each buyer. Buyers that produce more and get better results at the same time should be rewarded. Those that produce less or consistently obtain unsatisfactory supplier performance need to be improved.

## Evaluating Buyer Productivity

Because of differences in policies and procedures, and responsibility among different purchasing operations, it is just about meaningless to make any flat statement regarding how many hours are required to place a given number of purchase orders or how much time is required to order an item. There are just too many variables involved. For example, if your department is heavily involved in construction contracts or capital equipment purchases, it may take many hours to shop, obtain bids, negotiate, and write a complex order giving you full legal protection. On the other hand, if the majority of work is for items previously purchased, usually from the same source, or for shelf items that are readily obtainable from many sources, it may only take minutes to place an order.

Some purchasing departments are responsible to match receiving documents and invoices against purchase orders; most are not. Most buyers do some or all the follow-up work required to obtain material on order. Buyers in other companies do none because they have expeditors that are assigned that task. Some buyers are responsible to prepare specifications while most obtain their specifications from requisitioners or from engineers. You cannot depend on any figures that tell you a buyer should place so many orders per hour if those figures don't consider the above variables. There are no satisfactory industry standards. So how do you measure buyer productivity?

The answer lies in developing averages over a relatively long period of time. Records must be kept of which buyer handled each requisition, which buyer dealt with various suppliers, and which buyer placed each order and the value of those orders. Records need to be kept on the performance of suppliers that are used by each buyer.

Now, to compare buyer A with buyer B may tell you very little if buyer A handles MRO items and buyer B handles production material. Some companies periodically rotate their buyers for cross training and to avoid excessively close relationships between buyer and seller. In such cases how can you blame buyer B if he has inherited a supplier that was chosen by a previous buyer? After all, it is often very difficult to change suppliers quickly, especially if tooling is involved. The answer lies in looking at the trends. Has the supplier's performance improved since last time? Are shipments now on schedule? You can judge the relative merits of your staff if a new buyer takes on additional duties and still has time to spare while the previous buyer with the same products and suppliers could not get the work done and was always complaining about being overworked. Avoid making hasty judgments based on superficial data. Look at the figures and analyze what they mean. Be aware that conditions may be different during different seasons. That is why it is important to keep the records.

By studying the workflow you may pick up certain trends. The work may be seasonal. Perhaps the number of requisitions dramatically increases during January and falls off sharply near the end of the year when everyone has used all their budget. If the volume does fluctuate on a regular basis, you can plan to use available time during the slow periods to have buyers visit suppliers, or attend conventions, or attend seminars. If you are lucky enough to have work spread evenly throughout the year, your staffing job should be easy.

## ———— HOW TO MEASURE BUYER PERFORMANCE ————

As indicated in the previous section, one measurement of buyer performance is productivity, but that is not the most important. An incompetent buyer can outproduce a highly competent one. Good buyers do a lot more than produce an adequate quantity of work. They buy the proper goods at the right price and get those goods delivered on time without any problems developing later. They make sure the company has all the legal protection that is reasonably attainable. They help control unnecessary expenditures. They are concerned with long-term results and profit for the company as well as the immediate satisfaction of user requirements.

Thus it is not very easy to measure buyer performance, because even the best buyers occasionally have to step on a few toes and generate hostility from employees and suppliers that do not get what they want. You must keep this in mind when evaluating buyers, and it is sometimes necessary to defend a buyer's action by explaining the circumstances to your company executives or other members of the management team. Suppliers who have lost out in bidding for a particular order can be very spiteful and may approach the top management of your company with slanted stories of what the buyer said or did. Remember that under time pressures or when serious supply problems develop even a good buyer may make a thoughtless or an injudicious remark. However, if repeated complaints are received about the same buyer from different sources, you may want to take a close look at what is happening and take some corrective action.

Be particularly alert to allegations of dishonesty. For example, some suppliers have made unsupported and unverifiable claims about particular buyers. Those claims were made by suppliers who were unsuccessful bidders. Investigations revealed that excellent products were purchased from the lowest bidder. No problems with the purchases and no dishonest behavior was ever verified.

In another case, allegations against a particular buyer revealed an impropriety: the buyer was soliciting his suppliers for funds for a charity that he helped administer. The buyer was reprimanded and eventually reassigned to another department.

***Evaluating Prices Paid by Buyers.*** The most important measure of purchasing performance is price. We must hasten to add that it is the price paid for products and services meeting the required specification or need. Those who deny the importance of price are either hypocritical or naive. Prices paid have a direct bearing on profits and profit is the measure of business success. Individual buyers have the most influence on price determination. Therefore that must be the key measurement of their performance. That is not to say that other factors are not used to measure performance. It simply means price is paramount.

A particular price alone without comparison means very little. You must measure it against something else. You can measure it against prices bid by other suppliers providing all the prices are adjusted for other costs. But that is difficult and not often precise. A better method is to compare prices over a period of time. See what was paid for the product when last purchased. This also has difficulties. Changes in the economy and the marketplace result in price changes that make buyers look good or bad even though they had little if anything to do with the price change. Consequently unadjusted comparisons of price activity have little value for buyer evaluations.

What is the answer, you ask? The answer is like so many other things in purchasing: the data must be analyzed. The details must be looked at. Price analysis helps to determine if a supplier is offering a justifiable price and is a very valuable tool in negotiating. It is also a valuable tool in helping to measure buyer performance.

A large number of items can be analyzed more easily now by using a computer. Previously a selection of the most important items was made for continual analysis. The items selected were sometimes referred to as key items. Even with the computer, the analysis may be restricted to certain classes of items. Prices for the selected items are broken down to contributing costs. For example they might include labor, material, and administrative costs including profit. The reasons for a change in price can include economics, design, negotiations, and miscellaneous factors (overhead, administrative, taxes, and so on). An example of such a breakdown of the old price and the new price of a typical product is shown in Table 14-2.

Notice that the increments of the price change explain the increase with the exception of ten cents. Thus the ten cent differential must be attributable to the negotiating effort of the buyer. Realize that in practice there may be other reasons that are not apparent. For example, the market may have changed and become more competitive; thus the supplier felt it necessary to reduce his margin. Nevertheless, over the long run and on the average, this method will provide a very good guide to the results obtained by each buyer. It is especially effective when comparing one buyer to another since market conditions are generally changing for everyone.

Obviously this method is better suited to repetitive items that are not too complex in their design. Although in theory you could use the same type of analysis on a piece of capital equipment, the task would be very time consuming and probably would not justify the effort. However, if you build your data base of information into the computer and develop the proper programs, you will find analysis is possible in many more situations and easier and easier to use. This system has just as much if not more value as a tool in negotiating and cost justification as it does in measuring buyer performance.

Buyer performance also must be measured by the percentage of on time shipments and the percentage of rejections. It is far better to be able to judge performance by concrete figures rather than by vague and subjective feelings.

## CONTROLLING PURCHASES BEYOND THE PURCHASING DEPARTMENT

It is the primary responsibility of the controller or the chief financial officer to make sure that no misconduct affects the financial well being of the company, but the purchasing executive can be and possibly should be of

**TABLE 14-2. SAMPLE ANALYSIS OF PRICE CHANGE**

| | Components of Price | | | | Attributable to | | | | |
| | Old Price | | Calculated New Price | | Design | Economics | Other | Negotiation | Actual New Price |
|---|---|---|---|---|---|---|---|---|---|
| Labor | .75 | 3 minutes at $15/hr. | 5 minutes at $18/hr. | 1.50 | 2 minutes .60 | .15 | | | 1.50 |
| Material | .25 | 1/2 pound $0.50/pound | 5/8 pound $0.55/pound | .34 | 1/8 pound .07 | .02 | | | .34 |
| Administrative & Other | .25 | at 25% of direct | | .46 | | | .21 | 2.10 | .36 |
| Total | 1.25 | | | 2.30 | .67 | .17 | .21 | 2.10 | 2.20 |

great help. The very special knowledge of purchasing allows you to check and control material in ways that accounting personnel may not be aware of. We have discussed how you keep buyers honest, but it is not only the buyer that may affect company finances. Other personnel outside your department are often the cause of inappropriate expenditures and costly mistakes. Your company may be cheated through ignorance, through error, or by a deliberate effort to defraud or sabotage the business.

## Make Sure Accounts Payable Pays Invoices Accurately

One area of particular weakness in many companies is accounts payable. Incorrect invoices are common. Almost as common is the payment of such invoices. The purchase order system is designed to minimize this difficulty, but if the purchase order system is not enforced by the controller and the purchasing manager, it is easy to have inappropriate invoices paid.

Incorrect invoices get paid for a variety of reasons. First the volume of invoices is usually high in comparison to the number of people checking them. Secondly inexperienced and uninformed accounts payable personnel are often assigned the job of checking invoices. And finally, the purchase order system has been ignored or circumvented.

The solution to the first problem is to computerize accounts payable so that most invoices that are routine and uncomplicated are handled without the need for close scrutiny. The few that need more personal attention will then receive it. Just because you are using a computer to do the matching does not mean that all inappropriate invoices will be caught. The system must flag invoices that are ambiguous or might have hidden discrepancies because of the nature of the product. Internal audits and random checks supplement the system and reduce the need for large staffs.

Take the following example of an invoice that might be submitted. The invoice shows twelve cartons of paper towels. The purchase order shows twelve cartons of paper towels. A match? Maybe. Read on. The purchase order further states that each carton will contain one dozen rolls of towels. The invoice includes in the description that each carton contains ten rolls. Since the cartons match and the price per carton matches, the computer would allow the invoice to be paid unchallenged.

Sometimes the invoice will give insufficient information describing the product. In such cases the accounts payable function must depend on the document submitted by the receiving clerk or an inspector that verifies the product was received as ordered. But the receiving clerk is also very busy and may not check all the details even if he has the information at hand. A buyer can go on for years under these circumstances assuming he is getting a very good price for a good product that is delivered on time. In fact, he is being fooled, deliberately or not. He is paying 20% more than he thinks he is.

The second problem of using inexperienced and uninformed accounts payable personnel can be solved by making sure that the people are properly trained. You can assist in this by calling attention to unusual contracts or complex pricing formulas. Simply submitting copies of purchase orders does not accomplish this.

For example, there have been cases where accounts payable personnel were approving invoices (that is, claiming they matched the purchase order and receiving document) even though the units of measure were different in each of the documents. Furthermore, they were unaware of the complex formula that converted the units of measure so the invoices could be matched.

Active and interested purchasing managers can help solve these two problems by making the financial manager aware of the need to check invoices carefully and by conducting random checks on their own. They can do even more to eliminate the third and last reason for payment of inappropriate invoices, which is ignoring the purchase order system. Engineers, maintenance supervisors, foremen, sales managers, and any number of other people in an organization sometimes want supplies and contact a supplier before notifying purchasing. The supplier convinces the potential customer to place an order immediately and requests a purchase order. The requestor then tells the salesperson to hold on while he calls purchasing to get a purchase order number. The phone is answered by a clerk or buyer who is often intimidated by the position of the caller and obliges the caller by giving him a purchase order number. The more aggressive buyer or clerk will obtain a promise that a requisition will follow promptly.

In company after company, this same scenario plays. In some companies it is so prevalent that all semblance of control has been lost. In other companies, it happens infrequently. But when it happens the purchase order sytem has been circumvented. It is not as flagrant as when orders are placed without a number, but the consequence is similar.

## Make Sure Warehouse Personnel Receive the Right Goods

The receiving function also has a significant effect on purchasing performance and the profitability of the organization. When receiving department personnel collaborate with other individuals to defraud the company gigantic losses can occur, but we must assume that these cases are rarities and the perpetrators are usually caught and punished. While the losses may not be as great with honest receiving personnel, they can and often do cause various kinds of difficulty for the organization.

It is important to have well defined and clear procedures for receiving personnel. Receiving personnel should be selected carefully. They need to be intelligent and resourceful. Incomplete or incorrect records can cause the following problems in the purchasing department:

- *difficulty filing claims for damaged goods* because responsibility cannot be determined if records are insufficient. Was the damage caused by the supplier or the carrier, or the buying organization?

- *errors in inventory records* because of incorrect counts. Counts that are too low cause excess inventory to accumulate, because new orders are placed for unneeded merchandise. Counts that are too high cause shortages because of lack of material. Purchasing must then obtain material on a rush basis that often is more costly and may even incur extra transportation cost because higher cost shipping methods are used unnecessarily.

- *failure to identify incorrectly marked or wrong merchandise,* which may eventually cause the same inventory and cost problems described above.

- *failure to handle incoming shipments promptly* may result in the mistaken belief that larger inventories are needed because leadtime is thought to be longer than previously planned for.

- *less frequent or delayed deliveries*—this may occur when the receiving function makes unreasonable restrictions on trucking companies and their drivers. For example, there have been cases where drivers were required to stay overnight to get their truck unloaded because they arrived too close to quitting time. This was after they had driven several hundred miles and the material was urgently needed for the assembly line.

## Make Sure Quality Control Interprets Specifications Accurately

The quality control function also affects purchasing activities by either being too lax in its interpretation of the specifications or too strict or arbitrary. If inspections are not made promptly the results will be similar to those mentioned above for the receiving function.

## — IMPORTANT PURCHASING MANAGEMENT TECHNIQUES —

There are many management techniques that are useful in any management position. We find the following especially helpful in managing purchasing.

## Pareto Principle

Named after Vilfredo Pareto (1848-1923), Italian economist and sociologist, this principle is perhaps the most important management tool that a purchasing manager has.

Pareto applied mathematics to economic theory. His work illustrated that often a few causes or occurrences account for most of the variation. For example, most of the absences can be attributed to a small percentage of employees. This principle can be applied to many types of situations. For example, in purchasing, most late deliveries are caused by a small percentage of suppliers. Sometimes, this principle is erroneously referred to as the 80-20 rule, meaning that 80% of the occurrences are caused by 20% of the contributors. Actually the percentage figures may vary and be set at whatever you want them to be. You may use 90-10 or 85-15, etc. Often arbitrary percentages are chosen to make it simple, but you can conduct a Pareto analysis that will allow you to select a more appropriate split.

A particularly useful Pareto application is to concentrate your negotiating efforts where the greatest potential results will be achieved. Get a listing of all suppliers and the amounts spent with each for a prior period. Make sure the list is produced in descending order of dollar expenditures. You may have a list of five hundred or more suppliers, but you will immediately see that only a few account for most of the dollars spent. Because you have limited time, that is where you will spend your time. Table 14-3 provides a sample list of suppliers and the percentage of purchases from each supplier.

## Management by Exception

Once in a while you see managers obtaining large volumes of print outs of computer reports although this was more common when the use of the computer in business was relatively new. In some cases these reports were issued daily or weekly and the persons receiving them probably could not go through one report even if they devoted full time to it when the new report arrived. Obviously there must be a better way to manage. The answer is to look at the exceptions and the problem areas, not every detail. That is not to say that you don't need to look at details altogether. On the contrary, it is important to look at details, but you should have a reason for doing so and it should not be a routine practice that bogs the manager down with an impossible workload.

You check details randomly for mistakes or problems and you check totals, subtotals, and conclusions for reasonableness. If the larger picture does not make sense, then the details may reveal why.

**TABLE 14-3. SAMPLE ANALYSIS OF PURCHASES BY ANNUAL EXPENDITURES**

| Supplier | Purchases | % of Purchases | Accumulated Percent | % of Items |
|---|---|---|---|---|
| Pennsylvania Company | $10,979,842 | 38.26 | 38.26 | 4.2 |
| Brown Specialties | 8,765,241 | 30.54 | 68.80 | 8.3 |
| Target Industries | 5,211,989 | 18.16 | 86.96 | 12.5 |
| California Mill Supply | 2,101,345 | 7.32 | 94.28 | 16.7 |
| ABC Company | 631,776 | 2.20 | 96.48 | 20.8 |
| Smith and Jones | 399,211 | 1.39 | 97.87 | 25.0 |
| Blue Marble International | 191,105 | .67 | 98.54 | 29.2 |
| Fostoria Inc. | 95,009 | .33 | 99.87 | 33.3 |
| Max of Atlanta | 85,991 | * | | |
| Williams Works | 52,110 | | | |
| Alois Paper Products | 45,055 | | | |
| Quick Supplies | 35,001 | | | |
| Hanna Printing Company | 29,808 | | | |
| T. Edwards Company | 18,441 | | | |
| Best First Aid | 15,332 | | | |
| Crown Office Supply | 12,111 | | | |
| Miltons Automotive | 10,549 | | | |
| Ajax Janitorial Service | 7,625 | | | |
| McGuire Service | 3,900 | | | |
| Dalton Batteries | 2,444 | | | |
| Mike's Stationery | 1,990 | | | |
| R & J Products | 1,229 | | | |
| Florida Enterprises | 801 | | | |
| Grape and Fitzwater | 273 | | | |
| TOTAL | $28,698,178 | | 100.0 | 100.0 |

* Purchases from suppliers further down the list account for a negligible percentage spent. Note that only four suppliers account for over 94% of the dollars spent. Most companies have many more suppliers than are listed in this example but only a few suppliers still represent most of the expenditures.

## Management by Objectives

Management by Objectives (MBO) is somewhat out of vogue now at least compared with a few years back when most companies were talking about it. Nevertheless, it is an important concept and its use will contribute much to major accomplishments in purchasing or any other function of business.

Perhaps it has lost popularity and many companies have set the idea aside because it was inappropriately understood and applied. The idea entails top management having major or general objectives that are conveyed to the next level down so that level can make its own objectives that might be in more detail and that contribute toward the overall company objectives. That level in turn hands down its objectives and the next level makes its objectives in still greater detail toward helping its leaders achieve its objectives. This process continues to the lowest level.

The theory requires each individual to participate in establishing his or her objectives that are approved by the manager rather than being dictated. There may be some give and take involved and suggestions made, but the idea is to get everyone to feel fairly comfortable with the objectives. That is, they should neither be too easy or too difficult to attain. They should involve some challenge and require some effort, but not be so difficult that a person will give up.

There are two other important things to remember about MBO. Wherever possible, and in most cases, objectives should be quantified and have target dates for their attainment. For example, a purchasing manager might approve a buyer's objective of reducing the number of suppliers by 5% by December 1 of the following year.

Some employees fear and resent objectives, because they have been previously forced to accept unrealistic objectives that they had no part in establishing. If individuals help decide on their own objectives, they are usually fair and reasonable. In fact, sometimes, they will set goals much too high so that they are impossible to attain. In such cases, the manager should explain the importance of having the goal attainable. If the goals are exceeded, so much the better, although if they are exceeded by too great an extent, then you can conclude the goals were set too low.

MBO is an excellent way of getting everyone involved in the planning process. Make sure that everyone is working toward the overall goals of the organization and not at cross purposes with the company plan. Table 14-4 shows how company objectives are used to establish relevant departmental and buyer level objectives. Table 14-5 lists sample objectives that buyers might have.

## Motivating Personnel

Although MBO is a great help in motivating personnel there are other things that you can do to provide motivation to buyers to get the job done. There are also things you should not do unless you want to discourage and demotivate the people that work for you. Amazingly management often makes rules and procedures and issues statements that provide negative motivation. Listed below are various actions that improve motivation and dedication to the job and other actions that have the opposite effect.

**TABLE 14-4. RELATED OBJECTIVES AT VARIOUS ORGANIZATIONAL LEVELS**

| | |
|---|---|
| Company | Improve Percentage of Industry Sales by 10% by end of fiscal year. |
| Purchasing Department | Reduce average leadtime of components by two weeks by end of fiscal year. This will allow manufacturing to produce special items two weeks earlier than previously and consequently permit the sales department to offer two week earlier delivery promises. |
| Buyer | Negotiate with my major suppliers of raw material to obtain two or more weeks reduction in delivery time by the end of this fiscal year. |

Positive Motivators:

- Let buyers know what is expected of them and how they are doing. Nothing is worse than being ignored. When criticism is needed, keep it objective and restrict your remarks to the job that needs to be done. Quantify what you expect and where the deficiencies are. Avoid vagueness.
- Give praise publicly and criticism privately.
- Give praise when it is deserved. Some supervisors believe that when praise is given the employee then will demand a raise in pay. The two should not be directly connected. Even poor performers or

**TABLE 14-5. SAMPLE BUYER OBJECTIVES**

- Reduce the number of suppliers by 5% by December 31.
- Reduce the cost of plastic resin by 7.5% from ABC company by July 10.
- Improve leadtime by an average of 4 days by the end of October.
- Reduce the number of quality rejections by 15% per month by August 1.
- Improve on time delivery so that 98% of all suppliers are no more than one day earlier or one day later than the requested delivery date.
- Take a course or seminar in purchasing law before the end of this year.
- Find a new more competitive source for our folding cartons before the end of May.
- By the end of February visit the facilities of my three major suppliers and report what they are doing to plan for future product development.
- By January 15 complete an investigation into the possibilities of modifying the design of our products so that we can use the same fasteners for all six items. Then by March 1 determine the cost of implementing the revisions and compare it with the savings obtained by reduction of number of items inventoried and the economies of scale.

marginal employees are encouraged to do better when their improvements are recognized.

- Reward people for good performance. This provides positive reinforcement. That is, people will strive to duplicate the same action to obtain the reward.
- Give your buyers and clerks as much responsibility as they can handle. Allow them to sign purchase orders and contracts commensurate with their education, experience, and maturity.
- Pay people what they are worth and make sure that it is at least as much as the market for the same responsibility. It is a serious mistake to try to get people to work for the least you can get away with. This is especially true in purchasing where buyers are often exposed to high-salary sales and management personnel.
- Be impartial. Evaluate every individual equally regardless of gender, religion, or ethnic background. Failing to do so will generate resentment, disloyalty, and lack of dedication to the job.

Negative Motivators:

- Continual fault finding, especially on petty subjects—this results in poor performance and often high turnover. Vague criticism has the same effect. Make sure the buyers are given detailed instructions when you expect them to behave in a specific manner or carry out an assignment in a certain way.
- Failure to trust your staff—while it is important to check on the integrity of all buyers and make sure they follow your guidelines to insure control, you should not show open distrust. Your checking should be a routine procedure that buyers expect; it should not be looked upon as an invasion of privacy or as a trial.
- Criticizing in public or in front of one's peers—this is a great way to create resentment and demotivate employees.
- The reverse of any positive motivator has negative effect. Withholding deserved praise, inadequate salaries, inadequate recognition, withholding authority and responsibility, showing partiality, all generate negative reactions.

## Measuring and Quantifying Purchasing Activities

It is up to the purchasing manager to see that records are kept and data input into the computer so that purchasing activity can be measured. Before the advent of the computer it was often difficult and very costly to accumulate data to help make informed buying decisions. Much of purchasing activity was done on an arbitrary and subjective basis. This should no longer be the case.

To make the informed decisions that are necessary, purchasing activities need to be quantified. You cannot measure buyer performance objectively without statistics. Neither can you measure supplier performance. Table 14-6 provides a list of records that you need to keep and the statistics that are obtained from those records as well as the purpose or use for those figures.

## Allocating Time and Delegating Responsibility

A particular Vice President of Purchasing for a major division of a "Fortune 500" company insisted on opening all the mail himself. He would then deliver the mail to the appropriate buyer. We suppose this was his way of knowing what was going on and possibly he believed he was controlling purchases by using this method. He also made the rule that he was the only one in the department permitted to sign purchase orders regardless of amount.

There are several things wrong with using such a technique. First, it takes the responsibility away from the other people in the department. They are no longer as concerned with getting their work right, because as long as the boss signs it, he is approving the work. If the work is scanned the boss does not catch every error. If he reads and thoroughly checks everything before signing, it takes up most of his time.

Secondly, the boss is acting as a clerk or a buyer and not as a manager. So much of his time is being consumed by clerical duties that he lacks time to manage. In this real life situation, there was no purchase planning, no buyer training, no purchase analysis, no value analysis, or any of the other techniques that make up a modern purchasing department.

As previously mentioned many purchasing departments run with a purchasing manager in name only. The person with that title has little time to manage because he or she is either doing clerical work or buying. Generally clerks and buyers are paid much less than managers and general management should demand that the person appointed purchasing manager, manages. If he or she needs clerical help to get the job done, that expense is paid for over and over many times because of the management activity that is being done. Or to put it another way, if the so-called manager is really forced to do the clerical work or become an order placer, then the company is wasting thousands or perhaps millions of dollars that would be saved if the company spent the salary for a clerk or buyer and allowed the manager to do the work that the title implies.

If you are purchasing manager for a small company, you probably will need to do much of the buying and many of the buying functions yourself, but the minute you have help you should begin to shift away from these

**TABLE 14-6. NEEDED RECORDS FOR USEFUL STATISTICS**

| Record | Statistic | Use |
|--------|-----------|-----|
| Purchase Orders | | |
| | Number of orders | Work volume |
| | Average number orders | Work volume |
| | Number items per order | Work volume |
| | Orders per supplier | Supplier negotiations |
| | Dollars per order | Planning & analysis |
| | Dollars per supplier | Supplier negotiations |
| | Scheduled delivery date | Supplier compliance |
| | Price Paid | Buyer evaluation, comparison shopping |
| | Date of purchase order | Department efficiency, buyer efficiency |
| Requisitions | | |
| | Number requisitions | Work volume |
| | Number requisitioners | Volume per area |
| | Items per requisition | Work volume |
| | Date of requisitions | Department efficiency |
| Quote History/ Price History | | |
| | Number of bids obtained | Buyer thoroughness |
| | Quantity price breaks per supplier | Supplier comparisons |
| | Dates bids obtained | Planning, buyer effectiveness |
| | Percent increase/period | Supplier evaluation, negotiation |
| Quality Record | | |
| | Number of rejections | Supplier evaluation, buyer evaluation |
| | Number of rejections per supplier | Supplier evaluation |
| | Type of rejections | Problem solution |
| Receiving Record | | |
| | Quantity discrepancies | Supplier evaluation, buyer evaluation, supplier negotiations |
| | Date received | Schedule compliance, supplier evaluation |
| | Concealed discrepancies | Supplier evaluation |

routine functions and spend more and more time managing. While the buyer may look at the bigger picture and discover opportunities that are not directly related to his or her responsibility, it is not the buyer's primary concern. A professional purchasing manager should be concerned about the large picture and the long run. The professional manager should anticipate problems and plan to avoid them. He should be alert to new business opportunities.

The following is a list of some long-range concerns that purchasing managers should be aware of:

- Will other industries develop a new demand for products that we are now purchasing and create a shortage or increase the cost?

- Is an alternate material being developed or now available that can help us produce a better product for our customers or help us reduce our cost?

- Is our competitor taking up the production capacity of our source? Will our future deliveries be delayed? Will leadtimes be increased?

- Is the government considering raising or lowering duties on items that we now import or could import? How will this affect our cost?

- How will the exchange rate for the yen (or the pound, mark, etc.) change in the next year? Should we be looking for a new source in another country with a more favorable exchange rate?

- If our annual sales increase as forecasted, do we have enough trained purchasing personnel?

- Can our present suppliers handle the expected increased volume without problems? Do we have sufficient tooling to handle the volume? If we order more tooling now, will it be available in sufficient time?

- Would it be less expensive to produce our own components? If not, would the ability to control delivery dates be worth the investment?

- What companies that are for sale would complement our product line and make our company more profitable?

- How can general management be convinced that an investment in more engineering personnel to produce detailed specifications will be more than offset by lower purchasing cost and better quality?

- Will adding staff to spend more time expediting orders reduce inventory enough to pay for the added expense?

- Will rotating buying assignments reduce cost?

While these concerns are not restricted to purchasing alone, the purchasing manager often has the opportunity to discover ideas better than managers from other departments.

The management of the purchasing function obviously has much in common with the management of other business functions. You must remember not to get totally occupied in routine order processing and the operation of the department, but must look beyond the immediate every-day activities. At the same time, you must randomly check the details and question the transactions to make certain that the department is operating the way it is intended. It is not an easy job to be a good purchasing manager but you have the reward of knowing you are a key person in the success of the organization.

# CHAPTER FIFTEEN

# Common Purchasing Problems and How to Solve Them

There are a few purchasing problems that are unique to purchasing. In addition, buyers and purchasing managers experience other problems that other business functions also encounter. We will discuss both types. Some of the problems are so common that we are tempted to say that they are universal within the purchasing function.

Throughout this book we have tried to give you solutions to various problems that are likely to occur and methods that can be used to solve them. Problems that were covered previously will be covered only briefly here.

## PROBLEMS COMMON TO MOST BUSINESSES

### What You Should Know About Back-Door Selling

Purchasing professionals usually want salespeople to work with purchasing rather than having them try to sell their products to employees outside of the purchasing department. If sales contacts are necessary outside of purchasing, at least purchasing should be informed about what is being discussed. Some companies require salespeople to clear all contacts through purchasing and send copies of all correspondence to the purchasing department. Purchasing wants the option of attending meetings when suppliers are calling on other departments, such as engineering or plant operations.

The reason for this viewpoint is not an attempt to grab or retain power within the organization. Rather it is because good purchasing people feel they have special knowledge and skill in dealing with outside sources. Because of their experience in hearing many sales presentations they feel they are better able to judge what are facts from mere hype. Purchasing professionals know something about the law and what it takes to make a contract and protect the interest of the organization which people in other departments usually do not have. Good purchasing people have training and experience in conducting negotiations to obtain the most value for the company's dollar.

On the other hand, many salespeople prefer to deal with people outside of purchasing because they believe these other people have a great influence on the buying decision and can often veto purchasing's choice of supply. They believe the user or requisitioner will see the advantages of the product they are selling whereas the buyer may not. Many salespeople believe that purchasing people do not understand the specifications or technical aspects of the product they are selling whereas the user does. In some cases this may be true, but product knowledge is only one of many topics necessary to make a good buyer. Many, if not most, salespeople have little idea of the work that purchasing people do. They often think that it simply amounts to placing orders.

Consequently sales efforts are directed to employees at all levels within a company, from the maintenance person up to the chairman of the board. Buyers and purchasing managers are called by requisitioners from all levels to buy this brand product or that brand product only. They are asked to "Buy from Joe Smith, because he is my neighbor" or "Buy from Don Jones because he is my cousin and he needs the business." The more thoughtful requisitioner will be more discreet. He or she will say, "Buy from neighbor, Abe Brown if everything is equal." All of this is not to say that Joe Smith, Don Jones, or Abe Brown may not have the best product and be the best choice. It simply means that political pressure is being put on the buyer. Complete impartiality becomes difficult if not impossible.

***How to Control Backdoor Selling.*** How do you control backdoor selling? Make sure that general management understands the importance of impartiality in all buying decisions. Make sure you point out the possible cost penalties of sourcing to the wrong suppliers. Point out the consequences of having other suppliers know that true cost is not used as your company's basis for awarding business. The word will get out and it will spread to all potential suppliers. When suppliers find that business is not awarded on the basis of cost they use different selling techniques. Rather than cutting their cost, they make emotional appeals, they try to sell requisitioners through flattery or by offering entertainment or "gifts." Suppliers with high ethical standards may no longer be interested in trying to get your company's business.

After you convince general management and get its support of a company wide policy that purchasing will handle all purchasing matters and that no one outside of purchasing should conduct business with suppliers without the involvement and leadership of purchasing your job is still not over. Salespeople and employees will still discuss purchases. The employees may be new and not familiar with company policy or the employees may have vested interest in directing business to a particular supplier. You must constantly be alert to influences affecting the choice of a supplier. For example, you may find that goods received from certain suppliers are constantly being rejected for one reason or another but you can see little difference in the goods from another supplier which always pass inspection.

While negotiating with the representative from a certain supplier, you find that he seems to know more about your internal company operations than he should. Heaven forbid, but you suspect he even knows the price you are paying his competition.

You must maintain constant vigilance and take steps to overcome backdoor selling. Here are 9 ways to limit back-door selling:

1. Prepare written policies and procedures establishing purchasing guidelines. Indicate who has the authority to contact suppliers and the extent and involvement of non-purchasing personnel. Include a requirement that purchasing must be informed about any contacts. Obtain the approval of the highest level of management possible and publish the documents or a summation of the documents to any employee that might come in contact with suppliers.

2. If you have leaks or a major problem consider using sealed bids.

3. Keep prices confidential and inaccessible to all but those who must know.

4. Have receptionist keep a log of who enters the building, who they are seeing, and the purpose of the meeting.

5. Question the people involved with meetings or contacts outside of purchasing and educate them on company policies and procedures.

6. Give printed "supplier guides to purchasing" to any potential suppliers. Make sure the guides contain the rules for dealing with your company.

7. Send letters explaining your company's policy to the sales executives of potential suppliers.

8. Institute a supplier certification program. Base certification for existing and potential suppliers on financial stability, business reputation, history of performance, available facilities, and capabilities. (Chapter 11 discusses supplier certification in detail.)

9. Maintain an approved supplier list.

Do not assume that information obtained by a salesperson is being deliberately funneled to him or her to influence the buying decision. Sometimes, information is inadvertently given. Salespeople walking through your offices, your warehouse, or your manufacturing operation can learn a great deal by just being observant. Make sure that salespeople are accompanied by a responsible employee so they will not wander around. Keep them out of restricted areas. A smart salesperson can learn who his competition is by looking at packages arriving on your receiving dock. He or she can learn what you are paying if copies of purchase orders received by other departments contain pricing information. And, incidentally, indiscreet salespeople may talk too much to your competition. If they call on your competitor they may mention that they saw a package on your shipping dock going to so and so.

## Beware of Inappropriate Specifications

In Chapter 5 we discussed the importance of proper specifications and Chapter 9 discussed quality issues. These two subjects are interrelated. You will not find it easy to get proper quality without adequate specifications, and the specifications cannot be written without knowing what level of quality you need. The requisitioner needs to help establish definitions for quality and specifications, but many managers would agree that the requisitioner or user alone should not have full authority to decide what will be purchased. Neither should the buyer. It is a joint effort. Because we want purchasing to be the primary if not the only department that deals with suppliers, buyers must let the users and specifiers know what is available. They must obtain specification data from suppliers and make recommendations about suppliers based on hard facts, rather than subjective emotions.

Everyone in our society is subject to a barrage of advertising and marketing hype and such pseudo information influences sophisticated business people as well as the naive. The purchasing professional must try to remove himself or herself from these influences. As a buyer, you should be like the scientist, detached and impartial. You should not be influenced by brand name or company size alone. Sometimes, famous brands are represented by the best product, sometimes they are not. And as we have seen there are many other factors to consider beside the product itself (e.g., will the company be around to service it? Do we need the best available product? etc.).

Small volume purchases involving small expenditures need not have elaborate specification details, although the details should be sufficient to purchase the item that the requisitioner wants. If the user asks for a pen, you could interpret this as a pen for pigs if you happen to work in that industry. If your user works in the office you will need to know if the person wants a ball point or a felt tip and if he wants blue, red, or black. If you are going to buy writing pens for a company employing a hundred fifty thousand people, you might want more specifications. You might ask if the user is entitled to order a gold plated pen. But with low volume of low cost items you wouldn't always get detailed specification on how the product should be constructed.

Neither will you get details on highly complex items with many components and complicated manufacturing processes when you are buying low volume even if the item is somewhat expensive. Whenever possible, these types of items are best suited for a functional specification. A functional specification will spell out what you want the product to do.

If you are buying a large volume of an item or a great amount of money is involved it is better to have a technical specification giving a detailed description of what you want. In such a case, the best specification produces a product or service to meet the need, no more, no less.

Good technical specifications should conform to the following 7 criteria:

1. Gives enough information to produce or purchase the product without restricting the purchase to any certain supplier.

2. Does not mention a brand name or supplier name on drawings or in the specification.

3. Does not give tolerances tighter than required to perform the function.

4. Does not require a higher grade of material than necessary to perform the function and last as required.

5. Provides sufficient information to produce a product that meets the quality levels desired and that can be measured objectively.

6. Provides drawings and specifications that are numbered, dated, signed, and approved by competent and authorized technical personnel.

7. Provides all revised drawings or specifications with the original numbers and dates, the date of revision, the revision number, and the necessary signatures for approval by competent authorized technical personnel.

### The Problem of Unqualified Personnel and How to Solve It

One of the biggest problems in purchasing is the incompetence and lack of professionalism in the function. Twenty years ago there was little awareness of the necessary knowledge required to do a good job in purchasing. Even today there are some companies, particularly small companies, that appoint someone as buyer, purchasing manager, or even purchasing director with no experience and little knowledge of purchasing. The result is usually higher than necessary purchasing cost. When the problem is discovered a revolving door often develops, with one person after another being selected for the position and then dismissed because he or she was perceived as not doing a good job. The problem, more often than not, rests with the management who hired the person in the first place. They either hired someone who was ill equipped to handle the job or management failed to support the efforts of a purchasing professional.

Examine the former case. We see people appointed to purchasing positions who are transferred from other departments within the organization. Many of these people have little interest or understanding of the purchasing function. They become order placers rather than buyers. They are not interested in gaining knowledge about purchasing because they don't understand or don't believe why additional knowledge is needed. They are not interested in belonging to any professional association or taking any seminars or training courses. Rarely, if ever will they read a book about purchasing or a related field which will help them do a better job. There are some other people who may have sufficient interest but do not have the temperament or personality for purchasing activities. Sometimes these people are too timid or become embarrassed if they have to ask for a lower price. Others are so overbearing and aggressive that they irritate salespeople and destroy profitable business relationships.

The ideal buyer needs training in many subjects. Some knowledge of math, accounting, marketing, economics, psychology, business law, and engineering subjects should be required. There are books and seminars on negotiating techniques and every purchasing professional should read and absorb what they contain. Today it is almost essential that anyone in business have some knowledge about the computer. Anyone appointed to a position in purchasing management needs more, like a knowledge of management techniques as well.

If you are going to appoint someone to a buying position without any knowledge of these subjects, you should make it clear that he or she will be making up the deficiency in quick order. You should follow-up to see that this is done.

But the learning job does not stop with school or in taking a few courses. In our fast changing world it is necessary to continue the learning process. It is a lifetime endeavor.

When appointing someone without experience to a purchasing position, give that person limited responsibility and authority until he or she learns how business is conducted. Make sure of at least the necessary formal training so you reduce your risk. School training probably gives a minimum level of competence.

First general management and then purchasing management are responsible to see that buyers are properly trained and that training is a continual process. Informed companies realize that it is a wise investment to pay for training courses and seminars. One idea taken away from a seminar may save the company thousands of dollars year after year.

Seminar courses are offered by universities, independent consultants, and the professional associations such as the American Purchasing Society. Write to these associations for a list of courses offered. These associations also offer certification programs that qualify purchasing professionals. No person is eligible for certification by the American Purchasing Society who has ever been convicted of a felony. In addition, to obtain certification by APS, a candidate must pass an investigation into his or her business reputation. Then he or she must obtain a minimum number of points based on the extent of experience and educational background. Finally, the candidate must pass an examination that tests knowledge of the above mentioned subjects with emphasis placed on purchasing applications of those subjects.

## How to Handle Lack of Support from General Management

Perhaps the most frustrating thing to buyers and purchasing managers is the feeling that they are not appreciated, that the purchasing function is a necessary evil and that purchasing should take second place to other more important areas of the organization. Good purchasing people see their efforts to improve profits ignored or, worse yet, obstacles put in the way of achieving results that make the company more profitable.

When this is true it may be because the general manager sees purchasing as a contributor to expenses rather than as a contributor to revenue. Few in general management have had in-depth experience with well run professional purchasing operations. When they have had some purchasing experience it usually has been of a superficial nature.

Those in management who have had a background in sales have often been exposed to the lowest caliber of buyers and purchasing managers. There are many stories of buyers "on the take," buyers who could not calculate a simple percentage, and buyers who refused to shop or award business to a more favorable source. Admittedly, some of the resentment could stem from jealousy because a better supplier received the business over the storyteller, but the details and frequency of these stories lead one to believe many are true. When these same salespeople reach levels of senior management, they encourage their sales managers to go around the customer's purchasing department or do whatever it takes to get purchasing to buy. Traditionally they look at purchasing managers or purchasing directors as low level middle management.

*How to Gain General Management's Support and Respect*

If you expect general management to give you the support you deserve you must conduct yourself in an ethical and professional manner. You must earn respect by your attitude and behavior.

Here are 11 things you can do to gain the support of general management:

1. Always be dignified. Avoid emotional outbursts. Look and act the part of a professional business person.

2. Organize your work and your work place. Keep your office clean and free from clutter. Have things filed promptly and be accessible.

3. Keep up to date on the latest technology and information about your profession and your industry. Make sure you belong to one or more professional associations such as the American Purchasing Society or the American Production and Inventory Control Society.

4. Understand that education is a continual, never-ending process. Study and read about purchasing and your industry. Attend seminars and take courses to keep up to date and expand your knowledge. Become certified.

5. Make sure your department has written policy and procedures and that they are kept up to date and followed. Try to be flexible and understand that there are exceptions to all rules.

6. Make sure you report your activities, but don't exaggerate problems or your successes. Avoid talking or writing in generalities or being vague. Be specific and quantify facts wherever possible. Use examples. Be able to back-up what you say by proof.

7. Try not to be a know-it-all. Listen to all sides of an argument. Do not take the word of one person or be misled. Check out the facts and corroborate the story.

8. Use up-to-date technology and management techniques.

9. Seek advice when you need it.

10. Be interested in learning about your company and how it functions. Get to know the other managers and officers. Make sure you know what your company's objectives are and make sure your objectives support those of your company.

11. Learn modern selling techniques and apply them to convincing your boss and general management of the importance of purchasing and how it contributes to the profits and success of the company.

## PROBLEMS UNIQUE TO
## —————— CERTAIN TYPES OF BUSINESSES ——————

The following purchasing problems are limited to special types of businesses.

### How to Handle Uneconomical Split Sourcing

When a product requires a proprietary design, it usually requires an investment in duplicate tooling when more than one source is selected. With low value requirements, it may be uneconomical to make the investment. The single source, realizing this, may raise prices to the point just below where adding tooling would be justified. Changing the single source involves risks and may require some investment anyway to adapt tooling to different machinery at the new source before you and a second source try negotiating with your present supplier.

### Selecting Unique Supplier-Designed Products

This is a slight twist to the previous situation. When we use a product designed and which may be patented by the supplier, we cannot resource without changing the design. Our negotiating power is severely hampered by this type of sourcing decision. Normally it is forced on purchasing by another department such as engineering or marketing who fails to realize or wishes to ignore the problem. When large volumes are involved, especially when for resale, the restriction may severely limit the profitability of the buying company and may even result in the abandonment of the product. It is better to have your own design unless the product is widely available from many sources.

### Managing Security and Ethical Problems

Every company must be aware of possible fraud, misappropriation of funds, embezzlement, and graft. When instances of problems of this type are not clear cut we often call them ethical lapses. We may say someone has been indiscreet, or used poor judgment. Common practice in the business world is to figuratively slap someone on the hands for a minor infraction. Even more serious matters are often handled by termination rather than prosecution. But a company should not take these matters lightly and management needs to be alert and take measures to prevent actions that are against the company's interest. Controls should be established and audits conducted to make certain that the company is not being cheated. There have been many instances where employees were stealing from the company either directly or indirectly. In all cases the employees were apprehended but not before they harmed the company and in several cases the harm was very serious.

The controller is usually assigned the responsibility of maintaining financial controls that prevent theft or at least disclose possible theft. However, neither the internal accountants nor the public accounting firms always succeed. Often the theft is discovered outside of the accounting function. Rarely do the accountants properly audit the purchasing function. Rarely do they establish controls that make sure everyone in the purchasing function remains honest. Unfortunately, when a buyer is caught cheating the company, the purchasing manager may end up taking a portion of the blame. Therefore, it is extremely important for the purchasing manager to insist on the establishment of proper controls. A smart purchasing manager will conduct audits of his or her own department to ensure that things are being done properly.

In addition to potential theft problems within purchasing, buyers and purchasing managers should be alert to the more frequent problems of poor ethical conduct and theft in other departments. Here is a list of 15 actions buyers and purchasing managers can take to protect the company:

1. Make sure that all suppliers deal with purchasing.
2. Make sure that all agreements are negotiated and approved by purchasing before any purchase order number is given to a supplier.
3. Make sure that quantities ordered are reasonable for use within your company or by the requisitioner in performance of his or her duties. Question figures that seem extreme.
4. Make sure that a buyer within purchasing is the only person who has final authority to select a source and make sure the suppliers understand this.
5. Make sure that all product is delivered to a recognized location and is checked in by someone other than the requisitioner. When a product needs to be sent to a noncompany location, for example, for further processing, make sure it is checked and a delivery receipt is sent to the company. If sent to a non-company location on a regular basis it is a good idea to periodically send a company employee to do the checking. If outside sources store your material, periodically obtain inventory counts, preferably by your own people.

6. Make sure that sealed packages and cartons are randomly checked for the proper quantities and proper material.

7. Make sure the items, prices, and quantities, and the payment terms on all invoices, delivery receipts, and purchase orders match.

8. Make sure no one is authorized to sign agreements or contracts outside of purchasing with the possible exception of company officers. We have even seen company officers unwittingly sign detrimental agreements.

9. Make sure that requisition forms, purchase orders, and purchase order revisions are prenumbered and a record is kept of those numbers and who received the blank forms.

10. Require employee disclosure statements listing significant interest or investments in other companies. Have employees, especially purchasing employees, list relatives who work for companies that your company does business with. Make sure those employees are removed from any transactions or negotiations with those companies.

11. If a purchasing department employee or any other employee that comes in contact with outside suppliers is living beyond his or her apparent means, discreetly try to find out how this can be.

12. If your organization is large enough to have more than one or two buyers, rotate their responsibilities so they will not continue to deal with the same supplier for a long time.

13. Restrict price information and details of contracts to those who need to know. A buyer from one area need not know details about another area handled by a different buyer.

14. Make sure new buyers are certified by the American Purchasing Society. Candidates cannot be certified by the society if they have committed felonies, and the society checks the reputation of each applicant before awarding certification.

15. Conduct periodic operational audits or preferably have them conducted by third parties who fully understand the purchasing function and how to conduct purchasing audits.

## What to Do When You Only Have One Source Available or Limited Competition

Once in a while you may run across a situation where there is only one source available to give you the product you need. This is very rare except for repair parts needed for a certain piece of equipment. Repair parts are often although not always proprietary with the original equipment manufacturer.

When there is only one source, by definition there is no competition and you may feel forced to buy the item from that supplier. If the item has little value or if you are only going to buy one or two pieces, you are probably better off to pay what is asked even though the price is usually inflated. Keep in mind however, that all things change, and if the supplier is too greedy, other firms will enter the marketplace sooner or later.

What if you use high quantities and spend a sizable sum on the product? Now you have a real problem, but there are possible solutions.

Here are 6 ways to manage sole sourcing:

1. Think about revising your need to obtain a more competitive product.

2. Negotiate with the supplier. One tactic is not to let on that the supplier has no competition. Even when the supplier states, "You have no choice, you must buy from me," you might not admit it, or acknowledge his statement. Another tactic is to acknowledge that the supplier has a monopoly but tell him that you will change at the first opportunity, as soon as a new supplier is available unless you receive better treatment.

   There may be another supplier in the wings that is just about ready to enter the market. You don't know and the source you are dealing with may not know either. Try to negotiate a better agreement to get a better cost. If the supplier offers a long-term agreement, don't be too quick to accept. In that case, the supplier may know of competition that is coming into the market and wants to tie you up for future orders.

3. Do a cost analysis to see if the product is priced fairly. You may be surprised. Some suppliers with a captive market keep prices low to prevent others from entering the market.

4. Do a value analysis to understand what the function is that needs the product. Perhaps something can be substituted which may do the job better or almost as well at a lower cost.

5. If your resources are sufficient, try buying the supplying company or division. That way you will be able to control the supply and the cost.

6. Make sure you have searched worldwide. I purchased a product only made by one company in the U.S. and everyone in the U.S. thought it was the only source available. Eventually another company was located in Norway that made a similar product that was used for another purpose. Investigation disclosed the product would do our job better than our old product.

## How to Handle Insufficient Supply in the Market

When there is insufficient supply in the marketplace, whether by accident or by design, prices will go up and delivery may be delayed. You may even have trouble getting anyone to accept your order. Anyone who bought steel during the 1960s will remember this situation. At other times electronic components have been short in supply. Plastic resin and components are sometimes difficult to get or prices are high during periods when oil supply is short or threatened. There have been times when energy itself was limited.

The solution to this problem is to be well informed about the marketplace and industry patterns. Know what affects the market and supply and take action to protect your company. Long-term agreements help. Dual or multiple sourcing helps. Treating your supplier fairly and paying your bills when they are due makes you a good customer and suppliers want to help their good customers. I have been warned far ahead of time about price increases and about allocation of supply.

When you are warned you can weigh the pros and cons of taking different courses of action. You can add more inventory or you can look for alternative sources or alternative products that might be used in an emergency. Sometimes you may be forced to shop for sources in other parts of the world. Sometimes you may be forced to pay premium prices in order to maintain supply. The smartest buyers avoid such necessity or keep such situations to a minimum.

## Allowing Buyers to Make Personal Purchases

Many companies, especially small ones, allow or encourage purchasing department people to make personal purchases for the company's employees' personal use. The objective is to save employees time in shopping for the product or to get a discount that the employees may not be able to get for themselves. Companies handle these purchases in various ways. Some make the purchase in the company's name and have the bill sent to the company for payment. The company then collects from the employee.

Some call in the order to the supplier and tell the supplier the purchase is for a company employee. The employee then pays the supplier. Other purchasing departments simply give the employee the name of a supplier where they may get a discount.

Most large companies discourage or prohibit the use of purchasing for the personal requirements of employees. In practice these restrictions are violated to some extent, if only by company officers or high level executives.

There are several reasons for a restriction in the use of the organization's purchasing department for personal purchases. First, the more employees a company has the more time that will be spent helping employees.

If all employees are not helped to the same extent, favoritism becomes apparent and morale suffers.

Seldom do purchasing departments keep records of how much time is spent on helping employees with personal purchases, but it can and probably does amount to a sizable block of time. This time is charged against purchasing operations and interferes with the more important tasks of reducing material and service cost to the company.

Suppliers often feel that the small volume involved with personal purchases is unprofitable and a nuisance. They therefore handle these transactions as a goodwill gesture or favor to the buyer or purchasing manager. The buyer consciously or unconsciously is aware of the favor and must feel some small obligation to the supplier. Immediately, the impartiality of the buyer/seller relationship has been compromised. Ask yourself if it is possible that the buyer would be influenced to award future business to a supplier, if that supplier handled purchases for your employees. If you answer yes, then it is wrong to permit personal purchases unless your first interest is not for the company.

There is still another problem the buyers face when they help employees with purchases. The product is not always what the employee expected. Sometimes he or she wants to return it. Sometimes the employee claims it was defective. Sometimes the employee leaves the company before the bill is paid and the company is expected to make good on the transaction. Most of the time the problems are not this severe, but again the buyer's time is diverted from the important task of working to help produce profit for the company. If the buyer refuses to help the employee settle these problems, then the entire purchasing department is blamed and word spreads that purchasing does a poor job.

If the buyer can refuse to help in the first place because it is strictly against company policy, all these problems can be avoided.

## Managing Excessive Personnel Turnover

Every company that has been in business for more than a short time has people leave for better jobs or various other reasons. When the number of people leaving or being terminated is far above the average you have a problem. The problem is more apparent and does more harm when the turnover is in certain departments. One of those departments is purchasing.

When buyers are continually changing, proper control of the cost of purchased material is difficult to maintain. Time spent in developing sources and negotiating agreements that are not finalized is wasted and the cost associated with that time is often significant.

Suppliers are confused and reluctant to make concessions or new agreements because they do not know if they will be honored. They are unsure if they might get a better agreement by waiting until things are more stable.

Suppliers often mislead new buyers and claim that agreements or terms and conditions favorable to them have already been made by the previous buyer. Sometimes this is true, sometimes not. The new buyer should be obligated to honor agreements made by the legal representative of the company, but should not take the word of the supplier if documentation is not available. On the other hand, a bad relationship may result if the buyer is obviously calling the supplier a liar.

A constant turnover of buyers or purchasing managers sometimes results in a corresponding turnover of suppliers. Many purchasing people have their favorite suppliers which they bring into a new company as soon as they can. Suppliers should not be awarded business on the basis of personal preference. Selection should be done on an objective basis, but in the real world bias exists. Consequently, turmoil develops. Quality usually suffers.

High turnover results from many causes. Here are some that come to mind and how to solve them.

**Impossible Workload.** Buyers have too much to do in too little time. SOLUTION: Keep records of volume over time. As work increases personnel should increase to handle it. Report volume to those authorized to increase personnel and request what you need. Make sure your figures are accurate and be conservative with your request. Use a software program that measures workload.

**Low Remuneration.** Salaries are below the average for the job. SOLUTION: Compare salaries paid by other companies for the same responsibility and duties. Check organizations that conduct salary surveys such as *Purchasing* magazine and the American Purchasing Society. Make sure personnel managers or salary administrators understand the scope and responsibility of the job. Show them the results of the surveys published by specialists in the purchasing profession. Make certain that purchasing personnel are competent and properly trained.

**Improper Screening and Testing of Applicants.** Employees are transferred or hired into purchasing without the consent of the purchasing manager. SOLUTION: Make sure that nonpurchasing managers, personnel, and the appropriate executives understand the requirements necessary to do the job that benefits the company the most. Make sure they realize that paying a lower salary to incompetent or marginal people is false economy. Test the new people either formally or informally to see if they know the essentials and report your findings immediately if the candidates are not capable.

*Harrassment of Buyers and Purchasing Managers.* Other managers sometimes use purchasing as a scapegoat for their own deficiencies. SOLUTION: This can be a difficult problem to solve but several things help. Offer suggestions or help to the departments that need help, but use extreme diplomacy so that you are not perceived as trying to take over their operation. Point out to the problem people that you can do more to get the material they need quicker and at a lower cost if they will work with you for the good of the company. As a last resort only, point out the problem to the executives in charge of the operation. Make sure you state your case unemotionally and give specific examples. Document all correspondence and all the cases of errors and lack of cooperation. Be prepared to defend yourself with written records.

*Poor Work Environment.* For example, there may be a lack of ventilation, poor lighting, inadequate equipment, insufficient heat or cooling. SOLUTION: Make a verbal request for what you need to improve conditions. If there are many items, it might be better to make a written request listing the items. If action is not obtained the first time, submit a second request, and then a third, and so on. If funds are needed to improve the environment, make sure that the appropriate amounts are planned in the budget. Build a case for what you want justifying it in terms of higher productivity, fewer errors, less fatigue, and so forth.

*Unethical Conduct by Buyers or Management.* Remember, if you are a purchasing agent or purchasing manager, you can be held responsible if laws or contracts are broken. In the worst case scenario, you could go to jail or be sued by your company or a supplier even if you were doing what your boss asked you to do. Therefore, it is imperative that you abide by the law and honor contracts that you or your delegated buyers have made. You should not tolerate dishonesty or unethical behavior from your buyers or take part in such dealings yourself. Make sure you build in all the controls suggested earlier and make sure management understands the risks and costs of not supporting honesty and ethical practices.

*Personality Conflicts with Supervisors or Management.* SOLUTION: Learn the principles of psychology. Learn how to be tolerant of others. Try to look at each situation from the other person's point of view. Build up strong relationships with coworkers and others within the company that share your point of view. You may need their support if a showdown develops. Remember that everything changes. People move on to other jobs. Someone you befriend at a low level within your organization may someday be company president. On the other hand, someone you treat badly can also become your boss or the company president.

*Illness or Personal Problems.* SOLUTION: You must separate a temporary situation from a long-term problem. If an employee has been prompt and without absences for years and suddenly starts to be frequently late or absent, try to find out why before you make a harsh judgment. Make sure employees understand the importance of being on time and present everyday. Make sure they understand that they are needed and that their absence puts a burden on everyone else in the department. Keep a written record of all occurrences with the dates, time, and excuses made. Make certain you discuss the matter with the employee and warn all employees of any action you may take if the condition persists. Treat all employees equally, but be careful not to overreact and lose a valuable contributor to the company.

*Conclusion.* Hire someone only after he or she has been thoroughly checked and interviewed by someone who has a thorough knowledge of the purchasing function. Make sure that each applicant's background is checked. Make sure that new employees are treated with respect and given an opportunity to explain problems, and provide comfortable facilities that are necessary to do a professional purchasing job.

## What To Do About Constant Stock Shortages

Rarely are constant shortages the result of poor purchasing. True, once in a while a supplier habitually ships late or ships quantities that are less than requested and this creates an out-of-stock condition. In such a case, the buyer should take prompt action to investigate the reasons for the problem. If the supplier cannot or will not change, then a new supplier may do better.

However, in most cases, stock-outs are usually caused by poor forecasting, poor inventory control, or poor planning by requisitioners. Purchasing must make certain that requisitioners and others are properly informed of required leadtimes from suppliers (and don't forget time for processing orders and shipping the goods). If the planning department, inventory control, or production control gets incorrect sales forecasts from marketing or the sales department, then they need your support in devising an improved system. Many companies use "gut feel" forecasts rather than sophisticated statistical methods that yield far better results. Using proper software and the computer will improve forecasts and keep inventory levels low and stock-outs at an acceptable level.

## How to Solve the Problem of Late Shipments

Off-schedule shipments are a quality problem. Earlier we said you must tell the supplier what you expect before the first order. If you want on time shipments, you must make certain that the supplier understands what you mean by "on time." However, you must allow the supplier enough time to make the product. That leadtime needs to be given to your requisitioners and planners so that your schedules allow your supplier enough time.

If you have given your supplier the time needed to make and deliver the product and latenesses still occur, you need to investigate what is going wrong with the supplier. Is there a communication problem? Is the supplier having financial difficulties? Is the supplier favoring some other customer at your expense? In some of these cases you may be able to help and the problem will be solved with little effort. In others, you may have to get tough. As a last resort, you may be forced to look for a better source.

## How to Handle Excessive Design Changes

In the automotive industry, engineering drawings often had 20 revisions. It was not uncommon to have a dozen or more changes to a drawing before parts were delivered and changes continued to be made even after production started. Perhaps the automotive industry can afford this method with extremely high volumes being produced. Most companies find so many changes very costly. It makes purchasing's work difficult in the sense that it is difficult to negotiate and keep costs low. Every time a change is made there is a cost. It is understandable that there are many times when changes are necessary. Changes in design may be made to reduce the cost of the product or to improve the product's performance or to improve its appearance. Perhaps the most important reason for a change is to improve safety. No reasonable argument can be made for many of these changes.

However, before a change is made, some estimate should be made of the cost of the change compared with benefits derived. And the cost is not just the item or material being changed. It should include the adminstrative and other costs associated with making the change. Will tooling have to be changed? How much production will be lost by the supplier? How much inventory has been produced with the old design? Will it be used up or must it be scrapped? How long will the new design be used? Sometimes, a company will spend thousands, even millions to make a change, only to discontinue the sale of the item shortly thereafter. What a waste!

It is usually helpful to require the approval signature of various managers before a design change is approved. It is also a good idea to bring any affected suppliers into the discussions to learn what problems or cost are associated with the change before it is implemented. Also keep in mind that changing one item in an assembly often affects other items. Those other items may also need to be changed. In addition, when a change is made, the manufacturing time required to assemble the product may change.

## What To Do About Insufficient Leadtime

It used to be that leadtime for production items or those used by a manufacturing company was more than likely adequate. Because the items were frequently purchased and they were so important, an adequate inventory including safety stock was kept on hand. Today's trend toward "just in time" manufacturing and "stockless purchasing" changes that cushion. However, those who are successful with these newer methods have planned the system well and know what leadtime is necessary.

It is the responsibility of purchasing to keep all interested departments informed about leadtimes and changes in leadtimes. As previously mentioned, purchasing should prepare routine reports of required leadtimes.

Those areas that seem to ignore leadtimes the most are in the non-manufacturing departments. They mostly involve MRO supplies. They are items ordered by the various administrative departments, maintenance, and office areas. Although these areas may account for a small percentage of total dollars spent, they represent a very large number of requisitions and transactions. Many of the persons requesting material do so infrequently and have little knowledge or experience in dealing with suppliers. Therefore, it is up to the purchasing department to teach these people the necessity of ordering well in advance of their actual needs. Buyers and purchasing managers should learn to be patient with those not familiar with normal business practices.

When a department or individual continues to place requisitions at the last minute, they, rather than purchasing or the supplier, should be held accountable for the consequences. For example, if the accounts payable or payroll department waits to reorder checks until they are almost out of forms it costs the company unnecessary expense. Yes, you can get the forms in 24 hours, but you may pay double the price. If the using department is responsible for the excess expenditure and is made to explain why it spent the extra funds, it will not likely be tardy in ordering the next time.

## What to Do If Your Company Is Uncompetitive Because of High-Priced Supplies

This could be divided into two problems. The first is where management and possibly the employees do not realize they have a problem or do not know the reason for the problem. The second situation is when the problem and its cause are recognized but little is being done about it.

In most cases once the problem is recognized, it can be solved by using professional purchasing techniques such as shopping for more competitive costs, negotiating with suppliers, and using the various purchasing management policies and procedures recommended in this book.

Once in a while, the solution is more complicated, for one or more of the following reasons:

- Your competitor may make the products internally that you must obtain from outside sources at a higher cost.

- Your competitor may be buying in larger volumes so that per unit cost can be reduced for freight and volume discounts obtained.
- Your competitor may be closer to the source of supply and save on freight and save on the cost of carrying large inventories.
- Your competitor may hold patents on items that you cannot obtain or have a proprietary design whereas you must obtain alternate items that have a higher cost.

The first thing you must do is analyze the reasons for the higher cost. Then, look for possible solutions:

- You may need to invest to produce your own goods.
- You may have to order in larger quantities.
- You may have to give the supplier a long-term agreement to purchase from him.
- You may have to redesign your product to get around using a certain material or to use less of it.

The solution requires imagination and a concentrated effort. It may take an extended amount of time, but neglecting to solve the problem could cause your company to lose sales and become unprofitable. Eventually it could even lead to the failure of your company.

Seldom are the purchasing function or supply problems blamed for the failure of a company. Nor is the purchasing function given credit for high profits and the success of a company. However, the importance of purchasing is usually far underestimated and that performance can make all the difference in the success of a business enterprise.

## How to Delegate Effectively

Improper delegation may not be recognized as a problem, but it can result in commitments that cost you money and could expose your company to legal problems. It is common business practice to either deliberately delegate buying duties to secretaries, maintenance workers, and others, or delegate by default because these people are allowed to make purchases.

Nearly everyone thinks they know how to buy, but not so if you use our definition of buying. They know something about how to place an order, but rarely do they know the legal consequences of their actions or how to shop or how to negotiate.

When people outside of purchasing place orders, details of the purchase agreement are usually not documented and attempts to maintain accurate records of company expenditures are lost. When nonpurchasing people place orders, seldom do they ask about F.O.B. terms or payment terms.

If a junior person or an inexperienced or untrained buyer is assigned to make purchases, closely supervise him or her and limit any authority until the trainee has sufficient knowledge to protect the company's interest.

## ——— SPECIAL PROBLEMS FOR CERTAIN BUSINESSES ———

### What to Do if Your Company Pays Slowly or Has a Poor Credit Record

It can be a lot of fun to work in purchasing. It is also hard work if you do a good job, but it makes the job extremely difficult when your company has a poor credit record or pays bills long after they are due. Suppliers take several different courses of action with such customers. One course may not even be apparent to the buyer. Prices are higher, leadtime longer, and delivery slower. More obvious are tougher payment terms ranging from Net (payment upon delivery) to COD or payment in advance. In the worse cases a supplier may avoid doing business with you entirely.

You can help solve this problem. If you do it honestly and preserve your business reputation you should first ascertain the true condition of your company and the chances of a reversal of the reasons for the delayed payments. You should not promise improvement or guarantee payment if you know or doubt the truth of your statements.

Companies often get into a temporary credit crunch and need help. Suppliers can and often do help in return for the business they receive and the promise of future business. You should contact and deal with the key supplier people who have the authority to give concessions on credit terms. In a small- to medium-sized company, this may be the president or executive vice president. In a large company it may be a controller. In either case, decisions affecting large sums of credit often involve meetings and discussions with more than one manager or executive. Your negotiating strength comes from your promise for continuing business and future business. You may have to agree to a long-term contract which may not be particularly favorable. Much depends on how long you have been doing business with the supplier and your business relationship with the supplier. The state of the economy and the supplier's financial strength are key factors that affect the willingness to work with you.

To ease the pressure on your accounts payable and avoid unnecessarily damaging your credit rating, negotiate better credit terms with a limited and select number of suppliers. You may only want to pick a few of the biggest for discussions. In that way, most of the companies you deal with may never know that you had difficulties of any kind.

When you make your request, try to be specific about the terms you want and how long you expect relief. For example, you might request a temporary extension of sixty days. Or you might ask for an open credit line of one million dollars to be paid off in monthly installments during the next six months. Whatever you ask for, make sure you can live with those terms and are reasonably certain the supplier can give them if it so chooses.

Substantial credit concessions from suppliers are not given free. Once your financial problems are solved you may find the salespeople reminding you for years to come how they helped your company out of difficulties. The implication is that you are expected to buy or place orders with them even if their product is not always the best or the lowest in cost.

## What to Do When Costly Tooling Limits Multiple Sourcing

When you buy manufactured components produced to your specifications you also purchase the major unique tooling required to make those products. This is common when purchasing castings, injection moldings, printing, corrugated cartons and stampings. Some of this tooling may only cost hundreds of dollars while other items require the investment of thousands. Molds for castings can cost well over $100,000.

This investment is one reason to carefully select the suppliers for these items. Often the tooling is developed to fit the machinery available at the supplier and is not always easily transferable to another supplier without costly modifications. Suppliers know this and know that it is a major decision for you to have to move tooling. You should negotiate carefully the placement of orders where tooling is involved. You should include provisions in the agreement detailing when and how price changes are appropriate.

If your relationship with the supplier is not ideal you may consider obtaining a second backup source. The problem is that you must invest in a second set of tooling. If your volume does not warrant the cost of additional tooling you are locked in to your first choice.

A second supplier will also give you supply protection if the tooling with the first supplier breaks or if the first supplier cannot deliver because of a strike or another reason. Nevertheless, you must weigh the risk of these things happening against the cost of additional investment. You must consider how long you intend to use the product being made. Will both sets of tooling outlive the product life? You must ask your sales department how long it intends to sell the product, if there will be any changes in design, and what volume it expects to sell. A thorough analysis must be made to determine if additional tooling should be made and what type of tooling.

## How to Manage an Uneven Work Flow

If your company has seasonal sales cycles you may find periods when you are swamped with work and other periods when you are tempted to take it easy. A purchasing manager may request additional help when many hours of overtime are being used and the volume of work shows no indication of slackening. Companies may begin hiring to provide adequate staff during these peak periods. This results in either an excess of personnel present during slack periods or a continual fluctuation in the size of the purchasing staff. Neither of these situations is good for the company. In the former case, salary expenses are unnecessarily high. In the latter, morale suffers and it becomes increasingly difficult to obtain quality personnel because of the company's reputation for turnover.

The solution is to measure work volume and plan activities around the expected volume. During the slack periods, attend to the following functions:

- Spend more time negotiating long-term agreements and blanket orders to make it easier to place orders during peak periods.
- Shop for and analyze new vendors and products.
- Conduct training and visit suppliers.
- Develop computer systems.
- Write or revise policies and procedures.
- Prepare budgets and employee performance evaluations.

## How to Manage Buyers Who Have Insufficient Purchasing Workload

This is the opposite to the problem of an insufficient workforce previously discussed. It is more likely to occur in very small companies or at a branch location in companies with a decentralized purchasing system.

A common solution is to give someone dual responsibility. For example, a person may be assigned the responsibility for purchasing and personnel. While this setup is far from ideal, it is still better to have purchasing responsibility with a single person rather than spread to many nonspecialists. The selected individual should have some training in the purchasing function. He or she should be sent to seminars, encouraged to read about buying techniques, and encouraged to join professional associations.

Where a person has dual responsibility, one area is often favored to the detriment of the other. Therefore, clarify that the person's performance will be measured on both jobs and that the purchasing function is as important, if not more important, than other duties.

Outside third parties can be appointed to handle various facets of the purchasing operation. For example, the American Purchasing Society will conduct searches for suppliers, prepare custom policy and procedure manuals, and even negotiate major supplier agreements. This is an ideal solution when your work volume exceeds your work force but is not sufficient to hire another qualified person.

If the company grows so that more time is required for the purchasing function, a full-time person should be appointed at the first opportunity.

### How to Handle Potential Suppliers Who Are Slow to Respond or Visit Because of Your Size or Location

Some suppliers are slow to answer your inquiries or contact you after you leave word for them to call regardless of where your office is. Many more will neglect to contact you if you are located in a remote area, especially if your company is small. Keep in mind that sales calls are expensive. Some of the larger companies, for example big steel, have eliminated calling on smaller accounts simply because it doesn't pay.

If you are having trouble in getting quick response, here are some suggestions to improve your service.

- Avoid spreading your business among many suppliers. The more you spend with a supplier, the more attention you will get.
- Do not keep calling a supplier for information without really giving him or her a chance for business.
- If you buy or intend to buy a significant volume of goods either immediately or spread over a period of time, make sure the supplier knows it.
- Make sure the supplier knows if you have been in business for a long time and that you have a good record for prompt payment.
- If possible, take a trip to visit the supplier. Once you get to know him or her and vice versa, communications will be easier, and he or she will respond better.
- If suppliers still feel reluctant to visit you, offer to pay for their trip if you don't make a purchase. Chances are they will make the trip but refuse to accept payment (if payment is made, checks should be made out to the company only).

## CONCLUSION

There are no purchasing problems that cannot be resolved. It just takes imagination and a concentrated effort. In most cases the buyer, purchasing manager, or chief purchasing executive can solve the problem alone. In some cases assistance must be obtained from other departments. In a few cases outside consultants are necessary to reach a satisfactory conclusion.

No purchasing system, purchasing department, or purchasing practitioner is perfect. Errors will occur and there will always be the need to correct those errors. It is part of the purchasing manager's job to constantly look for ways to minimize the errors and improve the operation of the department.

# CHAPTER SIXTEEN

# International Purchasing: How to Succeed in Global Sourcing

Global sourcing, offshore purchasing, and importing are terms that refer to the procurement of goods and services outside the country. Such well-known companies as Schwinn, Black & Decker, Whirlpool, GE, IBM, and even Reebok have joined the global sourcing game. The first question that presents itself is why?

The reasons for a company to seek to purchase products outside the country are many:

- Lower prices
- Availability
- Special requirements
- Better quality
- Overseas marketing leverage

Due to increasing wages, benefits, standard of living, and so forth, prices of goods and services increased more rapidly in the United States than in other countries. If the competition for a company's products began to source off-shore and thereby gained lower costs, they were able to sell their products for less. Your company then, in turn, must meet those costs by also sourcing off-shore.

As more and more products ceased to be profitable to manufacture in the United States, companies either moved their manufacturing outside the country or bought subsidiaries in other countries. Some of these are Bourns (resistors), Zenith (electronics), Apple (computers). Nearly 20% of goods imported into the United States each year are manufactured by foreign branches of American companies. Even if you are still sourcing from the same supplier, you may find yourself involved in learning how to buy off-shore just to interface with your own company.

The shoddy imports of a few decades ago have been replaced with many products of a quality superior to those manufactured in the United States. German machinery, Japanese automobiles, and Korean steel are just a few examples. In order to maintain a high level of quality, therefore, you may be required to buy outside the United States.

In order for your company to sell its products in certain countries it may be appropriate or even necessary to buy some of your requirements from that country. Certainly Japan, known for its restrictive trade policies, would be one country where including components made in Japan in your product would be to your advantage when trying to market your products there. Another fairly new concept in international markets is called counter trade. Since the currency in some countries is not widely exchanged on the international markets, a paper barter system is instituted in order to maintain the exchange of goods and services. You may find yourself buying potatoes in the Soviet Union to facilitate the sale of your company's products there.

So you can see that there are many reasons why you might need to learn the idiosyncrasies of off-shore buying.

## ———— HOW TO FIND INTERNATIONAL SUPPLIERS ————

If you're just getting involved in global sourcing, the first thing you need to know is where the suppliers are. Traditional information sources such as the Thomas Register, Dun & Bradstreet, and trade magazines may not provide a full picture of off-shore manufacturers.

The following list provides a few generalizations of what type of products are manufactured where:

- Apparel, fashions, shoes—Europe
- Agricultural Products—Central & South America
- Electronics, Machinery—Pacific Rim
- Minerals, raw materials—Africa & S. America
- Petroleum & Chemicals—Middle East

These generalizations may be further researched through the U.S. Department of Commerce, which publishes dozens of lists outlining opportunities for foreign sources. The United Nations also publishes information that will assist you in identifying foreign sources. The *Foreign Trade Statistics of Asia and the Pacific* contains statistics on import/export trade and tables give data on overall trade and specific products. The *Industrial Statistics Yearbook* contains industrial information for over 94 countries.

A good source to get not only the names of manufacturers but also the names of company personnel is the foreign Chamber of Commerce in your country of interest. Through an embassy you can easily get the name of the Brazilian-American Chamber of Commerce or the Chinese-American Chamber of Commerce. Since a major reason for the existence of such organizations is to promote business, you can also use them as referral sources for in-country agents, brokers and the like.

With this general information in hand, you can contact the Commercial Division of a particular country's Embassy or Consulate. It can provide specific information on manufacturers and the products they wish to sell. Many larger embassies even have research libraries where you can view publications on various commodities that include pictures and specifications. Some can put you on a mailing list for future announcements. All provide a FAX service for information on your particular requirements.

## GETTING STARTED: UNDERSTANDING THE TERMINOLOGY ——— OF INTERNATIONAL PURCHASING DOCUMENTS ———

Once you establish a list of potential suppliers, the next step is to send Requests For Information and Quotations, just as you would do for a domestic supplier. However, you will want to delve a little deeper into details of the off-shore company's physical plant, your supplier's capabilities, time in business, employee skills, and so on.

Further, if you are dealing with sophisticated technology, you will need to know the types of testing and calibration equipment that are being used and what standards for calibration are used. For example, if your specifications are in thousandths of inches and all the supplier's equipment is in millimeters, you should provide drawings and specifications already converted to the metric system.

### Invoicing and Shipping Terms

An offshore supplier's response to an RFQ may often take the form of an invoice marked *Pro Forma* instead of a bid or quotation. The term *Pro Forma* means that the stated conclusions are based upon assumptions rather than facts. It is an international way of opening negotiations with the assumption that you will buy said merchandise. It is your call if you want to adjust the terms and conditions.

Within this Pro Forma Invoice will be the other terms that are different from those you are accustomed to. Traditionally, most companies purchase from prices quoted FOB (Free On Board) supplier's factory; freight and insurance is billed to you or shipped COD (Cash On Delivery). In international terms, this arrangement is referred to as *EX Factory* or *Ex Works* and is rarely used by buyers because the many costs of international shipping are most customarily borne by the supplier.

These other costs include international business terms as set forth either as INCOTERMS-1980 or the Revised American Foreign Trade Definitions - 1941. Copies of these documents may be obtained as follows:

- INCOTERMS—ICC Publishing Corporation, Inc.
  125 East 23rd Street, Suite 300
  New York, NY 10010
- Revised American Definitions—The National Council of
  American Importers
  1615 H Street, N.W.
  Washington, D.C. 20006

The most common shipping terms are as follows:

- *C.I.F. - Cost, (marine) Insurance & Freight* This includes the cost of the product, and that the seller is responsible to bear the costs of insurance and freight to your country's port of entry. You must bear the costs from the port of entry to your designated destination.
- *F.A.S. - Free Along Side* (X vessel at X port) The seller in this case only agrees to deliver the product to a designated port of embarkation. You bear all other costs such as loading the ship, marine insurance, freight, unloading the ship and so on.
- *F.O.B. (X port)* Here the seller can choose to quote all costs within the product price to include loading at his port, or, in some instances, freight and insurance to your port of entry. Unloading at your port is your expense. For example, FOB Amsterdam puts the product on a ship in Holland. Whereas FOB New York gets the product all the way to the US.

The major difference in these terms is to decide at what point the title (ownership) of the product passes from the supplier to the buyer. Figure 16-1 illustrates this difference.

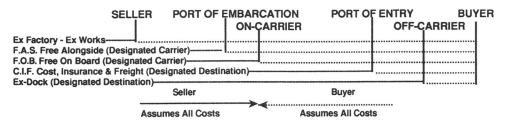

Figure 16-1. Shipping Terms for International Purchasing

## ASSESSING THE COSTS OF
## INTERNATIONAL PURCHASING

In addition to shipping costs, there are a myriad of other costs involved in off-shore sourcing as well. An attractive price of goods at the factory may not look so appealing once you tally these costs. Some of these extras might be:

- special packaging for ocean travel.
- customs brokerage fees.
- import duties.
- loading and handling costs at the port.
- export agent commissions.
- foreign agent commissions.
- freight forwarder fees.
- consular invoice fees.
- export documentary stamps.
- taxes.
- bank charges related to letters of credit.
- warehousing.
- repacking.

Special packaging may be required due to the products being subject to heat, moisture, and rough handling over a period of a month or so. In calculating the method of packaging, it is wise to consider the volume of a sea container as a unit of measure as opposed to a railroad car or trailer. How many cartons you can ship per full container should be your shipping strategy, as the extra costs for partial containers can sometimes be prohibitive.

Commissions and fees to those agents and freight handlers also add to your unit cost per product. On the other hand these experts may save you time in the long run and therefore be well worth the extra charges. Finance charges to banks and the government add small percentages to your total cost and must be calculated before a buy decision is made.

## How to Save Money on Importing

First, understand your commodity and how it relates to costs such as transportation and duty. The mis-classification of an item can cost you dearly. Since importing generally involves greater distances, the exact tariff classification of your product is of utmost importance.

***Customs Duties.*** The customs duty also can be over valued if the exact rate is not properly determined according to the Harmonized Tariff Schedule of the U.S. To receive a copy of this document, contact:

> Superintendent of Documents
>
> U.S. Government Printing Office
>
> Washington, D.C. 20402
>
> (202) 783-3238

It is not unusual to find a product, at different times, costed under several rates. The current tariff schedule was adopted in 1989. Therefore, those goods that have been coming into the country since before that time may bear a new look at the rate being charged. The imported goods classification is attached to the goods by the shipper, and you may have to negotiate with him as to what classification he is going to use. If you still disagree, you can get a binding ruling from U.S. Customs showing where you fall in the current schedule. This may be done against the shipper's classification or under a "protest of entry" against a U.S. Customs ruling. You can contest the valuation of the goods, the rate classification and the amount charged. Don't feel embarrassed about challenging this ruling. The U.S. Customs does not understand your product, its content, or uses as well as you do and rulings can be changed.

***Using the Free Trade Zone.*** If the final destination of the goods you are importing is not here in the United States, you have other alternatives to save money. One such method is to use a Free Trade Zone. Goods flowing into this so-called neutral soil within the United States are free from customs duties. In this zone you can repackage, modify, add to, or repair imported products without incurring duties coming into or out of this zone.

***Using a Bonded Warehouse.*** Another similar alternative to the Free Trade Zone is a bonded warehouse. Like a FTZ you can bring goods into a bonded warehouse without incurring duties. The bonded warehouse may be preferable due to its proximity or lack of a FTZ. Space in FTZs can also become a problem as in Miami in the late 1980s where a 6 month advance reservation requirement was common.

You are allowed to keep goods in a bonded warehouse for up to five years at which time you forfeit the goods to the government for resale. One of the advantages is importing during a time of high tariff rates coupled with lower unit pricing and withdrawing the goods from the warehouse and paying the duty after tariff rates have fallen. From time to time the U.S. Customs levies short term high tariff rates on certain goods from certain countries as leverage against an import/export imbalance. Computer parts is one historic example where in the 1980s some parts incurred a 100% duty.

***Requesting a Refund of Paid Duty.*** You may decide to sell some of your imported products outside the country long after you have purchased them and paid duty on them. In this instance you can file for a refund of previously paid duty. This is called "drawback" and is another cost savings.

If you maintain a repair service for your American made products sold outside the country, those items may re-enter the country duty free for the purpose of repair.

## —————— HOW TO PAY INTERNATIONAL SUPPLIERS ——————

Your familiar payment terms such as "Net 30 days" and "2% 10 days" go out the window when dealing overseas. You will now encounter terms of payment such as:

- Open Account
- Sight Draft
- Time Draft
- Letter of Credit

***Open Accounts.*** An open account is reserved for the most reputable companies who have established long term relationships within the supplier's country. As in the United States this means that your payment can be delayed until you receive the merchandise or later. However such arrangements are almost always "Ex-works" (FOB supplier's factory) and the buyer bears all costs of getting the product where it is needed.

***Sight Draft.*** A sight draft is a prewritten check to be presented to the supplier's bank when all the documentation validating the delivery of the products according to the terms of the contract is satisfied. One advantage is that the buyer may, for any reason, stop payment on the check. Another advantage is that the costs for such a transfer are less than a letter of credit.

***Time Drafts.*** Like a sight draft, a time draft is validated by the approval of documentation of delivery by the supplier's bank. However, at the time of approval, a time clock starts and, by contract, the supplier may be paid in 30, 60 or 180 days from the approval of documentation. This arrangement allows time for the buyer to sell the merchandise and then put money in the bank to cover the time draft. This psuedo-consignment form of payment is used extensively in the gift and novelty business. Again a trusting relationship must be established between the parties.

***Letters of Credit.*** The most common form of payment is in the form of a letter of credit (LC). LCs are managed under the terms and conditions of the Uniform Customs and Practice for Documentary Credits of the International Chamber of Commerce and is recognized by 156 countries. Like an escrow account, the buyer sequesters in a bank certain funds under a letter of credit until such time as the required documentation is presented to that bank. At that time the bank approves the documentation and releases the funds to the seller's bank.

There are also several rules that must be followed by the parties when using Letters of Credit, all having to do with the justification of keeping the bank out of contract disputes between buyer and seller. By following these rules the bank protects itself from making any judgments other than it is used to making such as the validity of the paper it handles.

Therefore the first rule states that the bank "deal in documents only." The bank is not concerned about the terms and conditions of the contract or the physical condition of the goods. If the shipping/delivery documents match the requirements stated in the letter of credit, the seller gets paid. Should a supplier ship the wrong parts, damaged parts or bogus parts, but the delivery documentation reflects the correct parts, the bank will pay the supplier. Your only remedy in such a case may be to sue the supplier for fraud. Therefore, the detail with which you prepare your letter of credit is paramount to obtaining the goods you paid for.

A second rule is the "rule of strict construction." This rule is designed to totally separate the LC transaction from any and all other documents or underlying transactions that may or may not pass between the buyer and seller. Again this makes the accuracy of the documentation or referred-to documentation absolutely necessary. If you specify that payment is to be made to "an agent" (an ambiguous description) of company XYZ and an agent of XYZ company shows up at the bank, certifies that he is an agent of the XYZ company, and demands payment (and this particular individual is not the intended beneficiary or the one you had in mind) he will receive payment. Generally it is wise to specify a corporate secretary, comptroller or other specific individual by name.

A third rule followed by banks is the "rule of independence." As with a bank's processing of checks, a bank is only bound to look at the validity of the issuing bank, the availability of sufficient funds in the issuing bank and the validity of the signature(s). The bank does not care if the amount of the check was unreasonable for the goods purchased, the merchantability of the goods or the condition of the goods involved in the transaction. Further, the bank is not interested in any underlying performance by either party to the transaction. Therefore the letter of credit is totally independent of any factors other than those described in the actual documentation.

The two most common forms of letters of credit are irrevocable and revocable. Since the LC is issued by the buyer's bank, the revocation is the privilege of the buyer. As you can imagine, the revocable LC is used only in circumstances of detailed product specification approval or for perishable items, the safety of which has been borne by the supplier.

## CURRENCY AND EXCHANGE RATES

The preferred international medium of exchange is the American dollar, followed by British sterling, French francs and German marks. However, in some areas the inflation is so rampant that other measures may be necessary.

During the late 1980s the Brazilian and Argentinean currency experienced an inflation rate in double digits per day in some cases. Brazilian buyers in this market could stand to pay double or triple for their materials during the course of a contract to sell to you and therefore the companies tried every means including exchange rate clauses in order to protect their profit margins.

This phenomenon also surfaced in Taiwan and Japan in the 1980s when the Japanese yen and the Taiwan NT dollar were rising against the U.S. dollar. Schemes were used such as sharing in the exchange rate variance, after the difference exceeded X%.

For example, the current rate of exchange for Japanese yen to the U.S. dollar is 155 yen = 1US$. When the rate drops by an average of 5 yen over a one month period (based on reports of currency rates in the Asian Wall Street Journal), the unit price will be adjusted accordingly. The parties will each share a 50% increase or decrease in the newly adjusted unit pricing.

**REMEMBER:** the Japanese company is thinking in yen.

| | | | |
|---|---|---|---|
| Exchange Rate Y155 = $1.00 | Unit Price | $225.00 | Y 34,875 |
| Exchange Rate Y150 = $1.00 | Unit Price | $232.50 | Y 34,875 |
| | Effect of Change | $ 7.50 | |
| | Sharing @ 50/50 | $ 3.75 | |
| Adjusted for sharing | New Unit Price | $228.75 | Y 34, 313 |

# UNDERSTANDING INTERNATIONAL
## ———————— PURCHASING CONTRACTS ————————

In the U.S. a valid contract is an agreement enforceable by law. The rules that govern domestic contracts are spelled out by the Uniform Commercial Code, U.S. Customs and other state and federal laws. Contracts sometimes refer to "governing law," "arbitration" and "breech of contract." In other countries these laws and clauses do not necessarily apply.

There has been a recent movement, especially in Korea and Japan, to have the governing law be the law of the supplier's country. Such changes can have a marked effect on such areas as worker liability, product liability and indemnification.

You should also be aware that in most countries, a contract is considered merely as a guideline of how the general business is to be done. For example, in the Middle East the signing of a contract may mean the beginning of negotiations. In Japan, religious meanings can hold sway over governmental meanings and when faced with a decision the Japanese businessmen may, very easily, hold harmony and "for the good of all" as a higher authority than the executed contract.

James J. Ritterskamp, Jr. covers some interesting highlights of foreign legal problems in *The Purchasing Manager's Desk Book of Purchasing Law.* In case of disputes it is wise to engage the services of legal counsel in the supplier's country.

# UNDERSTANDING THE CULTURE OF
## ———————— YOUR INTERNATIONAL SUPPLIER ————————

One final point must be made before you embark on international purchasing: study your destination country well. Read books on its culture, customs and mores. Learn and be cautious. When abroad, maintain control, be humble when necessary and respectful at all times of responses and methods that may seen new and unorthodox to you. Insistence on radical change, or "I'm doing it my way," will ensure that you will be doomed to failure with that supplier and, due to the overseas infrastructure, may have serious problems elsewhere as well.

Whereas American marketing and purchasing people consider themselves experts nonpareil here at home, they may become a staggering failure in the global marketplace. The Washington International Center says that without international training, only 20% of the Americans sent abroad can be expected to do well, and 40% to 60% will quit the assignment early or function far below their abilities. American companies may be losing more than $2 billion per year in direct costs because of their inappropriate business methods in dealing with international markets.

This great cost can be directly attributable to a lack of our acceptance of the differences involved in the international marketplace. Notwithstanding the fact that most foreign nationals engaged in business with the United States speak English, this in no way diminishes their sociological attachments to their cultural background. Furthermore, the assumption that a businessperson from Singapore who speaks English *understands* English is generally false. So too is the presumption that he understands American business practices and American psychological reasoning.

Americans are a product of many cultures. The very framework of our democracy has made the United States a melting pot for immigrants from all nations. Throughout our four hundred years or so, we have become knowledgeable, if not reasonably tolerant of our internal cultural differentials. And for the most part, the immigrants have assimilated themselves within our multi-cultural society.

However, when American business people do business within another country, another culture, another society, they tend to lose, forget or simply ignore the possibility of any potential problem. We must remember that most other countries enjoy homogeneity of not only language, but also religion, politics, social order, heritage and customs.

Whether a buyer or a seller, the business traveler must become knowledgeable of the caveats involved in the global marketplace. Predeparture cultural training is of utmost importance to the successful completion of any overseas dealings. The level of the importance of understanding another's culture is pointed out by the fervor with which those other cultures try to understand Americans.

Japanese manufacturing companies, such as Mitsubishi and Matsushita maintain literally hundreds of Japanese "point men" here in the United States solely for the purpose of understanding Americans, our markets and the trends of product acceptance. They duplicate this activity in virtually every country within which they seek to do business.

## USE A TRANSLATOR TO FACILITATE NEGOTIATIONS

When it comes down to the actual exchange of information with an overseas supplier it is often prudent to engage the services of a translator. Your contract and any other communications should be translated into the supplier's native language. When submitting the contract to the supplier, use one set of bound pages with the English version on the left hand page and the translation on the right page. This arrangement of the agreement will greatly facilitate the discussion of certain points at a later date.

It is wise to retain the services of two different translation firms if your budget allows. Once you have the first translation in hand, have the foreign language version *reverse translated* back to English. You will often be amazed at the variances between the two.

A further caveat when engaging the services of a translation firm is to be aware of the variances within a particular language. For example, Spanish has several distinct written forms. A translator from Cuba may present a document unintelligible to a supplier from Spain or Peru.

As it relates to the document itself, prepare an official-looking, neat, well-typed package preferably with a special cover that includes the supplier's name or company. Provide enough copies for all members of the negotiation teams on both sides plus several extra copies for those supplier executives that will not be present. One final note; use an excellent copy machine. Your attention to detail, or lack of it, will definitely be noticed.

We will assume that the spoken language of the negotiations will be in English. But, as we said before, you cannot assume that your supplier understands all English terminology as well as you do. Therefore, you need a technologically competent in-country translator to assist you in putting your points across. It is advised that you not rely on the services of the supplier's translator and especially not on a member of the supplier's team. It will probably not be necessary to have every sentence translated but it would be advisable to have the translator reiterate any important points as they become known.

## ───── NEGOTIATING WITH INTERNATIONAL SUPPLIERS ─────

We stressed preparation in Chapter 8 as it relates to negotiation. In the beginning of this chapter we stressed preparation and cultural knowledge. The actual negotiation, overseas, will require roughly twice the preparation as one here at home. Agreement, compromise and concession are important milestones in a supplier relationship, not to be taken lightly. Never compromise too quickly. Never agree without carefully considering all the facts and the consequences. Take heed of what was said as it relates to harmony and consensus.

For example, in the Far East, decisions involve much thought and many entities. Don't let it become known that you are easy or that you make all the decisions yourself. By taking time, even if you don't need it, you will give the impression that you have consulted others and have given the issue deep thought before you make your decision.

# Selected Bibliography

──────────── BOOKS ────────────

## Accounting and Finance

Dixon, Robert L. *The McGraw-Hill 36-Hour Accounting Course,* Second Edition, New York: McGraw-Hill Book Company, 1982.

Spurga, Ronald C. *Balance Sheet Basics, Financial Management for Nonfinancial Managers,* New York: MENTOR, published by Penguin Group, 1987.

## Law

Ambrose, Cunningham, Hancock, Rolitsky, and Victor *Legal Aspects of International Sourcing,* Chesterland, OH: Business Laws, Inc., 1986.

Babb, Hugh W. and Martin, Charles *Business Law,* Third Edition, New York: Barnes & Noble Books, a division of Harper & Row, Publishers, 1981.

*General information Concerning Patents,* Washington, DC: U.S. Department of Commerce, 1989.

Hancock, W. A. *The Law of Purchasing,* Chesterland, OH: Business Laws, Inc., 1982.

Prentice Hall Editorial Staff *Lawyer's Desk Book,* Ninth Edition, Englewood Cliffs, NJ: Prentice-Hall, Inc., 1989.

Ritterskamp, James Jr. *Purchasing Manager's Desk Book of Purchasing Law,* Englewood Cliffs, NJ: Prentice-Hall, Inc., 1987.

Ritterskamp, Jr. *1991 Supplement, Purchasing Manager's Desk Book of Purchasing Law*, Englewood Cliffs, NJ: Prentice-Hall, Inc., 1991.

Stone, Bradford *Uniform Commercial Code in a Nut Shell*, St. Paul, MN: West Publishing Co., 1975.

## Materials Management

Ammer, Dean S. *Materials Management and Purchasing*, 4th ed. Homewood, IL: Richard D. Irwin, Inc., 1980.

Hall, Robert W. with American Production & Inventory Control Society *Zero Inventories*, Homewood, IL: Dow Jones-Irwin, 1983.

Janson, Robert L. *Handbook of Inventory Management*, Englewood Cliffs, NJ: Prentice-Hall, Inc., 1987.

Mather, Hal *How To Really Manage Inventories*, New York: McGraw-Hill Book Company, 1984.

Orlicky, Joseph *Materials Requirements Planning*, New York: McGraw-Hill Book Company, 1975.

## Negotiating

Bazerman, Max H. and Neole, Margaret A. *Negotiating Rationally* New York: The Free Press a Division of Macmillan, Inc. 1992.

Fisher, Roger and Ury, William *Getting To Yes, Negotiating Agreement Without Giving In*, Boston, MA: Houghton Mifflin Company, 1981; Paperback New York: Penguin Books, 1983.

Fisher, Roger and Brown, Scott *Getting Together, Building Relationships As We Negotiate*, Boston, MA: Houghton Mifflin Company, 1988; Paperback New York: Penguin Books, 1989.

Cohen, Herb *You Can Negotiate Anything*, Secaucus, NJ: Lyle Stuart Inc., 1980.

Fuller, George *The Negotiator's Handbook*, Englewood Cliffs, NJ: Prentice-Hall, Inc., 1991.

Greenburger, Francis with Kiernan, Thomas *How To Ask For More and Get It, The Art of Creative Negotiation*, Garden City, NY: Doubleday & Company, Inc., 1978.

Griffin, Trenholme J. and Daggatt, W. Russell *The Global Negotiator* New York: Harper Business, a Division of Harper Collins, 1990.

Karrass, Chester L. *The Negotiating Game, How to Get What You Want*, New York: Thomas Y. Crowell Company, 1970.

Karrass, Chester L. *Give & Take, The Complete Guide to Negotiating Strategies and Tactics*, New York: Thomas Y. Crowell Company, 1974.

Karrass, Gary *Negotiate to Close, How to Make More Successful Deals*, New York: A Fireside Book published by Simon & Shuster, Inc., 1985.

Kellar, Robert E. *Sales Negotiating Handbook*, Englewood Cliffs, NJ: Prentice-Hall, Inc., 1988.

Koch, H. William, Jr. *Negotiator's Factomatic*, Englewood Cliffs, NJ: Prentice-Hall, Inc., 1988.

Kuhn, Robert Lawrence *Deal Maker* New York: John Wiley and Sons, 1988.

Leritz, Len *No-Fault Negotiating*, New York: Warner Books, Inc., 1987.

Mastenbroek, William. *Negotiate,* First translation Oxford and New York: Basil Blackwell Inc., 1989.

Nierenberg, Gerard I. *Fundamentals of Negotiating*, New York: Harper & Row Publishers, Inc., 1973. Available in paperback from Perennial Library Division of Harper & Row.

Raiffa, Howard *The Art & Science of Negotiation*, Cambridge MA and London, England: The Belknap Press of Harvard University Press, 1982.

Rubin, Jeffrey Z. and Brown, Bert R. *The Social Psychology of Bargaining and Negotiation*, New York: Academic Press, A Subsidiary of Harcourt Brace Jovanovich, Publishers, 1975.

Schatzki, Michael with Wayne R. Coffey *Negotiation, The Art of Getting What You Want*, New York: Signer, The New American Library, Inc., 1981.

Seligman, Scott D. *Dealing With The Chinese*, New York: Warner Books, Inc., 1989.

Warschaw, Tessa Albert *Winning By Negotiation*, New York: McGraw-Hill Paperbacks, 1980.

Young, H. Peyton, Editor, *Negotiation Analysis* Ann Arbor: The University of Michigan Press, 1991.

## Prices and Costs

*Armed Services Pricing Manual*, 2 volumes, Chicago, IL: Commerce Clearing House, Inc., 1987.

Figgie, Harry E. Jr. *Cutting Costs, An Executive's Guide to Increased Profits*, Paperback edition, New York: AMACOM Division, American Management Association, 1990.

## Purchasing, General

Burt, David N. *Proactive Procurement, The Key To Increased Profits, Productivity, and Quality*, Englewood Cliffs, NJ: Prentice-Hall, Inc., 1984.

Corey, E. Raymond *Procurement Management: Strategy, Organization, and Decision-Making*, Boston, MA: CBI Publishing Company, Inc., 1976.

*Federal Acquisition Regulation*, Chicago, IL: Commerce Clearing House, Inc., 1987.

Harding, Michael *Profitable Purchasing*, New York: Industrial Press, 1990.

Heinritz, Farrell, Giunipero, and Kolchin *Purchasing Principles and Applications*, Eighth Edition, Englewood Cliffs, NJ: Prentice-Hall, Inc. 1991.

Woodside, Arch G. and Vyas Nyren *Industrial Purchasing Strategies*, Lexington, MA: Lexington Books Division of D. C. Heath and Company, 1987.

Lee, Lamar, Jr. and Dobler, Donald W. *Purchasing and Materials Management, Text and Cases*, New York: McGraw-Hill Book Company, 1971.

Leenders, Fearon, and England *Purchasing and Materials Management*, Ninth Edition, Homewood, IL: Richard D. Irwin, Inc., 1989.

*Professional Purchasing Study Material and Certification Guidance Manual*, Port Richey, FL: American Purchasing Society, 1990.

Scheuing, Eberhard E. *Purchasing Management*, Englewood Cliffs, NJ: Prentice-Hall, Inc., 1989.

## Quality

Barra, Ralph *Putting Quality Circles To Work*, New York: McGraw-Hill Book Company, 1983.

Crosby, Philip B. *Quality Is Free, The Art of Making Quality Certain*, New York: McGraw-Hill Book Company, 1979.

Hart, Christopher W. L. and Bogan, Christopher E. *The Baldrige*, New York: McGraw-Hill, Inc., 1992.

Hutchins, Greg *Purchasing Strategies for Total Quality*, Homewood, IL, Business One Irwin, 1992.

Ingle, Sud *In Search of Perfection, How to Create/Maintain, Improve Quality*, Englewood Cliffs, NJ: Prentice-Hall, Inc., 1985.

## —————————————— PERIODICALS ——————————————

*Electronic Buyers' News*, Newsweekly for the electronics industry with information about suppliers to the electronic industry and buyers of electronic components. Manhasset, NY: CMP Publications, Inc., Published weekly.

*Professional Purchasing*, Newsletter providing information on how to buy and manage purchasing. Port Richey, FL: American Purchasing Society, Published monthly.

*Purchasing*, Magazine covers a wide variety of purchasing and purchasing related subjects. Newton, MA: Cahners Publishing Company, Semi-monthly

─────────────────────── **CASSETTES** ───────────────────────

Crosby, Philip B. *Quality Is Free, The Art of Making Quality Certain*, Fullerton, CA: McGraw-Hill, 1989.

Crosby, Philip B. *Quality Without Tears, The Art of Hassle-Free Management*, Fullerton, CA: McGraw-Hill, 1989.

Fisher, Roger and Ury, William. *Getting To Yes, How To Negotiate Agreement Without Giving In*, Six Audiocassettes and a study guide, New York: Simon & Schuster Audio Publishing Division, 1986.

Hough, Harry E. *Negotiating for Purchasing*, Port Richey, FL: American Purchasing Society, 1991.

Dawson, Roger *The Secrets of Power Negotiating*, Chicago, IL: Nightingale-Conant Corporation, 1990.

Hough, Harry E. *Purchasing and Accounting,* Transactions Between The Departments, Port Richey, FL: American Purchasing Society, 1991.

Hough, Harry E. *Purchasing and Engineering*, Port Richey, FL: American Purchasing Society, 1991.

Nierenberg, Gerard I. *The Art of Negotiation*, Holmes, PA: Sound Editions from Random House, 1987.

Reck, Ross R. and Long, Brian G. *The Win Win Negotiator*, Chicago, IL: Nightingale-Conant Corporation, 1985.

Warschaw, Tessa Albert *Negotiating To Win*, Fullerton, CA: TDM/McGraw-Hill, 1987.

# Appendixes

## *Appendix A: Price Information Sources*

### *Boardroom Reports*

Prices for Commodities

This general business newsletter publishes prices of various commodities, products, and services. Selected items are reported semimonthly. For subscription information contact Service Department, *Boardroom Reports,* Box 58415, Boulder, Colorado 80322.

### *Electronic Buyers' News*

Electronic Prices

Price announcements for electronic components and industry price news. Published weekly by CMP Publications Inc., 600 Community Drive, Manhasset, NY 11030-3875.

### *Purchasing* **Magazine**

Prices for Commodities

Transaction prices, price news, and trends are reported semi-monthly for commodities and other products. Good coverage for metals, wood, paperboard, chemicals, plastics, electrical and electronic items. For subscription information, write to *Purchasing,* 44 Cook Street, Denver, CO 80206-5800.

### U.S. Government

Producer Price Indexes
Consumer Price Indexes

Use these indexes to estimate price movements by applying the percentage change to particular commodities or items. Information available in monthly printed reports, on disk, and on tape. A particularly valuable report is the *CPI Detailed Report* which is published monthly by the U.S. Department of Labor, Bureau of Labor Statistics. To order this and other government publications contact the Superintendent of Documents, U.S. Government Printing Office, Washington, DC 20402.

### *The Wall Street Journal*

Commodity Prices
Foreign Currency
Price News

This newspaper, published Monday through Friday, is an excellent source for commodity prices and announcements of industry price changes. Also prints money exchange rates if you are involved with foreign trade. Order from Wall Street Journal, Dow Jones & Co., Inc. 200 Liberty Street, New York, NY 10281.

## Appendix B: Where to Find A Source

### Telephone Books

#### Yellow Pages
Check the Yellow Pages of the telephone book. If you are in a small town or a rural area, contact your telephone company to obtain the yellow pages of the largest city closest to you. Some purchasing departments obtain Yellow Pages for the major cities. New York, Los Angeles, Chicago, and Atlanta are among the cities that are selected.

### General Product Directories

#### MacRae'S Blue Book
Three volume set listing 50,000 manufacturers. Volume 1 has company and trade name index. Home office and branch office locations. Volume 2 & 3 list manufacturers by product. $145 and available from MacRae's Blue Book Inc., 817 Broadway, New York, NY 10003, 1-800-622-7237 Discount to members.

#### Thomas Register
The most common and perhaps most widely used directory for industrial buyers is the Thomas Register of American Manufacturers. It consists of twenty-three volumes. The first fourteen volumes lists the names and addresses of manufacturers and the products and services they offer. Volumes 15 and 16 describe the companies, and volumes 17 to 23 include catalogs of various companies. The biggest drawback to the Thomas Register is that it does not give the names of sales executives and officers of the companies that are listed. Neither does it give much financial data. The cost of all 23 volumes is $240 and may be ordered from the Circulation Department, Thomas Register, Thomas Publishing Company, One Penn Plaza, New York, NY 10117-0138.

### Special Product Directories
There are special directories for most categories of the products purchased. Some of these are published to be sold and others are sent as supplements to magazines or given out at trade shows. Some are offered by associations and professional societies. Listed below are but a few of the many that are available.

#### Appliance Industry Purchasing Directory
Includes products and suppliers for the appliance industry. Annual issue of Appliance Magazine published by Dana Chase. Contact Circulation Department, Appliance, 1000 Jorie Boulevard, CS5030, Oak Brook, IL 60521

#### Directory of Metal Suppliers
A supplement to Purchasing Magazine published by Cahners Publishing Co., 275 Washington St., Newton, MA 02158-1630

#### The Electronic Source Book
Seven regional editions are available at $22 each. Published by Professional Decision Making, Inc. 125 Wolf Road, Albany, NY 12205. Lists sources for electronic components. It is divided into a section for manufacturers, one for distributors, and one for value-added services. It also has a section listing representatives.

#### Kline Guide to the Paint Industry
Includes technical data and names of paint manufacturers, laboratories, and sources for information. Available from Charles H. Kline & Co., Inc. 330 Passaic Avenue, Fairfield, NJ 07006

#### Motivation
Includes names of companies exhibiting at the National Premium Incentive Show and the Incentive Travel and Meeting Executive Show. Contact APS for further information.

#### National Job Shop Directory I
Includes names of suppliers and the equipment they have available. Published by the Edwards Company who also publishes Job Shop Technology, P.O. Box 7193, 16 Waterbury Road, Prospect, CT 06712-1215

#### Official Directory & Buyers' Guide
Includes list of products and companies exhibiting at the National Plant Engineering & Maintenance Show and Conference. Published by Cahners Exposition Group, 999 Summer Street, P.O. Box 3833, Stamford, CT 06905-0833

#### Packaging Buyers Guide
An annual issue of Packaging Magazine published by Cahners Publishing Co., 275 Washington St., Newton, MA 02158-1630

#### Plastics Directory
Issued annually by Plastics World Magazine, Cahners Publishing Company, 275 Washington Street, Newton, MA 02158-1630. It includes resin and compound suppliers, additives and modifier suppliers, primary and auxiliary equipment suppliers.

#### Modern Plastics Encyclopedia
Published by McGraw-Hill. Provides technical information and the names of suppliers.

#### Sources for Iron Castings
A buyers guide and directory of members. Published by the Iron Castings Society, Cast Metals Federation Building, 10611 Center Ridge Road, Rocky River, OH 44116

AMERICAN PURCHASING SOCIETY, INC.

11910 Oak Trail Way, Port Richey, Fl 34668

## Sources of Supply/Buyers Guide

Includes sources for paper and paper products, cost $60, published annually by Advertisers and Publishers Service, Inc. P. O. Drawer 795, 300 N. Prospect Avenue, Park Ridge, IL 60068

## Who's Who In Electronics

Five regional editions with each edition including national and regional sources. Includes sections for distributors, manufacturers, and products. Available for $50 plus $5 for packaging and handling from Harris Publishing Company, 2057 Aurora Road, Twinsburg, OH 44087

## State Directories

Directories of manufacturers are available for most states. Prices range between $50 and $150. Available from Manufacturers' News, Inc., 4 East Huron St., Chicago, IL 60611-2793.

## Finding International Sources

There may be as many international directories as there are domestic directories. Listed below are a few. If you cannot locate a directory for the country you are interested in, contact the consulate for that country. Offices are in Washington, but many also have offices in other major cities. The consul will see which companies are interested in exporting to the U.S.or will give you a list of companies that you can directly contact.

## Directory of Hong Kong Industries

Includes advertisements, list of products and the Hong Kong companies that sell them. Description of companies is given with some giving names of key executives. For further information contact the Management & Industrial Consultancy Div., Hong Kong Productivity Council, 12/F., World Commerce Centre, Harbour City, Kowloon, Hong Kong

## European Eletronic Component Distributor Directory

Lists component distributors in seventeen European countries. Firms are listed by country, alphabetically, by products carried and by manufacturer represented. Price $150 and available from Harris Publishing Company, 2057 Aurora Road, Twinsburg, OH 44087

## International Electronics Directory

Provides detailed information of products and the companies that manufacture them. This specialized directory Includes listings for 28 countries, 1500 product lines, and 40,000 executives. Available for $387 from Harris Publishing Co., 2057 Aurora Road, Twinsburg, OH 44087

## Italian Yellow Pages for the U.S.A.

Contains Italian companies and the products they sell. Published by SEAT - Societa Elenchi Ufficiali Abbonati al Telefono, a cooperative effort of AT&T, ItalCable, and SEAT. Contact AT&T International Business Markets Group, 412 Mt. Kemble Avenue, Morristown, NJ 07960

## Irish Export Directory

Lists companies and products. Published on behalf of Coras Trachtala/Irish Export Board by Jemma Publication, Ltd. 22 Brookfield Avenue, Blackrock Co, Cublin, Ireland

## Japan Yellow Pages

Contains Japanese companies and the products they sell. To order or for price information contact Japan Yellow Pages Ltd., ST Bldg., 6-9 Iidabashi 4-chome, Chiyoda-ku, Tokyo 102, Japan

## Made in Europe, Monthly Import Guide and Continuous Trade Fair in Print

Includes advertisements for all type products produced in Europe. Published by Made in Europe Marketing Organization GmbH & Co. KG, 21-29 Unterlindau, D-6000 Frankfurt am Main 1, West Germany

## Taiwan Hardware Buyers' Guide

Includes advertisements, articles, and list of companies and the products they sell. Published by Trade Winds, Inc., P.O. Box 7-179, Taipei 10602, Taiwan, R.O.C.

## Financially Oriented Directories

Some directories primarily aimed at financial managers are useful guides for finding sources and at the same time evaluating the financial strength of the company. The two best examples are probably most accessible in public libraries include the Dun and Bradstreet Directories and the Standard & Poor's Directory.

## Standard & POOR'S Register of Corporations, Directors, and Executives

Includes company names, a general description of what they make or sell, the approximate sales volume, and the names of officers and directors. Available for lease only at $510 per year which includes updates throughout the year and a completely revised set annually. Price $510 from Standard & Poor's Corporation, 25 Broadway, New York, NY 10004

## Trade Associations

Look up the name of the appropriate association in National Trade and Professional Associations of the United States which is available in most libraries or purchase it for $55 from Columbia Books, Inc. 1212 New York Avenue, N.W., Suite 330, Washington, D.C. 20005

## Other Source Finding Techniques

Magazine advertisements, companies mentioned in magazine articles (if the address is not given, contact the editor).Other supplier referrals. If all else fails or you do not have the appropriate directory, contact the American Purchasing Society. We are glad to help you.

AMERICAN PURCHASING SOCIETY, INC.

11910 Oak Trail Way, Port Richey, Fl 34668

# PROFESSIONAL
# PURCHASING

REPORT NUMBER 8                                                          1989

### Analyzing a Supplier's
### Financial Strength

If you are going to depend on a company for goods or services of a significant amount, it is important to investigate its reputation. Check its technical capabilities, and make sure it has the proper facilities to produce and deliver the products you want. A physical inspection of the plant and offices is often desirable. It often reveals far more than any written report or references would provide.

However, even though a company has the required technical skill, a good reputation for high quality, and all the necessary equipment, it may have financial difficulties that threaten delivery of the product you order. At the least, the financial problems of your supplier can cause late delivery and poor quality. Even more seriously, the result may be the loss of your customers and financial loss to your company.

Professionals in purchasing routinely check the financial stability of new suppliers. Because conditions change many conduct periodic financial checks to avoid unpleasant surprises.

#### How you get financial information

A new supplier usually asks a buyer for credit references unless the buyer represents a large corporation that publicly discloses financial information. Even then, additional data may be

*Continued on page 3, Analyzing Financial*

## Analyzing the Financial Strength of Suppliers

*Continued from page 2*

requested if the transaction amount is very large. In addition the seller may get data from various credit information services such as Dun and Bradstreet. Purchasing managers for large corporations frequently give copies of their annual reports to their major suppliers.

The buyer or purchasing manager in turn can request financial reports from the supplier. The buyer can also obtain reports from D & B or other credit reporting services. Most suppliers will give bank references without any hesitation. A thorough financial analysis requires annual reports consisting of balance sheets and profit and loss statements going back three or more consecutive years from the present.

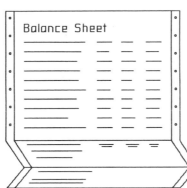

**What you check**

One of the first things you are interested in is how long the supplier has been in business. When was the company founded? When was it incorporated and in what state? Who founded the company? Who are the present owners? Is it a close corporation? Is the stock publicly traded? Is it listed on a major stock exchange? What is the history of the company?

Newer companies are riskier to do business with simply because most business failures occur within the first few years of a company's existence.

You should look at the amount of capitalization of the company. In other words, how much was invested and what is the net worth? It may be unwise to give an order worth more than the supplier's equity. Net worth is shown at the end of the balance sheet. We have seen companies give orders and large down payments to tool builders that have little more than a garage and equipment less than the advance they received. If something happens to the owner, there would be little chance to recoup the

*Continued at top*

*Continued from bottom*

amount given without much trouble and expense.

Sales volume is another important item to check. The figure may be shown as "sales" or "revenue" at the beginning of the profit and loss statement. Compare the amount of your business that you intend to give to the supplier with the total sales volume of the supplier. Be cautious if it represents a high percentage. The supplier may be so anxious to get that amount of business that costs have been under estimated or he may not have the capabilities to handle the volume.

One supplier kept delaying delivery of some plastic components. Each week the supplier got further and further behind on deliveries. A check of the available machinery and the speed of the machines revealed that it was physically impossible to produce the agreed upon quantity with the equipment available. The supplier seemed to be unaware of the cause of the problem.

You might also want to ask the supplier how the sales dollars are concentrated or dispersed among his other customers. If one or two customers account for most of the sales and one of those customers is lost, it could be disastrous.

One of the most important pieces of information you are looking for is to find out if the company is profitable. Net profit or loss is shown at the end of the profit and loss report. Compare the sales and earnings

## Analyzing the Financial Strength of Suppliers

*Continued from page 3*

for three or more years. Look to see if they are steadily improving or if they are steadily getting worse. If they show profitability one year followed by a loss the next and then another year of profitability, you may have to do a lot more analysis. Ask the supplier for explanations of such a cloudy picture. In particular, small privately held companies may seem unprofitable, but the owners are taking large sums in salaries and bonuses. Those sums are shown in the salary expense on the profit and loss report. Net profit is thereby reduced by the high salaries and in fact can even cause the company to show a loss.

Check the amount of working capital - the difference between total current assets and total current liabilities. Generally, an acceptable figure requires total current

assets to be twice as large as current liabilities. The amount of assets that can be quickly turned into cash, if need be, is a useful figure. Quick assets are current assets less inventory. The quick assets ratio is quick assets divided by current liabilities.

A thorough analysis will check inventory turnover. The annual sales volume divided by the value of the inventory shown on the balance sheet will give you the inventory turnover.

There are various other ratios you can check. To be meaningful, you will need to compare them with performance over time and with other companies in the same industry.

If you have not done a review before, the first one can take you an hour or more after you have gathered all the information you need. After you become experienced you may be able to reduce the time to a few minutes. ✠

## *Appendix D: Questions to Ask When Negotiating*

### *BUYERS CHECKLIST NUMBER 8*

## QUESTIONS TO ASK WHEN NEGOTIATING

**By Harry E. Hough**

Questions are one of the most useful tools while negotiating. Questions both give and get information. The type of questions you ask may indicate your interest or your concerns. Here are some samples you may use when you negotiate.

Do you have enough capacity to handle our business if we need 50% more next year?

Is your company flexible on payment terms?

Could you lower your price if we purchase the raw material for you? (This assumes that you have already been told what they allegedly pay for their raw material)

You say you cannot make the delivery date we require, but could you make it if we pay you overtime for working on the weekends?

You say your product is the best in the market place, yet you give a shorter warranty period than your competition. Why is that?

What ideas have you come up with to reduce cost during the last three years of doing business with you?

You say you need a 15% increase in price because inflation has eaten away your profit and you have not had an increase in three years. Doesn't that mean you were making an exorbitant profit all this time?

Are you aware of how much competition you have?

Which companies are your major competitors?

How much have you invested in research to solve our problem? Isn't our business worth it to you?

You say you have idle capacity and promise quick delivery, but won't you put us on the back burner when the economy improves and your high volume regular customers begin ordering again?

You require a large cash advance for this job even though we have top notch credit, does that mean you are financially shaky?

How is your business doing? Are you busy? How is business compared to last year? What is your forecast for next year?

Do you sell to any of our competitors?

Are you most efficient with high volume orders or smaller orders?
Do you prefer standard items or items produced to the customer's specifications?

How many customers do you have?

Are there any customers that account for the major portion of your business?

What salary do you pay your secretaries?

Do you have trouble keeping engineers?

Every few months a different salesperson calls on us. What is the problem in your company?

AMERICAN PURCHASING SOCIETY, INC.

11910 Oak Trail Way, Port Richey, Fl 34668

*Appendix E: Essential Mathematics for Purchasing*

## 1. The Use of Percentages

Every successful buyer must have a good understanding of percentages and how to use them. The reasonableness of price changes is best evaluated by comparing the percentage change with the percentage change of the consumer price index or the producer price index or some other criteria rather than looking at the absolute dollar amount of the change.

Percentages are used to show relative position of supplier performance or buyer performance.

*Problem:* If the price of a product is $250 and it is reduced through your effort to $235, what percentage savings did you obtain?

*Solution:* You obtain a $15 reduction in price. Divide 15 by 250 to obtain the answer of 6%.

*Problem:* The price of a product is $235 and the supplier announces an increase to $250 but you convince him to keep it at $235; what percentage additional cost have you avoided?

*Solution:* You divide the $15 saving by $235. The answer is 6.4%. It is important to remember which base to use when calculating percentages. If you (or the supplier) use the wrong base the answer can be misleading.

## 2. Calculating Price Discounts

Price discounts are widely used in business, particularly for shelf or stock items. There is little doubt that many companies make their pricing formulas and discount structures needlessly complex. One must assume that this is done to hide the true cost from those who may be timid or unwilling to dig for the facts. If possible, the buyer should try to negotiate simple formulas and easy-to-calculate discounts. In some cases, the buyer is forced to accept the price structure offered.

*Problem:* Argus States offers their high quality bond paper at $7.00 per ream. If you buy 2 to 9 reams, you get a 10% discount, if you buy 10 to 20 reams you get a 15% discount. You feel you can store 15 reams and use it before it deteriorates. However, you calculate your holding cost for 15 reams averages $4 and your order processing cost for an extra order at $12. Without considering other facts, which would be more economical, to make one purchase of 15 reams or to buy twice at lower quantities?

*Solution:* The cost of two orders totaling 15 reams will be $7 − (7 × .1) = $6.30 × 15 = $94.50 plus $12 for processing the extra paperwork = $106.50. The cost of one order of 15 reams will be $7 − (7 × .15) = $5.95 × 15 = $89.25 plus $4 for holding cost = $93.25. Therefore, the most economical cost based on these facts is one purchase with the higher discount. The saving is $13.25.

**Problem:** You request bids on your annual purchases of electrical switches, and No-Shock Switches, Inc. gives you the best offer with price discounts of 25, 15, and 10. You receive a requisition to buy the following switches.

| Part Number | Quantity | List Price Each |
|---|---|---|
| XY-101 | 25 | $3.40 |
| XY-107 | 50 | 2.75 |
| XY-109 | 35 | 2.90 |

What is the total value of the order after taking the price discounts?

**Solution:** There are at least two different ways of doing this problem. You can calculate the net price for each item and then multiply by the quantity. Finally you add the net totals for each item to get the value for the order. Or you can multiply each quantity times the list price, add the results, and then take the discounts off the total. When you do the latter make sure the same discounts apply to all items. With the latter method your total for the order before discounts is $324. Multiply this amount by .75, the result by .85, and that result by .9. The answer is $185.90 Answers may differ slightly because of rounding. Using the first method, we obtained $185.86.

## 3. Evaluating Payment Discounts

The most common payment term is Net 30. That means invoices received are due within thirty days. Next most common is a stated discount if paid within a short time period, usually ten days, but with the full amount due after a longer period, usually thirty days. A general description of this term might read X% Y, Net X. For example, 1% 10, Net 30 or 2% 10, Net 60. There are many other payment terms that are less frequently used.

The finance or accounting department usually is responsible to take or disregard the discount offered, but the purchasing manager should set a negotiating target to match what the financial people prefer. When a company is short of cash, it may be forced to forego taking profitable discounts.

**Problem:** The invoice from One & Only Plumbing Supply is in the amount of $1243 with payment terms of 2% 10, Net 30. If the discount is taken, how much should be paid?

*Solution:* Multiply .02 times $1,243 and subtract the result from $1,243 to get the net amount that should be paid. Or simply multiply .98 times $1,243. The answer is $1,218.14.

*Problem:* Assume the controller tells you that your company can borrow money at 14%. Should the above discount be taken? What is the rate of return on paying the bill in time to take the discount?

*Solution:* By paying the bill by the 10th day rather than waiting 30 days, the company gives up use of the money for an extra 20 days or, put another way, the company earns 2% for a period of 20 days. Dividing 365 by 20 equals 18.25. Multiply 18.25 times 2% equals 36.5% annually. If money can be borrowed at 14% the net return is 22.5%. If borrowing is not necessary, the return is 36.5%.

## 4. Using the Time Value of Money in Purchasing

Money has value over time..That is why it is best to put off paying taxes as long as legally possible. That is why a good buyer will negotiate a lower price for paying sooner. That is why, among other reasons, it is poor policy to pay for work or material in advance. Conversely, if you want to pay for something in the future, you should expect to pay more. The question is how much more should you be willing to pay.

*Problem:* A machine tool builder agrees to accept payment when the tool you need is completed but the price totals $268,000, with terms of 50% down and 50% when completed, whereas the builder wants $300,000 to do all the work before any payment. The current cost of money to you is 12.5%. The tool will be complete in two years. Which deal is best for you and how much will you save?

*Solution:* Use the present value formula $P = S/(1 + r)^n$

$$\text{where } P = \text{present value}$$
$$S = \text{future value}$$
$$r = \text{interest rate}$$
$$n = \text{periods}$$

Using $S = \$300,000$, $r = .125$, and $n = 2$, the value of $P$ is $237,037.

With our alternate price of $268,000, we know that we must pay 50 percent down or $134,000 and another $134,000 two years hence. Therefore, we need to know the present value of our future $134,000 payment. Inserting into the formula, $S = \$134,000$, $r = .125$, and $n = 2$, the value of $P$ becomes $105,876.54. Add our first up front payment and we get a total value of $239,876.54.

Thus the end payment of $300,000 has a present value of $237,037, whereas, the 50% down, plus 50% end payment totaling $268,000, has a present value of $239,876.54 or is $2839.54 more costly.

## 5. Calculating Economic Order Quantities and Economic Purchase Quantities

Some companies use eyeball methods of controlling inventory while others use complex forecasting and mathematical techniques to minimize inventory cost. However, even those companies with highly structured inventory control systems do not usually control all the items that purchasing buys. Consequently the buyer must often decide on the quantity to order. One commonly used method is application of an economic order quantity formula. Although these formulas do not allow for obsolescence, deterioration of stock, lack of storage space, or limited cash available, they do provide guidance. The buyer need not accept the derived answer blindly, but if other factors are not a problem, the calculated quantity is a much better figure than guesswork. The economic order quantity formula does not make allowances for volume discounts; therefore separate calculations are required for different price levels.

To solve the problems below use this formula to obtain the least costly quantity to buy.

$EOQ = (2AS/pI)^{1/2}$ where:    $A$ = the annual usage
$S$ = the ordering cost
$p$ = unit delivered price
$I$ = inventory carrying cost expressed as a
decimal fraction of average inventory

**Problem:** International Widgets supplies widgets to your company at $495 per thousand. Looking at your purchase history, you see you use about 23,000 per year. Your controller estimates that the carrying cost for inventory is 22% and you estimate your ordering cost at $45 per order. What is the economic order quantity?

**Solution:** Using the $EOQ$ formula $((23,000 \times 45/.495(.22))^{1/2}$

$$EOQ = 3,083$$

The most economical quantity to order is 3,083.

**Problem:** When you begin to place the order with International Widgets, the salesperson informs you that if you order 5000 or over you would get a 5% discount. Will it pay you to order 5,000?

**Solution:** A 5% discount changes the price to .470. Recalculating with the new price we get:

$$EOQ = ((23,000 \times 45/.470(.22))^{1/2}$$
$$EOQ = 3164$$

The most economical order quantity even at the lower price is still considerably under 5,000; therefore it is not a good idea to increase the size of the order beyond 3,083.

### 6. Separating Fixed and Variable Purchasing Cost

Fixed cost must be spread over the entire quantity that you order. Therefore when you order larger quantities the amount of fixed cost that applies to one unit is much smaller than at lower quantities. For example, much of the cost in printing is in make-ready and setting up the machine. That is why it does not cost much more to get much greater quantities of printed material than it does to order a small quantity and the unit cost is so much lower. For example, it might cost you $150 or ten cents each to order 1500 copies, whereas it will only cost $250 or six cents each to order 5,000 copies.

In many business situations suppliers will attempt to hide components of cost, but a good buyer will try to learn the details so that negotiations can provide the lowest cost. Once you know the cost details, you can make better sourcing decisions.

***Problem:*** Fantastic Plastics has a machine that cost $600,000 and the owners figure a cost of $60 per hour for the use of the machine. Labor to run the machine cost $16 per hour. Ten thousand of your products can be produced per hour but it takes one hour to set up the machine. Small Time Plastics has a machine that cost $80,000 and the owner figures a cost of $9 for the machine and labor at $12 per hour. The machine will produce 1,000 of your product per hour but it takes one half hour to set the machine up. Assuming the suppliers are equal in every other respect, at what quantity will it make no difference in cost who gets the order?

***Solution:*** Write an equation where the total production cost of Fantastic Plastics for the unknown quantity equals the total production cost of Small Time Plastics. Therefore:

Let $Q$ = the unknown quantity

On the left side of the equation add the various component costs for Fantastic Plastics.

60 = Cost for one hour use of machine during set-up

plus

16 = Cost for one hour labor to set up machine

$(60 \times Q)/10,000$ = Cost for use of machine to produce the unknown quantity

plus

$(16 \times Q)/10,000$ = Cost of labor to run unknown quantity

On the right side of the equation add the various component costs for Small Time Plastics.

9/2 = Cost for half hour use of machine during set-up

12/2 = Cost for half hour for labor to set up machine

$(9 \times Q)/1000$ = Cost for use of machine for unknown quantity

$(12 \times Q)/1000$ = Cost of labor to run unknown quantity

Thus:

60 + 16 + 60Q/10000 + 16Q/10,000 = 9/2 + 12/2 + 9Q/1000 + 12Q/1000
Solving for Q = 4888

## 7. The Use of Averages

In addition to an understanding of percentages, knowledge about the different types of averages and how to use them is most useful for the buyer. There are three different kinds of averages you should know: the mean, the mode, and the median. The mean is the average that is most commonly used although it is not necessarily always the most revealing. It is the sum of the variables divided by the number of items. If one or two items out of many have very high values, the answer is weighted toward the higher values.

The mode is the value of the most commonly repeated item and the median is the middle point where half of the items have higher values and half of the items lower values.

**Problem:** The M & P Company announces a price increase of all the items that it sells to your company averaging less than 4%. Your buyer is not satisfied with the announcement and tells the salesperson he must supply more detail. Your buyer ask for a list showing the old price, the new price, and the percentage price change for each item. M & P prepares the following list and gives it to the buyer as you requested.

| Part Number | Old Price | New Price | % Change |
|---|---|---|---|
| CX-1897 | .76 | .80 | 5.3 |
| BX-3099 | 1.18 | 1.23 | 4.2 |
| CX-6859 | .46 | .44 | −4.3 |
| CX-9660 | .92 | .96 | 4.3 |
| DX-1491 | .19 | .21 | 10.5 |
| XX-2595 | 2.38 | 2.50 | 5.0 |

Based on the information on the list alone, is the supplier's statement that the price changes average less than 4%. If not, what is the average (mean) price change?

**Solution:** The supplier is in error; the increase is not below 4%. Based on the information on this table alone, the average increase is 4.16%.

**Problem:** After negotiating, the buyer agreed to accept price changes somewhat lower than those shown in part A, but at the end of a month with the new prices in effect, the controller reported that material cost went up more than 4%. You investigate to find out what happened. You obtain the following information from accounts payable.

| Part Number | Quantity Purchased During Month | Price Paid |
|---|---|---|
| CX-1897 | 200 | .79 |
| BX-3099 | 250 | 1.23 |
| CX-6859 | 50 | .43 |
| CX-9660 | 400 | .96 |
| DX-1491 | 900,000 | .21 |
| XX-2595 | 85,000 | 2.50 |

You check with the buyer and find that the prices charged match the negotiated agreement. What happened? Was the buyer's negotiation successful? What is the actual percentage cost change?

***Solution:*** The buyer did not consider the volume of the items purchased. A good buyer will look at the history of purchases and try to forecast future needs based on information from sales, marketing, engineering, and operations. Smart suppliers gather as much information about future potential and price products accordingly. To obtain the effective cost increase, the buyer must multiply the expected usage of each item by the old price and total the cost for all items. The same process then needs to be done for the new prices. You then subtract the total old cost from the total new cost and divide the result by the total old cost. The weighted cost increase in this example is 7.5%, even though the average increase of the unweighted percentages is only 3.6%.

## 8. Understanding Foreign Rates of Exchange and Price Changes Using Foreign Sources

Although you can use international sources through representatives located in the United States and draw from stock stored in the United States, you may obtain your lowest cost by dealing directly with the source in the foreign location. Doing so requires an understanding of currency exchange rates and the effects those rates have on prices and cost. You may negotiate your purchase in the currency of the supplier or you may prefer to negotiate the purchase agreement with U.S. dollars. If you expect the foreign currency to become more valuable in relation to the dollar, you would be better off to make your agreement in dollars. If you expect the foreign currency to decline in value you would be better off making your agreement in the foreign currency. Whichever currency is used, the effect on long-term cost will still depend on the exchange rate.

***Problem:*** You were buying parts from Japan at 20 yen each when the exchange rate was 200 yen to the dollar and you expected the yen to decline in value so you made an agreement to buy for one year at the fixed price of 20 yen, but instead within six months the yen increased in value so that the exchange rate is 100 yen to the dollar. How much were you paying each in U.S. currency when the yen was 200 to the dollar and how much are you paying in U.S. currency when the yen is 100 to the dollar?

*Solution:* If 200 yen equals a dollar, then 20 yen is only 1/10 of a dollar. Thus you were paying ten cents each. Even though the yen increased in value (in other words it will take fewer yen to buy the same goods), you made a fixed price deal to pay 20 yen. Since 100 yen now equals a dollar, you divide 20 by 100 and your answer is .20 or 1/5. Multiply this by the dollar and your cost is .20 each. You avoid having to predict how the rates will change and the risk of being wrong by negotiating the price in U.S. dollars, but of course you would not gain if the foreign currency declined in value. Make sure you keep a record of what the exchange rate is at the time you make the agreement. You need this information to evaluate any price changes in the future.

*Problem:* You started buying a pump from Japan in U.S. dollars at a price of $2.60 and at the same time the yen was 245 to the dollar. The exchange rate has changed to 150 yen to the dollar and you are ready to place a new order. The supplier informs you the price is now $3.40. What percentage increase must you pay? What percentage change in revenue will the supplier incur?

*Solution:* Your price rises from $2.60 to $3.40, an increase of 30.8%. At the $2.60 price your supplier received 637 yen (2.60 × 245). When the exchange rate changed your supplier received 510 yen ($3.40 × 150). Thus even though you interpret the change in price as an increase, your supplier in effect is taking a reduction in price from 637 to 510 or −19.9% and must absorb the difference.

## 9. Converting Units of Measure

With the use of the computer for purchasing and accounting, problems with converting different units of measure are minimized. Nevertheless, it makes it easier if the units of measure are the same for quantities and prices on purchase orders, receiving documents, and invoices. This is not always possible because some requisitioners and suppliers use different methods.

*Problem:* The stationery supply clerk requisitions 282 pens from purchasing. When the buyer calls the supplier, she finds out that the pens sell for 89 cents each but come in boxes of 12 only and they will not break a box. When the shipment is received the receiving clerk checks the document and agrees that he did receive 4 cartons and each carton contained 5 dozen boxes. The invoice received by accounting is for 2 gross of pens for a total of $265.32. How many pens were ordered? What is the value of the order? How many pens were received? What should the invoice amount be?

***Solution:***

| | |
|---|---|
| Quantity Ordered by Requisitioner | 282 |
| Minimum Needed for Full Boxes | 288 |
| Purchase Order Amount 288 × .89 | $256.32 |
| Quantity Received 4 × 5 × 12 | 240 |
| Corrected Invoice 240 × .89 | 213.60 |

## 10. Cost Analysis of Purchased Products

There are two types of cost analysis of purchased goods. One involves the cost of obtaining the goods and includes packaging, transportation, and any other expense associated with delivery of the goods. The other type includes the cost of using the material and is essential to accurately evaluate the value of the goods received. The following problem illustrates the latter type.

***Problem:*** As buyer for Cosmopolitan Insurance you receive a requisition to buy floor wax for all the office floors. Your responsibility is to obtain the best value for funds expended. You ask six suppliers for quotations and receive five replies.

| | |
|---|---|
| Quick Shine | $4/gallon |
| Glo-Right | 6/gallon |
| Brite Floor | 8.40/gallon |
| Best Wax | 20.40/gallon |
| Luxury Shine | 21.50/gallon |

You have an impartial test conducted to see how easy it is to apply each product, how much product is needed, and to evaluate the durability of each product. You receive the following report.

**TEST REPORT FOR COSMOPOLITAN INSURANCE—COMPARISON OF WAXES**

| Supplier | Coverage per Gallon in Square Feet | Average Application Square Feet/Hour | Durability Estimated in Months |
|---|---|---|---|
| Quick Shine | 65 | 150 | 6 |
| Glo-Right | 126 | 108 | 12 |
| Brite Floor | 162 | 117 | 18 |
| Best Wax | 180 | 175 | 24 |
| Luxury Shine | 180 | 170 | 18 |

The maintenance workers that will apply the wax earn $8.50 per hour.

With this information alone and assuming the data is accurate, calculate exactly which product is your best buy.

*Solution:* Material plus Labor = Cost per Application

Cost per Application divided by Number of Years equals Cost per Year assuming 1,000 square feet of floor space.

|  | Material + Labor = | Cost per Application | Years (Months/12) | Cost per Year |
|---|---|---|---|---|
| Quick Shine | $\frac{(1000 \times 4.00)}{65} + \frac{(1000 \times 8.50)}{150}$ | = 118.20 | ÷ 6/12 | = $236.40 |
| Glo-Right | $\frac{(1000 \times 6.00)}{126} + \frac{(1000 \times 8.50)}{108}$ | = 126.31 | ÷ 12/12 | = $126.31 |
| Bright Floor | $\frac{(1000 \times 8.40)}{162} + \frac{(1000 \times 8.50)}{117}$ | = 124.50 | ÷ 18/12 | = $ 83.00 |
| Best Wax | $\frac{(1000 \times 20.40)}{180} + \frac{(1000 \times 8.50)}{175}$ | = 161.90 | ÷ 24/12 | = $ 80.95 |
| Luxury | $\frac{(1000 \times 21.50)}{180} + \frac{(1000 \times 8.50)}{170}$ | = 169.44 | ÷ 24/12 | = $ 84.72 |

*Problem:* After you reach your decision regarding which wax has the lowest per-year cost, the controller of Cosmopolitan Insurance stops by your office and tells you that the company guidelines for return on investment are 14% or more. With this additional information, which product is the best buy?

*Solution:* Without considering any cost of investment, the saving in selecting Best Wax as a source rather than Brite Floor is $2.05 per year. However, the additional investment required to purchase and apply the wax is $37.40 ($161.90 − $124.50). Therefore the return on the investment of $37.40 is 5.5%, that is $2.05 divided by $37.40. Since our controller wants a return of 14%, Brite Floor is a better choice.

## Appendix F: How A Supplier's Guide to Purchasing Helps You

A Supplier's guide to purchasing will make it easier for you to do a better job. Many companies give potential suppliers guides to purchasing. Sometimes these guides are referred to as "Welcome to Purchasing" guides. They come in various shapes and sizes. Some are simply lists of the buyers and purchasing managers with the product responsibility they have and perhaps their telephone numbers and extensions. Others are elaborate, containing the purchasing policies and procedures that the supplier should know to do business with that company.

Hewlett-Packard has a fifteen page two color glossy booklet entitled, "Selling To Hewlett-Packard, A Seller's Information Guide." It contains a message from the president, photos of Hewlett-Packard products and operations, a description of the purchasing organization, and the company's procurement policy. It also includes a section on the requirements to become an approved Hewlett-Packard Supplier.

Daniel A. Kasha, Director of Purchasing and Inventory for Middlesex County College and a certified member of the American Purchasing Society, prepared a ten page booklet entitled "How to do business with Middlesex County College." The booklet has been revised several times and each issue has been approved by the Board of Trustees of the College. It contains the institution's purchasing policy, describes the types of material and services purchased, and explains the competitive bidding procedures.

A "Suppliers Guide to Purchasing" from the Communications Systems Division of Motorola, Inc. is a one page folded brochure which simply list the names of the purchasing contacts and the products they are responsible for. It includes a short message to suppliers and a short policy statement about Motorola's supplier relationships. It also includes a small map showing how to get to the Motorola facility.

"Doing Business With Ford Purchasing" was a thirty-four page booklet with many illustrations and much information about Ford's purchasing operation. It had a map of the United States showing where each Ford facility was located. It went into detail on how Ford purchasing was organized and who purchased what. The large Ford guide is now out of print. In its place a six panel brochure is used. It briefly describes what Ford expects from a potential supplier and lists the addresses of the various purchasing activities around the U.S. Apparently, the larger book was expensive to produce and needed to be constantly revised because of the many changes that occur in a large organization.

Before writing a guide, think of yourself as a seller going to call on an unknown company for the first time. What would you like to know? What do you need to know? Here are some things that you might find helpful.

What does the company do or what does it sell?

How big is the company?

Where are its facilities?

Where will I find the person with buying authority?

Who would be the person that might buy my product?

What does the company normally buy?

Could there be a need for my product or service?

Is there a chance to get any business from this company?

Are there limited appointment hours for salespeople?

What is the company's policy on negotiating bids?

Do minority companies have a chance to get business?

Is supplier certification required?

Will the company accept third party certification?

What is the procedure for obtaining certification?

Does the company insist on any terms or conditions?

What is most important, price, quality, or delivery?

Of course salespeople would also like to know other things that you would not be willing to disclose. They would like to know who you are presently dealing with and how much you are paying. You should not include any information that would be harmful to your interest.

Some might wonder why they should be so concerned with giving salespeople any of this information at all. Why go to all this trouble to help the seller? Are the motives strictly altruistic? First of all, the effort required is only a few hours. Once the booklet is prepared, you can keep giving it out year after year with few changes necessary. More importantly, if the booklet is well prepared, it will make your job easier and help you do a better job in purchasing. Welcome to purchasing brochures help improve communications between buyer and seller. Here are some of the things a good supplier's guide will do for you.

1. Guides let suppliers know who to call on and helps eliminate back door selling. If your guide contains a statement that all sales contacts must be made through purchasing or that purchasing must be sent a copy of all letters to your company, your purchasing hand will be significantly strengthened.

2. Guides advise suppliers of your normal terms and conditions so they are prepared to accept or reject them. This saves you time by eliminating suppliers who are unwilling to negotiate.

3. Guides improve the image of purchasing both internally and to outside organizations. A supplier's guide to purchasing indicates that you have a professional department, and you gain all the advantages that implies.

4. Written policies and procedures given to the supplier save you time repeating the information to every potential supplier that comes in the door. By giving suppliers the same written material, you avoid the claim that they never were told about a particular policy.

You can reinforce the information in your guide by referring to it in conversation or written correspondence. You might even consider getting suppliers to initial a log indicating they received the guide. You can use the log to control inventory of the booklets so you will know how many have been given out and when to reorder. This system has the additional advantage of giving you statistics on how many suppliers are interested in your business.✠

Reprinted from *Professional Purchasing,* Journal of the American Purchasing Society, Vol. 8 (September 1991): 1–3.

## Appendix G: Metric Equivalent of U.S. Weights and Measures

### APOTHECARIES' WEIGHT

| | | |
|---|---|---|
| 1 scruple | = | 1.296 grams |
| 1 dram | = | 3.888 grams |

### AVOIRDUPOIS WEIGHT

| | | |
|---|---|---|
| 1 dram | = | 1.772 grams |
| 1 ounce | = | 28.3495 grams |
| 1 pound | = | 453.59 grams or 0.4536 kilogram |
| 1 hundredweight | = | 45.36 kilograms |
| 1 short ton | = | 907.18 kilograms or 0.9072 metric ton |
| 1 long ton | = | 1,016.05 kilograms or 1.0160 metric tons |

### TROY WEIGHT

| | | |
|---|---|---|
| 1 pennyweight | = | 1.555 grams |
| 1 ounce | = | 31.1035 grams |
| 1 pound | = | 373.24 grams or 0.3732 kilogram |

### CUBIC MEASURE

| | | |
|---|---|---|
| 1 cubic inch | = | 16.387 cubic centimeters |
| 1 cubic foot | = | 0.0283 cubic meter |
| 1 cubic yard | = | 0.7646 cubic meter |
| 1 cord | = | 3.625 cubic meters |

### LIQUID MEASURE

| | | |
|---|---|---|
| 1 fluid ounce | = | 0.0297 liter |
| 1 gill | = | 0.118 liter |
| 1 pint | = | 0.4732 liter |
| 1 quart | = | 0.9463 liter |
| 1 gallon | = | 3.7853 liters |

### DRY MEASURE

| | | |
|---|---|---|
| 1 quart | = | 1.1012 liters |
| 1 peck | = | 8.8096 liters |
| 1 bushel | = | 35.2383 liters |

### LINEAR OR LONG MEASURE

| | | |
|---|---|---|
| 1 inch | = | 2.54 centimeters |
| 1 foot | = | 0.3048 meter |
| 1 yard | = | 0.9144 meter |
| 1 rod | = | 5.029 meters |
| 1 furlong | = | 201.17 meters |
| 1 mile | = | 1.6093 kilometers |
| 1 league | = | 4.83 kilometers |

### MARINERS' OR NAUTICAL MEASURE

| | | |
|---|---|---|
| 1 fathom | = | 1.829 meters |
| 1 nautical mile | = | 1,853.248 meters |

### SQUARE MEASURE

| | | |
|---|---|---|
| 1 square inch | = | 6.452 square centimeters |
| 1 square foot | = | 929 square centimeters |
| 1 square yard | = | 0.8361 square meter |
| 1 square rod | = | 25.29 square meters |
| 1 acre | = | 40.4687 ares or 0.4047 hectare |
| 1 square mile | = | 259 hectares or 2.59 square kilometers |
| 1 township | = | 9,324 hectares or 93.24 square kilometers |

# Uniform Commercial Code

## TITLE
## AN ACT

To be known as the Uniform Commercial Code, Relating to Certain Commercial Transactions in or regarding Personal Property and Contracts and other Documents concerning them, including Sales, Commercial Paper, Bank Deposits and Collections, Letters of Credit, Bulk Transfers, Warehouse Receipts, Bills of Lading, other Documents of Title, Investment Securities, and Secured Transactions, including certain Sales of Accounts, Chattel Paper, and Contract Rights; Providing for Public Notice to Third Parties in Certain Circumstances; Regulating Procedure, Evidence and Damages in Certain Court Actions Involving such Transactions, Contracts or Documents; to Make Uniform the Law with Respect Thereto; and Repealing Inconsistent Legislation.

## ARTICLE 1/GENERAL PROVISIONS

### PART 1/SHORT TITLE, CONSTRUCTION, APPLICATION AND SUBJECT MATTER OF THE ACT

**Section 1—101. Short Title**

This Act shall be known and may be cited as Uniform Commercial Code.

**Section 1—102. Purposes; Rules of Construction; Variation by Agreement**

(1) This Act shall be liberally construed and applied to promote its underlying purposes and policies.

(2) Underlying purposes and policies of this Act are

    (a) to simplify, clarify and modernize the law governing commercial transactions;

    (b) to permit the continued expansion of commercial practices through custom, usage and agreement of the parties;

    (c) to make uniform the law among the various jurisdictions.

(3) The effect of provisions of this Act may be varied by agreement, except as otherwise provided in this Act and except that the obligations of good faith, diligence, reasonableness and care prescribed by this Act may not be disclaimed by agreement, but the parties may by agreement determine the standards by which the performance of such obligations is to be measured if such standards are not manifestly unreasonable.

(4) The presence in certain provisions of this Act of the words "unless otherwise agreed" or words of similar import does not imply that the effect of other provisions may not be varied by agreement under subsection (3).

(5) In this Act unless the context otherwise requires

    (a) words in the singular number include the plural, and in the plural include the singular;

    (b) words of the masculine gender include the feminine and the neuter, and when the sense so indicates, words of the neuter gender may refer to any gender.

### Section 1—103. Supplementary General Principles of Law Applicable

Unless displaced by the particular provisions of this Act, the principles of law and equity, including the law merchant and the law relative to capacity to contract, principal and agent, estoppel, fraud, misrepresentation, duress, coercion, mistake, bankruptcy, or other validating or invalidating cause shall supplement its provisions.

### Section 1—104. Construction Against Implicit Repeal

This Act being a general act intended as a unified coverage of its subject matter, no part of it shall be deemed to be impliedly repealed by subsequent legislation if such construction can reasonably be avoided.

### Section 1—105. Territorial Application of the Act; Parties' Power to Choose Applicable Law

(1) Except as provided hereafter in this section, when a transaction bears a reasonable relation to this state and also to another state or nation, the parties may agree that the law either of this state or of such other state or nation shall govern their rights and duties. Failing such agreement, this Act applies to transactions bearing an appropriate relation to this state.

(2) Where one of the following provisions of this Act specifies the applicable law, that provision governs and a contrary agreement is effective only to the extent permitted by the law (including the conflict of laws rules) so specified:

Rights of creditors against sold goods. Section 2—402.

Applicability of the Article on Bank Deposits and Collections. Section 4—102.

Bulk transfers subject to the Article on Bulk Transfers. Section 6—102.

Applicability of the Article on Investment Securities. Section 8—106.

Perfection provisions of the Article on Secured Transactions. Section 9—103.

### Section 1—106. Remedies to Be Liberally Administered

(1) The remedies provided by this Act shall be liberally administered to the end that the aggrieved party may be put in as good a position as if the other party had fully performed, but neither consequential or special nor penal damages may be had except as specifically provided in this Act or by other rule of law.

(2) Any right or obligation declared by this Act is enforceable by action unless the provision declaring it specifies a different and limited effect.

### Section 1—107. Waiver or Renunciation of Claim or Right After Breach

Any claim or right arising out of an alleged breach can be discharged in whole or in part without consideration by a written waiver or renunciation signed and delivered by the aggrieved party.

### Section 1—108. Severability

If any provision or clause of this Act or application thereof to any person or circumstances is held invalid, such invalidity shall not affect other provisions or applications of the Act which can be given effect without the invalid provision or application, and to this end the provisions of this Act are declared to be severable.

### Section 1—109. Section Captions

Section captions are part of this Act.

## PART 2/GENERAL DEFINITIONS AND PRINCIPLES OF INTERPRETATION

### Section 1—201. General Definitions

Subject to additional definitions contained in the subsequent Articles of this Act which are applicable to specific Articles or Parts thereof, and unless the context otherwise requires, in this Act:

(1) "Action" in the sense of a judicial proceeding includes recoupment, counterclaim, set-off, suit in equity and any other proceedings in which rights are determined.

(2) "Aggrieved party" means a party entitled to resort to a remedy.

(3) "Agreement" means the bargain of the parties in fact as found in their language or by implication from other circumstances including course of dealing or usage of trade or course of performance as provided in this Act (Sections 1—205 and 2—208). Whether an agreement has legal consequences is determined by the provisions of this Act, if applicable; otherwise by the law of contracts (Section 1—103). (Compare "Contract.")

(4) "Bank" means any person engaged in the business of banking.

(5) "Bearer" means the person in possession of an instrument, document of title, or security payable to bearer or indorsed in blank.

(6) "Bill of lading" means a document evidencing the receipt of goods for shipment issued by a person engaged in the business of transporting or forwarding goods, and includes an airbill. "Airbill" means a document serving for air transportation as a bill of lading does for marine or rail transportation, and includes an air consignment note or air waybill.

(7) "Branch" includes a separately incorporated foreign branch of a bank.

(8) "Burden of establishing" a fact means the burden of persuading the triers of fact that the existence of the fact is more probable than its nonexistence.

(9) "Buyer in ordinary course of business" means a person who in good faith and without knowledge that the sale to him is in violation of the ownership rights or security interest of a third party in the goods buys in ordinary course from a person in the business of selling goods of that kind but does not include a pawnbroker. All persons who sell minerals or the like (including oil and gas) at wellhead or minehead shall be deemed to be persons in the business of selling goods of that kind. "Buying" may be for cash or by exchange of other property or on secured or unsecured credit and includes receiving goods or documents of title under a preexisting contract for sale but does not include a transfer in bulk or as security for or in total or partial satisfaction of a money debt.

(10) "Conspicuous": A term or clause is conspicuous when it is so written that a reasonable person against whom it is to operate ought to have noticed it. A printed heading in capitals (as: NON-NEGOTIABLE BILL OF LADING) is conspicuous. Language in the body of a form is "conspicuous" if it is in larger or other contrasting type or color. But in a telegram any stated term is "conspicuous." Whether a term or clause is "conspicuous" or not is for decision by the court.

(11) "Contract" means the total legal obligation which results from the parties' agreement as affected by this Act and any other applicable rules of law. (Compare "Agreement.")

(12) "Creditor" includes a general creditor, a secured creditor, a lien creditor and any representative of creditors, including an assignee for the benefit of creditors, a trustee in bankruptcy, a receiver in equity and an executor or administrator of an insolvent debtor's or assignor's estate.

(13) "Defendant" includes a person in the position of defendant in a cross-action or counter-claim.

(14) "Delivery" with respect to instruments, documents of title, chattel paper or securities means voluntary transfer of possession.

(15) "Document of title" includes bill of lading, dock warrant, dock receipt, warehouse receipt or order for the delivery of goods, and also any other document which in the regular course of business or financing is treated as adequately evidencing that the person in possession of it is entitled to receive, hold and dispose of the document and the goods it covers. To be a document of title a document must purport to be issued by or addressed to a bailee and purport to cover goods in the bailee's possession which are either identified or are fungible portions of an identified mass.

(16) "Fault" means wrongful act, omission or breach.

(17) "Fungible" with respect to goods or securities means goods or securities of which any unit is, by nature or usage of trade, the equivalent of any other like unit. Goods which are not fungible shall be deemed fungible for the purposes of this Act to the extent that under a particular agreement or document unlike units are treated as equivalents.

(18) "Genuine" means free of forgery or counterfeiting.

(19) "Good faith" means honesty in fact in the conduct or transaction concerned.

(20) "Holder" means a person who is in possession of a document of title or an instrument or an investment security drawn, issued or indorsed to him or to his order or to bearer or in blank.

(21) To "honor" is to pay or to accept and pay, or where a credit so engages, to purchase or discount a draft complying with the terms of the credit.

(22) "Insolvency proceedings" includes any assignment for the benefit of creditors or other proceedings intended to liquidate or rehabilitate the estate of the person involved.

(23) A person is "insolvent" who either has ceased to pay his debts in the ordinary course of business or cannot pay his debts as they become due or is insolvent within the meaning of the federal bankruptcy law.

(24) "Money" means a medium of exchange authorized or adopted by a domestic or foreign government as a part of its currency.

(25) A person has "notice" of a fact when

(a) he has actual knowledge of it; or
(b) he has received a notice or notification of it; or
(c) from all the facts and circumstances known to him at the time in question he has reason to know that it exists.

A person "knows" or has "knowledge" of a fact when he has actual knowledge of it. "Discover" or "learn" or a word or phrase of similar import refers to knowledge rather than to reason to know. The time and circumstances under which a notice or notification may cease to be effective are not determined by this Act.

(26) A person "notifies" or "gives" a notice or notification to another by taking such steps as may be reasonably required to inform the other in ordinary course whether or not such other actually comes to know of it. A person "receives" a notice or notification when

(a) it comes to his attention; or
(b) it is duly delivered at the place of business through which the contract was made or at any other place held out by him as the place for receipt of such communications.

(27) Notice, knowledge or a notice of notification received by an organization is effective for a particular transaction from the time when it is brought to the attention of the individual conducting that transaction, and in any event from the time when it would have been brought to his attention if the organization had exercised due diligence. An organization exercises due diligence if it maintains reasonable routines for communicating significant information to the person conducting the transaction and there is reasonable compliance with the routines. Due diligence does not require an individual acting for the organization to communicate information unless such communication is part of his regular duties or unless he has reason to know of the transaction and that the transaction would be materially affected by the information.

(28) "Organization" includes a corporation, government or governmental subdivision or agency, business trust, estate, trust, partnership or association, two or more persons having a joint or common interest, or any other legal or commercial entity.

(29) "Party," as distinct from "third party," means a person who has engaged in a transaction or made an agreement within this Act.

(30) "Person" includes an individual or an organization (see Section 1—102).

(31) "Presumption" or "presumed" means that the trier of fact must find the existence of the fact presumed unless and until evidence is introduced which would support a finding of its nonexistence.

(32) "Purchase" includes taking by sale, discount, negotiation, mortgage, pledge, lien, issue or re-issue, gift or any other voluntary transaction creating an interest in property.

(33) "Purchaser" means a person who takes by purchase.

(34) "Remedy" means any remedial right to which an aggrieved party is entitled with or

without resort to a tribunal.

(35) "Representative" includes an agent, an officer of a corporation or association, and an trustee, executor or administrator of an estate, or any other person empowered to act for another.

(36) "Rights" includes remedies.

(37) "Security interest" means an interest in personal property or fixtures which secures payment or performance of an obligation. The retention or reservation of title by a seller of goods notwithstanding shipment or delivery to the buyer (Section 2—401) is limited in effect to a reservation of a "security interest." The term also includes any interest of a buyer of accounts or chattel paper which is subject to Article 9. The special property interest of a buyer of goods on identification of such goods to a contract for sale under Section 2—401 is not a "security interest," but a buyer may also acquire a "security interest" by complying with Article 9. Unless a lease or consignment is intended as security, reservation of title thereunder is not a "security interest" but a consignment is in any event subject to the provisions on consignment sales (Section 2—326). Whether a lease is intended as security is to be determined by the facts of each case; however, (a) the inclusion of an option to purchase does not of itself make the lease one intended for security, and (b) an agreement that upon compliance with the terms of the lease the lessee shall become or has the option to become the owner of the property for no additional consideration or for a nominal consideration does make the lease one intended for security.

(38) "Send" in connection with any writing or notice means to deposit in the mail or deliver for transmission by any other usual means of communication with postage or cost of transmission provided for and properly addressed and in the case of an instrument to an address specified thereon or otherwise agreed, or if there be none to any address reasonable under the circumstances. The receipt of any writing or notice within the time at which it would have arrived if properly sent has the effect of a proper sending.

(39) "Signed" includes any symbol executed or adopted by a party with present intention to authenticate a writing.

(40) "Surety" includes guarantor.

(41) "Telegram" includes a message transmitted by radio, teletype, cable, any mechanical method of transmission, or the like.

(42) "Term" means that portion of an agreement which relates to a particular matter.

(43) "Unauthorized" signature or indorsement means one made without actual, implied or apparent authority and includes a forgery.

(44) "Value." Except as otherwise provided with respect to negotiable instruments and bank collections (Sections 3—303, 4—208 and 4—209) a person gives "value" for rights if he acquires them.

    (a) in return for a binding commitment to extend credit or for the extension of immediately available credit whether or not drawn upon and whether or not a charge-back is provided for in the event of difficulties in collection; or

    (b) as security for or in total or partial satisfaction of a preexisting claim; or

    (c) by accepting delivery pursuant to a preexisting contract for purchase; or

    (d) generally, in return for any consideration sufficient to support a simple contract.

(45) "Warehouse receipt" means a receipt issued by a person engaged in the business of storing goods for hire.

(46) "Written" or "writing" includes printing, typewriting or any other intentional reduction to tangible form.

### Section 1—202. Prima Facie Evidence by Third Party Documents

A document in due form purporting to be a bill of lading, policy or certificate of insurance, official weigher's or inspector's certificate, consular invoice, or any other document authorized or required by the contract to be issued by a third party shall be prima facie evidence of its own authenticity and genuineness and of the facts stated in the document by the third party.

### Section 1—203. Obligation of Good Faith

Every contract or duty within this Act imposes an obligation of good faith in its performance or enforcement.

### Section 1—204. Time; Reasonable Time; "Seasonably"

(1) Whenever this Act requires any action to be taken within a reasonable time, any time which is not manifestly unreasonable may be fixed by agreement.

(2) What is a reasonable time for taking any action depends on the nature, purpose and circumstances of such action.

(3) An action is taken "seasonably" when it is taken at or within the time agreed or, if no time is agreed, at or within a reasonable time.

### Section 1—205. Course of Dealing and Usage of Trade

(1) A course of dealing is a sequence of previous conduct between the parties to a particular transaction which is fairly to be regarded as establishing a common basis of understanding for interpreting their expressions and other conduct.

(2) A usage of trade is any practice or method of dealing having such regularity of observance in a place, vocation or trade as to justify an expectation that it will be observed with respect to the transaction in question. The existence and scope of such usage are to be proved as facts. If it is established that such a usage is embodied in a written trade code or similar writing the interpretation of the writing is for the court.

(3) A course of dealing between parties and any usage of trade in the vocation or trade in which they are engaged or of which they are or should be aware give particular meaning to and supplement or qualify terms of an agreement.

(4) The express terms of an agreement and an applicable course of dealing or usage of trade shall be construed wherever reasonable as consistent with each other; but when such construction is unreasonable, express terms control both course of dealing and usage of trade and course of dealing controls usage of trade.

(5) An applicable usage of trade in the place where any part of performance is to occur shall be used in interpreting the agreement as to that part of the performance.

(6) Evidence of a relevant usage of trade offered by one party is not admissable unless and until he has given the other party such notice as the court finds sufficient to prevent unfair surprise to the latter.

### Section 1—206. Statute of Frauds for Kinds of Personal Property Not Otherwise Covered

(1) Except in the cases described in subsection (2) of this section, a contract for the sale of personal property is not enforceable by way of action or defense beyond five thousand dollars in amount or value of remedy unless there is some writing which indicates that a contract for sale has been made between the parties at a defined or stated price, reasonably identifies the subject matter, and is signed by the party against whom enforcement is sought or by his authorized agent.

(2) Subsection (1) of this section does not apply to contracts for the sale of goods (Section 2—201) nor of securities (Section 8—319) nor to security agreements (Section 9—203).

### Section 1—207. Performance or Acceptance Under Reservation of Rights

A party who with explicit reservation of rights performs or promises performance or assents to performance in a manner demanded or offered by the other party does not thereby prejudice the rights reserved. Such words as "without prejudice," "under protest" or the like are sufficient.

### Section 1—208. Option to Accelerate at Will

A term providing that one party or his successor in interest may accelerate payment or performance or require collateral or additional collateral "at will" or "when he deems himself insecure" or in words of similar import shall be construed to mean that he shall have power to do so only if he in good faith believes that the prospect of payment or performance is impaired. The burden of establishing lack of good faith is on the party against whom the power has been exercised.

### Section 1—209. Subordinated Obligations

An obligation may be issued as subordinated to payment of another obligation of the person obligated, or a creditor may subordinate his right to payment of an obligation by agreement with either the person obligated or another creditor of the person obligated. Such a subordination does not create a security interest as against either the common debtor or a subordinated creditor. This section shall be construed as declaring the law as it existed prior to the enactment of this section and not as modifying it.

## ARTICLE 2/SALES

### PART 1/SHORT TITLE, GENERAL CONSTRUCTION AND SUBJECT MATTER

### Section 2—101. Short Title

This Article shall be known and may be cited as Uniform Commercial Code—Sales.

### Section 2—102. Scope; Certain Security and Other Transactions Excluded From This Article

Unless the context otherwise requires, this Article applies to transactions in goods; it does not apply to any transaction which although in the form of an unconditional contract to sell or present sale is intended to operate only as a security transaction nor does this Article impair or repeal any statute regulating sales to consumers, farmers or other specified classes of buyers.

### Section 2—103. Definitions and Index of Definitions

(1) In this Article, unless the context otherwise requires,

(a) "Buyer" means a person who buys or contracts to buy goods.

(b) "Good faith" in the case of a merchant means honesty in fact and the observance of reasonable commercial standards of fair dealing in the trade.

(c) "Receipt" of goods means taking physical possession of them.

(d) "Seller" means a person who sells or contracts to sell goods.

(2) Other definitions applying to this Article or to specified Parts thereof, and the sections in which they appear are:

"Acceptance." Section 2—606.
"Banker's credit." Section 2—325.
"Between merchants." Section 2—104.
"Cancellation." Section 2—106(4).
"Commercial unit." Section 2—105.
"Confirmed credit." Section 2—325.
"Conforming to contract." Section 2—106.
"Contract for sale." Section 2—106.
"Cover." Section 2—712.
"Entrusting." Section 2—403.
"Financing agency." Section 2—104.
"Future goods." Section 2—105.

"Goods." Section 2—105.
"Identification." Section 2—501.
"Installment contract." Section 2—612.
"Letter of Credit." Section 2—325.
"Lot." Section 2—105.
"Merchant." Section 2—104.
"Overseas." Section 2—323.
"Person in position of seller." Section 2—707.
"Present sale." Section 2—106.
"Sale." Section 2—106.
"Sale on approval." Section 2—326.
"Sale or return." Section 2—326.
"Termination." Section 2—106.

(3) The following definitions in other Articles apply to this Article:

"Check." Section 3—104.
"Consignee." Section 7—102.
"Consignor." Section 7—102.
"Consumer goods." Section 9—109.
"Dishonor." Section 3—507.
"Draft." Section 3—104.

(4) In addition Article 1 contains general definitions and principles of construction and interpretation applicable throughout this Article.

### Section 2—104. Definitions: "Merchant"; "Between Merchants"; "Financing Agency"

(1) "Merchant" means a person who deals in goods of the kind or otherwise by his occupation holds himself out as having knowledge or skill peculiar to the practices or goods involved in the transaction or to whom such knowledge or skill may be attributed by his employment of an agent or broker or other intermediary who by his occupation holds himself out as having such knowledge or skill.

(2) "Financing agency" means a bank, finance company or other person who in the ordinary course of business makes advances against goods or documents of title or who by arrangement with either the seller or the buyer intervenes in ordinary course to make or collect payment due or claimed under the contract for sale, as by purchasing or paying

the seller's draft or making advances against it or by merely taking it for collection whether or not documents of title accompany the draft. "Financing agency" includes also a bank or other person who similarly intervenes between persons who are in the position of seller and buyer in respect to the goods (Section 2—707).

(3) "Between merchants" means in any transaction with respect to which both parties are chargeable with the knowledge or skill of merchants.

### Section 2—105. Definitions: Transferability; "Goods"; "Future" Goods; "Lot"; "Commercial Unit"

(1) "Goods" means all things (including specially manufactured goods) which are movable at the time of identification to the contract for sale other than the money in which the price is to be paid, investment securities (Article 8) and things in action. "Goods" also includes the unborn young of animals and growing crops and other identified things attached to realty as described in the section on goods to be severed from realty (Section 2—107).

(2) Goods must be both existing and identified before any interest in them can pass. Goods which are not both existing and identified are "future" goods. A purported present sale of future goods or of any interest therein operates as a contract to sell.

(3) There may be a sale of a part interest in existing identified goods.

(4) An undivided share in an identified bulk of fungible goods is sufficiently identified to be sold although the quantity of the bulk is not determined. Any agreed proportion of such a bulk or any quantity thereof agreed upon by number, weight or other measure may to the extent of the seller's interest in the bulk be sold to the buyer who then becomes an owner in common.

(5) "Lot" means a parcel or a single article which is the subject matter of a separate sale or delivery, whether or not it is sufficient to perform the contract.

(6) "Commercial unit" means such a unit of goods as by commercial usage is a single whole for purposes of sale and division of which materially impairs its character or value on the market or in use. A commercial unit may be a single article (as a machine) or a set of articles (as a suite of furniture or an assortment of sizes) or a quantity (as a bale, gross, or carload) or any other unit treated in use or in the relevant market as a single whole.

### Section 2—106. Definitions: "Contract"; "Agreement"; "Contract for Sale"; "Sale"; "Present Sale"; "Conforming" to Contract; "Termination"; "Cancellation"

(1) In this Article unless the context otherwise requires, "contract" and "agreement" are limited to those relating to the present or future sale of goods. "Contract for sale" includes both a present sale of goods and a contract to sell goods at a future time. A "sale" consists in the passing of title from the seller to the buyer for a price (Section 2—401). A "present sale" means a sale which is accomplished by the making of the contract.

(2) Goods or conduct, including any part of a performance, are "conforming" or conform to the contract when they are in accordance with the obligations under the contract.

(3) "Termination" occurs when either party pursuant to a power created by agreement or law puts an end to the contract otherwise than for its breach. On "termination" all obligations which are still executory on both sides are discharged but any right based on prior breach or performance survives.

(4) "Cancellation" occurs when either party puts an end to the contract for breach by the other and its effect is the same as that of "termination" except that the cancelling party also retains any remedy for breach of the whole contract or any unperformed balance.

### Section 2—107, Goods to Be Severed From Realty: Recording

(1) A contract for the sale of minerals or the like (including oil and gas) or a structure or its materials to be removed from realty is a contract for the sale of goods within this Article if they are to be severed by the seller, but until severance a purported present sale thereof which is not effective as a transfer of an interest in land is effective only as a contract to sell.

(2) A contract for the sale apart from the land of growing crops or other things attached to realty and capable of severance without material harm thereto but not described in

subsection (1) or of timber to be cut is a contract for the sale of goods within this Article whether the subject matter is to be severed by the buyer or by the seller even though it forms part of the realty at the time of contracting, and the parties can by identification effect a present sale before severance.

(3) The provisions of this section are subject to any third party rights provided by the law relating to realty records, and the contract for sale may be executed and recorded as a document transferring an interest in land and shall then constitute notice to third parties of the buyer's rights under the contract for sale.

## PART 2/FORM, FORMATION AND READJUSTMENT OF CONTRACT

### Section 2—201. Formal Requirements; Statute of Frauds

(1) Except as otherwise provided in this section, a contract for the sale of goods for the price of $500 or more is not enforceable by way of action or defense unless there is some writing sufficient to indicate that a contract for sale has been made between the parties and signed by the party against whom enforcement is sought or by his authorized agent or broker. A writing is not insufficient because it omits or incorrectly states a term agreed upon but the contract is not enforceable under this paragraph beyond the quantity of goods shown in such writing.

(2) Between merchants, if within a reasonable time a writing in confirmation of the contract and sufficient against the sender is received and the party receiving it has reason to know its contents, it satisfies the requirements of subsection (1) against such party unless written notice of objection to its content is given within 10 days after it is received.

(3) A contract which does not satisfy the requirements of subsection (1) but which is valid in other respects is enforceable.

    (a) if the goods are to be specially manufactured for the buyer and are not suitable for sale to others in the ordinary course of the seller's business and the seller, before notice of repudiation is received and under circumstances which reasonably indicate that the goods are for the buyer, has made either a substantial beginning of their manufacture or commitments for their procurement; or

    (b) if the party against whom enforcement is sought admits in his pleading, testimony or otherwise in court that a contract for sale was

made, but the contract is not enforceable under this provision beyond the quantity of goods admitted; or

    (c) with respect to goods for which payment has been made and accepted or which have been received and accepted (Sec. 2—606).

### Section 2—202. Final Written Expression: Parol or Extrinsic Evidence

Terms with respect to which the confirmatory memoranda of the parties agree or which are otherwise set forth in a writing intended by the parties as a final expression of their agreement with respect to such terms as are included therein may not be contradicted by evidence of any prior agreement or of a contemporaneous oral agreement but may be explained or supplemented

    (a) by course of dealing or usage of trade (Section 1—205) or by course of performance (Section 2—208); and

    (b) by evidence of consistent additional terms unless the court finds the writing to have been intended also as a complete and exclusive statement of the terms of the agreement.

### Section 2—203. Seals Inoperative

The affixing of a seal to a writing evidencing a contract for sale or an offer to buy or sell goods does not constitute the writing a sealed instrument and the law with respect to sealed instruments does not apply to such a contract or offer.

### Section 2—204. Formation in General

(1) A contract for sale of goods may be made in any manner sufficient to show agree-

ment, including conduct by both parties which recognizes the existence of such a contract.

(2) An agreement sufficient to constitute a contract for sale may be found even though the moment of its making is undetermined.

(3) Even though one or more terms are left open a contract for sale does not fail for indefiniteness if the parties have intended to make a contract and there is a reasonably certain basis for giving an appropriate remedy.

### Section 2—205. Firm Offers

An offer by a merchant to buy or sell goods in a signed writing which by its terms gives assurance that it will be held open is not revocable, for lack of consideration, during the time stated or if no time is stated for a reasonable time, but in no event may such period of irrevocability exceed three months; but any such term of assurance on a form supplied by the offeree must be separately signed by the offeror.

### Section 2—206. Offer and Acceptance in Formation of Contract

(1) Unless otherwise unambiguously indicated by the language or circumstances

    (a)  an offer to make a contract shall be construed as inviting acceptance in any manner and by any medium reasonable in the circumstances;

    (b)  an order or other offer to buy goods for prompt or current shipment shall be construed as inviting acceptance either by a prompt promise to ship or by the prompt or current shipment of conforming or non-conforming goods, but such a shipment of non-conforming goods does not constitute an acceptance if the seller seasonably notifies the buyer that the shipment is offered only as an accommodation to the buyer.

(2) Where the beginning of a requested performance is a reasonable mode of acceptance, an offeror who is not notified of acceptance within a reasonable time may treat the offer as having lapsed before acceptance.

### Section 2—207. Additional Terms in Acceptance or Confirmation

(1) A definite and seasonable expression of acceptance or a written confirmation which is sent within a reasonable time operates as an acceptance even though it states terms additional to or different from those offered or agreed upon, unless acceptance is expressly made conditional on assent to the additional or different terms.

(2) The additional terms are to be construed as proposals for addition to the contract. Between merchants such terms become part of the contract unless:

    (a)  the offer expressly limits acceptance to the terms of the offer;

    (b)  they materially alter it; or

    (c)  notification of objection to them has already been given or is given within a reasonable time after notice of them is received.

(3) Conduct by both parties which recognizes the existence of a contract is sufficient to establish a contract for sale although the writings of the parties do not otherwise establish a contract. In such case the terms of the particular contract consist of those terms on which the writings of the parties agree, together with any supplementary terms incorporated under any other provisions of this Act.

### Section 2—208. Course of Performance or Practical Construction

(1) Where the contract for sale involves repeated occasions for performance by either party with knowledge of the nature of the performance and opportunity for objection to it by the other, any course of performance accepted or acquiesced in without objection shall be relevant to determine the meaning of the agreement.

(2) The express terms of the agreement and any such course of performance, as well as any course of dealing and usage of trade, shall be construed whenever reasonable as consistent with each other; but when such construction is unreasonable, express terms shall control course of performance and course of performance shall control both course of dealing and usage of trade (Section 1—205).

(3) Subject to the provisions of the next section on modification and waiver, such

course of performance shall be relevant to show a waiver or modification of any term inconsistent with such course of performance.

### Section 2—209. Modification, Rescission and Waiver

(1) An agreement modifying a contract within this Article needs no consideration to be binding.

(2) A signed agreement which excludes modification or rescission except by a signed writing cannot be otherwise modified or rescinded, but except as between merchants such a requirement on a form supplied by the merchant must be separately signed by the other party.

(3) The requirements of the statute of frauds section of this Article (Section 2—201) must be satisfied if the contract as modified is within its provisions.

(4) Although an attempt at modification or rescission does not satisfy the requirements of subsection (2) or (3) it can operate as a waiver.

(5) A party who has made a waiver affecting an executory portion of the contract may retract the waiver by reasonable notification received by the other party that strict performance will be required of any term waived, unless the retraction would be unjust in view of a material change of position in reliance on the waiver.

### Section 2—210. Delegation of Performance; Assignment of Rights

(1) A party may perform his duty through a delegate unless otherwise agreed or unless the other party has a substantial interest in having his original promisor perform or control the acts required by the contract. No delegation of performance relieves the party delegating of any duty to perform or any liability for breach.

(2) Unless otherwise agreed, all rights of either seller or buyer can be assigned except where the assignment would materially change the duty of the other party, or increase materially the burden or risk imposed on him by his contract, or impair materially his chance of obtaining return performance. A right to damages for breach of the whole contract or a right arising out of the assignor's due performance of his entire obligation can be assigned despite agreement otherwise.

(3) Unless the circumstances indicate the contrary, a prohibition of assignment of "the contract" is to be construed as barring only the delegation to the assignee of the assignor's performance.

(4) An assignment of "the contract" or of "all my rights under the contract" or an assignment in similar general terms is an assignment of rights and, unless the language or the circumstances (as in an assignment for security) indicate the contrary, it is a delegation of performance of the duties of the assignor, and its acceptance by the assignee constitutes a promise by him to perform those duties. This promise is enforceable by either the assignor or the other party to the original contract.

(5) The other party may treat any assignment which delegates performance as creating reasonable grounds for insecurity and may without prejudice to his rights against the assignor demand assurances from the assignee (Section 2—609).

## PART 3/GENERAL OBLIGATION AND CONSTRUCTION OF CONTRACT

### Section 2—301. General Obligations of Parties

The obligation of the seller is to transfer and deliver and that of the buyer is to accept and pay in accordance with the contract.

### Section 2—302. Unconscionable Contract or Clause

(1) If the court as a matter of law finds the contract or any clause of the contract to have been unconscionable at the time it was made, the court may refuse to enforce the contract, or it may enforce the remainder of the contract without the unconscionable clause, or it may so limit the application of any unconscionable clause as to avoid any unconscionable result.

(2) When it is claimed or appears to the court that the contract or any clause thereof may be unconscionable, the parties shall be afforded a reasonable opportunity to present evidence as to its commercial setting, purpose and effect to aid the court in making the determination.

**Section 2—303. Allocation or Division of Risks**

Where this Article allocates a risk or a burden as between the parties "unless otherwise agreed," the agreement may not only shift the allocation but may also divide the risk or burden.

**Section 2—304. Price Payable in Money, Goods, Realty, or Otherwise**

(1) The price can be made payable in money or otherwise. If it is payable in whole or in part in goods each party is a seller of the goods which he is to transfer.

(2) Even though all or part of the price is payable in an interest in realty the transfer of the goods and the seller's obligations with reference to them are subject to this Article, but not the transfer of the interest in realty or the transferor's obligations in connection therewith.

**Section 2—305. Open Price Term**

(1) The parties, if they so intend, can conclude a contract for sale even though the price is not settled. In such a case, the price is a reasonable price at the time for delivery if

    (a) nothing is said as to price; or

    (b) the price is left to be agreed by the parties and they fail to agree; or

    (c) the price is to be fixed in terms of some agreed market or other standard as set or recorded by a third person or agency and it is not so set or recorded.

(2) A price to be fixed by the seller or by the buyer means a price for him to fix in good faith.

(3) When a price left to be fixed otherwise than by agreement of the parties fails to be fixed through fault of one party, the other may at his option treat the contract as cancelled or himself fix a reasonable price.

(4) Where, however, the parties intend not to be bound unless the price be fixed or agreed and it is not fixed or agreed, there is no contract. In such a case, the buyer must return any goods already received or if unable so to do must pay their reasonable value at the time of delivery and the seller must return any portion of the price paid on account.

**Section 2—306. Output, Requirements and Exclusive Dealings**

(1) A term which measures the quantity by the output of the seller or the requirements of the buyer means such actual output or requirements as may occur in good faith, except that no quantity unreasonably disproportionate to any stated estimate or in the absence of a stated estimate to any normal or otherwise comparable prior output or requirements may be tendered or demanded.

(2) A lawful agreement by either the seller or the buyer for exclusive dealing in the kind of goods concerned imposes, unless otherwise agreed, an obligation by the seller to use best efforts to supply the goods and by the buyer to use best efforts to promote their sale.

**Section 2—307. Delivery in Single Lot or Several Lots**

Unless otherwise agreed all goods called for by a contract for sale must be tendered in a single delivery and payment is due only on such tender; but where the circumstances give either party the right to make or demand delivery in lots, the price if it can be apportioned may be demanded for each lot.

**Section 2—308. Absence of Specified Place for Delivery**

Unless otherwise agreed

    (a) the place for delivery of goods is the seller's place of business or, if he has none, his residence; but

    (b) in a contract for sale of identified goods which to the knowledge of the parties at the time of contracting are in some other place, that place is the place for their delivery; and

    (c) documents of title may be delivered through customary banking channels.

**Section 2—309. Absence of Specific Time Provisions; Notice of Termination**

(1) The time for shipment or delivery or any other action under a contract if not provided in this Article or agreed upon shall be a reasonable time.

(2) Where the contract provides for successive performances but is indefinite in duration, it is valid for a reasonable time; but unless otherwise agreed may be terminated at any time by either party.

(3) Termination of a contract by one party, except on the happening of an agreed event, requires that reasonable notification be received by the other party and an agreement dispensing with notification is invalid if its operation would be unconscionable.

### Section 2—310. Open Time for Payment or Running of Credit; Authority to Ship Under Reservation

Unless otherwise agreed

    (a) payment is due at the time and place at which the buyer is to receive the goods even though the place of shipment is the place of delivery; and

    (b) if the seller is authorized to send the goods, he may ship them under reservation, and may tender the documents of title, but the buyer may inspect the goods after their arrival before payment is due unless such inspection is inconsistent with the terms of the contract (Section 2—513); and

    (c) if delivery is authorized and made by way of documents of title otherwise than by subsection (b), then payment is due at the time and place at which the buyer is to receive the documents regardless of where the goods are to be received; and

    (d) where the seller is required or authorized to ship the goods on credit, the credit period runs from the time of shipment but postdating the invoice or delaying its dispatch will correspondingly delay the starting of the credit period.

### Section 2—311. Options and Cooperation Respecting Performance

(1) An agreement for sale which is otherwise sufficiently definite (subsection (3) of Section 2—204) to be a contract is not made invalid by the fact that it leaves particulars of performance to be specified by one of the parties. Any such specification must be made in good faith and within limits set by commercial reasonableness.

(2) Unless otherwise agreed, specifications relating to assortment of the goods are at the buyer's option and, except as otherwise provided in subsections (1) (c) and (3) of Section 2—319, specifications or arrangements relating to shipment are at the seller's option.

(3) Where such specification would materially affect the other party's performance but is not seasonably made or where one party's cooperation is necessary to the agreed performance of the other but is not seasonably forthcoming, the other party in addition to all other remedies

    (a) is excused for any resulting delay in his own performance; and

    (b) may also either proceed to perform in any reasonable manner or after the time for a material part of his own performance treat the failure to specify or to cooperate as a breach by failure to deliver or accept the goods.

### Section 2—312. Warranty of Title and Against Infringement; Buyer's Obligation Against Infringement

(1) Subject to subsection (2), there is in a contract for sale a warranty by the seller that

    (a) the title conveyed shall be good, and its transfer rightful; and

    (b) the goods shall be delivered free from any security interest or other lien or encumbrance of which the buyer at the time of contracting has no knowledge.

(2) A warranty under subsection (1) will be excluded or modified only by specific language or by circumstances which give the buyer reason to know that the person selling does not claim title in himself or that he is purporting to sell only such right or title as he or a third person may have.

(3) Unless otherwise agreed a seller who is a merchant regularly dealing in goods of the kind warrants that the goods shall be delivered free of the rightful claim of any third person by way of infringement or the like but a buyer who furnishes specifications to the seller must hold the seller harmless against any such claim

which arises out of compliance with the specifications.

### Section 2—313. Express Warranties by Affirmation, Promise, Description, Sample

(1) Express warranties by the seller are created as follows:

(a) Any affirmation of fact or promise made by the seller to the buyer which relates to the goods and becomes part of the basis of the bargain creates an express warranty that the goods shall conform to the affirmation or promise.

(b) Any description of the goods which is made part of the basis of the bargain creates an express warranty that the goods shall conform to the description.

(c) Any sample or model which is made part of the basis of the bargain creates an express warranty that the whole of the goods shall conform to the sample or model.

(2) It is not necessary to the creation of an express warranty that the seller use formal words such as "warrant" or "guarantee" or that he have a specific intention to make a warranty, but an affirmation merely of the value of the goods or a statement purporting to be merely the seller's opinion or commendation of the goods does not create a warranty.

### Section 2—314. Implied Warranty: Merchantability; Usage of Trade

(1) Unless excluded or modified (Section 2—316), a warranty that the goods shall be merchantable is implied in a contract for their sale if the seller is a merchant with respect to goods of that kind. Under this section, the serving for value of food or drink to be consumed either on the premises or elsewhere is a sale.

(2) Goods to be merchantable must be at least such as

(a) pass without objection in the trade under the contract description; and

(b) in the case of fungible goods, are of fair average quality within the description; and

(c) are fit for the ordinary purposes for which such goods are used;

and

(d) run, within the variations permitted by the agreement, of even kind, quality and quantity within each unit and among all units involved; and

(e) are adequately contained, packaged, and labeled as the agreement may require; and

(f) conform to the promises or affirmations of fact made on the container or label if any.

(3) Unless excluded or modified (Section 2—316), other implied warranties may arise from course of dealing or usage of trade.

### Section 2—315. Implied Warranty: Fitness for Particular Purpose

Where the seller at the time of contracting has reason to know any particular purpose for which the goods are required and that the buyer is relying on the seller's skill or judgment to select or furnish suitable goods, there is unless excluded or modified under the next section an implied warranty that the goods shall be fit for such purpose.

### Section 2—316. Exclusion or Modification of Warranties

(1) Words or conduct relevant to the creation of an express warranty and words or conduct tending to negate or limit warranty shall be construed wherever reasonable as consistent with each other; but, subject to the provisions of this Article on parol or extrinsic evidence (Section 2—202), negation or limitation is inoperative to the extent that such construction is unreasonable.

(2) Subject to subsection (3), to exclude or modify the implied warranty of merchantability or any part of it, the language must mention merchantability and in case of a writing must be conspicuous, and to exclude or modify any implied warranty of fitness the exclusion must be by a writing and conspicuous. Language to exclude all implied warranties of fitness is sufficient if it states, for example, that "There are no warranties which extend beyond the description on the face hereof."

(3) Notwithstanding subsection (2)

(a) unless the circumstances indicate otherwise, all implied warranties are excluded by expressions like "as is," "with all faults" or other language which in common understanding calls the buyer's attention to the exclusion of warranties and makes plain that there is no implied warranty; and

(b) when the buyer before entering into the contract has examined the goods or the sample or model as fully as he desired or has refused to examine the goods, there is no implied warranty with regard to defects which an examination ought in the circumstances to have revealed to him; and

(c) an implied warranty can also be excluded or modified by course of dealing or course of performance or usage of trade.

(4) Remedies for breach of warranty can be limited in accordance with the provisions of this Article on liquidation or limitation of damages and on contractual modification of remedy (Sections 2—718 and 2—719).

### Section 2—317. Cumulation and Conflict of Warranties Express or Implied

Warranties whether express or implied shall be construed as consistent with each other and as cumulative, but if such construction is unreasonable the intention of the parties shall determine which warranty is dominant. In ascertaining that intention the following rules apply:

(a) Exact or technical specifications displace an inconsistent sample or model or general language of description.

(b) A sample from an existing bulk displaces inconsistent general language of description.

(c) Express warranties displace inconsistent implied warranties other than an implied warranty of fitness for a particular purpose.

### Section 2—318. Third Party Beneficiaries of Warranties Express or Implied

Note: *If this Act is introduced in the Congress of the United States this section should be omitted. (States to select one alternative.)*

### Alternative A

A seller's warranty whether express or implied extends to any natural person who is in the family or household of his buyer or who is a guest in his home if it is reasonable to expect that such person may use, consume or be affected by the goods and who is injured in person by breach of the warranty. A seller may not exclude or limit the operation of this section.

### Alternative B

A seller's warranty whether express or implied extends to any natural person who may reasonably be expected to use, consume or be affected by the goods and who is injured in person by breach of the warranty. A seller may not exclude or limit the operation of this section.

### Alternative C

A seller's warranty whether express or implied extends to any person who may reasonably be expected to use, consume or be affected by the goods and who is injured by breach of the warranty. A seller may not exclude or limit the operation of this section with respect to injury to the person of an individual to whom the warranty extends.

### Section 2—319. F.O.B. and F.A.S. Terms

(1) Unless otherwise agreed, the term F.O.B. (which means "free on board") at a named place, even though used only in connection with the stated price, is a delivery term under which

(a) when the term is F.O.B. the place of shipment, the seller must at that place ship the goods in the manner provided in this Article (Section 2—504) and bear the expense and risk of putting them into the possession of the carrier; or

(b) when the term is F.O.B. the place of destination, the seller must at his own expense and risk transport the goods to that place and there tender delivery of them in the manner provided in this Article (Section 2—503);

(c) when under either (a) or (b) the term is also F.O.B. vessel, car or other vehicle, the seller must in addition at his own expense and risk load the goods on board. If the term is F.O.B. vessel, the buyer must name the vessel and, in an appropriate case, the seller must comply with the provisions of this Article on the form of bill of lading (Section 2—323).

(2) Unless otherwise agreed, the term F.A.S. vessel (which means "free alongside") at a named port, even though used only in connection with the stated price, is a delivery term under which the seller must

    (a) at his own expense and risk deliver the goods alongside the vessel in the manner usual in that port or on a dock designated and provided by the buyer; and

    (b) obtain and tender a receipt for the goods in exchange for which the carrier is under a duty to issue a bill of lading.

(3) Unless otherwise agreed in any case falling within subsection (1) (a) or (c) or subsection (2) the buyer must seasonably give any needed instructions for making delivery, including, when the term is F.A.S. or F.O.B., the loading berth of the vessel and, in an appropriate case, its name and sailing date. The seller may treat the failure of needed instructions as a failure of cooperation under this Article (Section 2—311). He may also at his option move the goods in any reasonable manner preparatory to delivery or shipment.

(4) Under the term F.O.B. vessel or F.A.S., unless otherwise agreed, the buyer must make payment against tender of the required documents and the seller may not tender nor the buyer demand delivery of the goods in substitution for the documents.

### Section 2—320. C.I.F. and C. & F. Terms

(1) The term C.I.F. means that the price includes in a lump sum the cost of the goods and the insurance and freight to the named destination. The term C. & F. or C.F. means that the price so includes cost and freight to the named destination.

(2) Unless otherwise agreed and even though used only in connection with the stated price and destination, the term C.I.F. destination or its equivalent requires the seller at his own expense and risk to

    (a) put the goods into the possession of a carrier at the port for shipment and obtain a negotiable bill or bills of lading covering the entire transportation to the named destination; and

    (b) load the goods and obtain a receipt from the carrier (which may be contained in the bill of lading) showing that the freight has been paid or provided for; and

    (c) obtain a policy or certificate of insurance, including any war risk insurance, of a kind and on terms then current at the port of shipment in the usual amount, in the currency of the contract, shown to cover the same goods covered by the bill of lading and providing for payment of loss to the order of the buyer or for the account of whom it may concern; but the seller may add to the price the amount of the premium for any such war risk insurance; and

    (d) prepare an invoice of the goods and procure any other documents required to effect shipment or to comply with the contract; and

    (e) forward and tender with commercial promptness all the documents in due form and with any indorsement necessary to perfect the buyer's rights.

(3) Unless otherwise agreed, the term C. & F. or its equivalent has the same effect and imposes upon the seller the same obligations and risks as a C.I.F. term except the obligation as to insurance.

(4) Under the term C.I.F. or C. & F., unless otherwise agreed the buyer must make payment against tender of the required documents and the seller may not tender nor the buyer demand delivery of the goods in substitution for the documents.

### Section 2—321. C.I.F. or C. & F.: "Net Landed Weights"; "Payment on Arrival"; Warranty of Condition on Arrival

Under a contract containing a term C.I.F. or C. & F.

(1) Where the price is based on or is to be adjusted according to "net landed weights,"

"delivered weights," "out turn" quantity or quality or the like, unless otherwise agreed the seller must reasonably estimate the price. The payment due on tender of the documents called for by the contract is the amount so estimated, but after final adjustment of the price a settlement must be made with commercial promptness.

(2) An agreement described in subsection (1) or any warranty of quality or condition of the goods on arrival places upon the seller the risk of ordinary deterioration, shrinkage and the like in transportation but has no effect on the place or time of identification to the contract for sale or delivery or on the passing of the risk of loss.

(3) Unless otherwise agreed, where the contract provides for payment on or after arrival of the goods the seller must before payment allow such preliminary inspection as is feasible; but if the goods are lost, delivery of the documents and payment are due when the goods should have arrived.

### Section 2—322. Delivery "Ex-Ship"

(1) Unless otherwise agreed, a term for delivery of goods "ex-ship" (which means from the carrying vessel) or in equivalent language is not restricted to a particular ship and requires delivery from a ship which has reached a place at the named port of destination where goods of the kind are usually discharged.

(2) Under such a term, unless otherwise agreed

    (a) the seller must discharge all liens arising out of the carriage and furnish the buyer with a direction which puts the carrier under a duty to deliver the goods; and

    (b) the risk of loss does not pass to the buyer until the goods leave the ship's tackle or are otherwise properly unloaded.

### Section 2—323. Form of Bill of Lading Required in Overseas Shipment; "Overseas"

(1) Where the contract contemplates overseas shipment and contains a term C.I.F. or C. & F. or F.O.B. vessel, the seller unless otherwise agreed must obtain a negotiable bill of lading stating that the goods have been loaded on board or, in the case of a term C.I.F. or C. & F., received for shipment.

(2) Where in a case within subsection (1) a bill of lading has been issued in a set of parts, unless otherwise agreed, if the documents are not to be sent from abroad the buyer may demand tender of the full set; otherwise only one part of the bill of lading need be tendered. Even if the agreement expressly requires a full set.

    (a) due tender of a single part is acceptable within the provisions of this Article on cure of improper delivery (subsection (1) of Section 2—508); and

    (b) even though the full set is demanded, if the documents are sent from abroad the person tendering an incomplete set may nevertheless require payment upon furnishing an indemnity which the buyer in good faith deems adequate.

(3) A shipment by water or by air or a contract contemplating such shipment is "overseas" insofar as by usage of trade or agreement it is subject to the commercial, financing or shipping practices characteristic of international deep water commerce.

### Section 2—324. "No Arrival, No Sale" Term

Under a term "no arrival, no sale" or terms of like meaning, unless otherwise agreed,

    (a) the seller must properly ship conforming goods and if they arrive by any means he must tender them on arrival, but he assumes no obligation that the goods will arrive unless he has caused the non-arrival; and

    (b) where without fault of the seller the goods are in part lost or have so deteriorated as no longer to conform to the contract or arrive after the contract time, the buyer may proceed as if there had been casualty to identified goods (Section 2—613).

### Section 2—325. "Letter of Credit" Term; "Confirmed Credit"

(1) Failure of the buyer seasonably to furnish an agreed letter of credit is a breach of the contract for sale.

(2) The delivery to seller of a proper letter of credit suspends the buyer's obligation to pay. If the letter of credit is dishonored, the seller may on seasonable notification to the buyer require payment directly from him.

(3) Unless otherwise agreed, the term "letter of credit" or "banker's credit" in a contract for sale means an irrevocable credit issued by a financing agency of good repute and, where the shipment is overseas, of good international repute. The term "confirmed credit" means that the credit must also carry the direct obligation of such an agency which does business in the seller's financial market.

### Section 2—326. Sale on Approval and Sale or Return; Consignment Sales and Rights of Creditors

(1) Unless otherwise agreed, if delivered goods may be returned by the buyer even though they conform to the contract, the transaction is

    (a) a "sale on approval" if the goods are delivered primarily for use, and

    (b) a "sale or return" if the goods are delivered primarily for resale.

(2) Except as provided in subsection (3), goods held on approval are not subject to the claims of the buyer's creditors until acceptance; goods held on sale or return are subject to such claims while in the buyer's possession.

(3) Where goods are delivered to a person for sale and such person maintains a place of business at which he deals in goods of the kind involved, under a name other than the name of the person making delivery, then with respect to claims of creditors of the person conducting the business the goods are deemed to be on sale or return. The provisions of this subsection are applicable even though an agreement purports to reserve title to the person making delivery until payment or resale or uses such words as "on consignment" or "on memorandum." However, this subsection is not applicable if the person making delivery

    (a) complies with an applicable law providing for a consignor's interest or the like to be evidenced by a sign, or

    (b) establishes that the person conducting the business is generally known by his creditors to be substantially engaged in selling the goods of others, or

    (c) complies with the filing provisions of the Article on Secured Transactions (Article 9).

(4) Any "or return" term of a contract for sale is to be treated as a separate contract for sale within the statute of frauds section of this Article (Section 2—201) and as contradicting the sale aspect of the contract within the provisions of this Article on parol or extrinsic evidence (Section 2—202).

### Section 2—327. Special Incidents of Sale on Approval and Sale or Return

(1) Under a sale on approval, unless otherwise agreed

    (a) although the goods are identified to the contract, the risk of loss and the title do not pass to the buyer until acceptance; and

    (b) use of the goods consistent with the purpose of trial is not acceptance but failure seasonably to notify the seller of election to return the goods is acceptance, and if the goods conform to the contract acceptance of any part is acceptance of the whole; and

    (c) after due notification of election to return, the return is at the seller's risk and expense but a merchant buyer must follow any reasonable instructions.

(2) Under a sale or return, unless otherwise agreed

    (a) the option to return extends to the whole or any commercial unit of the goods while in substantially their original condition, but must be exercised seasonably; and

    (b) the return is at the buyer's risk and expense.

### Section 2—328. Sale by Auction.

(1) In a sale by auction, if goods are put up in lots each lot is the subject of a separate sale.

(2) A sale by auction is complete when the auctioneer so announces by the fall of the hammer or in other customary manner. Where a bid is made while the hammer is falling in acceptance of a prior bid, the auctioneer may in his discretion reopen the bidding or declare

the goods sold under the bid on which the hammer was falling.

(3) Such a sale is with reserve unless the goods are in explicit terms put up without reserve. In an auction with reserve, the auctioneer may withdraw the goods at any time until he announces completion of the sale. In an auction without reserve, after the auctioneer calls for bids on an article or lot, that article or lot cannot be withdrawn unless no bid is made within a reasonable time. In either case a bidder may retract his bid until his auctioneer's announcement of completion of the sale, but a bidder's retraction does not revive any previous bid.

(4) If the auctioneer knowingly receives a bid on the seller's behalf or the seller makes or procures such a bid, and notice has not been given that liberty for such bidding is reserved, the buyer may at his option avoid the sale or take the goods at the price of the last good faith bid prior to the completion of the sale. This subsection shall not apply to any bid at a forced sale.

## PART 4/TITLE, CREDITORS AND GOOD FAITH PURCHASERS

### Section 2—401. Passing of Title; Reservation for Security; Limited Application of This Section

Each provision of this Article with regard to the rights, obligations and remedies of the seller, the buyer, purchasers or other third parties applies irrespective of title to the goods except where the provision refers to such title. Insofar as situations are not covered by the other provisions of this Article and matters concerning title become material the following rules apply:

(1) Title to goods cannot pass under a contract for sale prior to their identification to the contract (Section 2—501), and unless otherwise explicitly agreed the buyer acquires by their identification a special property as limited by this Act. Any retention or reservation by the seller of the title (property) in goods shipped or delivered to the buyer is limited in effect to a reservation of a security interest. Subject to these provisions and to the provisions of the Article on Secured Transactions (Article 9), title to goods passes from the seller to the buyer in any manner and on any conditions explicitly agreed on by the parties.

(2) Unless otherwise explicitly agreed, title passes to the buyer at the time and place at which the seller completes his performance with reference to the physical delivery of the goods, despite any reservation of security interest and even though a document of title is to be delivered at a different time or place; and in particular and despite any reservation of a security interest by the bill of lading

    (a) if the contract requires or authorizes the seller to send the goods to the buyer but does not require him to deliver them at destination, title passes to the buyer at the time and place of shipment; but

    (b) If the contract requires delivery at destination, title passes on tender there.

(3) Unless otherwise explicitly agreed, where delivery is to be made without moving the goods,

    (a) if the seller is to deliver a document of title, title passes at the time when and the place where he delivers such documents; or

    (b) if the goods are at the time of contracting already identified and no documents are to be delivered, title passes at the time and place of contracting.

(4) A rejection or other refusal by the buyer to receive or retain the goods, whether or not justified, or a justified revocation of acceptance revests title to the goods in the seller. Such revesting occurs by operation of law and is not a "sale."

### Section 2—402. Rights of Seller's Creditors Against Sold Goods

(1) Except as provided in subsections (2) and (3), rights of unsecured creditors of the seller with respect to goods which have been identified to a contract for sale are subject to the buyer's rights to recover the goods under this Article (Sections 2—502 and 2—716).

(2) A creditor of the seller may treat a sale or an identification of goods to a contract for sale as void if as against him a retention of

possession by the seller is fraudulent under any rule of law of the state where the goods are situated, except that retention of possession in good faith and current course of trade by a merchant-seller for a commercially reasonable time after a sale or identification is not fraudulent.

(3) Nothing in this Article shall be deemed to impair the rights of creditors of the seller

    (a) under the provisions of the Article on Secured Transactions (Article 9); or

    (b) where identification to the contract or delivery is made not in current course of trade but in satisfaction of or as security for a preexisting claim for money, security or the like and is made under circumstances which under any rule of law of the state where the goods are situated would apart from this Article constitute the transaction a fraudulent transfer or voidable preference.

### Section 2—403. Power to Transfer; Good Faith Purchase of Goods; "Entrusting"

(1) A purchaser of goods acquires all title which his transferor had or had power to transfer except that a purchaser of a limited interest acquires rights only to the extent of the interest purchased. A person with voidable title has power to transfer a good title to a good faith purchaser for value. When goods have been delivered under a transaction of purchase, the purchaser has such power even though

    (a) the transferor was deceived as to the identity of the purchaser, or

    (b) the delivery was in exchange for a check which is later dishonored, or

    (c) it was agreed that the transaction was to be a "cash sale" or

    (d) the delivery was procured through fraud punishable as larcenous under the criminal law.

(2) Any entrusting of possession of goods to a merchant who deals in goods of that kind gives him power to transfer all rights of the entruster to a buyer in ordinary course of business.

(3) "Entrusting" includes any delivery and any acquiescence in retention of possession regardless of any condition expressed between the parties to the delivery or acquiescence and regardless of whether the procurement of the entrusting or the possessor's disposition of the goods have been such as to be larcenous under the criminal law.

(4) The rights of other purchasers of goods and of lien creditors are governed by the Articles on Secured Transactions (Article 9), Bulk Transfers (Article 6) and Documents of Title (Article 7).

## PART 5/PERFORMANCE

### Section 2—501. Insurable Interest in Goods; Manner of Identification of Goods

(1) The buyer obtains a special property and an insurable interest in goods by identification of existing goods as goods to which the contract refers even though the goods so identified are non-conforming and he has an option to return or reject them. Such identification can be made at any time and in any manner explicitly agreed to by the parties. In the absence of explicit agreement, identification occurs

    (a) when the contract is made, if it is for the sale of goods already existing and identified;

    (b) if the contract is for the sale of future goods other than those described in paragraph (c), when goods are shipped, marked or otherwise designated by the seller as goods to which the contract refers;

    (c) when the crops are planted or otherwise become growing crops or the young are conceived, if the contract is for the sale of unborn young to be born within twelve months after contracting or for the sale of crops to be harvested within twelve months or the next normal harvest season after contracting whichever is longer.

(2) The seller retains an insurable interest in goods so long as title to or any security interest in the goods remains in him; and where the identification is by the seller alone, he may until default or insolvency or notification to the buyer that the identification is final substitute other goods for those identified.

(3) Nothing in this section impairs any insurable interest recognized under any other statute or rule of law.

### Section 2—502. Buyer's Right to Goods on Seller's Insolvency

(1) Subject to subsection (2), and even though the goods have not been shipped, a buyer who has paid a part or all of the price of goods in which he has a special property under the provisions of the immediately preceding section may, on making and keeping good a tender of any unpaid portion of their price, recover them from the seller if the seller becomes insolvent within ten days after receipt of the first installment on their price.

(2) If the identification creating his special property has been made by the buyer, he acquires the right to recover the goods only if they conform to the contract for sale.

### Section 2—503. Manner of Seller's Tender of Delivery

(1) Tender of delivery requires that the seller put and hold conforming goods at the buyer's disposition and give the buyer any notification reasonably necessary to enable him to take delivery. The manner, time and place for tender are determined by the agreement and this Article, and in particular

    (a) tender must be at a reasonable hour, and, if it is of goods, they must be kept available for the period reasonably necessary to enable the buyer to take possession; but

    (b) unless otherwise agreed, the buyer must furnish facilities reasonably suited to the receipt of the goods.

(2) Where the case is within the next section respecting shipment, tender requires that the seller comply with its provisions.

(3) Where the seller is required to deliver at a particular destination, tender requires that he comply with subsection (1) and also, in any appropriate case, tender documents as described in subsections (4) and (5) of this section.

(4) Where goods are in the possession of a bailee and are to be delivered without being moved

    (a) tender requires that the seller either tender a negotiable document of title covering such goods or procure acknowledgement by the bailee of the buyer's right to possession of the goods; but

    (b) tender to the buyer of a nonnegotiable document of title or of a written direction to the bailee to deliver is sufficient tender unless the buyer seasonably objects, and receipt by the bailee of notification of the buyer's rights fixes those rights as against the bailee and all third persons; but risk of loss of the goods and of any failure by the bailee to honor the nonnegotiable document of title or to obey the direction remains on the seller until the buyer has had a reasonable time to present the document or direction, and a refusal by the bailee to honor the document or to obey the direction defeats the tender.

(5) Where the contract requires the seller to deliver documents

    (a) he must tender all such documents in correct form, except as provided in this Article with respect to bills of lading in a set (subsection (2) of Section 2—323); and

    (b) tender through customary banking channels is sufficient and dishonor of a draft accompanying the documents constitutes nonacceptance or rejection.

### Section 2—504. Shipment by Seller

Where the seller is required or authorized to send the goods to the buyer and the contract does not require him to deliver them at a particular destination, then, unless otherwise agreed, he must

(a) put the goods in the possession of such a carrier and make such a contract for their transportation as may be reasonable having regard to the nature of the goods and other circumstances of the case; and

(b) obtain and promptly deliver or tender in due form any document necessary to enable the buyer to obtain possession of the goods or otherwise required by the agreement or by usage of trade; and

(c) promptly notify the buyer of the shipment.

Failure to notify the buyer under paragraph (c) or to make a proper contract under paragraph (a) is a ground for rejection only if material delay or loss ensues.

### Section 2—505. Seller's Shipment Under Reservation

(1) Where the seller has identified goods to the contract by or before shipment:

(a) his procurement of a negotiable bill of lading to his own order or otherwise reserves in him a security interest in the goods. His procurement of the bill to the order of a financing agency or of the buyer indicates in addition only the seller's expectation of transferring that interest to the person named.

(b) a nonnegotiable bill of lading to himself or his nominee reserves possession of the goods as security but except in a case of conditional delivery (subsection (2) of Section 2—507) a nonnegotiable bill of lading naming the buyer as consignee reserves no security interest even though the seller retains possession of the bill of lading.

(2) When shipment by the seller with reservation of a security interest is in violation of the contract for sale it constitutes an improper contract for transportation within the preceding section but impairs neither the rights given to the buyer by shipment and identification of the goods to the contract nor the seller's powers as a holder of a negotiable document.

### Section 2—506. Rights of Financing Agency

(1) A financing agency by paying or purchasing for value a draft which relates to a shipment of goods acquires to the extent of the payment or puchase, and in addition to its own rights under the draft and any document of title securing it, any rights of the shipper in the goods, including the right to stop delivery and the shipper's right to have the draft honored by the buyer.

(2) The right to reimbursement of a financing agency which has in good faith honored or purchased the draft under commitment to or authority from the buyer is not impaired by subsequent discovery of defects with reference to any relevant document which was apparently regular on its face.

### Section 2—507. Effect of Seller's Tender; Delivery on Condition

(1) Tender of delivery is a condition to the buyer's duty to accept the goods and, unless otherwise agreed, to his duty to pay for them. Tender entitles the seller to acceptance of the goods and to payment according to the contract.

(2) Where payment is due and demanded on the delivery to the buyer of goods or documents of title, his right as against the seller to retain or dispose of them is conditional upon his making the payment due.

### Section 2—508. Cure by Seller of Improper Tender or Delivery; Replacement

(1) Where any tender or delivery by the seller is rejected because non-conforming and the time for performance has not yet expired, the seller may seasonably notify the buyer of his intention to cure and may then within the contract time make a conforming delivery.

(2) Where the buyer rejects a non-conforming tender which the seller had reasonable grounds to believe would be acceptable with or without money allowance, the seller may if he seasonably notifies the buyer have a further reasonable time to substitute a conforming tender.

### Section 2—509. Risk of Loss in the Absence of Breach

(1) Where the contract requires or authorizes the seller to ship the goods by carrier

(a) if it does not require him to deliver them at a particular destination, the risk of loss passes to the buyer when the goods are duly delivered to the carrier even though the shipment is under reservation (Section 2—505); but

(b) if it does require him to deliver them at a particular destination and the goods are there duly tendered while in the possession of the carrier, the risk of loss passes to the buyer when the goods are there duly so tendered as to enable the buyer to take delivery.

(2) Where the goods are held by a bailee to be delivered without being moved, the risk of loss passes to the buyer

(a) on his receipt of a negotiable document of title covering the goods; or

(b) on acknowledgment by the bailee of the buyer's right to possession of the goods; or

(c) after his receipt of a nonnegotiable document of title or other written direction to deliver, as provided in subsection (4) (b) of Section 2—503.

(3) In any case not with subsection (1) or (2), the risk of loss passes to the buyer on his receipt of the goods if the seller is a merchant; otherwise the risk passes to the buyer on tender of delivery.

(4) The provisions of this section are subject to contrary agreement of the parties and to the provisions of this Article on sale on approval (Section 2—327) and on effect of breach on risk of loss (Section 2—510).

### Section 2—510. Effect of Breach on Risk of Loss

(1) Where a tender or delivery of goods so fails to conform to the contract as to give a right of rejection, the risk of their loss remains on the seller until cure or acceptance.

(2) Where the buyer rightfully revokes acceptance, he may to the extent of any deficiency in his effective insurance coverage treat the risk of loss as having rested on the seller from the beginning.

(3) Where the buyer, as to conforming goods already identified to the contract for sale, repudiates or is otherwise in breach before risk of their loss has passed to him, the seller may to the extent of any deficiency in his effective insurance coverage treat the risk of loss as resting on the buyer for a commercially reasonable time.

### Section 2—511. Tender of Payment by Buyer; Payment by Check

(1) Unless otherwise agreed, tender of payment is a condition to the seller's duty to tender and complete any delivery.

(2) Tender of payment is sufficient when made by any means or in any manner current in the ordinary course of business unless the seller demands payment in legal tender and gives any extension of time reasonably necessary to procure it.

(3) Subject to the provisions of this Act on the effect of an instrument on an obligation (Section 3—802), payment by check is conditional and is defeated as between the parties by dishonor of the check on due presentment.

### Section 2—512. Payment by Buyer Before Inspection

(1) Where the contract requires payment before inspection, non-conformity of the goods does not excuse the buyer from so making payment unless

(a) the non-conformity appears without inspection; or

(b) despite tender of the required documents, the circumstances would justify injunction against honor under the provisions of this Act (Section 5—114).

(2) Payment pursuant to subsection (1) does not constitute an acceptance of goods or impair the buyer's right to inspect or any of his remedies.

### Section 2—513. Buyer's Right to Inspection of Goods

(1) Unless otherwise agreed and subject to subdivision (3), where goods are tendered or delivered or identified to the contract for sale, the buyer has a right before payment or acceptance to inspect them at any reasonable place and time and in any reasonable manner. When the seller is required or authorized to

send the goods to the buyer, the inspection may be after their arrival.

(2) Expenses of inspection must be borne by the buyer but it may be recovered from the seller if the goods do not conform and are rejected.

(3) Unless otherwise agreed and subject to the provisions of this Article on C.I.F. contracts (subdivision (3) of Section 2—321), the buyer is not entitled to inspect the goods before payment of the price when the contract provides

    (a) for delivery "C.O.D." or on other like terms; or

    (b) for payment against documents of title, except where such payment is due only after the goods are to become available for inspection.

(4) A place or method of inspection fixed by the parties is presumed to be exclusive but, unless otherwise expressly agreed, it does not postpone identification or shift the place for delivery or for passing the risk of loss. If compliance becomes impossible, inspection shall be as provided in this section unless the place or method fixed was clearly intended as an indispensable condition, failure of which avoids the contract.

### Section 2—514. When Documents Deliverable on Acceptance; When on Payment

Unless otherwise agreed, documents against which a draft is drawn are to be delivered to the drawee on acceptance of the draft if it is payable more than three days after presentment; otherwise, only on payment.

### Section 2—515. Preserving Evidence of Goods in Dispute

In furtherance of the adjustment of any claim or dispute

    (a) either party on reasonable notification to the other, and for the purpose of ascertaining the facts and preserving evidence, has the right to inspect, test and sample the goods including such of them as may be in the possession or control of the other; and

    (b) the parties may agree to a third party inspection or survey to determine the conformity or condition of the goods and may agree that the findings shall be binding upon them in any subsequent litigation or adjustment.

## PART 6/BREACH, REPUDIATION AND EXCUSE

### Section 2—601. Buyer's Rights on Improper Delivery

Subject to the provisions of this Article on breach in installment contracts (Section 2—612) and unless otherwise agreed under the sections on contractual limitations of remedy (Sections 2—718 and 2—719), if the goods or the tender of delivery fail in any respect to conform to the contract, the buyer may

    (a) reject the whole; or

    (b) accept the whole; or

    (c) accept any commercial unit or units and reject the rest.

### Section 2—602. Manner and Effect of Rightful Rejection

(1) Rejection of goods must be within a reasonable time after their delivery or tender. It is ineffective unless the buyer seasonably notifies the seller.

(2) Subject to the provisions of the two following sections on rejected goods (Sections 2—603 and 2—604),

    (a) after rejection any exercise of ownership by the buyer with respect to any commercial unit is wrongful as against the seller; and

    (b) If the buyer has before rejection taken physical possession of goods in which he does not have a security interest under the provisions of this Article (subsection (3) of Section 2—711), he is under a duty after rejection to hold them with reasonable care at the seller's disposition for a time sufficient to permit the seller to remove them; but

    (c) the buyer has no further obligations with regard to goods rightfully rejected.

(3) The seller's rights with respect to goods wrongfully rejected are governed by the provisions of this Article on Seller's remedies in general (Section 2—703).

### Section 2—603. Merchant Buyer's Duties as to Rightfully Rejected Goods

(1) Subject to any security interest in the buyer (subsection (3) of Section 2—711), when the seller has no agent or place of business at the market of rejection, a merchant buyer is under a duty after rejection of goods in his possession or control to follow any reasonable instructions received from the seller with respect to the goods and in the absence of such instructions to make reasonable efforts to sell them for the seller's account if they are perishable or threaten to decline in value speedily. Instructions are not reasonable if on demand indemnity for expenses is not forthcoming.

(2) When the buyer sells goods under subsection (1), he is entitled to reimbursement from the seller or out of the proceeds for reasonable expenses of caring for and selling them, and if the expenses include no selling commission then to such commission as is usual in the trade or, if there is none, to a reasonable sum not exceeding ten percent on the gross proceeds.

(3) In complying with this section, the buyer is held only to good faith and good faith conduct hereunder is neither acceptance nor conversion nor the basis of an action for damages.

### Section 2—604. Buyer's Options as to Salvage of Rightfully Rejected Goods

Subject to the provisions of the immediately preceding section on perishables, if the seller gives no instructions within a reasonable time after notification of rejection the buyer may store the rejected goods for the seller's account or reship them to him or resell them for the seller's account with reimbursement as provided in the preceding section. Such action is not acceptance or conversion.

### Section 2—605. Waiver of Buyer's Objections by Failure to Particularize

(1) The buyer's failure to state in connection with rejection a particular defect which is acertainable by reasonable inspection precludes him from relying on the unstated defect to justify rejection or to establish breach

   (a) where the seller could have cured it if stated seasonably; or

   (b) between merchants when the seller has after rejection made a request in writing for a full and final written statement of all defects on which the buyer proposes to rely.

(2) Payment against documents made without reservation of rights precludes recovery of the payment for defects apparent on the face of the documents.

### Section 2—606. What Constitutes Acceptance of Goods

(1) Acceptance of goods occurs when the buyer

   (a) after a reasonable opportunity to inspect the goods signifies to the seller that the goods are conforming or that he will take or retain them in spite of their nonconformity; or

   (b) fails to make an effective rejection (subsection (1) of Section 2—602), but such acceptance does not occur until the buyer has had a reasonable opportunity to inspect them; or

   (c) does any act inconsistent with the seller's ownership; but if such act is wrongful as against the seller it is an acceptance only if ratified by him.

(2) Acceptance of a part of any commercial unit is acceptance of that entire unit.

### Section 2—607. Effect of Acceptance; Notice of Breach; Burden of Establishing Breach After Acceptance; Notice of Claim or Litigation to Person Answerable Over

(1) The buyer must pay at the contract rate for any goods accepted.

(2) Acceptance of goods by the buyer precludes rejection of the goods accepted and if made with knowledge of a non-conformity cannot be revoked because of it unless the acceptance was on the reasonable assumption that the non-conformity would be seasonably cured but acceptance does not of itself impair any other remedy provided by this Article for non-conformity.

(3) Where a tender has been accepted
- (a) the buyer must within a reasonable time after he discovers or should have discovered any breach notify the seller of breach or be barred from any remedy; and
- (b) if the claim is one for infringement or the like (subsection (3) of Section 2—312) and the buyer is sued as a result of such a breach, he must so notify the seller within a reasonable time after he receives notice of the litigation or be barred from any remedy over for liability established by the litigation.

(4) The burden is on the buyer to establish any breach with respect to the goods accepted.

(5) Where the buyer is sued for breach of a warranty or other obligation for which his seller is answerable over
- (a) he may give his seller written notice of the litigation. If the notice states that the seller may come in and defend and that if the seller does not do so he will be bound in any action against him by his buyer by any determination of fact common to the two litigations, then unless the seller after seasonable receipt of the notice does come in and defend he is so bound.
- (b) if the claim is one for infringement or the like (subsection (3) of Section 2—312), the original seller may demand in writing that his buyer turn over to him control of the litigation including settlement or else be barred from any remedy over and if he also agrees to bear all expense and to satisfy any adverse judgment, then unless the buyer after seasonable receipt of the demand does turn over control the buyer is so barred.

(6) The provisions of subsections (3), (4) and (5) apply to any obligation of a buyer to hold the seller harmless against infringement or the like (subsection (3) of Section 2—312).

### Section 2—608. Revocation of Acceptance in Whole or in Part

(1) The buyer may revoke his acceptance of a lot or commercial unit whose non-conformity substantially impairs its value to him if he has accepted it
- (a) on the reasonable assumption that its non-conformity would be cured and it has not been seasonably cured; or
- (b) without discovery of such non-conformity if his acceptance was reasonably induced either by the difficulty of discovery before acceptance or by the seller's assurances.

(2) Revocation of acceptance must occur within a reasonable time after the buyer discovers or should have discovered the ground for it and before any substantial change in condition of the goods which is not caused by their own defects. It is not effective until the buyer notifies the seller of it.

(3) A buyer who so revokes has the same rights and duties with regard to the goods involved as if he had rejected them.

### Section 2—609. Right to Adequate Assurance of Performance

(1) A contract for sale imposes an obligation on each party that the other's expectation of receiving due performance will not be impaired. When reasonable grounds for insecurity arise with respect to the performance of either party, the other may in writing demand adequate assurance of due performance and until he receives such assurance may, if commercially reasonable, suspend any performance for which he has not already received the agreed return.

(2) Between merchants, the reasonableness of grounds for insecurity and the adequacy of any assurance offered shall be determined according to commercial standards.

(3) Acceptance of any improper delivery or payment does not prejudice the aggrieved party's right to demand adequate assurance of future performance.

(4) After receipt of a justified demand, failure to provide within a reasonable time, not exceeding thirty days, such assurance of due performance as is adequate under the circum-

stances of the particular case is a repudiation of the contract.

### Section 2—610. Anticipatory Repudiation

When either party repudiates the contract with respect to a performance not yet due, the loss of which will substantially impair the value of the contract to the other, the aggrieved party may

- (a) for a commercially reasonable time await performance by the repudiating party; or
- (b) resort to any remedy for breach (Section 2—703 or Section 2—711), even though he has notified the repudiating party that he would await the latter's performance and has urged retraction; and
- (c) in either case suspend his own performance or proceed in accordance with the provisions of this Article on the seller's right to identify goods to the contract notwithstanding breach or to salvage unfinished goods (Section 2—704).

### Section 2—611. Retraction of Anticipatory Repudiation

(1) Until the repudiating party's next performance is due, he can retract his repudiation unless the aggrieved party has since the repudiation cancelled or materially changed his position or otherwise indicated that he considers the repudiation final.

(2) Retraction may be by any method which clearly indicates to the aggrieved party that the repudiating party intends to perform, but must include any assurance justifiably demanded under the provisions of this Article (Section 2—609).

(3) Retraction reinstates the repudiating party's rights under the contract with due excuse and allowance to the aggrieved party for any delay occasioned by the repudiation.

### Section 2—612. "Installment Contract"; Breach

(1) An "installment contract" is one which requires or authorizes the delivery of goods in separate lots to be separately accepted, even though the contract contains a clause "each delivery is a separate contract" or its equivalent.

(2) The buyer may reject any installment which is non-conforming if the non-conformity substantially impairs the value of that installment and cannot be cured or if the non-conformity is a defect in the required documents; but if the non-conformity does not fall within subsection (3) and the seller gives adequate assurance of its cure, the buyer must accept that installment.

(3) Whenever non-conformity or default with respect to one or more installments substantially impairs the value of the whole contract, there is a breach of the whole. But the aggrieved party reinstates the contract if he accepts a non-conforming installment without seasonably notifying of cancellation or if he brings an action with respect only to past installments or demands performance as to future installments.

### Section 2—613. Casualty to Identified Goods

Where the contract requires for its performance goods identified when the contract is made, and the goods suffer casualty without fault of either party before the risk of loss passes to the buyer, or in a proper case under a "no arrival, no sale" term (Section 2—324) then

- (a) if the loss is total the contract is avoided; and
- (b) if the loss is partial or the goods have so deteriorated as no longer to conform to the contract the buyer may nevertheless demand inspection and at his option either treat the contract as avoided or accept the goods with due allowance from the contract price for the deterioration or the deficiency in quantity but without further right against the seller.

### Section 2—614. Substituted Performance

(1) Where without fault of either party the agreed berthing, loading, or unloading facilities fail or an agreed type of carrier becomes unavailable or the agreed manner of delivery otherwise becomes commercially impracticable but a commercially reasonable substitute is available, such substitute performance must be tendered and accepted.

(2) If the agreed means or manner of payment fails because of domestic or foreign governmental regulation, the seller may withhold or stop delivery unless the buyer provides a means or manner of payment which is commercially a substantial equivalent. If delivery has already been taken, payment by the means or in the manner provided by the regulation discharges the buyer's obligation unless the regulation is discriminatory, oppressive or predatory.

### Section 2—615. Excuse by Failure of Presupposed Conditions

Except so far as a seller may have assumed a greater obligation and subject to the preceding section on substituted performance:

    (a) Delay in delivery or nondelivery in whole or in part by a seller who complies with paragraphs (b) and (c) is not a breach of his duty under a contract for sale if performance as agreed has been made impracticable by the occurrence of a contingency the nonoccurence of which was a basic assumption on which the contract was made or by compliance in good faith with any applicable foreign or domestic governmental regulation or order whether or not it later proves to be invalid.

    (b) Where the causes mentioned in paragraph (a) affect only a part of the seller's capacity to perform, he must allocate production and deliveries among his customers but may at his option include regular customers not then under contract as well as his own requirements for further manufacture. He may so allocate in any manner which is fair and reasonable.

    (c) The seller must notify the buyer seasonably that there will be delay or nondelivery and, when allocation is required under paragraph (b), of the estimated quota thus made available for the buyer.

### Section 2—616. Procedure on Notice Claiming Excuse

(1) Where the buyer receives notification of a material or indefinite delay or an allocation justified under the preceding section he may by written notification to the seller as to any delivery concerned, and where the prospective deficiency substantially impairs the value of the whole contract under the provisions of this Article relating to breach of installment contracts (Section 2—612), then also as to the whole,

    (a) terminate and thereby discharge any unexecuted portion of the contract; or

    (b) modify the contract by agreeing to take his available quota in substitution.

(2) If, after receipt of such notification from the seller, the buyer fails so to modify the contract within a reasonable time not exceeding thirty days, the contract lapses with respect to any deliveries affected.

(3) The provisions of this section may not be negated by agreement except insofar as the seller has assumed a greater obligation under the preceding section.

## PART 7/REMEDIES

### Section 2—701. Remedies for Breach of Collateral Contracts Not Impaired

Remedies for breach of any obligation or promise collateral or ancillary to a contract for sale are not impaired by the provisions of this Article.

### Section 2—702. Seller's Remedies on Discovery of Buyer's Insolvency

(1) Where the seller discovers the buyer to be insolvent, he may refuse delivery except for cash including payment for all goods theretofore delivered under the contract, and stop delivery under this Article (Section 2—705).

(2) Where the seller discovers that the buyer has received goods on credit while insolvent, he may reclaim the goods upon demand made within ten days after the receipt, but if misrepresentation of solvency has been made to the particular seller in writing within three months before delivery the ten day limitation does not apply. Except as provided in

this subsection, the seller may not base a right to reclaim goods on the buyer's fraudulent or innocent misrepresentation of solvency or of intent to pay.

(3) The seller's right to reclaim under subsection (2) is subject to the rights of a buyer in ordinary course or other good faith purchaser under this Article (Section 2—403). Successful reclamation of goods excludes all other remedies with respect to them.

### Section 2—703. Seller's Remedies in General

Where the buyer wrongfully rejects or revokes acceptance of goods or fails to make a payment due on or before delivery or repudiates with respect to a part or the whole, then with respect to any goods directly affected and, if the breach is of the whole contract (Section 2—612), then also with respect to the whole undelivered balance, the aggrieved seller may

  (a) withhold delivery of such goods;
  (b) stop delivery by any bailee as hereafter provided (Section 2—705);
  (c) proceed under the next section respecting goods still unidentified to the contract;
  (d) resell and recover damages as hereafter provided (Section 2—706);
  (e) recover damages for non-acceptance (Section 2—708) or in a proper case the price (Section 2—709);
  (f) cancel.

### Section 2—704. Seller's Right to Identify Goods to the Contract Notwithstanding Breach or to Salvage Unfinished Goods

(1) An aggrieved seller under the preceding section may

  (a) identify to the contract conforming goods not already identified if at the time he learned of the breach they are in his possession or control;
  (b) treat as the subject of resale goods which have demonstrably been intended for the particular contract even though those goods are unfinished.

(2) Where the goods are unfinished an aggrieved seller may, in the exercise of reasonable commercial judgment for the purposes of avoiding loss and of effective realization, either complete the manufacture and wholly identify the goods to the contract or cease manufacture and resell for scrap or salvage value or proceed in any other reasonable manner.

### Section 2—705. Seller's Stoppage of Delivery in Transit or Otherwise

(1) The seller may stop delivery of goods in the possession of a carrier or other bailee when he discovers the buyer to be insolvent (Section 2—702) and may stop delivery of carload, truckload, planeload or larger shipments of express or freight when the buyer repudiates or fails to make a payment due before delivery or if for any other reason the seller has a right to withhold or reclaim the goods.

(2) As against such buyer, the seller may stop delivery until

  (a) receipt of the goods by the buyer; or
  (b) acknowledgment to the buyer by any bailee of the goods except a carrier that the bailee holds the goods for the buyer; or
  (c) such acknowledgment to the buyer by a carrier by reshipment or as warehouseman; or
  (d) negotiation to the buyer of any negotiable document of title covering the goods.

(3) (a) To stop delivery the seller must so notify as to enable the bailee by reasonable diligence to prevent delivery of the goods.
  (b) After such notification the bailee must hold and deliver the goods according to the directions of the seller, but the seller is liable to the bailee for any ensuing charges or damages.
  (c) If a negotiable document of title has been issued for goods, the bailee is not obliged to obey a notification to stop until surrender of the document.
  (d) A carrier who has issued a non-negotiable bill of lading is not obliged to obey a notification to stop received from a person other than the consignor.

### Section 2—706. Seller's Resale Including Contract for Resale

(1) Under the conditions stated in Section 2—703 on seller's remedies, the seller may resell the goods concerned or the undelivered balance thereof. Where the resale is made in good faith and in a commercially reasonable manner, the seller may recover the difference between the resale price and the contract price together with any incidental damages allowed under the provisions of this Article (Section 2—710), but less expenses saved in consequence of the buyer's breach.

(2) Except as otherwise provided in subsection (3) or unless otherwise agreed, resale may be at public or private sale including sale by way of one or more contracts to sell or of identification to an existing contract of the seller. Sale may be as a unit or in parcels and at any time and place and on any terms but every aspect of the sale including the method, manner, time, place and terms must be commercially reasonable. The resale must be reasonably identified as referring to the broken contract, but it is not necessary that the goods be in existence or that any or all of them have been identified to the contract before the breach.

(3) Where the resale is at private sale, the seller must give the buyer reasonable notification of his intention to resell.

(4) Where the resale is at public sale
  (a) only identified goods can be sold except where there is a recognized market for a public sale of futures in goods of the kind; and
  (b) it must be made at a usual place or market for public sale if one is reasonably available and except in the case of goods which are perishable or threaten to decline in value speedily the seller must give the buyer reasonable notice of the time and place of the resale; and
  (c) if the goods are not to be within the view of those attending the sale, the notification of sale must state the place where the goods are located and provide for their reasonable inspection by prospective bidders; and
  (d) the seller may buy.

(5) A purchaser who buys in good faith at a resale takes the goods free of any rights of the original buyer even though the seller fails to comply with one or more of the requirements of this section.

(6) The seller is not accountable to the buyer for any profit made on any resale. A person in the position of a seller (Section 2—707) or a buyer who has rightfully rejected or justifiably revoked acceptance must account for any excess over the amount of his security interest, as hereinafter defined (subsection (3) of Section 2—711).

### Section 2—707. "Person in the Position of a Seller"

(1) A "person in the position of a seller" includes, as against a principal, an agent who has paid or become responsible for the price of goods on behalf of his principal or anyone who otherwise holds a security interest or other right in goods similar to that of a seller.

(2) A person in the position of a seller may as provided in this Article withhold or stop delivery (Section 2—705) and resell (Section 2—706) and recover incidental damages (Section 2—710).

### Section 2—708. Seller's Damages for Nonacceptance or Repudiation

(1) Subject to subsection (2) and to the provisions of this Article with respect to proof of market price (Section 2—723), the measure of damages for nonacceptance or repudiation by the buyer is the difference between the market price at the time and place for tender and the unpaid contract price together with any incidental damages provided in this Article (Section 2—710), but less expenses saved in consequence of the buyer's breach.

(2) If the measure of damages provided in subsection (1) is inadequate to put the seller in as good a position as performance would have done, then the measure of damages is the profit (including reasonable overhead) which the seller would have made from full performance by the buyer, together with any incidental damages provided in this Article (Section 2—710), due allowance for costs reasonably incurred and due credit for payments or proceeds of resale.

**Section 2—709. Action for the Price**

(1) When the buyer fails to pay the price as it becomes due, the seller may recover, together with any incidental damages under the next section, the price

(a) of goods accepted or of conforming goods lost or damaged within a commercially reasonable time after risk of their loss has passed to the buyer; and

(b) of goods identified to the contract if the seller is unable after reasonable effort to resell them at a reasonable price or the circumstances reasonably indicate that such effort will be unavailing.

(2) Where the seller sues for the price, he must hold for the buyer any goods which have been identified to the contract and are still in his control except that if resale becomes possible he may resell them at any time prior to the collection of the judgment. The net proceeds of any such resale must be credited to the buyer and payment of the judgment entitles him to any goods not resold.

(3) After the buyer has wrongfully rejected or revoked acceptance of the goods or has failed to make a payment due or has repudiated (Section 2—610), a seller who is held not entitled to the price under this section shall nevertheless be awarded damages for nonacceptance under the preceding section.

**Section 2—710. Seller's Incidental Damages**

Incidental damages to an aggrieved seller include any commercially reasonable charges, expenses or commissions incurred in stopping delivery, the transportation, care and custody of goods after the buyer's breach, in connection with return or resale of the goods or otherwise resulting from the breach.

**Section 2—711. Buyer's Remedies in General; Buyer's Security Interest in Rejected Goods**

(1) Where the seller fails to make delivery or repudiates or the buyer rightfully rejects or justifiably revokes acceptance, then with respect to any goods involved, and with respect to the whole if the breach goes to the whole contract (Section 2—612), the buyer may cancel and whether or not he has done so may in addition to recovering so much of the price as has been paid

(a) "cover" and have damages under the next section as to all the goods affected whether or not they have been identifed to the contract; or

(b) recover damages for nondelivery as provided in this Article (Section 2—713).

(2) Where the seller fails to deliver or repudiates, the buyer may also

(a) if the goods have been identified recover them as provided in this Article (Section 2—502); or

(b) in a proper case obtain specific performance or replevy the goods as provided in this Article (Section 2—716).

(3) On rightful rejection or justifiable revocation of acceptance, a buyer has a security interest in goods in his possession or control for any payments made on their price and any expenses reasonably incurred in their inspection, receipt, transportation, care and custody and may hold such goods and resell them in like manner as an aggrieved seller (Section 2—706).

**Section 2—712. "Cover"; Buyer's Procurement of Substitute Goods**

(1) After a breach within the preceding section, the buyer may "cover" by making in good faith and without unreasonable delay any reasonable purchase of or contract to purchase goods in substitution for those due from the seller.

(2) The buyer may recover from the seller as damages the difference between the cost of cover and the contract price together with any incidental or consequential damages as hereinafter defined (Section 2—715), but less expenses saved in consequence of the seller's breach.

(3) Failure of the buyer to effect cover within this section does not bar him from any other remedy.

**Section 2—713. Buyer's Damages for Nondelivery or Repudiation**

(1) Subject to the provisions of this Article with respect to proof of market price (Section 2—723), the measure of damages for non-

delivery or repudiation by the seller is the difference between the market price at the time when the buyer learned of the breach and the contract price together with any incidental and consequential damages provided in this Article (Section 2—715), but less expenses saved in consequence of the seller's breach.

(2) Market price is to be determined as of the place for tender or, in cases of rejection after arrival or revocation of acceptance, as of the place of arrival.

### Section 2—714. Buyer's Damages for Breach in Regard to Accepted Goods

(1) Where the buyer has accepted goods and given notification (subsection (3) of Section 2—607), he may recover as damages for any non-conformity of tender the loss resulting in the ordinary course of events from the seller's breach as determined in any manner which is reasonable.

(2) The measure of damages for breach of warranty is the difference at the time and place of acceptance between the value of the goods accepted and the value they would have had if they had been as warranted, unless special circumstances show proximate damages of a different amount.

(3) In a proper case any incidental and consequential damages under the next section may also be recovered.

### Section 2—715. Buyer's Incidental and Consequential Damages

(1) Incidental damages resulting from the seller's breach include expenses reasonably incurred in inspection, receipt, transportation and care and custody of goods rightfully rejected, any commercially reasonable charges, expenses or commissions in connection with effecting cover and any other reasonable expense incident to the delay or other breach.

(2) Consequential damages resulting from the seller's breach include

    (a) any loss resulting from general or particular requirements and needs of which the seller at the time of contracting had reason to know and which could not reasonably be prevented by cover or otherwise; and

    (b) injury to person or property proximately resulting from any breach of warranty.

### Section 2—716. Buyer's Right to Specific Performance or Replevin

(1) Specific performance may be decreed where the goods are unique or in other proper circumstances.

(2) The decree for specific performance may include such terms and conditions as to payment of the price, damages, or other relief as the court may deem just.

(3) The buyer has a right of replevin for goods identified to the contract if after reasonable effort he is unable to effect cover for such goods or the circumstances reasonably indicate that such effort will be unavailing or if the goods have been shipped under reservation and satisfaction of the security interest in them has been made or tendered.

### Section 2—717. Deduction of Damages From the Price

The buyer on notifying the seller of his intention to do so may deduct all or any part of the damages resulting from any breach of the contract from any part of the price still due under the same contract.

### Section 2—718. Liquidation or Limitation of Damages; Deposits

(1) Damages for breach by either party may be liquidated in the agreement but only at an amount which is reasonable in the light of the anticipated or actual harm caused by the breach, the difficulties of proof of loss, and the inconvenience or nonfeasibility of otherwise obtaining an adequate remedy. A term fixing unreasonably large liquidated damages is void as a penalty.

(2) Where the seller justifiably withholds delivery of goods because of the buyer's breach, the buyer is entitled to restitution of any amount by which the sum of his payments exceeds

    (a) the amount to which the seller is entitled by virtue of terms liquidating the seller's damages in accordance with subsection (1), or

    (b) in the absence of such terms, twenty percent of the value of the total performance for which the buyer is obligated under the contract or $500, whichever is smaller.

(3) The buyer's right to restitution under subsection (2) is subject to offset to the extent that the seller establishes

    (a) a right to recover damages under the provisions of this Article other than subsection (1), and

    (b) the amount or value of any benefits received by the buyer directly or indirectly by reason of the contract

(4) Where a seller has received payment in goods, their reasonable value or the proceeds of their resale shall be treated as payments for the purposes of subsection (2); but if the seller has notice of the buyer's breach before reselling goods received in part performance, his resale is subject to the conditions laid down in this Article on resale by an aggrieved seller (Section 2—706).

### Section 2—719. Contractual Modification or Limitation of Remedy

(1) Subject to the provisions of subsections (2) and (3) of this section and of the preceding section on liquidation and limitation of damages,

    (a) the agreement may provide for remedies in addition to or in substitution for those provided in this Article and may limit or after the measure of damages recoverable under this Article, as by limiting the buyer's remedies to return of the goods and repayment of the price or to repair and replacement of non-conforming goods or parts; and

    (b) resort to a remedy as provided is optional unless the remedy is expressly agreed to be exclusive, in which case it is the sole remedy.

(2) Where circumstances cause an exclusive or limited remedy to fail of its essential purpose, remedy may be had as provided in this Act.

(3) Consequential damages may be limited or excluded unless the limitation or exclusion is unconscionable. Limitation of consequential damages for injury to the person in the case of consumer goods is prima facie unconscionable but limitation of damages where the loss is commercial is not.

### Section 2—720. Effect of "Cancellation" or "Rescission" on Claims for Antecedent Breach

Unless the contrary intention clearly appears, expressions of "cancellation" or "rescission" of the contract or the like shall not be construed as a renunciation or discharge of any claim in damages for an antecedent breach.

### Section 2—721. Remedies for Fraud

Remedies for material misprepresentation of fraud include all remedies available under this Article for non-fraudulent breach. Neither rescission or a claim for rescission of the contract for sale nor rejection or return of the goods shall bar or be deemed inconsistent with a claim for damages or other remedy.

### Section 2—722. Who Can Sue Third Parties for Injury to Goods

Where a third party so deals with goods which have been identified to a contract for sale as to cause actionable injury to a party to that contract

    (a) a right of action against the third party is in either party to the contract for sale who has title to or a security interest or a special property or an insurable interest in the goods; and if the goods have been destroyed or converted, a right of action is also in the party who either bore the risk of loss under the contract for sale or has since the injury assumed that risk as against the other;

    (b) if at the time of the injury the party plaintiff did not bear the risk of loss as against the other party to the contract for sale and there is no arrangement between them for disposition of the recovery, his suit or settlement is, subject to his own interest, as a fiduciary for the other party to the contract;

    (c) either party may with the consent of the other sue for the benefit of whom it may concern.

### Section 2—723. Proof of Market Price: Time and Place

(1) If an action based on anticipatory repudiation comes to trial before the time for performance with respect to some or all of the goods, any damages based on market price (Section 2—708 or Section 2—713) shall be determined according to the price of such goods prevailing at the time when the aggrieved party learned of the repudiation.

(2) If evidence of a price prevailing at the times or places described in this Article is not readily available, the price prevailing within any reasonable time before or after the time described or at any other place which in commercial judgment or under usage of trade would serve as a reasonable substitute for the one described may be used, making any proper allowance for the cost of transporting the goods to or from such other place.

(3) Evidence of a relevant price prevailing at a time or place other than the one described in this Article offered by one party is not admissible unless and until he has given the other party such notice as the court finds sufficient to prevent unfair surprise.

### Section 2—724. Admissibility of Market Quotations

Whenever the prevailing price or value of any goods regularly bought and sold in any established commodity market is in issue, reports in official publications or trade journals or in newspapers or periodicals of general circulation published as the reports of such market shall be admissible in evidence. The circumstances of the preparation of such a report may be shown to affect its weight but not its admissibility.

### Section 2—725. Statute of Limitations in Contracts for Sale

(1) An action for breach of any contract for sale must be commenced within four years after the cause of action has accrued. By the original agreement, the parties may reduce the period of limitation to not less than one year but may not extend it.

(2) A cause of action accrues when the breach occurs, regardless of the aggrieved party's lack of knowledge of the breach. A breach of warranty occurs when tender of delivery is made, except that where a warranty explicitly extends to future performance of the goods and discovery of the breach must await the time of such performance the cause of action accrues when the breach is or should have been discovered.

(3) Where an action commenced within the time limited by subsection (1) is so terminated as to leave available a remedy by another action for the same breach, such other action may be commenced after the expiration of the time limited and within six months after the termination of the first action unless the termination resulted from voluntary discontinuance or from dismissal for failure or neglect to prosecute.

(4) This section does not alter the law on tolling of the statute of limitations nor does it apply to causes of action which have accrued before this Act becomes effective.

# Index

**Q**

**R**